Fortran 77 with Applications for Scientists and Engineers

FORTRAN 77
with Applications for Scientists and Engineers

RAMA N. REDDY
University of Arkansas–Little Rock

CAROL A. ZIEGLER
Former Faculty Member
University of Arkansas–Little Rock

West Publishing Company

St. Paul · New York
Los Angeles · San Francisco

About the Cover:
The diagram is a computer simulation of fluid flow over an airfoil from
the dissertation of Dr. Rama N. Reddy.

Production Credits:
Copyeditor *Sheryl Rose*
Designer *Joyce C. Weston*
Compositor *G & S Typesetters*
Cover Designer *David J. Farr, Imagesmythe, Inc.*

Library of Congress Cataloging-in-Publication Data

Reddy. Rama N.
  Fortran 77 with applications for scientists and engineers / Rama
N. Reddy. Carol A. Ziegler.
      p.   cm.
  Includes index.
  ISBN 0-314-48135-4
1. FORTRAN (Computer program language)   I. Ziegler, Carol A.
II. Title.
QA76.73.F25R42   1989
005.13'3--oc19   88-26734   CIP

To my late grandfather
Sonna P. Reddy

To my parents
Max B. Alcorn
Ruth B. Alcorn

Contents

2 Basic Concepts of FORTRAN

3 Input/Output Specifications

4 Control Structures

5 Modular Design and Subprograms

6 One-Dimensional Arrays

7 Multidimensional Arrays

8 Character Data Manipulation

9 File and Data Manipulation

10 Additional FORTRAN Features

Preface

FORTRAN remains the most versatile modern programming language for scientific, engineering, and industrial applications. We think the majority of students studying FORTRAN are math, science, computer science, and engineering majors; rather than aiming for a general audience, our text was written with this in mind. FORTRAN 77, the latest version of FORTRAN, is compatible with previous versions. However, some of the inherited features are stylistically undesirable. These we have chosen to deemphasize (for example, all types of GO TO statements and the logical and arithmetic IF statements). We stress program structure and the explicit declaration of variables and array types, which enhance the reliability and maintenance of programs, and we include a discussion of character data manipulation facilities.

FORTRAN 77 allows a modern approach to structured programming with sequence, selection, and repetition control structures, as well as function and subroutine subprograms. FORTRAN was one of the earliest languages to introduce the concept of modular programming. In this text, we emphasize the development of modularized programs from top-down design. Basic control sturctures such as DO WHILE and REPEAT UNTIL are simulated. We discuss the simulation of complex data types such as lists as well as the special data types such as logical, double precision, and complex, which are available in FORTRAN 77. Most importantly, we introduce subroutines earlier than most texts do—in Chapter 5, before studying arrays. This allows us to take advantage of FORTRAN's modular character.

Text Organization

This text is designed for a one-semester course in FORTRAN programming. The text includes those ANSI standard features that are supported by most FORTRAN 77 compilers. In many compilers, additional features are available. The syntax and semantics of the full ANSI language are presented in the appendices. No previous background in a high-level programming language is assumed.

Over a period of years, during the development of this text, we used the manuscript to teach FORTRAN to students of computer science, physical science, and engineering. All of the examples have been tested on a university computer. The exercises and review questions have also been tested.

The text is organized into ten chapters. Chapter 1 presents basic computer terminology pertaining to hardware, software, programming, and system environments. A thorough systematic approach to problem solving is introduced with the development of algorithms in pseudocode, hierarchy charts, and flowcharts. Reliability and documentation of programs is stressed throughout the book.

Chapter 2 presents the concept of structured programming in FORTRAN, and the semantic and syntactical rules used to form variable names and arithmetic and logical expressions. List-directed and formatted input/output are presented in depth in Chapter 3. We decided to include all the aspects of input/output in a single chapter to make them easily accessible. Some of the basic concepts of files are also presented in Chapter 3.

Control structures are covered in depth in Chapter 4. Iterative DO-loops and IF statements are presented as examples of block structure.

The heart of the book is its presentation of modular programming and subroutines in Chapter 5. Argument and parameter passing is illustrated with diagrams, which emphasize what actually happens inside the computer. This chapter prepares the student early in the course to write subprograms.

We stress the use of subroutines in Chapters 6 and 7, which deal with arrays. Variable dimensioning is also presented in these chapters. One criterion used in developing examples is that the functions and subroutines should be as general as possible with respect to the size of arrays handled.

Character data is presented in Chapter 8, emphasizing the use of subroutines in character data manipulation. Chapter 9 presents a comprehensive treatment of sequential and direct files. Chapter 10 contains some additional facilities available in FORTRAN 77, including the treatment of double-precision and complex numbers. Most of the other features in this chapter are primarily of historical interest and are included for the sake of completeness. They may be of use to the maintenance programmer.

Chapter Organization and Features

Throughout the text, we emphasize algorithm development and reliability and give programming hints and warnings at appropriate places. We use structured charts consistently throughout the text to stress structure in programming. Review questions at the end of each section reinforce the concepts presented in that section. These hints, warnings, and reviews enhance the depth of the student's understanding. Answers to the odd-numbered review questions can be found in Appendix D.

Each chapter includes a summary highlighting the most important concepts, followed by a variety of exercise problems in physics, chemistry, mathematics, and engineering, with a few business problems.

We have chosen the sample programming problems found at the end of the chapters from our experience in science and engineering. The problems are presented with complete solutions, pseudocode, flowcharts, and documentation. The programs were executed on a Digital Equipment Corporation VAX 11/780 four-processor clustered computer system. Most of the programs have been run interactively; the interactive input and output are shown.

Complete sample programs, fully documented, are placed at the end of each chapter. These programs illustrate the use of FORTRAN features presented in the chapter.

Ancillaries

An instructor's manual contains a brief description of each section of the textbook with pedogogical hints for presenting the material. Each description is followed by the complete set of answers for the review questions at the end of that section. A package of 100 transparency masters makes it easy to discuss flowcharts, pseudocode, diagrams, and sample programs from the book.

In addition, seventy of the sample programs along with input data files are available on a diskette. These programs have been thoroughly debugged and tested on several machines. They can be transferred to a mainframe or minicomputer for use as demonstration programs.

Acknowledgments

The authors wish to express their sincere thanks to the editors, Jerry Westby, Bill Gabler, Tammy Moore, Elizabeth Lee and Beth Kennedy of West Publishing Company for their interest, enthusiasm, criticisms and fruitful dissensions throughout the development of this book. The authors also wish to thank the following reviewers for their selfless suggestions. Their constructive criticisms improved the content and organization of this book:

Dr. James Allert—University of Minnesota–Duluth
Dr. James A. Ball—Indiana State University
Dr. John Buck—Indiana University
Bart Childs—Texas A & M University
Dr. Grady Early—Southwest Texas State University
Dr. David Fields—Eastern Kentucky University
Dr. Martin Granier—University of Northern Colorado
Prof. Abraham Kandell—Florida State University
Dominic Magno—William Rainey Harper College
Jane Wallace Mayo—University of Tennessee–Knoxville
Prof. Herbert A. Morris—Bradley University
Thomas Murtagh—San Jacinto College–South Campus
Dr. Linda M. Ott—Michigan Technological University
Dr. Judith Palagallo—University of Akron
Dr. Frederick M. Phelps—Central Michigan University
Dr. Richard A. Rink—Eastern Kentucky University
Dr. Sandra Schleiffers—Colorado State University
Dr. Henry S. Todd—Brigham Young University
Dr. Ronald Dale Williams—Central Piedmont Community College
Dr. Michael Zieger—Eastern Michigan University

The authors also wish to thank Glenn Geiger, a computer science major, for helping to run and document the programs; also Robin E. Ziegler and Wyndolyn J. Smith for assisting in the preparation of the instructor's manual.

Finally, we wish to express our sincere thanks to our students for their willingness to serve as guinea pigs for our pedagogical experiments and to study from an unfinished manuscript, and for their many suggestions and assistance in a multitude of ways. We are grateful to the Computer Science Department and the University of Arkansas at Little Rock for their encouragement. Last but most importantly, we thank our spouses and children for bearing with us during the long and demanding hours of work devoted to completing this book.

Rama N. Reddy

Carol A. Ziegler

Fortran 77 with Applications
for Scientists and Engineers

1 Introduction to Computers and Programming

Objective: To understand the basic concepts of program development, program generation, and the FORTRAN run-time environment.

*C*omputers and computer programming are an essential part of modern society because problem solving, especially in business and science, has become too complex for paper and pencil solutions. Computers can handle large amounts of data and complex calculations quickly and accurately and efficiently share the resulting information. Solid-state electronics and integrated circuits revolutionized the computer industry, making it possible to build increasingly powerful computers at less expense. These machines are efficient, affordable, and almost indispensable in most areas of modern industry.

Computers are used in educational institutions for teaching and research; in industry for research, design, and production; in medical science for diagnosis and treatment; in banking, aeronautics and space, the exploration of natural resources, weather prediction, and other such fields. Special types of computer systems are used for engineering analysis and design, to construct intelligent decision systems, to process natural language documents, in expert diagnostic systems, speech recognition, image processing, robotics, and production control.

Because computers and computer programs are widely used in critical applications, cost effectiveness and reliability are very important factors. The degree of reliability needed depends on the problem being solved. For applications such as space exploration, nuclear power production, and medical technology, failure of computerized devices is not acceptable. A high degree of reliability of the entire system is essential. The concept of reliability has led to the development of *fault-tolerant* computer systems. Such systems are designed not to fail under any circumstances. A critical part of these systems is the reliable computer programs.

1.1 Concepts of Computers

Computers are electromechanical devices that function semiautomatically and are capable of accepting instructions and data, performing computations, and manipulating the data to produce useful results. The term *computer* applies to the *hardware,* the collection of all the physical components. *Software* is the collection of all the programs that run on the hardware. Each program consists of a sequence of instructions, which directs the computer in analyzing data and calculating a solution to a problem.

Computer systems consist of both hardware and software. They are categorized according to their size, function, and area of application. *General-purpose computers* can run many different programming languages and solve many different types of problems. *Special-purpose computers* use a single programming language designed for a special type of application. Computers that have been developed for specialized use include LISP machines used for artificial intelligence research, database machines used for expert system applications, and CAD/CAM systems for engineering design.

Computers are broadly classified as mainframe, super, mini, or micro, based on memory size, word size, processing speed, number of peripheral devices supported, and other aspects. *Mainframe computers* are found in installations where there is a high demand for computer power and large amounts of data are processed. *Supercomputers* are extremely fast machines used primarily for complex calculations. *Minicomputers* are found in smaller installations and laboratories where there are fewer users and less data to process. Generally, minicomputers provide powerful computational capabilities. *Microcomputers* are used primarily in small businesses and for personal use.

Computers can also be classified according to the ways they organize the processing of instructions, or their basic architectural style. Most current computers are *von Neumann machines,* which process instructions one at a time in a predetermined sequence. Pipeline and parallel architectures are becoming more common. Computers with *pipeline* architecture handle several sets of data simultaneously, combining them as though the data streamed through pipelines into a processor and out through other pipelines. Computers with *parallel* architecture contain several processors wired together to work on the same data at the same time. Parallel and pipeline computers are expected to someday be much faster and more capable than present-day computers because they can process many data values at the same time, selecting the most efficient order for processing. One way of building fault-tolerant computers is to use redundancy, duplicating the hardware and building checking procedures into the software, sacrificing efficiency for reliability. The best way to accomplish this may be by using hardware with parallel or pipeline architecture. Software reliability is one of the programming quality areas addressed in this text.

1.1.1 Hardware Components and Functions

The primary hardware components are the input/output devices, memory units, and processing elements. The *central processing unit* (*CPU*) consists of main memory and the processor. The processor consists of the arithmetic and logic unit (ALU) and the control unit (CU). A typical system is shown in Fig. 1.1. Large systems also have support hardware, which performs additional specialized functions such as graphics, image processing, or managing secondary storage.

Input/Output Devices

Input devices are used to input instructions and data to the computer in character form. Some installations use *card reader* input devices to read instructions and data punched on cards and transmit it to the computer memory. Card readers are rarely used any more, but they are historically important. *Key entry devices* such as interactive terminals are the most common form of input device used today. Instructions and data are typed at the keyboard and the characters are transmitted directly or indirectly to main memory.

Output devices produce the processed information in the form of printouts, screen displays, or graphics. The most common output devices are printers, CRT displays, and graphics terminals. A *printer* prints on paper the output information that was stored in main memory. Some printers print characters one at a time like typewriters; others print one line at a time. Dot matrix printers are usually used for rough drafts. Higher quality output is produced by laser, chain, daisy wheel, and other special printers, which are used with specialized software for desktop publishing.

Figure 1.1

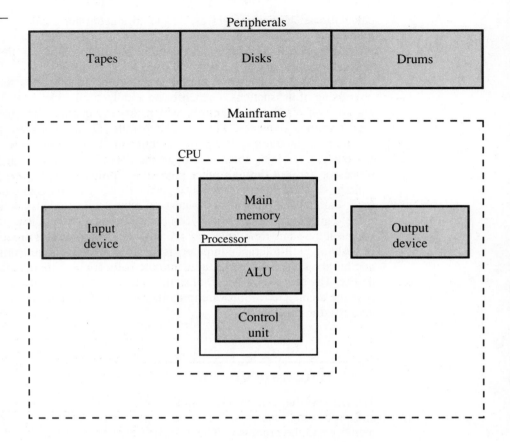

Magnetic storage devices such as tape drives, disk drives, drums, and floppy disks are used for both input and output. Although they are peripheral devices, they are internal to the system. Magnetic storage devices provide secondary storage. They hold large volumes of data in very little physical space. The data is coded as magnetic dots, each representing a zero or a one. Magnetic devices are convenient and cost effective, but the data stored on them can only be read by computers. These devices come in many different forms, with different access speeds and storage capacities.

Memory Devices

Memory devices store both data and program instructions as shown in Fig. 1.2. The information is stored in binary form as strings of 0's and 1's. Because information is entered through the input devices in character form, it must be converted to binary codes before being stored in memory.

The smallest unit of memory, known as a *bit* (binary digit), is a memory cell with an electronic state that can be interpreted as either 0 or 1. The electronic state of the cell can be copied and changed when necessary. (Special memory known as read-only memory or ROM cannot be changed.) Memory cells are grouped ac-

*Figure 1.2 Main
memory.*

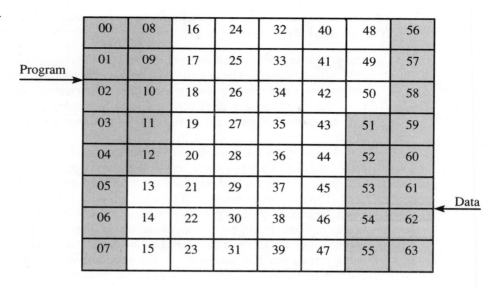

*Figure 1.3
Structure of
memory
locations.*

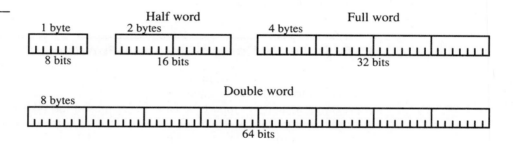

cording to the number of bits needed to code a character. Such a group of bits is called a *byte*. Typical memory sections are shown in Fig. 1.3.

Two, four, or eight bytes are grouped together for different purposes. These are called halfwords, fullwords, and double words. The organization of bits into words differs depending on the computer being used.

Bytes have unique locations in the memory, called *byte addresses*. Like post office box numbers, the addresses locate the places to store and retrieve information.

The main memory is used for instructions currently being executed and data currently being processed. The processor communicates directly with the main memory, following instructions from it and fetching and storing data.

The development of solid-state electronic technology and VLSI (very large-scale integrated) circuit technology has made it possible to build extremely compact memories having very large capacity at low cost. VLSI also made it possible to build parallel processing machines and compact memory chips. Many of today's desktop microcomputers are more powerful and have greater speeds and capacities than the roomsize computers of only a few years ago.

Central Processing Unit

The central processing unit consists of the main memory, the control unit, and the arithmetic-logic unit. The *control unit* contains electronic circuitry that fetches the instructions from memory and decodes them. It sends signals to the arithmetic-logic unit, directing it to carry out the arithmetic and logic operations. The control unit stores the results in main memory. It also supervises the input and output of data.

The *arithmetic-logic unit* contains the electronic circuitry that performs standard arithmetic operations and makes logic decisions by comparing values. The arithmetic circuits can add, subtract, multiply, and divide, using two numbers at a time. Their output is numeric. The logic circuits can compare either numeric or character values. The output of the logic circuits is interpreted as a logical value of true or false. In large mainframes and supercomputers, the ALU often contains coprocessors so that logic decisions may be made at the same time calculations are being carried out. Coprocessors are also very common on microcomputers, especially when using mathematically-oriented languages such as FORTRAN. All computer instructions are based on these elementary operations of arithmetic, comparison, fetching, and storing.

1.1.2 Software Components and Functions

A program is a sequence of instructions written in a programming language that directs a computer in problem solving. The software in a computer system consists of programs written to support the basic operations of the system and programs to carry out an application. There are several levels of software active at all times. Fig. 1.4 shows some of these software systems and their hierarchy.

The software that controls the execution of an application program is called *system software*. The major system software components are the operating system, file management systems, and programming language systems, which include utility programs and library routines. These programs keep the computer functioning efficiently and provide a comfortable environment for the user. They allow the user to access data in a variety of forms and to set up filing systems for data.

Application software consists of programs written to analyze data and solve specific problems. Application programs produce output concerning the exterior world, while system programs produce output concerning the state of the computer system.

Figure 1.4

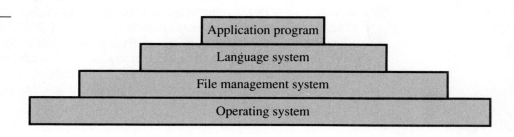

The *operating system* makes the system facilities available to the application programs and controls their use. It provides access to a variety of programming and debugging tools and interfaces between the user and the computer hardware. It schedules program execution and directs traffic through the computer. The operating system manages all the system resources, allocating and deallocating memory, processor, devices, and files to particular application programs as they need them. Operating systems have their own nonstandardized languages, known as *job control languages*. Instructions in these languages direct the computer to undertake tasks and make resources available to the tasks. Every programmer needs at least minimum knowledge of the job control language of the computer being used.

System management is designed to balance processing and input/output, with the aim of providing reasonable minimum turnaround and maximum throughput. *Turnaround* is the amount of time elapsing between a request to the computer to execute a program and the availability of output. *Throughput* is the number of jobs that are completed in a given time period.

System utility programs are the data management and device management software. The data management software manages the formatting of the input/output. The device management software makes the devices available as though they were extensions of memory.

The *system library* contains graphics packages, mathematical packages, statistical packages, database management routines, and data communication and networking software.

The *file management system* controls the storage and retrieval of records from program and data files, which are normally stored on magnetic devices such as disks or drums. It provides instructions and data to memory as the processor needs them.

Compilers are translators that translate programs written in high-level languages such as FORTRAN, Ada, or PL/I into machine language, which the hardware can interpret and execute directly. Languages that are reasonably machine independent and people oriented are called *high-level languages*. Assembly language and other machine-oriented languages are called *low-level languages*. Programs written in assembly language are assembled (translated) to machine code also. Compilers that translate source code into particularly efficient machine code are called *optimizing compilers*.

Application software programs are often written by users. Programmers may write a program to compute a payroll, for example, or to implement automatic navigation for an aircraft. When adequate application software can be purchased, programmers often modify it to their company's special needs. Application software installed with equipment that it controls is known as an *embedded system*. Current examples of embedded systems are the autopilot systems for aircraft, missile guidance systems, and the space shuttle navigation systems. In the future, embedded systems will become more popular.

Many computer systems come with permanently programmed software known as *firmware*. When software functions can be built into the hardware or programmed as firmware, the computers are more efficient. Firmware is often stored in read-only memory (ROM).

Figure 1.5

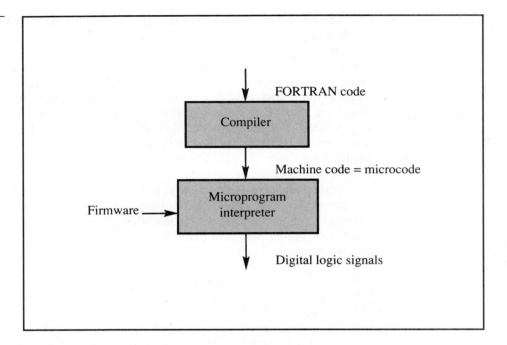

1.1.3 Integration of Hardware and Software

Hardware cannot function by itself without software, and software cannot function unless it has hardware to run on. Both are necessary to make a computer system work properly. The lowest level of hardware is the digital logic level. Application programmers do not write programs for this level. Instead, programs written in high-level languages go through several levels of translation and interpretation before the machine can execute them. The levels for a FORTRAN program are shown in Fig. 1.5. Application programs written in FORTRAN are translated by compilers into machine language, which is understood as microprograms and interpreted for execution by the digital logic, using firmware routines.

1.1.4 Review Questions

1. A computer system consists of both _____ and _____ .

2. What are the three major hardware components of a computer?

3. A compiler translates a high-level language program to _____ .

4. The arithmetic-logic unit of a computer performs _____ and _____ operations.

5. Machine language instructions are fetched and decoded by the _____ unit.

6. Input/output operations are controlled by the _____ unit.

7. The input devices handle instructions and data in _____ form.

8. Common secondary storage devices are _____ , _____ , and _____ .

9. Programs written to manipulate data and solve a problem are called _____ software.

10. The central processing unit consists of _____ , _____ , and _____ .

11. What kinds of resources does the operating system manage?

12. The program in a computer system that manages the computer resources is called _____ software.

13. Software that is permanently embedded in general-purpose computer hardware is called _____ .

14. Software programs permanently installed to control equipment are called _____ systems.

15. How does a computer with von Neumann architecture execute instructions?

16. How does a computer with parallel architecture execute instructions?

1.2 Algorithms and Program Development

Solving a problem on a computer requires a thorough analysis of the problem and the potential data. Once the problem has been analyzed, a detailed procedural solution can be developed. One of the steps in developing a computerized solution to a problem is to create an algorithm.

1.2.1 Concept of an Algorithm

An *algorithm* is a procedure consisting of a finite number of precisely defined steps for solving a problem. Each step of an algorithm must be an unambiguous instruction which, when written in a computer language, can be executed by a computer. The order of steps is important, because most computers can only execute one instruction at a time. Algorithms written for FORTRAN application programs must terminate.

There may be several different algorithms that can solve a single problem. The programmer should choose an algorithm on the basis of efficiency, accuracy, and clarity. The algorithm should be efficient with respect to computational time, storage requirements, and response time. The accuracy required is specified by the user. Clarity means an understandable programming style. Sometimes a compromise between these factors is necessary. For example, efficiency may be sacrificed for the sake of increased reliability.

The design of algorithms for simple problems can be straightforward, but the design of those for large, complex problems can be difficult and time consuming. Although this text can only deal with simple problems, the techniques we use are important in the design of algorithms for complex problems.

One common approach to complicated problems is to use top-down design. *Top-down design* starts with a general statement of the problem written in a precise, formal way to provide a *high-level specification* of the algorithm. This is broken into separate parts, and general specifications for the solutions of these parts are given. These parts correspond to major modules in the final algorithm. The parts are then further subdivided and specifications are drawn up. Finally the algorithm reaches a stage where the specifications consist of things that can be programmed without further explanation.

An example of a high-level problem specification is:

Calculate the total amount of steel needed to build a rectangular tank that has four cylindrical steel columns 50 ft long for support and that can hold 1200 cu ft of water.

This can be decomposed into the following parts:

1. Calculate the optimum dimensions of the tank.
2. Calculate the thickness of the steel needed in the tank.
3. Calculate the total compression load on each column.
4. Calculate the optimum size of the columns.
5. Calculate the total volume of steel needed to build the tank and the support columns.

Each stage of the algorithm should be carefully checked before the algorithm is tested on a computer. If the design is not validated at each stage, it may contain errors that make it necessary to start over. Careful validation during the design process leads to a more nearly correct solution procedure.

1.2.2 Concepts of Programs and Data

A *program* is a meaningful sequence of executable, unambiguous instructions written in a computer language. The computer can understand instructions of various types: input/output instructions to enter data into the computer and output answers from it; move instructions to rearrange data, control instructions to control selection and repetition of actions; arithmetic instructions to perform calculations; logic instructions to help the computer make choices. These types of instructions are available in most programming languages.

Both instructions and data are input or entered into the computer through terminals. Commands to the operating system are also input by the user. Instructions are entered and stored through the use of a *system editor* and processed by the compiler. Data is entered directly into an executing application program or stored in a file to be used later by an executing program (see Fig. 1.6). Commands are sent directly to the operating system. Input also refers to data sent to the computer processor from a file on an automatic storage device.

Output refers to data sent out from the computer processor to automatic storage devices or to the outside world. Output may be printed, displayed on a CRT screen, spooled to a disk or diskette, written on a tape, or plotted on a graphics terminal.

The internal rearrangement of data, during which values are moved from one memory location to another, is achieved primarily through *assignment instructions,* which look like simple equations. For example, the FORTRAN instruction

X = Y

Figure 1.6

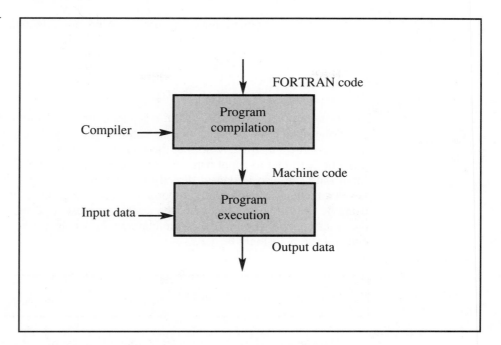

does not mean that X and Y have the same value, but rather that the value of Y is being copied to the location named X. *Arithmetic instructions* consist of the basic arithmetic operations of addition, subtraction, multiplication, division, and exponentiation (raising to a power), as well as moving the answer to a new place in memory. Thus,

```
X = 2.0 + 3.5 / 5.0
```

means that the value 2.7 is calculated and stored in the location named X. Arithmetic expressions are evaluated by the computer the same way they are evaluated in mathematics. In this example, the division is performed before the addition.

Control instructions are used to switch from one set of instructions to another depending on the logical comparison of data values. For example, the computer might choose between addition or subtraction depending on whether a number is positive or negative. Control instruction always involve the comparison of one value with another for equality or relative size. All comparisons result in an answer of true or false, which becomes the basis for a control decision.

Concept of data

The collection of related information to be processed by an application program is known as *data*. Data can be numeric or both numeric and alphabetic, known as alphanumeric. Numeric data can be written as numbers with fractional parts, as integers, in scientific notation, or as complex numbers. Numeric data is treated as numeric values. Alphanumeric data is treated as strings of characters. Data can also represent the logic values true and false.

Numeric data	Alphanumeric data
25	'JOHN SMITH'
-17.3	'(501)327-5691'
.029	'PX394'
+45.37	'+45.37'
.314159E+01	'33SE'

Data is stored in files. A *data file* is a structured collection of data.

Input data must be structured in a systematic way. The program includes a description of the structure so that the computer knows how to interpret it. If the program is to find its input data on a disk, the data must be keyed into a data file. Input data can also be keyed directly into an executing program. When data is keyed directly, it is particularly important that the program validate the data before using it. In either case, the end of the input data must be recognizable. Therefore, data files contain specific end-of-file markers. When data is keyed directly, a special end symbol should be used.

*Programming
Hint*

> Check input data for accuracy.

Data generated by the computer for output can be of many types: solutions to mathematical equations, pictures, graphs, textual material, or special symbols. Output data must be formatted properly for the output device by having appropriate vertical and horizontal spacing. It must be in usable form. Numbers printed or displayed should be arranged and labeled with headings and subheadings and whatever other identification is helpful.

Output should be understandable, easy to use, and attractive. Good quality output is worth the time expended in designing it.

*Programming
Hint*

> Make output readable and visually attractive. Use titles and column headings. Align data. Put the date and time on reports.

Not all values calculated by a program are part of the output data. Such values as counts, intermediate computational results, and logical values that control processing are *internal* data. Internal data also includes status flags for various pieces of equipment and for functions of the operating system.

1.2.3 Procedure for Problem Analysis

To analyze a program, besides writing a precise specification of the algorithm, the user should write precise specifications for the input and output data. This should include boundary conditions and initial conditions, such as those associated with mathematical models, and the equations or formulas to be used. Some problems do not have exact solutions. These should be analyzed for ways of obtaining approximate solutions and determining the quality of these solutions. Side effects, options, and possible disastrous cases must be considered. Once the problem is clearly understood and the associated side effects are resolved, programming can begin.

Problem Types

There are three basic types of solutions. First, when a closed-form solution to a problem is known, the appropriate equations can be used in a program. Second, when no closed-form solution is known or when the mathematical solution involves trial and error, numerical methods can be used. For example, numerical methods are used to solve ordinary differential equations, partial differential equations, systems of equations, and numeric integration. Third, some types of problems have so many independent variables that rather than a single answer, a variety of possible solutions is desired. In this case, mathematical modeling may be appropriate.

Development of the algorithm and the input and output formats depends on the type of solution to be developed. Remember that although the computer can perform calculations quickly, handle large sets of data, maintain a high degree of mathematical accuracy, and test many possible solutions, it cannot guess at answers.

Data Types

The procedure for problem analysis includes analyzing categories of possible input data. In some cases the input data is external to the program, in other cases, it is generated internally. When external data is used, the input must be validated by the computer according to clearly defined specifications, as the computer cannot guess the intent of the person entering the data. Data specifications include such requirements as the type of data expected (numeric or alphanumeric), the form of the data (integers, real numbers, double-precision numbers, complex numbers, logical data, character strings, etc.), the size of the data (number of digits or characters), and the arrangement of the data (lists, tables, records, etc.).

Problem analysis should include designing the layout, and label of the output, and selecting the output medium. Output design also includes indentifying the number of copies and how the output will be distributed.

1.2.4 Procedure for Solution Design

Once the problem has been clearly stated and analyzed, the solution must be developed. This involves the actual design of the input, output, and internal data, the development of an algorithm, and the development of test data for testing the algorithm. For example, the computer must know whether the data consists of integers or real numbers, whether it is in normal decimal notation or scientific notation. It must know how many data values there are or how to identify the end of the data values.

Design step: Describe the input and output data formats.

At the design stage, the algorithm can be represented by pseudocode, hierarchy charts, flowcharts, or by other logic representation techniques. Consider the simple problem of calculating and printing the average value of a set of samples of air pollution. The basic steps in this calculation are:

1. Add the data values, at the same time counting how many values there are.
2. Divide the total by the number of values.
3. Print the result.

The first of these steps includes repeated addition. The computer needs more detail on adding the values and counting them. The instructions given to the computer resemble instructions that would be given to someone who is a beginning user of a pocket calculator. Following is a pseudocode description of this algorithm:

    Initialize the total and the tally to zero
    For each data value
        Add the data value to the total
        Add 1 to the tally
    End for
    Divide the total by the tally to get the average
    Print the average
    Stop

Pseudocode is a semiformal description of each step to be carried out by the computer, including steps that are to be repeated and decisions that are to be made. There is more than one way of writing an algorithm in pseudocode. Another way of describing this algorithm in pseudocode would be:

    Total ← 0
    Tally ← 0
    For each sample
        Total ← total + sample
        Tally ← tally + 1
    End for
    Average ← total / tally
    Print the average
    Stop

A *hierarchy chart* is a tree structure that corresponds to the levels of the pseudocode. At the highest level of the chart is the general statement of the problem solution. The next level contains the major modules that correspond to the main steps in the solution. Below these are their submodules, down to as many levels as necessary. Fig. 1.7 shows a hierarchy chart for the problem of finding the average value in a set of data. The bottom row of the hierarchy chart describes the processing of a single data value. The circular arrow indicates the repetition of part of the hierarchy chart.

Figure 1.7

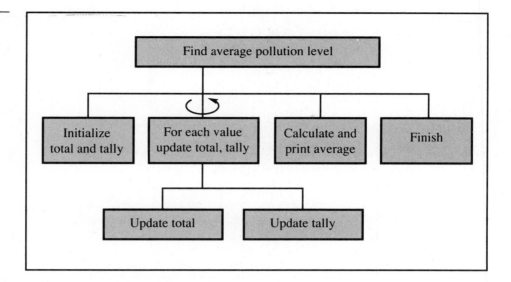

A *flowchart* uses standard symbols to show different operations and the order of execution of the submodules of the hierarchy chart. These are the steps that are followed to reach the subgoals. Lines and arrows are used to show the flow of control. Fig. 1.8 shows a flowchart for the problem of finding the average value in a set of data.

A flowchart must show a step indicating input of a data value followed by a check to determine whether the input attempt was successful. The values are to be processed one at a time, so they must be input one at a time. The flowchart loop that indicates the processing of individual data values is exited only when there are no more values.

At this stage of the design process, working with both words and diagrams provides more insight into the solution than would either method by itself. Errors found when working with the diagrams can be used to correct the specifications, which in turn leads to changes in the diagrams. This feedback and correction process should be repeated until the designer is satisfied that the solution is feasible with available computer resources. Any errors not found during the design phase can be very expensive to correct later on.

Programming Hint

Design step: Draw the hierarchy diagram, draw the flowchart, or write the pseudocode.

Once the design is complete, the computer program can be written. This consists of *computer code,* or data specifications and instructions supplied to the computer, and *documentation* or comments that document the process as an aid to people who may later read the program.

Figure 1.8

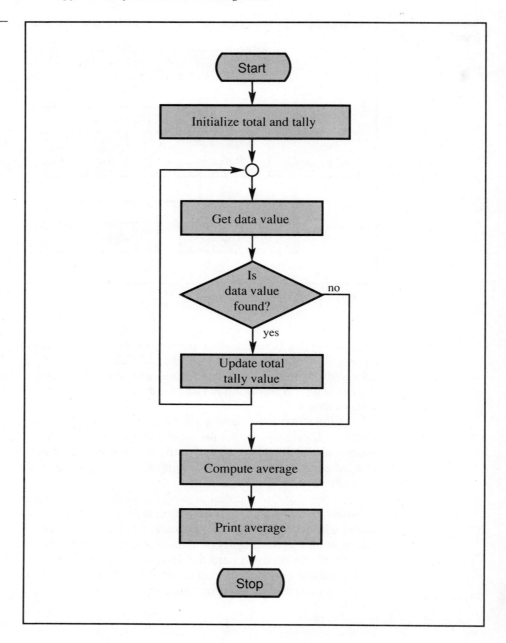

Implementation step: Desk check the program code before executing it.

The computer code should be written and tested module by module, corresponding to the submodules of the hierarchy chart or flowchart. It should be carefully read and tested by hand before being tested on the computer.

The final part of the design involves writing any necessary control statements in the system command language of the computer. In general these will be statements to direct data to and from programs; to control the compilation, linkage (collecting routines), and execution of programs; and to save output from the compilation, linkage and execution steps in appropriate files for later use.

1.2.5 Review Questions

1. What is an algorithm?

2. What is a program?

3. Explain top-down design methodology.

4. Why is it important to validate algorithm design?

5. What does a move instruction do?

6. Name some different forms of computer output.

7. What are the fundamental types of instructions in any programming language?

8. What kind of data can computers process besides numbers?

9. Information supplied to an application program is called _____ .

10. Information produced by an application program is called _____ .

11. Data generated within a program which is not part of the output is called _____ data.

12. What is data validation?

13. What is pseudocode used for?

14. What is a hierarchy chart used for?

15. What is a flowchart used for?

16. Why is the format of the output data important?

17. Why should a program be tested?

18. Why are reliability and efficiency important?

19. What are control instructions used for?

1.3 Program Compilation, Debugging, and Testing

Once the program code has been written and desk checked, it must be tested on the computer.

1.3.1 The Compilation Process

The first step in testing a program on the computer is compilation. During this process, the computer checks whether the program is understandable and accurately typed. If it appears to be all right, it is translated to machine code. All

Figure 1.9

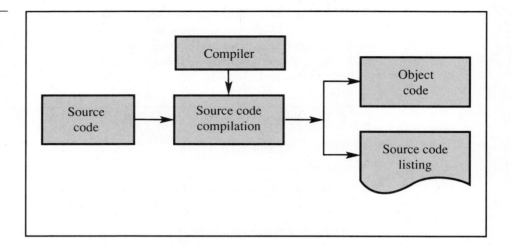

FORTRAN 77 programs are written in symbolic code known as FORTRAN *source code*. This symbolic code, written according to the grammatical rules of the FORTRAN language, is designed to make it easy for programmers to read and write programs. It must be processed by a FORTRAN 77 compiler in order to be translated into machine code, which is designed for the specific computer being used. The machine code generated during compilation is called *object code*. The compilation process is shown in Fig. 1.9.

Programming Rule

Implementation step: Compile the source code in order to test its syntactic correctness.

In FORTRAN, programs may be written in separate pieces called *modules,* each of which is designed to do a specific task. These program modules are compiled separately. This means that they can be developed, implemented, and tested separately. For each major module, a separate source code listing and object code module are stored in temporary files. The programmer must keep track of all the files and maintain backup files, at least of the source code. A *backup file* is a reserve copy of the file which can be used if the working copy is damaged or destroyed. Backup copies of data files should also be made if the data files are to be updated periodically. Errors detected in the source code during the compilation process must be corrected before compilation is tried again. Programs cannot be executed until they compile correctly.

Programming Warning

Linking and execution of a program must be attempted only after the program is compiled without errors.

1.3.2 Program Execution

After the main program module and any submodules have been written and compiled correctly, the resulting object modules are linked along with any mathematical or other library routines needed, and a single executable module is built. The
process of building an executable module, or *linking,* is shown in Fig. 1.10. The
linkers and loaders of the operating system are responsible for building the executable module and executing it. If these system routines detect errors, corrections
must be made to the appropriate source code module, any changed modules recompiled, and the linking done again.

When the program is finally run, the computer carries out the programmer's
instructions in sequence, accepts the designated input, performs the required calculations, and produces the desired output. The output includes messages indicating whether the execution contained errors and statistics about the computer resources used. When there are execution errors, the source code must be corrected
and the program recompiled, relinked, and reexecuted. The program is finished
only when it terminates normally and produces correct answers without any execution errors.

Figure 1.10

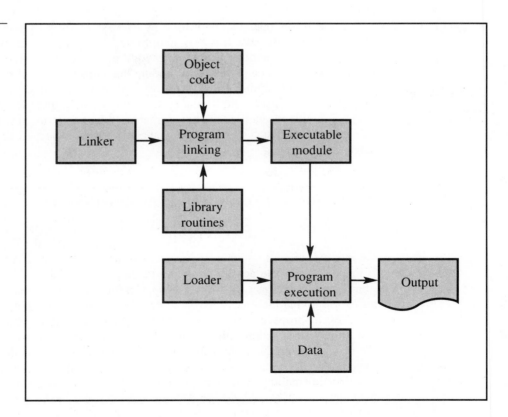

1.3.3 Errors and Debugging Methods

Program development is almost never error free. Errors may be of many types: specification and program design errors, implementation errors, typing errors, logic errors, data input errors. Errors are detected at different stages as specification and design errors, compilation errors, linkage errors, or execution errors. The errors in a program are called *bugs,* and the process of detecting and removing them is called *debugging.* It is desirable to detect any errors as early as possible in the programming process to minimize the changes and avoid extra implementation cost and effort.

Logic errors are the hardest to detect, since programs may produce answers without producing correct answers. To check the accuracy of the logic, it is necessary to know in advance what the answers should be for certain sets of *test data.* Before a program can be used to produce new answers, it must be run with typical data for which the answers are known. It must also be run with unusual data that has known answers. If the computer does not produce the correct answers, there is probably something wrong with the specifications or the design of the program.

Programming Hint

> Debug the program using specially designed test data.

Logic errors may also be caused by careless copying of numbers, formulas, or data formats. Because it is very hard to find typographical errors, sometimes it is helpful to have another programmer look at the code. Explaining the code to someone else is also a good way of finding logic errors.

Some programming languages have built-in tools that are useful for debugging, and some installations have system and software tools for debugging. Use debugging aids whenever they are available. When they are not, build programs using extra output statements so that you can see what is happening at intermediate stages of processing.

1.3.4 Program Testing and Documentation

Testing is a process intentionally designed to find errors in programs. This must be done systematically. Each module must be separately tested for errors and when the modules are put together, the result must be tested further. Any time a change is made, there is the possibility of introducing more errors. Not only must a program give correct answers to correct input, it must be able to detect incorrect input and avoid giving incorrect answers to possible but unlikely input.

Testing procedures for large, complex systems are extensive and detailed. The test cases must be carefully designed to check the entire system. In general, the people testing the system should not be the same ones who design and implement it.

Documentation, an important part of software development, should be carried out simultaneously, with design. Documentation is used to keep track of the design procedure and to keep track of implementation and testing. It becomes part of the final system, where it is used by the programmers who will maintain or modify the system. There are two types of documentation, system documentation and program documentation. System documentation includes functional descriptions, introductory manuals, reference manuals, installation manuals, user manuals, and so forth. Program documentation includes all phases of program development documents. It should include:

> Statement of the problem
> Glossary of input and output variables
> Description of each module of the program
> Error messages produced by the program
> Security measures to be incorporated in the program to protect the programs and data
> Test data to be used in program modification

Some of the program documentation is part of the source code of the program.

Programming Rule

> Program source code must be documented.

The total documentation package must include everything anyone who uses the system needs to know about the system. It should be organized according to the needs of the various people who deal with the system.

Documentation may need to be changed any time changes are made to the software program. Just as there are various versions of the source code on the computer, so there will be various versions of the documentation.

Programming Objective

> Write easy-to-maintain source code and easy-to-understand documentation.

During the life of a production program, further modifications will be needed to meet changing situations and to correct previously undetected errors. All useful programs can be expected to evolve to meet changing circumstances.

1.3.5 Review Questions

1. What does a linker do?

2. The code in which the program is written is called _____ code.

3. The compilation process produces _____ code.

4. What does a loader do?

5. List the types of errors according to developmental stages.

6. Give two reasons documentation is important.

7. The process of locating and correcting errors is called _____ .

8. Why can't program testing guarantee the absence of errors?

9. Why is it important to test a program with data that intentionally contains errors?

1.4 Program Processing Environment

There are two ways to look at a processing environment: as a computer system environment or a programming environment. The system environment in which the program runs is characterized as single job, time-sharing, multiprogramming, or multiprocessing. The programming environment is batch, interactive, or real time.

1.4.1 Computer System Environment

A *single-job environment* is one in which only one program at a time can be loaded into the computer. All the system resources in such an environment, such as disk, memory, and processor, are allocated to a single job. Once the job is completed, all the system resources are released.

Most mainframe computers and minicomputers and some microcomputers support a time-sharing environment. A *time-sharing environment* is one in which several users can have access to the computer at the same time, running different programs. Multiprogramming, multiprocessing, and parallel processing are all different forms of time-sharing environments.

In a *multiprogramming environment,* several executable programs can exist in memory at the same time, but only one program is executed at any given instant. The programs that are loaded for execution will take turns using the time and resources available within the time limit allocated to each. In a *multiprocessing environment* there is more than one CPU, making it possible to execute several programs simultaneously. Alternately, several processors may be working on the same program at the same time.

1.4.2 Programming Environment

Programming environments are designed for different user needs. In batch processing, programs are executed when it is convenient for the computer installation. Usually large amounts of data are involved and the actual time of execution is not critical. In interactive processing, programs are executed while the user waits for the output. Real-time processing is used to directly control equipment.

Batch Processing

In multiprogramming and multiprocessing environments, the batch processing mode is commonly used for program testing and for numeric applications. In *batch processing,* the operating system takes control of the program. The computer schedules and controls program execution. Several jobs may be entered through terminals, or loaded from disk files and left to be executed when sufficient time is available.

Jobs submitted in a batch environment are stored on the disk (spooled) and scheduled by the operating system according to the priority of the job and the resources it needs. Once begun, processing continues until the program is completed. The output is spooled to the disk print file so that it can be printed once the program has terminated and the printer is available.

Batch processing is used when there are large amounts of data to be processed, or when time is not critical. The output usually consists of dated reports. It is not useful when the user must interact with the program, processing transactions, correcting drawings, or directing choices. Batch processing is used, however, for updating an online transaction system when the transactions can be collected and processed at a single time, for example, at the end of the day.

Interactive Processing

In *interactive processing,* the user is in communication with the computer system. Data is entered through terminals and the user expects an immediate response from the system. Output design may differ from that sent to a printer. Interactive processing is primarily used for transaction processing, changing permanently stored data, and retrieving information.

Several terminals can be connected to a large computer system, each one having access to the computer hardware and software resources. If there are several users at the same time, the CPU will share its time with all of them. There are various strategies for allocating time to a job. The operating system attempts to keep all the hardware operating as near capacity as possible without causing any user to wait very long.

FORTRAN is primarily designed for batch processing applications, but it is also used for interactive processing.

Real-time processing

In *real-time processing,* computer response must be nearly instantaneous. The computer is used to directly control equipment. Embedded computer systems are real-time systems. Examples include a computer on board an aircraft that controls the autopilot, or computers that control nuclear reactor cooling systems, space shuttles, pacemakers, power fluctuations, and automobile ignition systems. Real-time systems are online systems which must respond immediately to changing needs. They have critical time constraints. Such systems are dedicated to single job applications. FORTRAN may be used for real-time applications only in special hardware and software environments.

1.4.3 Review Questions

1. What is meant by time-sharing?

2. What is a batch-processing environment?

3. What is multiprogramming?

4. A multiprocessing system will have more than one _____ .

5. Why is real-time processing important?

6. Is interactive processing the same as real-time processing? Explain.

7. Why is programming for interactive processing different from programming for batch processing?

1.5 Examples of Algorithms

The following examples show the development of algorithmic procedures. Each step of the algorithm must perform a single function. Together the steps must arrive at the desired solution.

1.5.1 Stress in Steel Bar

Problem

Write an algorithm to compute the stress in a circular steel bar of diameter D subject to a tensile force of P tons.

Method

The stress is defined as force of resistance per unit area. To compute the stress, the area is computed first. Then the tensile force of P tons is divided by the area.

Algorithm in Pseudocode

Input the diameter D in inches
Compute the radius
 $R \leftarrow D/2$
Compute the cross-sectional area of the circular rod
 $Area \leftarrow \pi R^2$
Input the tensile force P in tons
Compute the tensile stress
 $f \leftarrow P/Area$ (computed in tons/sq in.)
Output D, P, and f
Stop

Figure 1.11

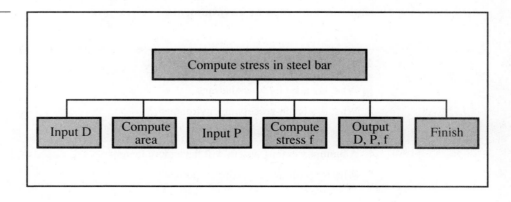

The algorithm is shown as a hierarchy chart in Fig. 1.11. The algorithm is shown as a flowchart in Fig. 1.12.

The input is done in two stages, as the values are needed. As the algorithm is written, the stress can be calculated for only one size of rod and only one tensile force. If the effects of several different forces were to be calculated for the rod, the algorithm would be as follows.

Figure 1.12

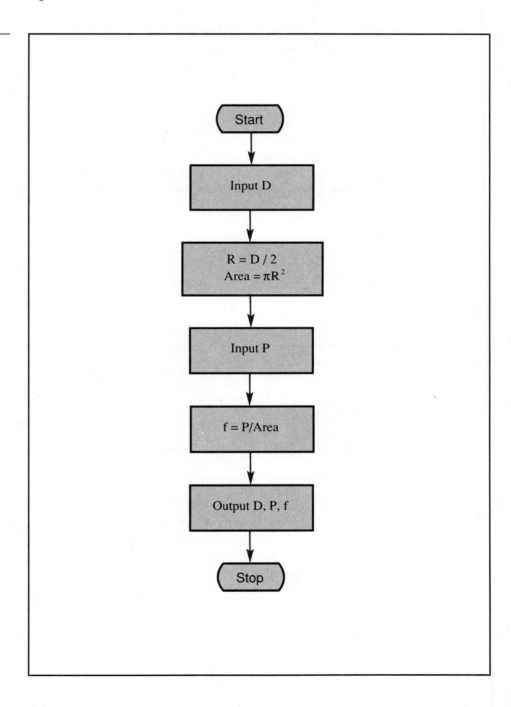

Algorithm in Pseudocode

Input the diameter D in inches
Compute the radius
   R ← D/2
Compute the cross-sectional area of the circular rod
   Area ← πR^2
For each tensile force,
   Input the tensile force P in tons
   Compute the tensile stress
     f ← P/Area (computed in tons/sq in.)
   Output D, P, and f
End for
Stop

The Algorithm is shown as a hierarchy chart in Fig. 1.13. The algorithm is shown as a flowchart in Fig. 1.14.

Next, various stresses on each of several different rods are to be calculated. The data values are presented in pairs: the diameter of the rod and the tensile force applied.

Figure 1.13

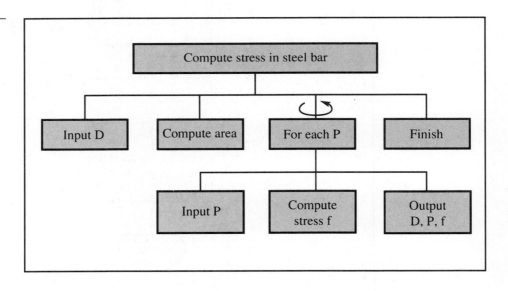

Figure 1.14

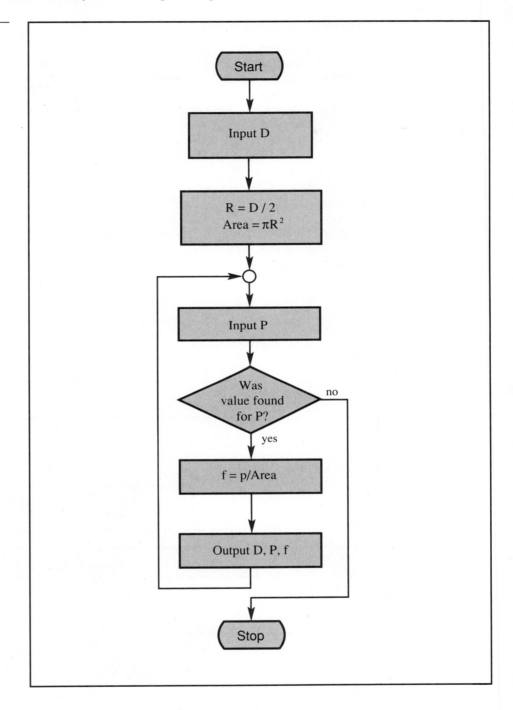

Algorithm in Pseudocode

For each data pair
   Input the diameter D in inches, and the force P in tons
   Compute the radius
     $R \leftarrow D/2$
   Compute the cross-sectional area of the circular rod
     Area $\leftarrow \pi R^2$
   Compute the tensile stress
     $f \leftarrow P/\text{Area}$ (computed in tons/sq in.)
   Output D, P, and f
End for
Stop

The algorithm is shown as a hierarchy chart in Fig. 1.15. The algorithm is shown as a flowchart in Fig. 1.16.

Figure 1.15

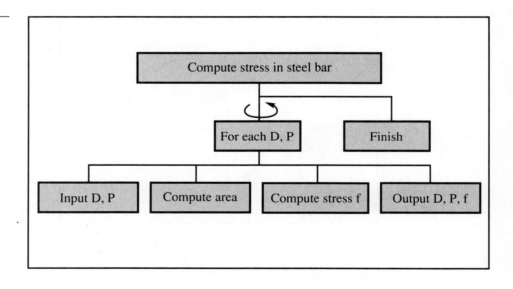

Figure 1.16

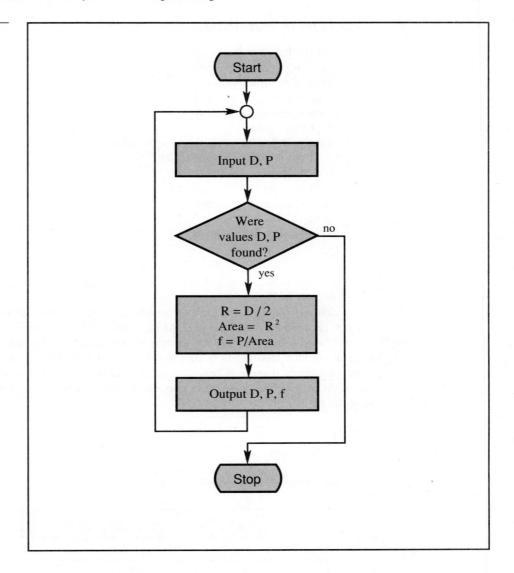

1.5.2 Largest and Smallest Values

Problem

Write an algorithm to compute the largest and the smallest integers in a given list of integers.

Method

Assume that the first number is both the largest and the smallest. Then, as each number is read, compare it to the smallest and largest already found. If the number is smaller than the previous smallest, save it. It if is larger than the previous largest, save it. Repeat the process until all the numbers have been processed.

Algorithm in Pseudocode

Input the first number
Save it as
   largest ← first number
   smallest ← first number
For each remaining number
   Input the number
   Compare it with the largest and smallest
     If the number > largest then
       largest ← number
     If the number < smallest then
       smallest ← number
End for
Output largest and smallest
Stop

The algorithm is shown as a hierarchy chart in Fig. 1.17. The algorithm is shown as a flowchart in Fig. 1.18.

Each number is compared with both the largest and smallest. The numbers are not retained in the computer. At any time, only the current number and the current largest and smallest are known to the computer. By initializing both the largest and smallest values to be the same as the first number, the algorithm will work accurately if there is only one number in the list, but it will be inaccurate if the list is empty. This method of processing data is used when there is no need to save the data.

Figure 1.17

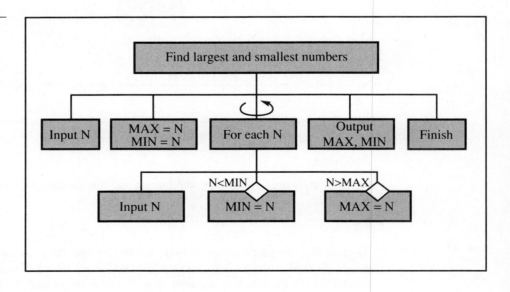

Figure 1.18

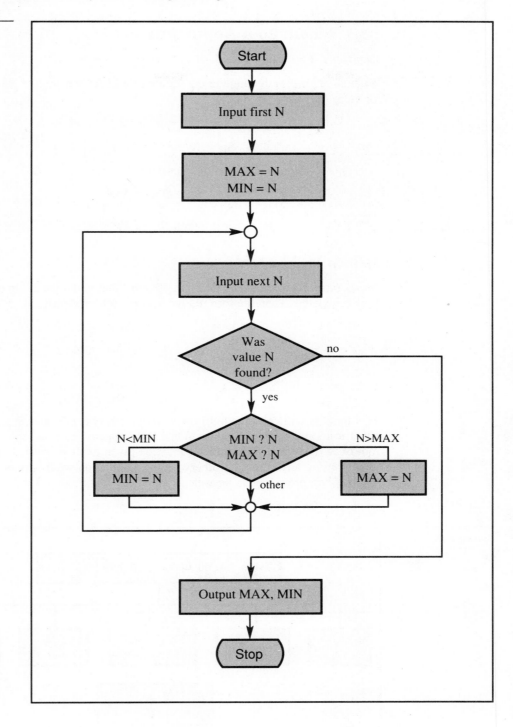

1.5.3 Square Root Approximation

Problem

Write an algorithm to compute the square root of X by using the Newton-Raphson formula:

$$S_{k+1} = (S_k + X/S_k)/2 \qquad k \geq 1$$

$$S_1 = X/2 \qquad X > 0$$

This formula is based on the fact that

$$\text{given } S_k \approx \sqrt{X}$$

$$\text{then } S_k^2 \approx X$$

Method

The iterative solution of the problem assumes that given the value of X, the value S_1 is calculated. Then the formula for S_{k+1} is used repeatedly.

$$\text{for } k = 1 \qquad S_2 = (S_1 + X/S_1)/2$$

$$k = 2 \qquad S_3 = (S_2 + X/S_2)/2$$

$$\cdots$$

$$k = n \qquad S_{n+1} = (S_n + X/S_n)/2$$

This process will continue until the difference between S_k and S_{k-1} is less than or equal to a predetermined value. When this happens, S_k is accepted as the square root of X. Note that the computer must be given explicit instructions about when to stop an iterative process, otherwise the calculation would continue indefinitely without ever providing an answer.

Figure 1.19

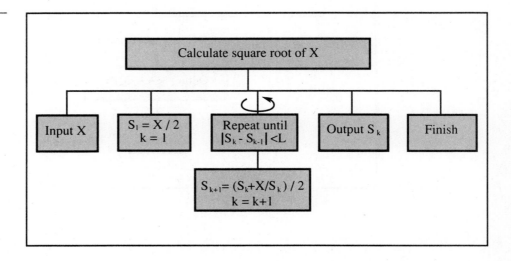

Figure 1.20

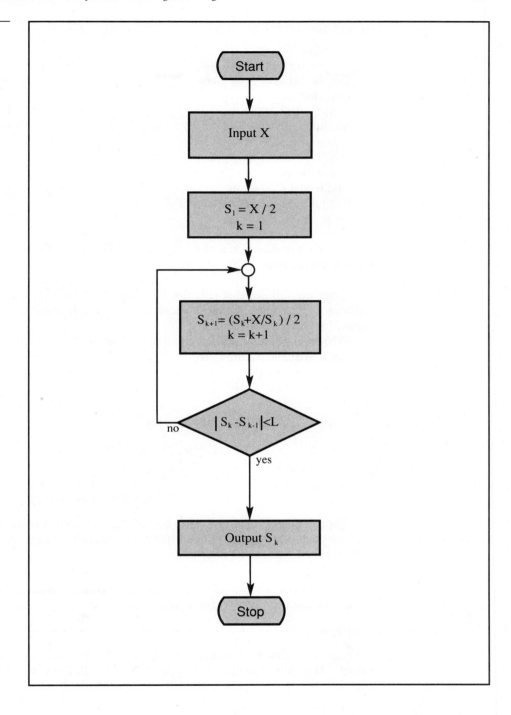

Algorithm in Pseudocode

Initialize limit
   $L \leftarrow 0.0001$
Get the value of X as input
Calculate S_1
   $S_1 \leftarrow X/2$
Starting with $k \leftarrow 1$
repeat until $|S_k - S_{k-1}| < L$
   $S_{k+1} \leftarrow (S_k + X/S_k)/2$
   $k \leftarrow k + 1$
End repeat
Output S_k as the square root of X
Stop

The algorithm is shown as a hierarchy chart in Fig. 1.19. The Algorithm is shown as a flowchart in Fig. 1.20.

Later we will see that it is not necessary to have all the different S values available at the same time. It is possible to write this algorithm using only two names, for example, SK and SNEXT.

Whenever possible, an algorithm should be hand checked before a computer program is written. Assume that

$$X = 25.0$$

Then

$$S_1 = 25.0/2 = 12.5$$

$$S_2 = (12.5 + 25.0/12.5)/2 = 7.25$$

$$S_3 = (7.25 + 25.0/7.25)/2 = 5.349$$

$$S_4 = (5.349 + 25.0/5.349)/2 = 5.0113$$

The calculated value appears to be converging to 5.0, the correct square root. The computer iteration will stop when two successive values of S are within a predetermined distance of each other.

1.5.4 Velocity of Water Through Pipes

Problem

Write an algorithm to compute the velocity of water flowing through a pipe of diameter D inches. The rate of flow of water is Q cubic feet per second.

Method

For each pipe size, for Q varying from Q1 to Q2, compute the velocity of water flowing through the pipe per second. First compute the cross-sectional area of the pipe in square feet. Divide the rate of flow of the water by the cross-sectional area of the pipe to obtain the velocity.

Algorithm in Pseudocode

For each diameter D
  Input diameter D in inches and Q1 and Q2 cu ft/sec
  Compute the radius
    R ← D/24 ft
  Compute the cross-sectional area
    Area ← πR² sq ft
  Q ← Q1
  Do while Q ≤ Q2
    Compute the velocity
      Vel ← Q/Area (ft/sec)
    Output Q, D, Vel
    Q ← Q + 1
  End do
End for
Stop

The algorithm is shown as a hierarchy chart in Fig. 1.21. The algorithm is shown as a flowchart in Fig. 1.22.

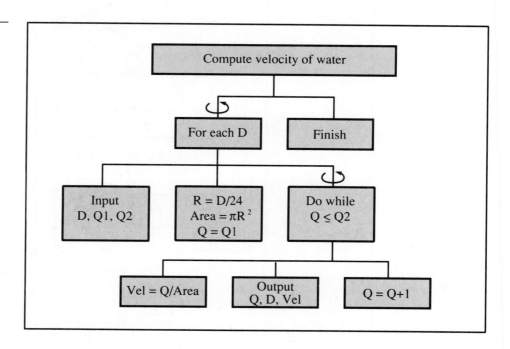

Figure 1.21

Figure 1.22

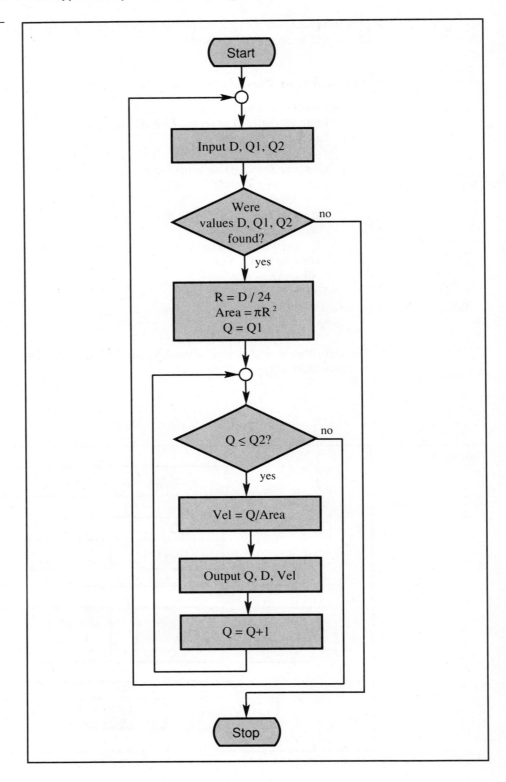

1.5.5 Monthly Sales Report

Problem

Write a program which prints a daily sales summary for a scientific instrument company.

Method

There is a record for each day of the month of the dollar sales of balances, pumps, meters, and scopes. Compute the total monthly sales of each type of item, and the total sales for the month. Print the daily sales and monthly totals.

Algorithm in Pseudocode

```
TBAL ← 0
TPUMP ← 0
TMETER ← 0
TSCOPE ← 0
For each day of the month
    Input BAL, PUMP, METER, SCOPE
    Print BAL, PUMP, METER, SCOPE
    Add BAL, to TBAL
    Add PUMP to TPUMP
    Add METER to TMETER
    Add SCOPE to TSCOPE
end for
TOTAL ← TBAL + TPUMP + TMETER + TSCOPE
Print TBAL, TPUMP, TMETER, TSCOPE
Print TOTAL
Stop
```

Figure 1.23

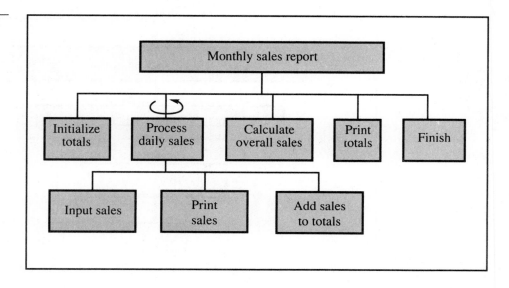

Figure 1.24

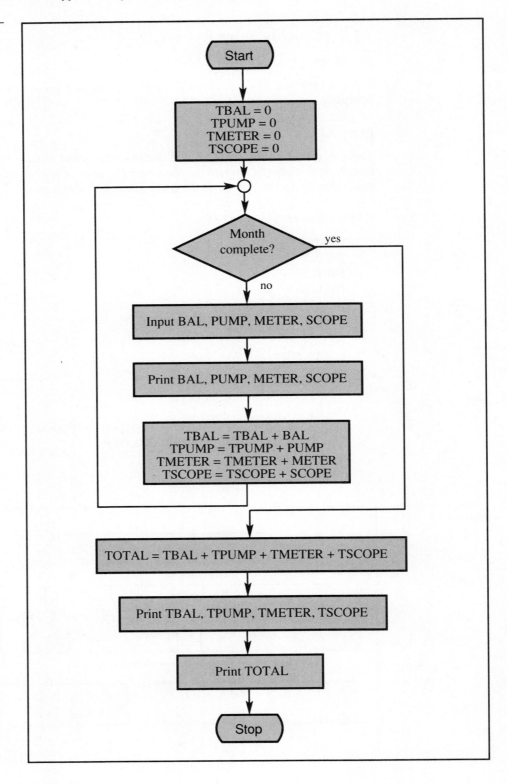

The algorithm is shown as a hierarchy chart in Fig. 1.23. The algorithm is shown as a flow chart in Fig. 1.24.

Chapter Summary

Modern computers are used to solve problems accurately and quickly. They can handle large amounts of data. Computers come in different sizes, from personal computers to minicomputers to large mainframes. A computer system consists of hardware components, software modules, and firmware, which is software embedded in the hardware. The hardware components are the input and output devices, memory, and processor and peripheral devices such as disk drives, tape drives, graphic display devices, and plotters. Input devices send information to be processed into the computer. Output devices return the processed information from the computer system. The processor performs arithmetic and logic operations on the information stored in memory under the commands of a control unit.

The major system software component is the operating system, which manages all the system resources and interfaces between the system and the user. Other software components are the system utilities, file management routines, and compilers. Programs written to solve problems are called application software. These programs are written in a high-level language, compiled and debugged to eliminate errors, and then linked and executed.

Solving problems on a computer involves several steps: design, implementation, testing, production use, and maintenance. The design step includes design of data formats, a procedural algorithm, and test data. The steps are repeated until a program is obtained that produces correct results.

An application program may run in a batch or interactive environment. The environment may be single job, time sharing, or real time.

Exercises

1. Write an algorithm to compute the sum and average of a list of input numbers.

2. Write an algorithm to compute the root of a given polynomial,

$$X^3 + 5X^2 + 6X + 7 = 0$$

using the Newton-Raphson iteration scheme,

$$X_{n+1} = X_n - f(X_n)/K$$

where $K = 3X^2 + 10X + 6$ the derivative of $f(X)$

3. Write an algorithm to compute the roots of a quadratic equation $AX^2 + BX + C = 0$ whose solutions are:

$$X_1 = \frac{-B + \sqrt{B^2 - 4AC}}{2A}$$

$$X_2 = \frac{-B - \sqrt{B^2 - 4AC}}{2A}$$

4. Write an algorithm to compute the distance S fallen by an object in free fall. The formula is:

$$S = S_0 + V_0 t + \frac{1}{2} a t^2$$

where S_0 is the initial position in feet, V_0 is the initial velocity in ft/sec, t is the time in seconds, and a is 32 ft/sec².
Make a table of S for t = 1, 5, 10, 15, 20, . . ., 100.

5. Write an algorithm to compute the distance covered in 20 min, 40 min, 60 min, 80 min, 100 min, . . . if an airplane is traveling at a speed of 600 miles per hour. Stop at 1000 miles.

6. Write an algorithm to compute the amount of accumulated principal P_n for n years, at the interest rate of r, for an initial investment of P_0, if the interest is compounded annually. The formula for compound interest is:

$$P_n = P_0 (1 + r)^n$$

Print a table showing the amount at the end of each year. Base each year's amount on the previous year rather than using the exponential formula.

7. Write an algorithm to compute the compressive stress on a circular hollow steel rod of inner diameter D_i and outer diameter D_o subject to a compressive load of P tons for P = 1, 2, 3, . . . 10. The formulas are:

$$R_o = D_o/2$$

$$R_i = D_i/2$$

$$\text{area} = \pi(R_o^2 - R_i^2)$$

$$\text{stress} = P/\text{area}$$

8. Write an algorithm to compute the flow in gallons per second through a pipe of diameter D ft with the velocity of V ft/sec. The formula for the flow rate Q in cubic ft/sec is:

$$Q = \pi R^2 V$$

where R = D/2 and where 1 cu ft = 7.481 gallons. Input data consists of pairs of values D and V.

9. Write pseudocode, draw a hierarchy chart and a flowchart for a sales report for a copying shop. The copying shop charges different rates per page for copying different size documents. The input consists of the number of copies made of each of three different document sizes, and the cost per copy for each order. Compute and print the total cost of each order and the total for the day.

10. Write pseudocode, draw a hierarchy chart and a flowchart for a production report for a machine shop. The input consists of the number of pieces of each part made, the unit production cost and the sales price for each part made. Compute the net sales for the day. Print the cost, sales price, and profit per part, and the total cost, total sales, and total net sales.

2 *Basic Concepts of FORTRAN*

Objective: To learn the logical, syntactic, and physical structure of a FORTRAN program and the types of data that can be processed.

*O*f the high-level programming languages, FORTRAN has become the most widely used for scientific programming. It was the first high-level programming language developed, and because of its simplicity and versatility it has been extended to meet evolving needs of the scientific and engineering communities. The name FORTRAN stands for FORmula TRANslation, reflecting its development for efficient handling of mathematical formulas and equations.

FORTRAN has been revised many times. The popular present version is known as FORTRAN 77. (The 77 refers to 1977 when it was targeted for release for general use.) This process has been guided by the introduction of various standards, starting with ANSI (American National Standards Institute) FORTRAN in 1966. Standardization makes programs more portable from one computing system to another. In practice, most compiler developers follow the standards but add proprietary extensions. Therefore the programmer who wishes to write portable programs must be familiar with standard FORTRAN as well as with the version available on the computer being used.

The structured programming concepts introduced in the 1970s to increase programmer productivity were included in the ANSI standard for FORTRAN 77, which appeared in 1978. This standard forms the basis of the FORTRAN presented in this text, although common extensions are also discussed. The extensions are clearly marked so that the programmer wishing to write standardized programs may avoid them.

2.1 Structured Programming

In structured programming design any algorithm can be written using three basic structures. This develops naturally from top-down algorithm development methodology and results in programs that have a clear structure and are both reliable and maintainable.

2.1.1 Concepts of Structured Programming

The development of algorithms in a top-down approach should use only the basic control structures. Recall that a program is a sequence of steps, each of which is an instruction or a group of instructions to be carried out by the computer. Some of these instructions are to be done exactly once; others are to be repeated many times; others offer alternatives. The steps in the sequence are to be followed in order. Each represents a single statement or a program module consisting of a group of statements, which is entered from the step above it and exited to the step below it.

2.1.2 Structured Constructs

The three basic structured constructs are sequence structure, selection structure, and repetition structure.

Figure 2.1

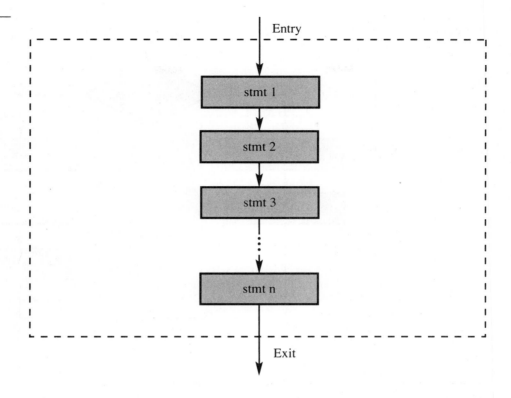

Sequence Structure

A sequence structure is one in which control flows down from one step to the next in sequence, without skipping any of the steps, executing each step exactly once. This is shown in the diagram in Fig. 2.1. An example of this structure written in pseudocode and FORTRAN is given below:

```
statement 1        A = 12.5
statement 2        B = 6.5
statement 3        C = A + B
    . . .              . . .
statement N        D = A * B - C / .016
```

Selection Structure

The selection structure gives the computer a choice of executing one of a set of statements. Usually there are two alternatives. Exactly one of them must be chosen and executed one time. FORTRAN 77 has special commands for the selection structure. A diagram for a selection structure with two alternatives is shown in Fig. 2.2. The following example of this structure shows both the general form in pseudocode and a FORTRAN equivalent:

Figure 2.2

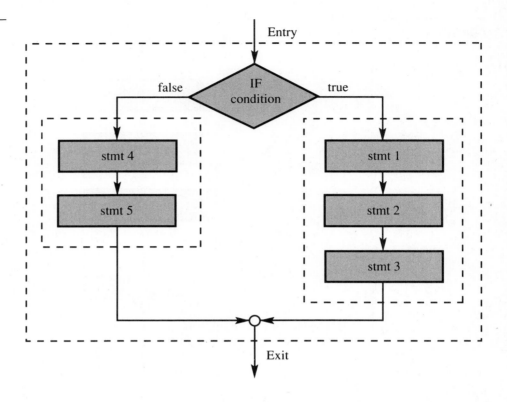

```
If condition then        IF (A .EQ. B) THEN
    statement 1              B = 2.0 * A
    statement 2              C = 3.0 * A
    statement 3              D = 4.0 * A
else                     ELSE
    statement 4              B = 0.0
    statement 5              C = 7.0
end if                   ENDIF
```

Repetition Structure

The repetition structure has one or more instructions that must be executed many times. These control constructs may be nested; for example, to instruct the computer to repeat a sequence of instructions, to repeat choices from a selection, or to select one of several repetitions. A diagram of this structure is shown in Fig. 2.3. A pseudocode equivalent and a FORTRAN example follow. FORTRAN 77 has special commands for the repetition structure. The DO WHILE is not a standard FORTRAN structure, but it exists in many compilers.

```
Do while condition       DO WHILE (A .GT. B)
    statement 1              A = A - .5
    statement 2              PRINT *, A
    statement 3              C = C + A
end do                   END DO
```

Figure 2.3

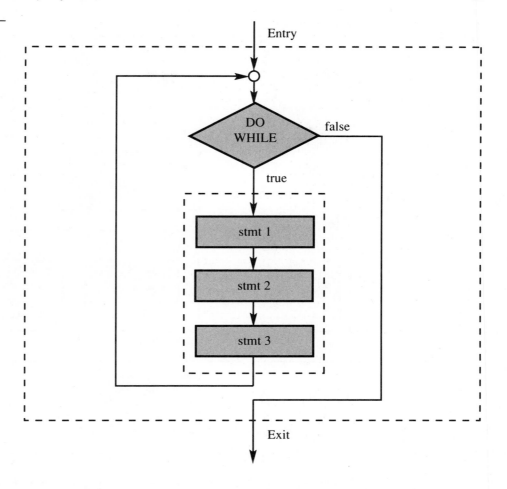

A structured chart is frequently used in the algorithm design stage and in documentation. This type of chart is a variation of a general flowchart that emphasizes the forms of the structures being used.

2.1.3 Design of Structured Programs

Use a hierarchy chart when developing the solution to a complex problem. The top level of the chart represents the problem statement, as in Fig. 2.4. The major modules in the next level each represent a structured construct. Usually the first and last modules represent sequences and any middle modules represent repetitions or selections, as in Fig. 2.5. Any selections are likely to appear at the third level, as in Fig. 2.6.

Programming
Hint

Design step: The design should be thoroughly tested before starting the programming.

Figure 2.4

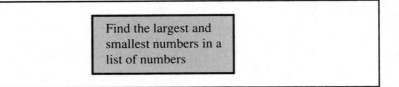

Figure 2.5

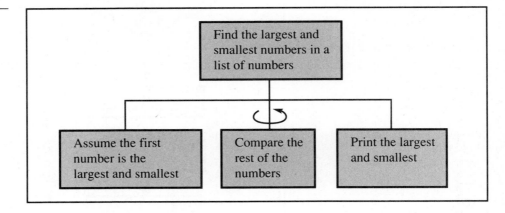

Figure 2.6

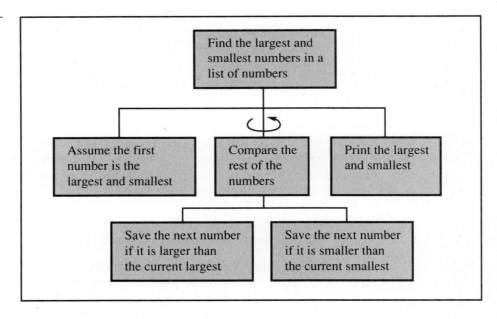

A hierarchy chart may have many levels and many modules at each level. As a design aid, it is a visual way of presenting an algorithm in general terms.

After developing the hierarchy chart, review the design to make sure that everything is included. You can then construct structured flowcharts to show the algorithm in more detail, and a glossary that assigns a name to each item. The names are generally used in the flowchart, as in Fig. 2.7. This structured chart

Figure 2.7

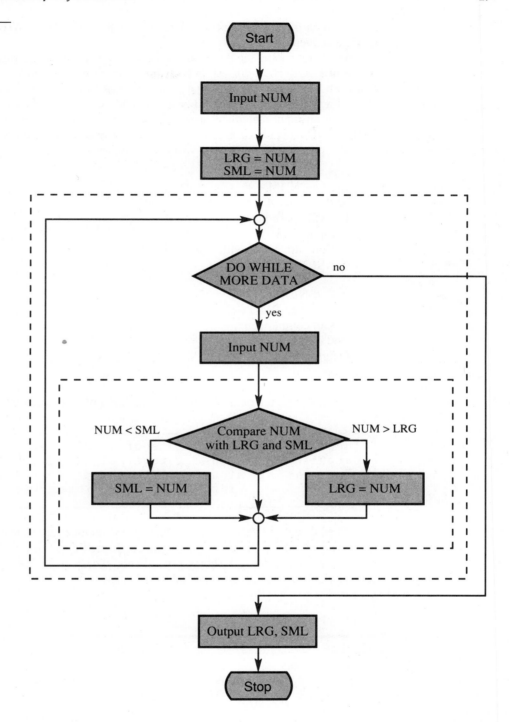

also shows a three-way selection statement nested inside a DO WHILE repetition inside a sequence.

While reviewing the flowchart for correctness, check to see that every module of the hierarchy chart corresponds to one or more modules of the flowchart, and that each module of the flowchart only belongs to one module of the hierarchy chart. Each name used in the flowchart should be given a value, that is, it should appear in an input statement or on the left side of an assignment (e.g., SML in SML = NUM) before it appears on the right side or in an output statement.

The pseudocode equivalent of Fig. 2.7 follows:

```
Input NUM
LRG ← NUM
SML ← NUM
Do while more data
   Input NUM
   Compare NUM with LRG and SML
      If NUM > LRG
         then LRG ← NUM
      If NUM < SML
         then SML ← NUM
   End comparison
End do
Output LRG, SML
Stop
```

Next, design the details of the input and output, for example:

```
Input:    NUM  signed integer of at most 5 digits
Output:   LRG  signed integer of at most 5 digits
          SML  signed integer of at most 5 digits
               largest = ±XXXXX   smallest = ±XXXXX
```

Then design the test data. Test data should include representative values, extreme values, and other values that might cause problems. Develop more than one set of test data. Table 2.1 shows several sets. These sets of test data have been carefully constructed to have the following properties:

Table 2.1

	SET A	SET B	SET C	SET D	SET E	SET F
	+425	+425	−425	+425	−1234	+425
		+99999	−99999	+0	−0	+99999
		+37	−3960	+1234	−425	−99999
						−425
max	+425	+99999	−425	+1234	−0	+99999
min	+425	+37	−99999	+0	−1234	−99999

set A: a list with only a single number

set B: a list with only positive numbers, the maximum in the middle and the minimum at the end

set C: a list with only negative numbers, the minimum in the middle and the maximum at the beginning

set D: a list of nonnegative numbers, the maximum at the end and the minimum in the middle

set E: a list of nonpositive numbers, the maximum in the middle and the minimum at the beginning

set F: a list of positive and negative numbers, the maximum and minimum both in the middle

If the program being developed is to be used interactively, you should include data that intentionally violates the descriptions in the glossary. For example:

1234 (without a sign), $+2X5$ (not all numeric), -123456 (too long)

Each of these sets of test data can be used to test both the hierarchy chart and the flowchart. Eventually they can be used to test the program.

Programming Hint

> Debugging: For cost effectiveness, use test data at the design stage.

This particular hierarchy chart and flowchart do not include any data validation steps. In later chapters, after the basic elements of FORTRAN have been presented, data validation modules will be included in the examples.

2.1.4 Review Questions

1. Indicate whether each of the following statement is true or false.

   a. Any program can be written using only three basic structures.
   b. In structured programming the control flow is top-down.
   c. Structured programs develop naturally from a top-down design methodology.
   d. Hierarchy charts are used in the beginning stages of program design.
   e. Each module in a hierarchy chart may result in several modular structures in a flowchart.
   f. If programs are written carefully, they do not have to be tested.
   g. A program must be able to distinguish good data from bad data.

2. The three basic structures used in structured programming are _____ , _____ , and _____ .

3. How are the structures represented in a hierarchy chart?

4. How are the structures represented in a structured flowchart?

5. What is in a glossary?

6. Why should more than one set of test data be used?

7. Test data should include numbers that differ in _____ , _____ , and _____ .

2.2 Constants and Variables

In FORTRAN 77, there are two ways of writing constants: as literal numbers or character strings, e.g., 3.715 or 'ABC'; or by using names that stand for single values, e.g, PI or ZERO. Variables are similar to variables in mathematical formulas. They have names (e.g., X or AREA) that can have different values at different times. When names are used for constants and variables, the programmer is responsible for assigning values to the names. Until a value is assigned, a variable is said to be *undefined*. A name can have only one value at a time. Both names and values must be written according to the rules of the FORTRAN language.

2.2.1 Character Set

Like any other language, FORTRAN 77 has a finite set of symbols called the *character set*. This includes all the symbols that may be used in names, literals, instructions, data descriptions, and so on. The FORTRAN character set consists of alphabetic characters, numeric digits, and special characters.

Alphabetic Characters

These are the 26 capital letters of the English alphabet. Many recent FORTRAN compilers also accept lowercase letters.

A B C D E F G H I J K L M N O P Q R S T U V W X Y Z

Numeric Characters

These are the numeric digits of the decimal number system.

0 1 2 3 4 5 6 7 8 9

Special Characters

arithmetic operators	+ − * /
assignment operator	=
grouping symbols	( )
punctuation symbols	, . ' :
blank space	ƀ
currency symbol	$

For purposes of alphabetizing names, addresses, and other data, an order known as the *collating sequence* is assigned to these symbols. The collating sequence depends on the character code being used by the computer. The most common codes are ASCII and EBCDIC, shown in Appendix A. In all the codes, the blank space precedes the alphabetic characters, and the alphabetic characters are in alphabetic order.

The characters from the character set are used to form symbolic names for many things besides constants and variables. The FORTRAN language has rules for the formation of names.

2.2.2 Identifiers (INTEGER, REAL, and PARAMETER statements)

Identifiers are the symbolic names that represent quantities in the program, whether they are constants or variables. An identifier must consist of one to six alphabetic or numeric characters. The first character must be alphabetic.

Since the period and hyphen are not alphabetic or numeric characters, they cannot be used in names. The blank space is not alphabetic or numeric, either. If it is used in a name, it will be ignored.

Valid identifiers	*Invalid identifiers*	*Comment*
DISTAN	DIAMETER	too long
VALUE5	5CONST	first character not alphabetic
TIME8	TOTßAL	blank ignored
B57C	VAL*C1	illegal char
MAXIM	MAX,MU	illegal char

In some FORTRAN compilers, data names may have more than six characters, but the computer will use only the first six. Because of this limitation, the examples in this text use data names of at most six characters. Technically, FORTRAN ignores all blanks that are not within quotations. However, it is confusing to have blanks included in data names or to have data names that are not separated by blanks. Therefore, the examples in this text are spaced for maximum readability.

It is important to use meaningful names when creating the glossary. Because of the restriction on the length of a name, when names must be abbreviated, standard abbreviations or a standard method of abbreviation should be used. Names might be shortened by eliminating the vowels, for example. Names that differ by one character or that are similar in appearance should not be used. You can see that using both names of each of the following pairs could easily lead to confusion and logical errors.

PRINTR	PRNTER	
Z00	ZOO	(0 and O are difficult to distinguish)
LIEF	LEIF	
AREA1C	AREA2C	
TRI	TRIA	

Declaration of Variables

All FORTRAN program variables should be declared in order to increase the reliability and maintainability of the program. Declaring a variable allocates space in memory to store data, identifies the type of data to be stored, and provides a name for the data.

Explicit Declaration of INTEGER Names

The general form of the declaration statement is:

```
INTEGER var1,var2,. . .,varn
```

Examples:

```
INTEGER CONST,ITEM,VALUE,VELCT1
INTEGER SUM,TOTAL,AVG,NUMB
```

Several names may be typed in a single declaration. If several declarations are being used, names may be grouped by function or alphabetically for easy access.

Explicit Declaration of REAL Names

The general form of the declaration statement is:

```
REAL var1,var2,. . .,varn
```

Examples:

```
REAL ACON,JVAL,KMAX
REAL ICNT,JCNT,KCNT,XCNT
```

Several names may be typed in a single declaration. Notice that declarations may contain names that would implicitly be of the type being declared as well as names that would implicitly be of a different type.

The explicit declaration of names makes the programmer more aware of their use, in turn making the program easier to debug and thus increasing its reliability. The computer must know the type of each name before the name is used in any other way. Therefore the declaration statements must be placed at the beginning of the program, before any executable instructions.

Programming Hint

> Declare all variable and constant names explicitly.

Variable Types Implicit to the Language

As in all computer languages, it is important to distinguish between different types of values and identify the type of each name, both in the glossary of the design stage and in the FORTRAN program. In FORTRAN 77 two types of numbers are frequently used, integers and real numbers. If the types of their names are not identified in the program in a type declaration statement, an implicit assumption of type is made for each name. The identifier is assumed to be real or integer based on the first letter of the name.

Integer variables and constants that are not explicitly typed must have names starting with one of the characters I through N. Real variables and constants that are not explicitly typed must have names starting with one of the characters A through H or O through Z.

Integer names	Real names
JVALUE	CONSTN
MAXM1	VALUE
I	X
K9	QBK5

Integer values and real values are distinguished by the presence of a decimal point in real values. Only integer values can be given integer names.

Integer values	Real values
285	285.0
-1709	-13.681
0	.0

Because program readability and reliability are important, it is customary to require the explicit typing of names. This ensures more appropriate naming of variables and constants.

PARAMETER Statement

The PARAMETER statement is used to assign names to constants. Because the constants remain the same throughout the program, the values assigned to constants can be stored at compile time. This saves time during execution. The general form of the PARAMETER statement is:

```
PARAMETER (name1=value1,name2=value2,...,
           namen=valuen)
```

The general type of the name and the constant must be the same, that is, only numeric values may be assigned to numeric names, only character string values to character names, and only logical values to logical names. The PARAMETER statement may be used with either implicit or explicit typing of names.

```
INTEGER N,K,L
REAL PI,HALFPI,GRAV,ZERO
PARAMETER (N=50)
PARAMETER (K=80,L=60,PI=3.14159)
PARAMETER (GRAV=32.0,ZERO=0.0)
PARAMETER (PI=3.1416,HALFPI=PI/2.0)
```

Programming Hint

> Values should have the same type as the variables to which they are assigned.

Some versions of FORTRAN do not support the PARAMETER statement.

2.2.3 FORTRAN Data Types

There are six standard data types in FORTRAN 77: integer, real, double precision, complex, logical, and character. Some FORTRAN systems allow the programmer to define other data types. Only integer and real are recognized by the computer as implicit data types. The programmer may want to use double-precision numbers when very accurate computations with high-precision numeric values are required. Complex numbers are needed in some types of mathematical and scientific computations. Logical data types are convenient in problems that manipulate and structure stored data. Character data is used in the processing of text and pictures.

Integer, real, double-precision, and complex values can all be used in arithmetic. They may be unsigned or written with leading signs. An unsigned number is assumed to be positive. Real values may also be written in modified scientific notation using exponents. The following examples show the data types of various numeric literals.

Literal	*Type*
48567	integer
12.8654	real
−687	integer
−687.0	real
−0.687E03	real, same as −687.0
0.000375	real
0.375E−03	real, same as 0.000375
5.0E2	real, same as 500.0

Note that when the letter E is used in a numeric literal, that value is never an integer. The letter E stands for exponent. The number following it is an exponent of 10. Therefore:

−0.687E03	means	-0.687×10^{03}
0.375E−03	means	0.375×10^{-03}

Modified scientific notation is used for numbers that would otherwise require a lot of zeros but are within a range determined by the computer hardware. For example, IBM 360/370 computers can handle numbers in the range 10^{-77} to 10^{+75} while the VAX 11/780 restricts them to the range 10^{-38} to 10^{+38}. Supercomputers such as the CRAY series or the CYBER 208 handle numbers in a much larger range, such as 10^{-2950} to 10^{2950}.

2.2.4 Review Questions

1. There are _____ characters in a FORTRAN 77 character set.

2. The arithmetic operators in FORTRAN for addition, subtraction, multiplication, and division are _____ , _____ , _____ , and _____ .

3. A variable name in FORTRAN 77 is limited to _____ characters.

4. A variable name must start with one of the _____ characters.

5. A data name starting with I, J, K, L, M, or N has the implicit type _____ .

6. A data name starting with a character from A through H or O through Z has the implicit type _____ .

7. State whether each of the following names is valid or invalid in FORTRAN 77:

CONSTANT	$MONEY
MAXIM	COUNT
5VALUE	VAL8X
N57*XY	BLN+5
BALƀNC	MANY6

8. State whether each of the following values is integer or real:

+38954.0	−18.754
67532.75	0.00185
−95	2.395E02
0	756.814E−02

9. Write a statement declaring the following names to be integer:

   AMAX, ACON, BSTR, CVAL, CONST1, AMIN5

10. Write a statement declaring the following names to be real:

    ICON1, KMAX5, NMIN1, LVAL6, JCON10

11. Write a PARAMETER statement to assign the value 10 to N and 25 to K.

12. Write the statements necessary to assign the integer value 10 to constant X and the real value 57.02 to constant N.

2.3 Arithmetic Expressions and Operations

The basis of scientific computing is arithmetic calculations. In FORTRAN, arithmetic operations can only be performed on numeric data types: integer and real numbers, double-precision numbers, and complex numbers. If numbers are stored in other data types, such as a telephone number stored as numerals in a character string, they cannot be used in calculations.

2.3.1 Basic Arithmetic Operations

The basic arithmetic operations are represented in FORTRAN 77 by the following symbols:

exponentiation	**
multiplication	*
division	/
addition	+
subtraction	−

The symbol for exponentiation (**) is understood as a whole; there can be no blank space between the asterisks. Following the rules of algebra, the addition and subtraction symbols can be used with either one operand (as a unary plus or minus) or two operands (to indicate addition or subtraction). Two operators cannot be side by side; they must be separated by an operand or parentheses. The following examples show the use of the operators.

	Expression	*Value*
Unary plus:		
	$+(+5)$	5
Addition operation:		
	$4 + 7$	11
	$-3 + 9$	6
	$+8+11$	19
	$-5+(-7)$	-12
	$14.36+7.2$	21.56
	$.028+(-.41)$	$-.382$
Unary minus:		
	$-(-0.25)$	0.25
Subtraction operation:		
	$8 - 3$	5
	$+9 - 6$	3
	$3-(-6)$	9
	$6.2-4.9$	1.3
Multiplication operation:		
	$3*5$	15
	$-5 * 8$	-40
	$9 *(-5)$	-45
	$2.5*1.1$	2.75
Division operation:		
	$18/2$	9
	$-20/2$	-10
	$17/(-8)$	-2
	$6.4/.4$	16.0

Programming Warning

> Division of integers produces an integer result.

When both operands are integers, the result is also an integer. This may lead to undesired results in division. The integer quotient is found by truncating the answer rather than rounding it.

$21/3$	7	
$21/4$	5	
$21/5$	4	
$21/6$	3	
$21/7$	3	
$-21/4$	-5	
$-21/6$	-3	
$21/22$	0	(truncated)

Exponentiation operation:

$5 ** 4$	625	(same as $5*5*5*5$)
$5**4.0$	625	
$2 ** (-3)$	0	(.125 truncated)
$36 ** 0.5$	6.0	

$$-8 ** 2 \qquad -64 \qquad \text{(same as } 0 - 8*8)$$
$$(-8)**2 \qquad 64 \qquad \text{(same as } (-8)*(-8))$$
$$-16**0.5 \qquad -4.0$$
$$(-16)**0.5 \qquad \text{error}$$

Mode of Arithmetic Results

If arithmetic is performed on integer operands only, the result is integer. If it is perfomed on real operands only, the result is real. If the operand types are mixed, the arithmetic is known as *mixed mode,* and the result will be the more complex of the two operand types, which is the real type. For example:

Expression	*Result*
18 + 2	20
18 + 2.0	20.0
18 − 9.5	8.5
12 * 2	24
6.3 * 2.1	13.23
13/2	6
(− 13)/2.0	−6.5
13.0/2.0	6.5
13.0/2	6.5
9**2	81
9**(0.5)	3.0

Programming Hint

> Efficiency: When possible, avoid mixed mode arithmetic.

When arithmetic (other than exponentiation) is done using both integer and real operands, the computer has to change the integer operand to a real number before performing the arithmetic.

18 + 5.0	becomes	18.0 + 5.0	with the result	23.0
15.2/4	becomes	15.2/4.0	with the result	3.8

When exponentiation is written using an integer exponent, the computer changes it into a series of multiplications.

5**4	becomes	5*5*5*5	with the result	625
5.0**4	becomes	5.0*5.0*5.0*5.0	with the result	625.0

But when exponentiation is written using a real exponent, the computer must change the base to a real number if it is not already real and use a logarithmic approximation.

$$5**4.0 \qquad \text{becomes} \qquad e^{4.0(\ln 5.0)} \qquad = 625.0$$

Table 2.2 gives the resulting type for mixed mode arithmetic other than exponentiation.

Note that blank spaces may be placed between elements of the FORTRAN language to make it more readable, but they cannot be placed within numbers or

Table 2.2

	INTEGER	REAL	DOUBLE PRECISION	COMPLEX
Integer	integer	real	double	complex
Real	real	real	double	complex
Double precision	double	double	double	not allowed
Complex	complex	complex	not allowed	complex

the exponentiation operator. Parentheses may be used to clarify the meaning of an expression.

Double precision and complex arithmetic are presented in later chapters.

2.3.2 Arithmetic Expressions

So far, only arithmetic expressions using numeric literals have been shown. In numerical computations for scientific and engineering problems, it is more common to use arithmetic expressions with variables. Numeric literals, constants, and variables may be mixed. The type of the result depends on the types of the operands. An expression can be used in FORTRAN programming wherever a value of the same type can be used. Also, following the rules of algebra, an expression may contain many operations.

FORTRAN expression	*Result type*
3 + 5 * 6 − 8 / 5	integer constant
3.0 − 5.6 + 7.3 / 2.0	real constant
J * I * K − L	implicit integer variable
A3 − BOT * C + DIM	implicit real variable
A * I + J9 − C/6.0	mixed mode, real result

An algebraic expression that does not have parentheses, complicated fractions, or complicated exponents can be written in FORTRAN by using the FORTRAN symbols in place of the algebraic symbols. Note that symbols must always be used for multiplication and exponentiation.

Algebraic expression	*FORTRAN expression*
$a + bc - \dfrac{d}{e} + f$	A + B * C − D / E + F
lwh	L * W * H
$3.14\ r^2$	3.14 * R ** 2
$ps + r^2 - tl + \dfrac{k}{4.0}$	P*S + R**2 − T*L + K/4.0
$\dfrac{a}{-5} + 7$	A/(−5) + 7
$x^{-2} + y^{-2}$	X**(−2) + Y**(−2)

These expressions are parentheses-free except around a unary operation. The computer evaluates the FORTRAN expressions in the same way that the algebraic expressions are evaluated, with operations performed from left to right depending on the precedence of the operators. Examples of computer evaluation are given in Section 2.3.4.

2.3.3 Assignment Statement

The assignment statement is a fundamental statement in most computer languages, including FORTRAN. Although the equal sign (=) is used in the FORTRAN assignment statement, this symbol does not have the same meaning that it does in algebraic expressions. The meaning of the symbol in FORTRAN is like its meaning in mathematical formulas where it indicates that the value computed from the expression on the right of the equal sign should be assigned to the variable name on the left.

A = 0.5∗B∗H   means   calculate $\dfrac{BH}{2}$ and assign the result to A. That

is, find the area of a triangle by taking half the base times the height.

An assignment statement prescribes actions to be taken. A calculation may be performed. If necessary, the result is converted to the data type of the variable where it is to be stored, and then it is stored. Therefore assignment statements such as the following are meaningful:

X = 6.0   before   after

X = X + 5.0   X $\boxed{6.0}$ $\boxed{11.0}$

This means retrieve the current value of X, which is 6.0, add 5.0 to it, and store the result back in X, replacing the value 6.0 with the new value, 11.0. In doing this, the computer loses the old value of X, replacing it with the new computed value.

The expression on the right side of an assignment statement may be of any appropriate type and may be a literal or constant, another variable that has already been given a value, or a valid FORTRAN expression to be evaluated. The following are examples of valid assignment statements:

Assignment statement	*Comment*
BB = 18.0	assuming BB is real, it takes the value 18.0
C = X	C is given the same value as X
T = 'HEADING'	assuming T is a character variable, it takes 'HEADING' as its value
X = 0.5 ∗ Y ∗ Z	using the values of Y and Z, 0.5∗Y∗Z is calculated and the result is stored in X
A = A∗C − A/B + A	the old value of A is replaced by a value calculated using the old value of A, B, and C

Each assignment statement is carried out in three steps.

1. The computer evaluates the expression on the right side of the equal sign.
2. If the result is not of the same type as the variable on the left side, it is converted to the proper type.
3. The computer assigns the resulting value to the variable on the left side. In effect, the value is stored in the memory location assigned to that variable.

When in integer value is assigned to a real variable, it is converted to a real value having a fractional part of .0 before being stored. When a real value is assigned to an integer variable, the fractional part of the value is discarded before the value is stored.

Assignment statement	Calculated value		Value assigned
M = 16.0/3.0	5.333333		5
K = − 19.0/4.0	−4.75		−4
N = 3 ∗ 5 ∗ 1.1	16.5		16
X = 2/3	0		0.0
A = 4.0∗∗(1/2)	1.0	(4.0∗∗0)	1.0
B = 4.0∗∗(1.0/2.0)	2.0	(4.0∗∗0.5)	2.0

2.3.4 Order of Evaluation

The order of evaluation of operations in arithmetic expressions depends on the precedence of the operations. This order is:

highest   ( )
           ∗∗
           ∗ /
lowest   + −

Operations of the same precedence are performed left to right except for exponentiation, which is performed right to left. Therefore the following are equivalent:

A + B + C	(A + B) + C	
X − Y − 7	(X − Y) − 7	
A + B − Z	(A + B) − Z	
15 ∗ Q ∗ R	(15 ∗ Q) ∗ R	
14 / 7 / 2	(14 / 7) / 2	value is 1
24 / 6 ∗ 3	(24 / 6) ∗ 3	value is 12
4∗∗3∗∗2	4 ∗∗ (3 ∗∗ 2)	

Observing both precedence and direction of calculation, in the following cases,

```
      4 ** 2 + 5 ** 3 + 6 **2
is    16  + 125  +   36
is        141      + 36
is             177
```

and

```
         24 / 3 / 2 − 14 * 6 − 3 ** 2 ** 2
is   24 / 3 / 2 − 14 * 6 − 3 **    4
is   24 / 3 / 2 − 14 * 6 −     81
```

$$\text{is} \qquad 8 \quad / 2 - 14 * 6 - \quad 81$$
$$\text{is} \qquad 4 \quad - 14 * 6 - \quad 81$$
$$\text{is} \qquad 4 \quad - \qquad 84 - \quad 81$$
$$\text{is} \qquad -80 \qquad - \quad 81$$
$$\text{is} \qquad\qquad -161$$

This is a slight oversimplification of the actual order of calculation used by the computer, but the result is the same. The following example shows the details of the step-by-step evaluation of an algebraic expression:

$$w + xy - \frac{g}{h} + e^2 + cd$$

	$W + X * Y - G / H + E ** 2 + C * D$	FORTRAN expression
step 1	$W + X * Y - G / H + \quad R1 \quad + C * D$	where $R1 = E ** 2$
step 2	$W + \quad R2 \quad - \quad R3 \quad + \quad R1 \quad + \quad R4$	where $R2 = X * Y$
		$R3 = G / H$
		$R4 = C * D$
step 3	$R5 \qquad\quad - R3 \quad + \quad R1 \quad + \quad R4$	where $R5 = W + R2$
step 4	$R6 \quad + \quad R1 \quad + \quad R4$	where $R6 = R5 - R3$
step 5	$R7 \qquad + \quad R4$	where $R7 = R6 + R1$
step 6	$R8$	where $R8 = R7 + R4$

R1, R2, . . . R7 are the intermediate results calculated by the computer before it reaches the final result R8. R2, R3, and R4 have been included in the same step because they are independent calculations and can be carried out in any order. R5, R6, R7, and R8 must be calculated one after the other and so are shown as separate steps. At each step, the computer uses the current values of the variables to calculate the new value. If the types don't match, it converts the values to the type needed to carry out the operation. This is shown in the following example:

Let $A = 10.0, B = 5.0, I = 6, K = 8, C = 12.0, D = 6.0$

		FORTRAN 77 expression
	$A * B + C / D + K - I ** 2$	FORTRAN 77 expression
step 1	$A * B + C / D + K - \quad 36$	$I ** 2$ is evaluated
step 2	$50.0 + \quad 2.0 \quad + K - \quad 36$	$A * B$ is evaluated
		C / D is evaluated
step 3	$52.0 \qquad + \quad K - \quad 36$	$50.0 + 2.0$ is computed
step 4	$60.0 \quad - \quad 36$	K is converted to real
		$52.0 + 8.0$ is computed
step 5	24.0	36 is converted to real
		$60.0 - 36.0$ is computed

The final result of the computation is a real value of 24.0.

2.3.5 Use of Parentheses

The order of evaluation used in the previous section is based on the hierarchy of operators when there are no parentheses in the expression. In some algebraic expressions in FORTRAN, parentheses are necessary to retain the meaning. For example, the algebraic expression

$$\frac{w + x}{y + z}$$

becomes the FORTRAN expression

$$(W + X) / (Y + Z)$$

Parentheses are generally necessary when an algebraic expression has fractions or exponents. The unparenthesized FORTRAN expression

$$W + X / Y + Z$$

is the equivalent of

$$w + \frac{x}{y} + z$$

All possible ways of parenthesizing this FORTRAN expression and their algebraic equivalents are shown below:

Algebraic expression	*FORTRAN expression*
$\dfrac{w + x}{y + z}$	$(W + X) / (Y + Z)$
$w + \dfrac{x}{y + z}$	$W + X / (Y + Z)$
$\dfrac{w + x}{y} + z$	$(W + X) / Y + Z$
$w + \dfrac{x}{y} + z$	$W + X / Y + Z$

Programming Hint

Use extra parentheses when there is any doubt as to how the expression should be parenthesized.

The general rule is to place the numerator and denominator of a fraction in parentheses if they are not positive numbers or simple variables. Parentheses are also required whenever there is an exponent with more than a single unsigned number or variable. If the exponent contains the division operator, unless integer division is intended, the exponent must be explicitly made real. When parentheses are used in an algebraic expression, they are also needed in the equivalent FORTRAN expression. The following examples show some critical cases:

Algebraic expression	*FORTRAN expression*
$a^{1/2}$	$A ** (1.0/2.0)$ or $A ** 0.5$
a^{-2}	$A ** (-2)$
$(-3)^6$	$(-3) ** 6$
-3^6	$-3 ** 6$ or $-(3 ** 6)$
$(-3)(-5)$	$(-3) * (-5)$ or $-3 * (-5)$
x^{y-1}	$X ** (Y - 1)$
$(X + 1)^3$	$(X + 1) ** 3$
$x^{k/n}$	$X ** ((1.0*K)/N)$

The hierarchy of operators shows that when an expression contains parentheses, the parentheses subexpressions must be evaluated first. When there are nested parentheses, the expression inside the inner parentheses is evaluated first, according to the hierarchical order of the operators, resulting in the removal of the inner parentheses. Then the innermost remaining expression is evaluated and its parentheses removed, and so on until there are no parentheses left and the remaining parentheses-free expression can be evaluated.

Programming Warning

> Proper nesting of parentheses is essential for correct computations.

The following example shows the evaluation of an algebraic expression containing nested parentheses:

$$\frac{s + t}{w + x + \dfrac{y + z}{p + q}}$$ Algebraic expression

	(S + T) / (W + X + (Y + Z) / (P + Q))		FORTRAN expression
step 1	R1 / (W + X + R2 / R3)	where R1 = S + T
		R2 = Y + Z
		R3 = P + Q
step 2	R1 / (W + X + R4)	where R4 = R2 / R3
step 3	R1 / (R5 + R4)	where R5 = W + X
step 4	R1 / R6	where R6 = R5 + R4
step 5	R7	where R7 = R1 / R6

In this example, all the parentheses shown in the FORTRAN expression are necessary to retain the meaning of the algebraic expression. As each set of parentheses is evaluated, the operations are performed according to the hierarchical precedence of operations.

2.3.6 Review Questions

1. The symbol used for the exponentiation operation is _____ .

2. Write the equivalent FORTRAN expression for each of the following algebraic expressions:

   a. $a + b - cd + \dfrac{g}{f}$

   b. $\dfrac{a + b}{c} + d - e$

   c. $\dfrac{5(x + y)}{8z} - km$

   d. $8a^2 + b^2 c$

   e. abc^2

   f. $-x + y \times (-z)$

   g. $-y^3 + z$

   h. $(x + y)^3 + z^2$

i. $\frac{1}{3}bh + \frac{1}{4}ik$

j. $bh^{1/2} - k^2p^{1/2}$

3. Given the values of A = 5.0, B = 10.5, C = 6.0, and I = 2, compute the value of each of the following:

a. A ** 2 + C ** 2

b. −5 ** I

c. B * A ** 2

d. A ** 2 * 3

e. A ** 3 − C ** 2

4. Given the values of X = 5.0, Y = 6.0, Z = 10.0, W = 8.0, compute the value of each of the following:

a. Y / X * Z

b. Y * X / Z

c. X * Y * Z / W

d. X * Y / Z * W

e. X / Y * Z / W

f. Z / X / W

5. Given the following algebraic expressions, write the equivalent FORTRAN expressions:

a. $\dfrac{w + x}{y + z} + xt$

b. $\dfrac{a + b + c}{d + e - \dfrac{f + g}{h + i}}$

c. $ax^3 + bx^2 - cx + d$

d. force = mass . acceleration

e. volume = length . width . height

6. Given the values of A = 10.5, B = 12.0, C = 8.5, I = 10, J = 6, determine the value computed and the value stored in each of the following assignment statements:

a. X = A − B * 2 − C / 2 + 5.0

b. Y = A * I + J − B / 2.0

c. Z = 15/2 * A + B

d. K = A * 5 + B − C / 2.0

e. L = I / 3 + J * 2.0 + C

7. Write the FORTRAN expression for each of the following equations used in engineering applications, where p is pressure, V is volume, m is moles, R is the universal gas constant, and t is temperature:

a. $p = \dfrac{mRt}{V}$

b. $p1 = \dfrac{p2\ v2}{v1}$ gives the pv constant for Boyle's law

c. Given the equation pv = mRt, write a FORTRAN statement to calculate the mass, given p, v, R, and t.

d. Given the formula a = $4\pi r^2$ for the surface area of a sphere, write a FORTRAN statement to calculate the radius r of a sphere given the surface area.

e. The moment of inertia of a disk about its fixed axis of rotation is a = $0.5\ m\ r^2$. Write a FORTRAN statement to calculate the mass, given a and r.

    f. The state equation for an ideal gas is $p = \rho R t$, where p is absolute pressure, ρ is mass density, t is absolute temperature, and R is the gas constant. Write a FORTRAN statement to find the pressure for gasses at 100° Celsius.

    g. The pressure loss in a pipe is given by:

$$h = \frac{f\, l\, v^2}{d\, 2g}$$

where f is the friction coefficient, l is length, v is velocity, d is diameter, g is gravitational acceleration. Write this as a FORTRAN statement.

    h. The discharge over a rectangular weir is given by:

$$q = k\sqrt{2gl}\; h^{3/2}$$

Write this as a FORTRAN statement.

    i. The effective resistance of a parallel circuit with five parallel resistances is given by:

$$r = \cfrac{1}{\dfrac{1}{r1} + \dfrac{1}{r2} + \dfrac{1}{r3} + \dfrac{1}{r4} + \dfrac{1}{r5}}$$

Write this as a FORTRAN statement.

2.4 FORTRAN 77 Library Functions

Library functions are predefined function modules built into the FORTRAN compiler. FORTRAN library functions include a large number of trignometric functions, character manipulation functions, logarithmic functions, and other mathematical functions. Some of these are standard, available with every FORTRAN implementation; others are offered by specific computer systems. Other mathematical functions can be found in scientific subroutine packages which are not part of standard FORTRAN. For the complete list of functions available on a specific computer, refer to the FORTRAN reference manual of the particular computer being used.

    The standard library functions in FORTRAN are also called intrinsic functions because they are built into the FORTRAN system and provided by the compiler. Only a few of the common functions are presented here. Others may be found in Appendix B.

2.4.1 Use of Functions

The names of the library functions are in most cases the same as the common mathematical abbreviations, but some of them have been altered to indicate the data type of the result of the function. The form used for library functions is:

```
fname(arg list)
```
                                      fname is a function name
                                        arg list is a list of arguments

There is no space between the function name and the parentheses enclosing the argument list. If there is more than one argument, the arguments are separated by commas. There is no space between the last argument and the closing right parenthesis.

Some of the function names are generic in that they represent more than one version of the same function; for example, a version for integers and one for real numbers. Other function names are type specific, that is, they may only be used with a single type of argument. When a generic name is used, any appropriate type may be used for the argument, and the type of the result after the evaluation of the function is the same as the type of the argument or arguments used. If the arguments are integers, the result will be an integer. If the arguments are real, the result will be real. When a generic function has more than one argument, all the arguments must be of the same type.

For example, the square root function SQRT is generic. There is a single argument which can be real, double precision, or complex. When the argument is real, for example 25.0, the square root 5.0 is real too. When the argument is double precision or complex, the square root is double precision or complex, respectively. In this example,

$$Y = SQRT(X)$$

if X is real, then SQRT(X) results in a real value. Therefore Y should be real too. If X is double precision, Y should be declared as double precision or the extra precision will be lost.

Because functional notation is a shorthand way of expressing a calculation, it is written in place of the calculation. For example:

Y = SQRT(X)	instead of	Y = X ** 0.5
C = 2.5 * SQRT(A + B)	instead of	C = 2.5 * (A + B) ** 0.5
WRITE (*,*) SQRT(X)	instead of	WRITE (*,*) X**0.5

A call on a library function may be used in any position in FORTRAN where an arithmetic expression may be used.

A library function may be used anyplace in a FORTRAN statement where an expression may be used. In addition, the argument or arguments of library functions may be expressions, provided they are of the correct type. This is seen in the following examples:

```
Y = SQRT(25.786)
Y = SQRT(13.7*X − 41.0)
Y = SQRT(SQRT(X))
Y = 3.1709 * SQRT(X)
Y = 5.0*SQRT(X − 1.7)/2.0
Y = SQRT(X)**3                    [this is  Y = (SQRT(X))**3]
Y = SQRT(X**3)
```

2.4.2 Common Functions

In this section we discuss the most commonly used functions. All the standard FORTRAN 77 functions are given in Appendix B.

Square Root Function (SQRT)

This function computes the square root of a real, double-precision, or complex number. It is a generic function with a single argument. The value returned by the function has the same type as the argument. The following program segment shows its use.

With a simple variable as an argument:

          X = 25.0
          Y = SQRT(X)   Y is 5.0

With a numeric literal as an argument:

          Y = SQRT(38.44)   Y is 6.2

With an expression as an argument:

          X = 4.0
          Y = 3.0
          Z = SQRT(X**2 + Y**2)   Z is 5.0

Because the expression is in parentheses, it is evaluated first. The actual argument of the square root function is 25.0.

Absolute Value Function (ABS)

This is a generic function that returns the absolute value of its argument. The argument may be real, double precision, or complex. The following examples show the use of this function.

With a real variable as an argument:

          X = −25.0
          Y = ABS(X)   Y is 25.0

With an expression as an argument:

          X = −45.0
          Y = 12.5
          Z = ABS(Y + X)   Z is 32.5
          Z = ABS(Y − X)   now Z is 57.5
          Z = ABS(X − Y)   Z is still 57.5

Exponential and Logarithmic Functions (EXP and LOG)

The generic function EXP returns a power of e. EXP(X) is the FORTRAN way of writing e^x, where e is 2.71828 . . . , the base of natural logarithms. The argument of the function may be real, double precision, or complex. The following examples show its use.

With a numeric literal as the argument:

          Y = EXP(1.0)   Y is e = 2.71828 . . .

With a real variable as the argument:

          X = −1.0
          Y = EXP(X)   Y is 0.36787

The generic function LOG returns the natural logarithm of a number. Its argument may be real, double precision, or complex. The following example shows its use:

$$Y = LOG(X)$$

The related generic function LOG10 returns the common logarithm of its argument. Its argument can only be real or double precision and must have a value greater than zero.

Algebraic expression	*FORTRAN expression*
e^x	EXP(X)
ln x or $\log_e x$	LOG(X)
log x or $\log_{10} x$	LOG10(X)

Modulo Function (MOD)

With positive integer arguments, this type-specific function computes the modulus of the two arguments, that is, the integer remainder after division of the first argument by the second. The formula used for the calculation is:

$$K = I - (\frac{I}{J} * J)$$

Both arguments must be integer. The following examples show the use of the function:

```
I  = 15
J  = 4
K  = MOD(I,J)          K is 3
K  = MOD(8,2)          K is 0
K  = MOD(-5,3)         K is -2
K  = MOD(-7,-4)        K is -3
K  = MOD(14,-5)        K is 4
K  = MOD(73,2)         K is 1
```

The related function for real numbers is AMOD.

Maximum and Minimum Functions (MAX and MIN)

The generic functions MAX and MIN may have two or more arguments. These arguments may be of any numeric type, provided that they are all of the same type. The MAX function returns the largest of its argument values, and the MIN function returns the smallest of its argument values. The following examples show the use of these functions.

With integer arguments:

```
K = MAX(5,8,9,4,3)     K is 9
K = MIN(5,8,9,4,3)     K is 3
K = MAX(-11,-23)       K is -11
K = MIN(-11,-23)       K is -23
```

With real arguments:

```
A = MAX(3.5,4.8,16.5,8.9,12.0)     A is 16.5
A = MIN(3.5,4.8,16.5,8.9,12.0)     A is 3.5
```

The related type-specific functions can be found in Appendix B.

Trignometric and Inverse Trignometric Functions

Trignometric and inverse trignometric functions are generic functions requiring appropriate real or double-precision values for arguments and returning a result of the same type. The SIN and COS functions will also take complex arguments. They are as follows:

Algebraic expression	FORTRAN expression
sin(x)	SIN(X)
cos(x)	COS(X)
tan(x)	TAN(X)
arcsin(x) or $\sin^{-1}(x)$	ASIN(X)
arccos(x) or $\cos^{-1}(x)$	ACOS(X)
arctan(x) or $\tan^{-1}(x)$	ATAN(X)

The argument of the SIN, COS, or TAN function is understood as being measured in radians. The ASIN, ACOS, and ATAN functions return the size of the angle in radians.

When an angle X is measured in degrees,

$$180° = \pi \text{ radians}$$

therefore

$$1° = \frac{\pi}{180} \text{ radians}$$

PI/180 * X is the size of the angle in radians, where PI = π = 3.14159

SIN(PI/180 * X) is the sine of the angle

When Y is the sine of an angle, where $-1.0 \leq Y \leq 1.0$,

ASIN(Y)   is arcsin(y), the size of the angle in radians
180 * ASIN(Y) / PI gives the angle in degrees

Type Conversion Functions (INT, NINT, and REAL)

There are two ways to convert a noninteger number to an integer in FORTRAN. One way is to assign it to an integer variable, for instance:

N = 45.968   N is 45

The other is to use the INT function. This function differs from the others being discussed in that the argument may be of any numeric type, but the result is integer. For instance:

N = INT(45.968)   N is 45

The value of the argument is truncated at the decimal point and the fractional part is discarded. If the number is to be rounded to the nearest integer rather than truncated, the function NINT should be used:

N = NINT(45.968)   N is 46
K = NINT(-271.4)   K is -271

There are also two ways in FORTRAN to convert a nonreal number to real. One way is to assign it to a real variable, for instance:

A = 26   A is 26.0

The other is to use the REAL function. This function will also accept any numeric type of argument. It returns a real result, for instance:

$$A = REAL(26) \qquad A \text{ is } 26.0$$

Specific forms of these functions are available.

2.4.3 Table of Functions

The functions we have discussed are summarized in Table 2.3. Many have the same names as the generic functions.

The functions marked with an asterisk in the table should be available in all versions of FORTRAN 77; the other result types may not be available. When the functions are not available in a generic form, the equivalents given in Appendix B can be used.

Table 2.3

FUNCTION	DESCRIPTION	ARGUMENT TYPE	RESULT TYPE
ABS	absolute value	integer	integer
		*real	real
		double precision	double precision
		complex	complex
ACOS	arccosine	*real	real
		double precision	double precision
		complex	complex
ASIN	arcsine	*real	real
		double precision	double precision
		complex	complex
ATAN	arctangent	*real	real
		double precision	double precision
		complex	complex
COS	cosine	*real	real
		double precision	double precision
		complex	complex
EXP	exponential of e	*real	real
		double precision	double precision
INT	integer	*real	real
		double precision	double precision
		complex	complex
LOG	natural logarithm	real	real
		double precision	double precision
LOG10	common logarithm	real	real
		double precision	double precision
MAX	maximum	integer	integer
		real	real
		double precision	double precision
		complex	complex
MIN	minimum	integer	integer
		real	real
		double precision	double precision
		complex	complex

Table 2.3 (*continued*)

FUNCTION	DESCRIPTION	ARGUMENT TYPE	RESULT TYPE
MOD	modulo	*integer	integer
REAL	real	*integer	real
		double precision	double precision
		complex	complex
SIN	sine	*real	real
		double precision	double precision
		complex	complex
SQRT	square root	*real	real
		double precision	double precision
		complex	complex
TAN	tangent	*real	real
		double precision	double precision
		complex	complex

2.4.4 Review Questions

1. Evaluate the following functions, given the values A = 28.0, B = 53.0, C = −18.0, D = 64.6, E = 37.5, K = 45:

   a. SQRT(ABS(A − B))
   b. ABS(E − D * 2.0)
   c. MAX(A,B,C,D,E)
   d. MIN(A,B,C,D,E)
   e. INT(D)
   f. NINT(D)
   g. REAL(K)
   h. MOD(B,A)
   i. MOD(C,4.0)

2. Write the equivalent FORTRAN statements for the following algebraic formulas:

   a. $x = y + \sqrt{z + w}$
   b. $a = b\,c + d\,|b-c| + \sqrt{f + |g-h|}$
   c. $s = t\,\sqrt{\sin x + \cos x}$
   d. $b = k + \dfrac{\sqrt{x - y}}{y - z}$
   e. $x = |a - b| + \sqrt{x^2 + y^2 - 2xy}$
   f. $w = x\,y\,|a - b| + \sqrt{b^2 - c}$

2.5 FORTRAN 77 Structures

FORTRAN 77 is standardized, but this only means that a program developed in one environment should be able to run in another environment with a minimum number of modifications. However, even if a program runs unaltered, the results may not be identical. The output of a program is affected by the word size of the computer, the underlying numeric and character representations used, the details of the arithmetic and logic operations, and the details of the input/output handling. In addition, different environments require different job control statements.

2.5.1 Statement and Data Formatting

FORTRAN statements and data are generally keyed into an interactive terminal using an editor. Although there are variations in the forms permitted, the standard format is still needed in many interactive systems. For program portability, its restrictions should be followed.

Each FORTRAN statement must be typed on a separate line. If a statement is too long to fit on a single line, continuation lines may be used. The line layout is as follows:

position	1	* or C for comment
		ƀ for FORTRAN statement
	1 to 5	A number identifies a place in the program. The allowable range is 1 through 99999. The same number may not be used twice in the same module.
	6	Any nonblank character other than 0 indicates a continuation line. A statement may be continued to a maximum of 19 lines.
	7 to 72	FORTRAN statement

```
1 2 3 4 5|6|7 8                    72|73          80
|                |                   |            |
|                |                   |            |
|                |                   |            |

                    for FORTRAN statements
                for continuation symbols
            for statement labels
    * or C for comment lines
```

Each nonblank line must have either a FORTRAN statement or a comment. A blank line will be ignored by the computer. Statement labels and continuation symbols are used only when needed. IDs can be used to identify the program, programmer, date, program line number, or anything else, as positions beyond 72 are ignored by the compiler.

Because FORTRAN is sensitive to the positioning on the line, it is important to use tab positions in interactive editing. Characters that are in the wrong position will be misinterpreted by the compiler.

Input data does not follow the format used for FORTRAN statements. It can be typed anywhere from position 1 to position 80, except that a single data value may not be split between two lines. The details of data values formatting depend on the formats written in the program.

Programming Warning

FORTRAN statements must be within positions 7 to 72.

2.5.2 Program Structure

Program instructions and data values must not be mixed. Just as each variable in a program has a name, there must be names for the program file and the data file. The name of the program file is known to the operating system. The data file may be known to the operating system by the name used to refer to it inside the program, or it may have two different names. Control statements used to compile, link, and execute a program refer to the names of the program and data files.

A large FORTRAN program may have several program files, each containing a function or subroutine. It is the function of the linker to find all these program parts, as well as the library functions needed, and combine them to form the executable code.

Special control statements are needed to indicate the written end of the program and the termination of execution. The END statement must be the last physical statement of every program module, because it is a signal to the compiler that the entire module has been found. There should also be at least one STOP statement placed where the computer is to stop execution. A STOP statement at the written end of the program may be omitted. The general form of a program is:

```
comments describing program module
data declarations
    .
    .         FORTRAN source code
    .
STOP        (this may be omitted)
END
```

This is the form of the main module, corresponding to the top module in a hierarchy chart. If the lower modules of the chart are implemented separately rather than as part of the main program, their structure differs slightly:

```
subprogram header
comments describing program module
data declarations
    .
    .         FORTRAN source code
    .
RETURN
END
```

2.5.3 Review Questions

1. Show the column position layout for the following small FORTRAN program:

```
C      THIS IS AN EXAMPLE
       A = 5.0
       STOP
       END
```

2. Identify the different positions of the FORTRAN statement line.

2.6 Sample Programs

The following sample programs illustrate the use of arithmetic operations. These programs have been run on the Digital Equipment Corporation (DEC) computer model VAX 780. Their output follows the source code. Some simple input/output statements are used, which are not explained in detail until Chapter 3. However, the form of the input data is shown for the interactive programs so that you can try these programs on the computer. The line numbers are for reference only and should not be considered part of the programs.

2.6.1 Volume of a Sphere

Problem

Write a program to calculate the volume of a sphere, given a data value for the radius.

Method

The volume of a sphere is given by the formula $V = \frac{4}{3} \pi r^3$. To calculate the volume, the radius must be known. This program inputs a data value for the radius. It prints the values of the radius and the volume. Because the value of π is not known to the computer, it is provided as a constant.

Program

```
***************************************************************
*                                                             *
*   CALCULATE THE VOLUME OF A SPHERE                          *
*                                                             *
***************************************************************
*                                                             *
*   CONSTANT: PI = 3.1415                                     *
*                                                             *
*   INPUT VARIABLES:                                          *
*                                                             *
*       RADIUS - RADIUS OF THE SPHERE                         *
*                                                             *
*   OUTPUT VARIABLES:                                         *
*                                                             *
*       VOLUME - COMPUTED VOLUME OF SPHERE                    *
*                                                             *
***************************************************************

1       REAL PI,RADIUS,VOLUME
2       PARAMETER (PI=3.14159)
```

```
3        PRINT*,'INPUT THE RADIUS OF THE SPHERE:'
4        READ*, RADIUS
5        VOLUME = 4.0 / 3.0 * PI * RADIUS ** 3
6        PRINT*, 'RADIUS=',RADIUS,'VOLUME =',VOLUME
7        STOP
8        END
```

Output

```
INPUT THE RADIUS OF THE SPHERE:
13

RADIUS =      13.00000        VOLUME =      9202.765
```

Statement 1   declares the type of the variables and constant.

Statement 2   assigns a value to the constant PI.

Statement 3   is an output statement used in interactive programming to prompt the user to input a value for the radius. This statement would be omitted for batch programming.

Statement 4   is an input statement that obtains the value of the radius and stores it in the location RADIUS.

Statement 5   is an assignment statement that calculates the volume of the sphere and stores it in the location VOLUME. Having the computer calculate the value 4.0 / 3.0 provides greater accuracy than using the number 1.333.

Statement 6   is an output statement that prints the labeled values for the RADIUS and VOLUME.

Statement 7   stops the execution of the program.

Statement 8   indicates to the compiler the physical end of the program.

When the program runs, the computer prompts the user to enter an input value. The value of the radius is entered interactively, followed by a carriage return. The output displays on the terminal screen.

2.6.2   Volume of Metal in a Hollow Steel Cylinder

Problem

Write a program to compute the volume of metal in a hollow steel cylinder, given data values for the inner radius, outer radius, and length.

Method

Let the hollow cylinder have an outer radius of r_o, an inner radius of r_i, and a length of l. The formula for the volume is:

volume = (area of outer circle − area of inner circle) length

This could be calculated as a single equation, but instead it will be done in steps.

The formula for the area of a circle is:

area of circle $= \pi r^2$

but for efficiency, multiplication is being used instead of exponentiation.

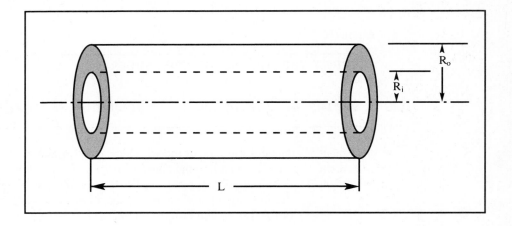

Program

```
*****************************************************************
*                                                               *
*   COMPUTE THE VOLUME OF METAL IN A HOLLOW CYLINDER            *
*                                                               *
*****************************************************************
*                                                               *
*   CONSTANT:  PI = 3.14159                                     *
*                                                               *
*   INPUT VARIABLES:                                            *
*                                                               *
*       RO      - RADIUS OF OUTER CIRCLE (INCHES)               *
*       RI      - RADIUS OF INNER CIRCLE (INCHES)               *
*       L       - LENGTH OF CYLINDER (INCHES)                   *
*                                                               *
*   OUTPUT VARIABLES:                                           *
*                                                               *
*       VOLUME - COMPUTED VOLUME OF HOLLOW CYLINDER             *
*                                 (CUBIC INCHES)                *
*                                                               *
*****************************************************************

1       REAL  PI, RO, RI, L, OAREA, IAREA, VOLUME
2       PARAMETER (PI=3.14159)

3       PRINT*, 'INPUT THE OUTER RADIUS, INNER ',
        1       'RADIUS, AND LENGTH:'
4       READ*, RO, RI, L
5       OAREA = PI * RO * RO
6       IAREA = PI * RI * RI
```

```
7         VOLUME = (OAREA - IAREA) * L
8         PRINT*
9         PRINT*, 'OUTER RADIUS =', RO
10        PRINT*, 'INNER RADIUS =', RI
11        PRINT*, 'LENGTH =', L
12        PRINT*, 'VOLUME OF CYLINDER =', VOLUME
13        STOP
14        END
```

Output

```
INPUT THE OUTER RADIUS, INNER RADIUS, AND LENGTH:
7.5,2.5,15

 OUTER RADIUS =    7.500000
 INNER RADIUS =    2.500000
 LENGTH =    15.00000
 VOLUME OF CYLINDER =     2356.193
```

Statement 1   declares the types of all of the variables and constants. Without this
               statement, L and IAREA would be of the wrong type.
Statement 2   assigns a value to the constant PI. The computer does not remem-
               ber values from one program to the next.
Statement 3   prompts the interactive user to input the data.
Statement 4   is an input statement that obtains three values and stores them in
               locations RO, RI, and L respectively.
Statement 5   is an assignment statement that computes the area of the outer circle
               and stores it in the location OAREA.
Statement 6   is an assignment statement that computes the area of the inner circle
               and stores it in the location IAREA.
Statement 7   is an assignment statement that computes the volume of the hollow
               cylinder and stores it in the location VOLUME.
Statement 8   is an output statement that leaves a blank line in the output.
Statements 9–12 are output statements that print the four values stored in locations
               RO, RI, L, and VOLUME, labeling them.
Statement 13   causes the execution to stop.
Statement 14   indicates to the compiler the physical end of the program.

The three input values would be entered at a terminal on a single line, separated by blank spaces and terminated by a carriage return. The output values would
have default spacing, appearing on a single line if possible.

2.6.3 Resistance and Voltage of a Parallel Circuit

Problem

Compute the effective resistance and voltage of a circuit containing two resistances
in parallel, with the current and resistances as input data.

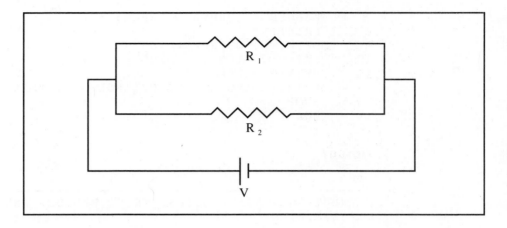

Method

The formulas for the effective resistance of a parallel circuit with resistances R_1 and R_2 and the voltage assuming a current of I are as follows:

$$\frac{1}{R} = \frac{1}{R_1} + \frac{1}{R_2}$$

Solved for R, this is:

$$R = \frac{R_1 * R_2}{R_1 + R_2}$$

$$V = I\,R$$

Program

```
*************************************************************
*                                                           *
*   COMPUTE THE EFFECTIVE RESISTANCE AND VOLTAGE OF         *
*   A PARALLEL CIRCUIT.                                     *
*                                                           *
*************************************************************
*                                                           *
*   INPUT VARIABLES:                                        *
*                                                           *
*       R1       - RESISTANCE (OHMS)                        *
*       R2       - RESISTANCE (OHMS)                        *
*       I        - CURRENT (AMPS)                           *
*                                                           *
*   OUTPUT VARIABLES:                                       *
*                                                           *
*       R        - COMPUTED EFFECTIVE RESISTANCE (OHMS)*
*       V        - COMPUTED VOLTAGE (VOLTS)                 *
*                                                           *
*************************************************************
```

```
      REAL I, R, R1, R2, V
      PRINT*, 'INPUT THE RESISTANCES R1 AND R2 IN',
     1         ' OHMS:'
      READ*, R1, R2
      R = R1 * R2 / (R1 + R2)
      PRINT*,'R1 =', R1,' R2 =', R2
      PRINT*,'EFFECTIVE RESISTANCE R =',R
      PRINT*
      PRINT*, 'INPUT THE CURRENT I IN AMPS:'
      READ*, I
      V = I * R
      PRINT*, 'CURRENT I =', I, ' VOLTAGE V =', V
      STOP
      END
```

Output

```
INPUT THE RESISTANCES R1 AND R2 IN OHMS:
100,300
R1 =    100.0000      R2 =    300.0000
EFFECTIVE RESISTANCE R =    75.00000

INPUT THE CURRENT I IN AMPS:
12
CURRENT I =    12.00000      VOLTAGE V =    900.0000
```

For variation, this program has two READ statements, two PRINT statements for output, and two PRINT statements to prompt the interactive user. Values needed in a formula must be obtained before the formula is used, but they do not need to be obtained at the beginning of the program. When the first READ statement is executed, two values are entered, separated by a comma and terminated by a carriage return. When the second READ statement is executed, the value for I is entered, terminated by a carriage return. Each of the PRINT statements produces one output line.

2.6.4 Hypotenuse of a Right Triangle

Problem

Given the lengths of the legs of a right triangle, calculate the length of the hypotenuse.

Method

The formula for the hypotenuse c of a right triangle in terms of the legs a and b is:

$$c = \sqrt{a^2 + b^2}$$

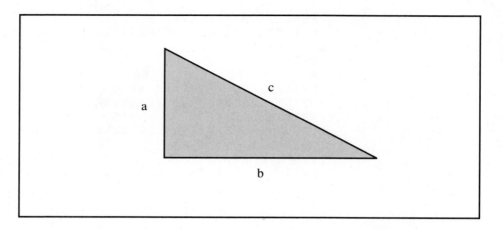

Program

This program computes the hypotenuse of three different triangles.

```
***************************************************************
*                                                             *
*   COMPUTE THE HYPOTENUSE OF A RIGHT TRIANGLE                *
*                                                             *
***************************************************************
*                                                             *
*   INPUT VARIABLES:                                          *
*                                                             *
*        A       - LEG OF RIGHT TRIANGLE                      *
*        B       - LEG OF RIGHT TRIANGLE                      *
*                                                             *
*   OUTPUT VARIABLES:                                         *
*                                                             *
*        C       - COMPUTED HYPOTENUSE OF RIGHT               *
*                    TRIANGLE                                 *
*                                                             *
***************************************************************

1      REAL A, B, C

2      PRINT*,'   LEG A            LEG B',
      1        '            HYPOTENUSE C'
3      PRINT*
4      READ*,A,B
5      C = SQRT(A*A + B*B)
6      PRINT*, A, B, C

7      READ*,A,B
8      C = SQRT (A*A + B*B)
9      PRINT*, A, B, C
```

```
10      READ*,A,B
11      C = SQRT(A*A + B*B)
12      PRINT*, A, B, C
13      STOP
14      END
```

Output

LEG A	LEG B	HYPOTENUSE C
3.000000	4.000000	5.000000
12.00000	33.00000	35.11410
5.000000	15.00000	15.81139

Statement 2   prints column headings for the output.

Statements 7–12 repeat statements 4–6 for the second and third triangle. In Chapter 4 we will see how a sequence of statements can be repeated any number of times by using a repetition construct.

This program is designed for batch processing, so no prompts are included in the code.

2.6.5 Amount of Paint and the Cost

Problem

Write a program to estimate the number of gallons of paint needed to paint the interior of a building and the cost of the paint. Each gallon of paint covers 250 sq. ft. and costs $10.50. All the walls have the height h. There are n1 walls of width w1, n2 walls of width w2, n3 walls of width w3, and n4 walls of width w4.

Pseudocode

Input the values n1, n2, n3, n4, w1, w2, w3, w4, h, cost
Compute the total width
    width ← n1 * w1 + n2 * w2 + n3 * w3 + n4 * w4
Compute the total wall area
    area ← h * width
Estimate the number of gallons of paint needed
    paint ← area / 250 + 1
Compute the total cost
    total cost ← paint * cost
Output the values paint, total cost
Stop

Program

```
**************************************************************
*                                                            *
*   COMPUTE THE AMOUNT OF PAINT AND COST TO PAINT A           *
*   BUILDING.                                                 *
*                                                            *
**************************************************************
*                                                            *
*   INPUT VARIABLES:                                          *
*                                                            *
*       N1,N2,N3,N4 - NUMBER OF WALLS                         *
*       W1,W2,W3,W4 - CORRESPONDING WIDTHS OF WALLS           *
*                     (FEET)                                  *
*       H           - HEIGHT OF WALLS (FEET)                  *
*       COST        - COST OF PAINT PER GALLON                *
*                     (DOLLARS)                               *
*                                                            *
*   OUTPUT VARIABLES:                                         *
*                                                            *
*       PAINT  - AMOUNT OF PAINT NEEDED (GALLONS)             *
*       TCOST  - TOTAL COST OF PAINT (DOLLARS)                *
*                                                            *
**************************************************************

        INTEGER N1,N2,N3,N4,AREA,PAINT
        REAL W,W1,W2,W3,W4,H,COST,TCOST

*   INPUT DATA VALUES

        READ*, N1,N2,N3,N4
        READ*, W1,W2,W3,W4
        READ*, H,COST

*   COMPUTE AMOUNT OF PAINT AND COST

        W = N1 * W1 + N2 * W2 + N3 * W3 + N4 * W4
        AREA = W * H
        PAINT = AREA / 250 + 1
        TCOST = PAINT * COST

*   OUTPUT AMOUNT OF PAINT AND TOTAL COST

        PRINT*
        PRINT*, 'NUMBER OF GALLONS OF PAINT =', PAINT
        PRINT*, 'TOTAL COST OF PAINT (IN DOLLARS) =',
       1          TCOST
        STOP
        END
```

Output

```
1,4,2,4
8,10,9,8
8,10.5

NUMBER OF GALLONS OF PAINT =              4
TOTAL COST OF PAINT (IN DOLLARS) =   42.00000
```

The amount of paint needed is an integer variable because a whole number of gallons of paint must be purchased. The integer division used to find the amount of paint truncates the fractional part of the answer; therefore an extra gallon is added to provide the extra amount of paint needed. If one gallon of paint painted exactly 250 sq ft and the area to be painted was an exact multiple of 250, the extra gallon of paint would not be needed.

2.6.5 Farm Grain Production Costs

Problem

Compute the total expenditures of a farmer raising a grain crop.

Method

The input consists of the amount spent on each of the following: seed, fertilizer, pesticide, equipment maintenance, labor, grain storage. Print the total cost.

Pseudocode

Input cost of seeds, fertilizer, pesticide, equipment, maintenance,
     labor, and storage
Calculate the total cost
Print the itemized costs
Print the total cost
Stop

Program:

```
***********************************************************
*                                                         *
*   REPORT ON FARM GRAIN PRODUCTION COSTS                 *
*                                                         *
***********************************************************
*                                                         *
*   INPUT VARIABLES:                                      *
*                                                         *
*     CSTSED - COST OF SEED                               *
*     CSTFRT - COST OF FERTILIZER                         *
*     CSTPST - COST OF PESTICIDE                          *
*     CSTEQP - COST OF EQUIPMENT MAINTENANCE              *
*     CSTLAB - COST OF LABOR                              *
*     CSTSTR - COST OF GRAIN STORAGE                      *
*                                                         *
*   OUTPUT VARIABLES:                                     *
*                                                         *
*     TOTCST - TOTAL COST OF GRAIN PRODUCTION             *
*                                                         *
***********************************************************
        REAL CSTSED,CSTFRT,CSTPST,CSTEQP,CSTLAB,CSTSTR,
     1          TOTCST
       PRINT*, 'INPUT THE DATA'
       PRINT*
       READ(*,*) CSTSED,CSTFRT,CSTPST,CSTEQP,CSTLAB,
     1          CSTSTR
       TOTCST = CSTSED + CSTFRT + CSTPST + CSTEQP +
     1          CSTLAB + CSTSTR
       PRINT*
       PRINT*, 'OUTPUT OF THE COSTS AND TOTAL COST'
       PRINT*
       PRINT*, 'COST OF SEED =',CSTSED
       PRINT*, 'FERTILIZER COST =',CSTFRT
       PRINT*, 'PESTICIDE COST =',CSTPST
       PRINT*, 'EQUIPMENT COST =', CSTEQP
       PRINT*, 'COST OF LABOR =',CSTLAB
       PRINT*, 'STORAGE COST =',CSTSTR
       PRINT*
       PRINT*, 'TOTAL COST =', TOTCST
       STOP
       END
```

Output

```
INPUT THE DATA

2500.0,1700.0,900.0,5000.0,2000.0,1000.0

OUTPUT OF THE COSTS AND TOTAL COST

COST OF SEED  =    2500.000
FERTILIZER COST =   1700.000
PESTICIDE COST =    900.000
EQUIPMENT COST =   5000.000
COST OF LABOR =    2000.000
STORAGE COST  =    1000.000

TOTAL COST  =    13100.00
```

Chapter Summary

FORTRAN 77 is designed for use in scientific and engineering applications. Because of this, it has a variety of numeric data types: integer, real, double precision, and complex. Variables have implicit types. All variables are real unless the first letter in their names is in the range I through N, or they are explicitly declared.

Declaration of types should be explicit:

```
INTEGER v1,v2,...,vn
REAL v1,v2,...,vn
DOUBLE PRECISION v1,v2,...,vn
COMPLEX v1,v2,...,vn
```

Named constants are given values through a PARAMETER statement:

```
PARAMETER (v1=c1,v2=c2,...,vn=cn)
```

The basic executable statement is the assignment statement. It uses a form very similar to that of algebraic equations, but it is interpreted in three steps: calculating the value of the expression on the right, converting it to the proper type, and storing it in the variable on the left.

A library of built-in functions is provided for mathematical computations. The more common of these are available on most compilers, although the function names may take one of several forms. The full FORTRAN 77 language supports both generic and type-specific functions.

The program and the data are prepared and entered into the computer as two separate files under the control of job control statements. Input formats differ for program statements and for data. Program statements have designated fields, which are interpreted in specific ways by the compiler. Data format is controlled by the program. In this chapter only free-format data input was used. The corresponding form of data output is given a default format by the computer. Program statements are restricted to columns 7–72 while input data may use any columns.

Exercises

1. Write a program to convert Fahrenheit temperature to Celsius temperature for one input value. Output both the Fahrenheit and the Celsius values. The conversion formula is:

$$C = \frac{5(F - 32)}{9}$$

2. Write a program to compute the volume of water held by a cylindrical tank of internal diameter D and height H for one value of D and one of H. Print all values.

3. Write a program to evaluate the polynomial

$$y = x^4 + 6x^3 - 2x^2 + 5x + 6$$

   for x = 5.0

   Assign the value 5.0 to x before calculating the value of the polynomial.

4. Write a program to compute the distance between the points P1(x1,y1) and P2(x2,y2), given values for x1, y1, x2, and y2.

$$\text{distance} = \sqrt{(x_2 - x_1)^2 + (y_2 - y_1)^2}$$

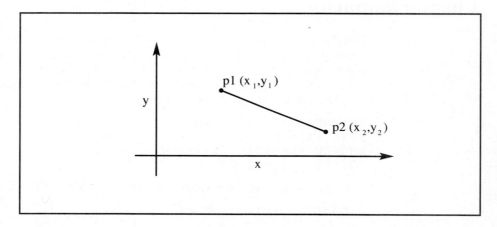

5. Write a program to compute the components of a resultant force F_R with an angle Θ to the horizontal. The components are given by:

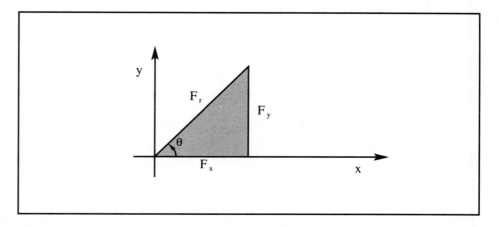

$F_X = F_R \cos \Theta$

$F_Y = F_R \sin \Theta$

6. Write a program to compute the area of a scalene triangle. The formula for the area, given sides a, b, and c, is:

$$area = (s(s-a)(s-b)(s-c))^{1/2}$$

$$where \ s = (a+b+c)/2.$$

7. Write a program to solve a set of simultaneous equations:

$$ax + by = c$$

$$dx + ey = f$$

where a, b, c, d, e, and f are input values.
The formulas for the solution are:

$$x = \frac{ce - bf}{ae - bd}$$

$$y = \frac{af - cd}{ae - bd}$$

Output all the input vaulues a, b, c, d, e, f and the computed values x and y.

8. Write a program to write an order for textbooks for a class. The input consists of ISBN numbers and unit costs and number of copies ordered for four different textbooks. Print the ISBN number, unit cost, number of copies, and total cost for each textbook, and the overall total cost.

9. Write a program to keep records on purchases of common stock in an investment portfolio. Input consists of the number of shares purchased and the total purchase price of XYZ common stock. Assume the price per stock purchased includes a 1% sales commission and $7.0 registration fee. Calculate the amount of the commission and the price per share of the purchase. Print the number of shares purchased, the price per share, the commission, and the total price.

3

Input/Output Specifications

Objective: Learn how to instruct the computer as to what data to process and what to do with the results.

*I*n Chapter 2 we discussed basic assignment statements, but we gave examples of input and output with very little explanation. These examples were of the most general type, providing quick answers for short programs. This general input and output format is unsatisfactory for longer programs or large amounts of data such as tables, because the output would be unreadable without careful structuring. For a program to be useful, careful input and output specification is necessary.

The details of the specifications depend on the devices being used for input and output. Data entered at a keyboard and displayed on a screen is usually limited to 80 characters per line, or *record,* including spaces. Printed data may be limited to 80, 120, or 132 characters per record. Data stored on a disk file may have records of any predetermined size, and data stored on magnetic tape may have records of a variety of sizes.

Input specifications may be designed for an interactive terminal, disk, or other device. Output specifications may be designed for interactive terminal screen, printer, disk, or tape devices. If a disk is used, it will serve as both an output and an input medium.

In scientific and engineering applications, input usually consists of actual or theoretical measurements, experimental design parameters that are being varied, and/or initial and boundary conditions for solving equations. Output usually consists of tables showing the effect of varying conditions, results from formulas, or statistical computations. Output should also contain titles, dates, a copy of the input data, and keys to any special symbols. If there is more than one page of output, the pages should be numbered and have document IDs. All of this requires careful data specifications.

In FORTRAN 77 there are two ways of organizing input and output data: as list directed or formatted. An implicit default format is used for *list-directed input/ output.* The programmer specifies the variables being used, but not the spacing of the input or output. In *formatted input/output* the programmer specifies both the variables being used and the spacing of the input or output. The examples in Chapter 2 used list-directed input/output, which is satisfactory for debugging programs. It is also used in small programs written to obtain quick answers.

Programming Hint

> Use list-directed input/output for debugging and for quick results. Use formatted input/output for professional-looking application programs.

Basic input and output statements are called *data transfer statements:*

READ   inputs data into the computer from any input device
WRITE   outputs data from the computer to any output device
PRINT   outputs data from the computer to a printer or terminal screen

The following are auxiliary input/output statements:

OPEN   makes data in a file available to the program through a logical unit number
CLOSE   closes a file so the data is no longer available to the program through the logical unit number

3.1 List-Directed Input/Output Statements

The list-directed input/output statements in FORTRAN programs are known as data transfer statements because they involve the transfer of data between a storage or I/O device and the CPU. The CPU uses the input data in the data manipulation steps in the program to produce the results, which are printed or displayed under the control of the output statements in the program. The input/output statements also control the extraction of data from a record and, in most cases, the conversion of data from one type to another. Data entered by a user consists of characters separated by blank spaces or commas. Data printed or displayed on a screen also consists of groups of characters. On input, the computer identifies the various groups of characters and, if they represent numeric literals, converts them to the proper internal numeric form. On output, the numeric values are converted to characters and spaced according to default specifications.

3.1.1 Simple Input Statements (READ statement)

The general form of the list-directed input statement is:

```
READ (*,*) var1,var2, . . . ,varn
```

For example:

```
READ (*,*) VAL
```

causes a group of characters representing a number to be read from the input device, converted to a real number (if VAL is REAL), and assigned to the variable VAL. If the input record is

```
86.54
```

then the value stored in the variable VAL is 86.54. Thus the READ statement above is approximately equivalent to this assignment statement:

```
VAL = 86.54
```

The input statement is used instead of the assignment statement when the value is unknown at the time the program is written.

The input statement

```
READ (*,*) MAX,CONS,AVAL,BCON
```

causes four groups of characters representing numbers to be read one at a time from the input device, converted to the proper numeric types, and assigned, the first to MAX, the second to CONS, the third to AVAL, and the fourth to BCON. If the input record is

```
120,  12.83,18.0,  25.62
```

or

```
120  12.83   18.0 25.62
```

then the value of MAX is 120, of CONS, 12.83, of AVAL, 18.0, and of BCON, 25.62.

The first character used in the READ statements (∗) directs the computer to take the input from the standard system input file. The second character (∗) directs the computer to use the default formatting rules. This means that the programmer does not control the data spacing. The actual spacing of the data in the input records is unimportant provided that the numbers are separated so that the computer can identify the characters that belong to each one. Data values in the list may be separated either by commas or blank spaces. Because the spacing is unimportant, the values of MAX, CONS, AVAL, and BCON could be entered instead on four separate records, as follows:

```
120
```

```
12.83
```

```
18.0
```

```
25.62
```

Programming Hint

Readability: The type of the data should match the type of the variable in which it will be stored.

Because input data is converted by the computer from characters to a numeric value, the form of the data does not have to match the type of the input variables. If MAX is integer and CONS, AVAL, and BCON are real, the following input data would result in the same numbers being assigned to the variables:

```
120.0  0.1283E02  18  25.62000
```

Since many different devices can be used for input, it must be possible to use the READ statement to direct the computer to any of them.

READ (∗,∗) varlist refers to the standard system input
READ (n,∗) varlist refers to input device n

Input devices are assigned integer numbers as IDs. The use of that number or an integer variable with that number in the READ statement directs the computer to the specific device wanted. Refer to the programmer's manual of the computer you are using to determine the correct number.

If the input statement is

```
READ (*,*) AMAX,BALNC,ICON,JVAL
```

and the input record is

```
28.75, 13.96, 48, 96
```

then AMAX is 28.75, BALNC is 13.96, ICON is 48, and JVAL is 96 after the statement is executed.

The variable list in the input statement directs the computer to expect a certain number of values. In interactive processing, the computer waits until that number of values has been entered. In batch processing, if the values are not there or there are too few of them, the processing halts with an error condition, unless the error option of the READ statement is used. This form of the input statement transfers control to a prespecified statement when there are not enough input values to read. For example,

```
READ (*,*,ERR=80) CONST,VAR,NUM,MAXIM
```

directs the computer to expect four numbers on standard input, use default rules to locate them, and transfer control to the line of the program labeled 80 if fewer than four numbers are found. Line 80 can be used to output an appropriate message. The end-of-file option can be used for the same purpose. For example,

```
READ (*,*,END=80) CONST,VAR,NUM,MAXIM
```

It is better programming style to use the error option for a data error and the end-of-file option when the end of the file is anticipated.

There are three important default rules for input:

1. When the computer fetches a READ statement to execute, it also looks for a new input record. Therefore, not all the numbers in a record may be used.
2. When the input list of a READ statement contains more variables than there are numbers on the input record, the computer reads several input records until it finds enough numbers or, in interactive mode, waits until the numbers have been entered.
3. When the input list of a READ statement contains more variables than there are numbers in the data file, the processing stops with an error condition unless the ERR= option is used.

For example, given this program segment,

```
READ (*,*) A, B, C
READ (*,*) X, Y, Z
```

and this data,

```
17.5  -23.09
```

```
.0572 1.68
```

```
45.7  31.0
```

A is assigned the value 17.5, B is assigned -23.09, C is assigned .0572. The second READ statement uses the third input record and the value 1.68 is not used. X is assigned the value 45.7, Y is assigned the value 31.0, and there is nothing left for Z. This raises the error condition. As a precaution, the ERR= option should have been used, for example as:

```
READ (*,*,ERR=100)  A,B,C
READ (*,*,ERR=100)  X,Y,Z
```

Then line 100 might be: *Error go to label 100.*

```
100  WRITE (*,*)'DATA MISSING'
```

With batch processing, the input comes from a disk file. The computer recognizes the end of the data in a disk file by finding the actual end of the file, which is marked with a special symbol known as an *end-of-file marker*. In interactive processing, when the READ statement is executed, the computer waits for the user to enter data through the terminal. The end-of-file marker is system dependent. The user must enter a special symbol to indicate the end of the input. On some systems, Ctrl/Z is used for this; on other systems, Ctrl/D or a simple carriage return. When the computer reads an end-of-file marker where one is not expected, it raises the error condition or the end condition.

The input of character data using list-directed input is shown in the following example:

```
READ (*,*) STR1,STR2
```
Keyboard format

```
'THIS IS A CAT', 'THIS IS A ROSE'
```

Notice that the character strings are enclosed in single quotation marks. The variables STR1 and STR2 must be declared as character variables. (The details of character variable declarations and input/output will be discussed in Chapter 8.) For all types of data, the form used for input is the same as that used for literals within the program.

3.1.2 Input from Data Files

Input to the program can come from a data file stored on a secondary storage device such as a disk instead of from the standard input device. Recall that a file is a collection of data records and each data record is a collection of data items or data values. A data file can be built from an editor by entering data records to the file. This data file can be used as an input file in the program. A data file can also be created by a program when it writes records to an output file that is to be used as an input file in the same or another program. In this section, we discuss some basic concepts of file use. More detailed discussion of files can be found in Chapter 9.

FORTRAN 77 has two types of files: sequential and direct access. Sequential files may be formatted or unformatted. Both list-directed and formatted input/output files are formatted files; list-directed files use default formatting while formatted input/output files are formatted by the program. Only sequential, formatted files are used in this chapter. By default, a data file that is not otherwise identified is sequential and formatted.

In order to access the records in a file, it must be connected to the program through a logical unit number associated with the device. This logical connection between a file, usually on a disk, and the program is established by using an OPEN statement. The logical connection is removed by using a CLOSE statement.

OPEN Statement

The OPEN statement with minimum control parameters is written as follows:

```
OPEN (UNIT=integer, FILE=character string,
STATUS=character string)
```

where   UNIT = integer expression   provides a logical unit number,

             FILE = character string   provides an external file name,

and   STATUS = character string   assigns a status of 'OLD', 'NEW', or 'UNKNOWN'.

A file has NEW status when it does not exist yet, but is being created by the program. A file has OLD status when it already exists and is being used by the program. UNKNOWN status means that the file does not exist yet, is being created and used by the program, but is temporary, existing only while the program is executing.

The unit numbers chosen by the programmer are the program's link to the file. They must be positive integers. Often numbers are assigned by an installation to specific devices.

The following OPEN statement,

```
OPEN (UNIT=10,FILE='MATDAT',STATUS='OLD')
```

associates the logical unit number 10 with the file having the external name 'MATDAT'. The file is assumed to exist already and be organized as a formatted sequential file.

CLOSE Statement

The CLOSE statement with minimum control parameters is written as follows:

```
CLOSE (UNIT=integer, STATUS=character string)
```

where   UNIT = integer expression   provides a logical unit number and

             STATUS = character string   assigns a status of 'DELETE' or 'KEEP'.

A file has KEEP status when it contains data that must be kept for future use. DELETE status means that the file will not be wanted after program execution terminates. The default status is KEEP.

The following CLOSE statement,

```
CLOSE (UNIT=10,STATUS='DELETE')
```

closes the file that was associated with logical unit 10 by the OPEN statement and releases the disk space used by the file.

The following CLOSE statement,

```
CLOSE (UNIT=10)
```

closes the file associated with logical unit 10 and saves it for future use.

List-Directed Input Statement

The general form of a list-directed input statement for input from an external named file is:

```
READ (list of control parameters) input list
```

The following statement,

```
READ (unit,*) input list
```

can be written in minimal form as, for example,

```
READ (10,*) A,B,C
```

Any program reading input data from an external named file should contain the three types of file statements shown in the following example:

```
OPEN (UNIT=10,FILE='MATDAT',STATUS='OLD')
. . .
READ (10,*) A,B,C
. . .
CLOSE (UNIT=10)
```

The file should be opened before any attempt is made to read data from it, and it should be closed when it is not needed any more in the program.

A more complete form of the READ statement tests for missing data through the use of the end-of-file and error options. In the following example,

```
OPEN (UNIT=12,FILE='DATF1',STATUS='OLD')
READ (12,*,END=50,ERR=80) X,Y,Z
```

the processing will continue at line 50 if the end-of-file marker was read by the computer, indicating that there is no input data available. The processing will continue at line 80 if an error occurs during the input operation.

Assume that the file 'SAMPLE' contains the following records:

28,	18,	12,	16
30,	50,	81,	95
78,	82,	35,	62
12,	98,	11,	65
13,	55,	49,	58

Given the following FORTRAN program,

```
      INTEGER A, B, C, D

      OPEN (UNIT=10,FILE='SAMPLE',STATUS='OLD')
   5  READ (10,*,END=50) A,B,C,D
        WRITE (*,*) A,B,C,D
      GO TO 5

  50  WRITE (*,*) 'INPUT FROM THE FILE IS COMPLETE'
      CLOSE (UNIT=10,STATUS='KEEP')
      STOP
```

all the records from the file will be read and printed.

3.1.3 Simple Output Statements (PRINT, WRITE statements)

Two different FORTRAN statements are used for list-directed output. The standard FORTRAN 77 statement is WRITE, but PRINT, from earlier versions of FORTRAN, may still be used. With these statements, the programmer can control page ejects and vertical spacing (overstrike and single, double, or triple spacing) as desired. The programmer also has control over horizontal spacing on the output line.

PRINT Statement

A commonly available but nonstandard list-directed PRINT statement has the general form

```
      PRINT*, value1,value2,...,valuen
```

This statement may be used for quick programs testing and for statements used in debugging; however, it does not give the programmer any control over the form of the output. The asterisk indicates the use of a default format. This format is a standard one determined by the compiler, rather than by the program. The output is sent to the standard system output device, either a printer or terminal screen. It may be a disk file that will eventually be printed or displayed on a terminal screen.

   The output list is not limited to variables, but may contain variables, literals, and expressions. For example, given A = 12.5, B = 18.6, C = 12.8, D = 18.95, and the output statement

```
      PRINT*, A,B,C,D
```

the output is:

```
  12.5        18.6        12.8        18.95
```

Given CONS = 125.6 and the output statement

    PRINT*, 'THIS IS A CONSTANT:',CONS

the output is:

```
THIS IS A CONSTANT:    125.6
```

Given A = 5.0, B = 10.0, and C = 8.5 and the output statement

    PRINT*, 'THIS IS A COMPUTED VALUE:',A*B-C

the output is:

```
THIS IS A COMPUTED VALUE: 41.5
```

There are two important default rules for output:

1. When the computer fetches a PRINT statement to execute, it also starts a new output record.
2. When the output list of a PRINT statement contains more values than can be placed on the output line, the computer continues to the next line.

For example, given A = 1.5, B = 12.5, C = 18.7, D = 9.8, E = 1739.4, F = .0645, G = −9.862 and the output statement

    PRINT*, A,B,C,D,E,F,G

then the output is:

```
1.5      12.5      18.7      9.8      1739.4
.0645    -9.862
```

According to the default specifications, the output line is divided into five fields. Each output value is placed in a new field. Within the field, the values are aligned. The only control the programmer has on the horizontal spacing of the values is by using character strings consisting of blanks in the output list. For example, given A = 12.85, B = 6.0, C = 13.8 and the output statement

    PRINT*, A,'b',B,'b',C

then the output is:

```
12.85                 6.0                 13.8
```

Programming Hint

> With list-directed output, use blank character strings in the output list for horizontal spacing.

WRITE Statement

The general form of the list-directed WRITE statement is:

```
WRITE (*,*) value1,value2,...,valuen
```

or

```
WRITE (n,*) value1,value2,...,valuen
```

where n is the unit number of the logical output device being used. When an asterisk is used for the logical unit number, the output defaults to the system output file. Again, the second asterisk indicates the use of default format specifications. For example, given A = 285.62, B = 18.75, C = 378.94 and the output statement

```
WRITE (*,*) A,B,C
```

then the output is:

```
285.62    18.75    378.94
```

Given A = 64.2, B = −98.7 and

```
WRITE (*,*) 'THESE ARE VARIABLES:',A,B
```

then the output is:

```
THESE ARE VARIABLES:  64.2    −98.7
```

Given A = 98.32 and

```
WRITE (*,*) 'A VARIABLE AND A CONSTANT:',A,28.75
```

then the output is:

```
A VARIABLE AND A CONSTANT:  98.32    28.75
```

Given A = 5.0, B = 10.5, C = 2.0, D = 10.75 and

```
WRITE (*,*) 'THIS IS AN EXPRESSION:', A−B*C+D
```

then the output is:

```
THIS IS AN EXPRESSION:        -5.25
```

When there is the possibility of an output error, the ERR= option can be used. The following statement,

```
WRITE (*,*,ERR=200) A,B,C,D
```

outputs the values of A, B, C, and D. If there is an error during the output process, control will transfer to line 200 of the program. This line may be used to print an error message before the execution stops.

3.1.4 Output to Data Files

Output can be written to a data file instead of a printer or a terminal screen. The file may already exist, or it may be newly created. It is connected to the program by association with a logical unit number in an OPEN statement. After the complete set of data has been written to the file, it is disconnected from the program with a CLOSE statement. The OPEN and CLOSE statements are the same as those used for input files. The following example shows how they would be used in a program:

```
OPEN (UNIT=10, FILE='OUTFIL', STATUS='NEW')
.  .  .
WRITE (10,*) A,B,C
.  .  .
CLOSE (UNIT=10, STATUS='KEEP')
```

When a file has been used for output, the CLOSE statement causes an end-of-file marker to be written to it. The file can then be used for input in the same or a different program. The following program segment shows three records written to a data file, followed by reading the same three records from the file. As the records are read, they are printed. The same file is used in both the output and input sections of the program because the external file name is the same, even though the logical unit numbers are different.

```
      OPEN (UNIT=10, FILE='DATFIL', STATUS='NEW')
      WRITE (10,*) 1,2,3
      WRITE (10,*) 4,5,6
      WRITE (10,*) 7,8,9
      CLOSE (UNIT=10, STATUS='KEEP')

      OPEN (UNIT=12, FILE='DATFIL', STATUS='OLD')
    5 READ (12,*,END=50) A,B,C
        PRINT*, A,B,C
      GO TO 5

   50 CLOSE (UNIT=12, STATUS='KEEP')
```

Notice that the file status is 'NEW' when the file is first created and 'OLD' when the already existing file is read. After the file is created, it must be closed and reopened before it is used in input. Opening the file a second time repositions it at the beginning so that the same three records will be read. The END= option of the READ statement detects the end of the file after three records have been read, and control passes to statement 50. Notice that when the file is used for output and input, it is opened before any records are processed and is not closed until after all the records are processed.

Programming Hint

> Reliability: Use the ERR= options on all output statements.

3.1.5 Review Questions

1. Write the list-directed input statements to input the following variables and show input records for the values shown:
   $$p = 10.5, K = 18, L = 11, R = 28.75$$

2. Write the list-directed output statement using the PRINT form for the variables shown. Also show how the output would appear.

   a. ST = 798.5, MAX = 218, JMAX = 9875
   b. VAL = -135.8, CON = 'AXBCRT', JMAX = 875
   c. LENGTH = 80, WIDTH = 10.75, AREA = LENGTH*WIDTH

3. Write the list-directed output statement using the WRITE form for the variables shown. Also show how the output would appear.

   a. UBOUND = 18.35, LBOUND = 19, KVA = 7854
   b. A = 17.0, B = -1.0, C = $\sqrt{A+B}$
   c. X = -45.9, Y = -13.11, MAX(X,Y)

4. Write a fault-tolerant, list-directed input statement to read the variables A, B, and N (use END= and ERR=).

5. Write a fault-tolerant, list-directed output statement to output the values of A, B, and A*B (use ERR=).

3.2 Formatted Input Statements

Formatted input/output statements should be used for program control over the appearance and spacing of data. The general form of the formatted input statement and the possible options are:

```
READ  n, variable list
READ  (lun,n) variable list
READ  (lun,n,END=m) variable list
READ  (lun,n,END=m,ERR=k) variable list
```

where lun is the unit number and n, m, and k are numbers of lines in the FOR-TRAN program. Line n is the format description; line m is the statement to which control transfers when the end of the input file is reached; line k is the statement to which control transfers when an error occurs during input processing. Examples of this statement using input assigned to unit number 5 are:

```
READ 5, A,B,C,D
READ (5,1000) A,B,C,D
READ (5,1000,END=150) A,B,C,D
READ (5,1000,END=150,ERR=200) A,B,C,D
```

Usually the line numbers selected for the format descriptions are much greater than the line numbers of executable statements. Then all the formats are placed together in the program. Alternately, each format description may be placed with the input/output statement that refers to it. The format statement is a nonexecutable statement that describes the spacing and type of data for a single input or output statement. It is possible to use a single format statement with several I/O statements, but this is not recommended. When the same format is being used with more than one input/output statement, separate format statements should be used for ease in maintaining the program.

Programming Hint

> Maintainability: Provide a separate FORMAT statement for each input/output statement. Number the FORMAT statements differently from the executable statements.

The general form of the format statement is:

```
line number FORMAT (specification list)
```

Here the line number is in columns 1–5 of the instruction line. The format itself, like other instructions and descriptions in FORTRAN, is in columns 7–72. The specification list consists of specifications for data and spacing, which contain the general information for each input group: type code, field width, and fractional digits.

3.2.1 Integer Input (I specification)

The general form for the data specification for integer data is:

```
Iw
```

where w is the field width. This specification must match both the variable in the input list and the form of the data on the input record. It indicates to the computer that the next w input positions of the input record contain an integer that is right justified in the field (possibly leading blanks, but no trailing blanks). For example:

```
      READ (*,1000) ICON,JMAX,KVAL
1000  FORMAT(I8,I5,I6)
```

expects an input record with this structure:

> cols.   1–8 first number
>   9–13 second number
>   14–19 third number

Any input characters beyond the 19th position are ignored. The input data might be as follows:

```
|b|b|5|6|8|7|3|2|6|9|5|7|3|b|8|5|4|6|2|
```

The value 568732 is stored in ICON, 69573 in JMAX, and 85462 in KVAL. Notice that there are no commas in the data between the values. There may be blank spaces for readability, but they are not necessary. If blank spaces are present, it is customary to include them in the field width of the number they precede; for example, five spaces followed by four digits would be specified as I9.

When standard input spacing is used, a repeat factor may be used in the specification, giving it the form

```
rIw
```

which is equivalent to r occurrences of Iw; e.g., Iw, Iw, . . ., Iw. This is shown in the following examples. Given the program segment

```
       READ (*,1000) M,K,L,N
 1000  FORMAT(I6,I5,I5,I7)
```

or

```
       READ (*,1000) M,K,L,N
 1000  FORMAT(I6,2I5,I7)
```

and the data

```
|b|b|3|8|5|4|b|b|-|4|5|b|b|9|8|5|b|b|7|5|4|3|2|
```

execution of the input statement assigns 3854 to M, −45 to K, 985 to L, and 75432 to N. The second and third values are both in fields of width 5 so their specification can be given as either I5, I5, or 2I5.

Given the program segment

```
       READ (*,1000) M,K,L
 1000  FORMAT(3I10)
```

appropriate data would be:

```
|b|b|b|b|b|b|3|8|5|4|b|b|b|b|b|b|b|-|4|5|b|b|b|b|b|b|b|b|9|8|5|
```

Since it is difficult to type input into a terminal with the correct spacing, there are two directives, BN and BZ, which permit trailing blanks in fields and indicate to the computer how they should be treated. BN means to ignore trailing blanks, and BZ means to treat trailing blanks as zeros.

Given this input data:

| ƀ | ƀ | 8 | 5 | 4 | 3 | ƀ | ƀ | ƀ | ƀ | ƀ | 3 | 9 | 5 | ƀ | ƀ | ƀ | ƀ | 1 | 8 | ƀ | ƀ | ƀ | ƀ |

and the input statement

```
READ (*,1000) ICON,JMAX,KVAL
```

and if the format is

```
1000  FORMAT(BN,3I8)
```

then

```
ICON = 8543, JMAX = 395, KVAL = 18
```

But if the format is

```
1000  FORMAT(BZ,3I8)
```

| ƀ | ƀ | 8 | 5 | 4 | 3 | ƀ | ƀ | ƀ | ƀ | ƀ | 3 | 9 | 5 | ƀ | ƀ | ƀ | ƀ | 1 | 8 | ƀ | ƀ | ƀ | ƀ |

then

```
ICON = 854300, JMAX = 39500, KVAL = 180000
```

The directive BN or BZ applies to the data specifications that follow in the same format until a new directive is given. For example, if the format is

```
1000  FORMAT(BN,2I8,BZ,I8)
```

| ƀ | ƀ | 8 | 5 | 4 | 3 | ƀ | ƀ | ƀ | ƀ | ƀ | 3 | 9 | 5 | ƀ | ƀ | ƀ | ƀ | 1 | 8 | ƀ | ƀ | ƀ | ƀ |

then

```
ICON = 8543, JMAX = 395, KVAL = 180000
```

Programming Hint

> Validity: Use BN and large field specifications for interactive input.

The rule for designing an I format is:

let f = maximum number of whole digits expected
    w ≥ f + 1 (1 position for sign)
then Iw is the format specification to be used

There is a limit to the number of digits that can be stored in an integer variable. This limit depends on the word length of the machine being used. If the input contains a number that is too big, an overflow error occurs. The I format may specify a field width greater than the machine limit, but no error will occur unless a particular input value is too big, as shown in the following examples:

Format	Input value	Result
I5	31472	31472
I15	ɓ12345678ɓɓɓɓɓɓ	12345678
I15	123456789012345	error (too long)

3.2.2 Real Input (F and E specifications)

Data being read into real variables must be described using either an F or an E format specification. The E format is used when the data is in exponential form, otherwise the F format is used. Each of these specifications has several forms:

Fw.0   w is field width
       explicit data decimal point is expected
Fw.d   w is field width
       d is number of fractional digits
       explicit data decimal point is optional
Ew.0   w is field width
       explicit data decimal point is expected
Ew.d   w is field width
       d is number of fractional digits
       explicit data decimal point is optional

If the data does not contain an explicit decimal point, the number of fractional digits must be indicated in the specification. If both the specification and the data indicate the position of the decimal point, the position of the decimal point in the actual data value overrides the specification. If the format is Fw.0 and there is no decimal point in the data, the data is understood to be a whole number. For example:

Format	Input value	Result
F5.0	ɓ2761	2761.0

F Specification

The rules for matching the F specification with the data value are as follows:

Format	Input	Comment
Fw.0	decimal point	value given by data
Fw.d	no decimal point	point inserted d from right end
Fw.d	decimal point	value given by data

The following examples show the use of the F specification with various data values:

Format	Input value	Result
F5.0	25314	25314.0
F5.0	ƀƀ213	213.0
F5.0	918ƀƀ	91800.0
F5.0	ƀ3.47	3.47
F5.0	91.6ƀ	91.6
F5.0	ƀ63.ƀ	63.0
F5.2	12345	123.45
F5.2	−371ƀ	−37.10
F5.2	ƀ1.4ƀ	1.40
F5.2	−.669	−.669
F5.2	ƀ3.ƀƀ	3.00

A repetition number may be included in the specification. Given the FORTRAN program segment

```
READ (*,1500) AVAL, BCON, CVAL
```

then suppose AVAL is 159.845, BCON is −3975.12, CVAL is 7.0893. If the input data is given a standardized field size (9) and a standard number of decimal places (4), either of these formats,

```
1500  FORMAT(F9.4,F9.4,F9.4)
```

or

```
1500  FORMAT(3F9.4)
```

with this data

input the same values. The arrows indicate where the decimal point is placed. Because there are no decimal points in the data, the format specification is used to identify the last four digits as fractional digits. Trailing blanks are treated as zeros.

If minimum field sizes are specified and explicit decimal points used with either of these formats:

```
1500  FORMAT(F7.3,F8.2,F6.4)
```

or

```
1500  FORMAT(F7.0,F8.0,F6.0)
```

and the input data is:

> |1|5|9|.|8|4|5|−|3|9|7|5|.|1|2|7|.|0|8|9|3|

the values are the same.

    If standard field sizes are specified and explicit decimal points are used,

    1500 FORMAT(F9.3,F9.2,F9.4)

or

    1500 FORMAT(3F9.0)

and the input data is:

> |b|b|1|5|9|.|8|4|5|b|−|3|9|7|5|.|1|2|b|b|7|.|0|8|9|3|b|

the values are the same. Note that the decimal point in the data overrides any decimal point specification. Also, with explicit data decimal points, leading and trailing blanks have no effect. The BN and BZ directives may be used with the F specification, but they are less useful than with the I specification.

    The rule for designing an F format is:

    let f = maximum number of whole digits expected
      d = maximum number of fractional digits expected
      $w \geq f + d + 2$ (1 position each for sign and decimal point)
    then Fw.d is the format to be used

    When the data contains very large or very small numbers, they may be written in exponential form even when an F format is used. In this case, the F specification should show only the field width. Given this program segment:

        READ (*,2000) P, Q, R
    2000 FORMAT(F8.0,F7.0,F6.0)

and this input data:

> |5|4|.|3|2|E|0|2|2|5|8|.|E|−|5|.|8|2|E|0|4|

then P is 54.32E02 or 5432.0, Q is 258.E − 5 or .00258, and R is .82E04 or 8200.0.

    Because computers are based on a binary number system, real values with fractional parts that are not powers of two are only approximately equal to the decimal number found in the input. The number of significant digits depends on the word length of the computer and the internal form used for the number. A typical machine retains six or seven significant digits. If the input has more digits than the machine can use, the computer will accept them and store as accurate a number as possible. If an exponent is near the machine limit, an input error of exponent overflow or underflow may occur.

<table>
<tr><td>*Programming*
Hint</td><td>Use format specification Fw.0 when there are decimal points in the data, Fw.d when there are no decimal points in the data.</td></tr>
</table>

E Specification

The rules for the use of the E specification are the same as those for the F specification:

Specification	Input	Comment
Ew.0	no decimal point	point assumed to be at right end
Ew.0	decimal point	value given by data
Ew.d	no decimal point	point inserted d from right end
Ew.d	decimal point	value given by data

The following examples show the use of the E specification with various data values:

Format	Input value	Result
E8.0	16815E00	16815.0
E8.0	5314E−02	53.14
E8.0	ƀƀƀ213E5	21300000.0
E8.0	ƀ3.47E01	34.7
E8.0	−91.6E+3	−91600.0
E8.0	ƀ63.E−01	6.3
E8.0	ƀ21.3E1ƀ	213000000000.0
E8.2	ƀ12345E3	123450.
E8.2	−371E−01	−.371
E8.2	ƀƀƀ1.4E2	140.0
E8.2	ƀƀ1.E−1ƀ	.0000000001

As with other format specifications, if the data value is not right justified in its field, trailing blanks are understood to be zeros unless BN is specified.

Given this program segment,

```
READ (*,1000) AVAL,BMIN,CMAX
```

then the format

```
1000  FORMAT(BN,E11.0,E11.0,E11.0)
```

or

```
1000  FORMAT(BN,3E11.0)
```

fits the data:

|8|9|3|.|7|5|4|E|0|2|b̷|b̷|.|0|3|2|5|4|E|0|2|b̷|b̷|b̷|1|5|.|4|7|E|–|0|2|

Note that the exponent may be either signed or unsigned. When the exponent is signed, the letter E may be omitted. Therefore the following data is equivalent:

|8|9|3|.|7|5|4|+|0|2|b̷|b̷|.|0|3|2|5|4|+|0|2|b̷|b̷|b̷|1|5|.|4|7|–|0|2|b̷|

The rule for designing an E format is:

let f = maximum number of whole digits expected
   d = maximum number of fractional digits expected
   w ≥ f + d + 6 (1 position each for sign and decimal point
                           4 positions for signed exponent)
then Ew.d is the format to be used

If the input has more digits than the machine can use, the computer will accept them and store as accurate a number as possible. If an exponent is near the machine limit, an input error of exponent overflow or underflow may occur. The actual limits on the exponent depend on the machine.

*Programming
Hint*

Validity: Design input data formats to make the data visually attractive and easy to read.

3.2.3 Input Control (X, T, and / specifications)

Horizontal and vertical spacing of the input data are controlled by using the X specification and the slash (/) in the input format. The X specification, which is used for horizontal spacing, has the form

   rX

where r is a repetition number and a field width of one is understood. It is used to indicate positions in the input that are not to be read. These positions may contain blanks or other characters.

Given this program segment:

```
        READ (*,1000) IMAX,ICON,KVAL
   1000 FORMAT(I3,5X,I4,5X,I3)
```

and this data:

|7|5|4|ƀ|ƀ|ƀ|ƀ|ƀ|8|9|0|5|ƀ|ƀ|ƀ|ƀ|3|8|5|

then IMAX is 754, ICON is 8905, and KVAL is 385.

The X specification makes it possible to label online data, yet read only the data values. For example, given this program segment:

```
      READ (*,1000) IMAX, ICON, KVAL
1000  FORMAT(I3,5X,I4,5X,I3)
```

and this data:

|7|5|4|I|C|O|N|=|8|9|0|5|K|V|A|L|=|3|8|5|

then IMAX is 754, ICON is 8905, and KVAL is 385.

The fields of the input line that are specified by the X specification may be blank or may contain extraneous characters. The computer ignores them.

When data is evenly spaced, the X specification and a standard data specification can be grouped in parentheses and a repetition number used with the entire group. Given the program segment

```
      READ (*,5000) A, B, C, D
5000  FORMAT(F5.2,2X,F6.2,2X,F6.2,2X,F6.2)
```

or

```
5000  FORMAT(F5.2,3(2X,F6.2))
```

and the data

|3|2|8|6|5|ƀ|ƀ|2|5|9|7|6|2|ƀ|ƀ|ƀ|1|2|7|3|6|ƀ|ƀ|-|5|8|1|3|2|

then A is 328.65, B is 2597.62, C is 127.36, and D is -581.32.

The T specification directs the computer to "tab" to specific columns. The general form of the T specification is:

```
Tn
```

where n is an integer that specifies the column of the input record where reading is to resume. In tabbing to column n, earlier columns are ignored. The following examples show the use of the T specification. Given the program segment

```
      READ (*,1000) A,B,C
1000  FORMAT(F5.3,T11,F8.2,T24,F7.4)
```

and the data

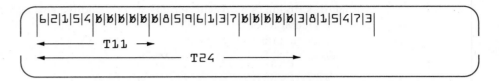

then A is 62.154, B is 85961.37, and C is 381.5473. Notice that the data for B is read from columns 11 through 18. The field of width 8 starts in position 11 of the input record. Similarly the data for C is read from the seven columns in positions 24 through 30.

The T specification can be used to read data in an order different from the order in which it is entered. Given the program segment

```
      READ (*,1000) A,B
1000  FORMAT(T21,F5.2,T11,F5.4)
```

and the data

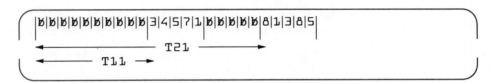

then A is 813.85 and B is 3.4571. The number from columns 21 through 25 is read first and assigned to A; then the number from columns 11 through 15 is read and assigned to B.

The slash is used in formatted input to specify several input records in the same format. With list-directed input, the computer automatically advanced to a new record when there were not enough data values in the current record. With formatted input, the computer does not advance unless it is instructed to do so.

Given the program segment

```
      READ (*,1000) I,J,K,L,M
1000  FORMAT(I3,I4,I2/I3,I6)
```

and the data

| 2|8|0| |1|5|0|1|8| |

| 1|5|8| | |3|8|5|6| |

then I is 280, J is 150, K is 18, L is 158, and M is 3856. There are two descriptions in the format, I3,I4,I2 and I3,I6, which match the two data records. The first format description is used with the first record and the second format description with the second record.

Given the program segment

```
      READ (*,1500) I,J,K,L,M
 1500 FORMAT(I5,I6//I4,I2,I4)
```

and the data

ƀ	2	8	6	5	ƀ	-	3	9	7	2	ƀ	ƀ	1	7

blank line or card

ƀ	3	9	7	ƀ	ƀ	ƀ	1	3	6

then I is 2865, J is −3972, K is 397, L is 0, and M is 136.

Programming Hint

> Use blank lines to separate sets of data. The end of each set of data is detected when all the input values are zero.

The format statement describes three input records. The first one has the description I5,I6. The third value in the record is not used because it is outside the bounds of the description. No field is described in the second record, but if there were any data on it, there would be a field specification between the two slashes of the format. The third record is described as I4,I2,I4. The second field contains only blanks, but it is understood to be 0. The slash may be used in a repeated specification. The program segment

```
      READ (*,1000) F,G,H,P,Q,R
 1000 FORMAT(2F6.0/2F8.0/2F8.0)
```

or

```
 1000 FORMAT(2F6.0,(/2F8.0))
```

describes the data

2	8	9	.	7	2	6	3	1	5	.	7

2	8	3	2	.	8	5	4	7	8	9	.	3	1	7	6

| b | b | 1 | 8 | . | 2 | 8 | 9 | b | b | - | . | 8 | 3 | 4 | 2 |

Since the format statement does not specify six fields for the six variables, it is repeated from the rightmost left parenthesis. As a general rule, the format is repeated from the repetition count preceding the left parenthesis that matches the right parenthesis following the last field specification.

Ending a format statement with a slash would be meaningless because the slash *separates* record descriptions. However, starting a format with a slash would tell the computer to ignore a record and advance to the next one. Note that with interactive input, a slash would be meaningful only if data at the end of an input line were to be ignored.

3.2.4 Review Questions

1. Write the input and format statements to read the following integer data. Also show the data layout. Assume I = 389, J = 793, K = −3915, L = 85, M = −9.

   a. Exact field specification.
   b. Overspecification of field widths to include five blank spaces between the numbers (but not before the first number).
   c. A repeat specification that will accommodate all the values.
   d. Exact field specifications, but the use of X specifications to leave five blank spaces between values.
   e. I,J on one line, K, L, M on a second line with exact specifications and one READ statement.

2. Write the input and format statements to read the following integer data for IMAX, KVAL, MCON, and NMIN, given the input data specifications for all numbers:

| 8 | 9 | 5 | b | b | b | b | b | 7 | 9 | 3 | 7 | 5 | b | b | 6 | 9 | 5 | 4 | 2 | b | b | - | 1 | 5 | 8 | 6 | 7 | b |

   Left justify the numbers in the data record. Suppress the trailing blanks for MCON and NMIN, but treat them as zeros for the other values. What are the values of IMAX, KVAL, MCON, and NMIN?

3. Write the input and format statements to read the following real numbers. Also show the layout of the data. Assume ACON = 3856.854, BMAX = −31.085, CVAL = 785.984, BMIN = 0.00375.

   a. Exact specification when the data does not contain explicit decimal points.
   b. Overspecification of the fields using F12.7 for all values when the data does not contain explicit decimal points.
   c. Exact specification when the data does not contain explicit decimal points and there are five blanks between values. (Use the X format.)
   d. Exact specification when there are explicit decimal points in the data, but no spaces between values.
   e. Use F12.0 format for all values and explicit decimal points when the values are left justified in the fields.

4. Write the format statement to read the values of P = 13.6E02, Q = $-32.76E - 03$, R = 5.678E03. Also show the form of the input.

   a. Use exact specifications and no explicit decimal points.
   b. Use the standard specification E15.6 for each value, but no explicit decimal points
   c. Use exact specifications and explicit decimal points.
   d. Use the standard specification E15.6 for each value and explicit decimal points.

5. Given the following input data and instructions, what values are assigned to the variables?

   a. |1|2|3|4|5|6|7|8|9|0|1|2|3|4|5|6|7|8|9|0|1|

   ```
         READ (*,1000) K,L,M,N
   1000  FORMAT(I5,I6,I7,I3)
   ```

   b. |6|2|5|4|1|7|6|9|3|5|2|1|7|3|1|8|9|3|2|1|1|6|0|7|5|

   ```
         READ (*,1000) A,B,C,D
   1000  FORMAT(F5.3,F8.5,F7.3,F5.2)
   ```

   c. |3|1|2|6|7|2|E|0|3|1|8|9|5|4|E|0|2|

   ```
         READ (*,1000) X,Y
   1000  FORMAT(E9.3,E8.2)
   ```

   d. |+|1|2|3|−|4|5|6|7|8|9|−|1|3|5|+|7|

   ```
         READ (*,1000) P,Q
   1000  FORMAT(E6.1,E8.2)
   ```

3.3 Formatted Output Statements

Formatted input statements are used primarily with data files. Formatted output statements are used for most output, including interactive output. The format specifications are similar to those for input, the major difference being that special directives are available for spacing on printer pages. These directives must be used with PRINT instructions. Otherwise, we can study the PRINT and WRITE instructions together.

Printer Directives

Line printers generally have a standard line length, 80, 120, or 132. (This text assumes a length of 80 character positions.) When an output format is specified, the computer sets up the entire line before sending it to the printer, using a buffer that contains one position more than the length of the printer line. This first position contains the spacing directive character. When a formatted output statement is executed, first the entire buffer is filled with blanks, then the programmer places a spacing directive character (carriage control character) in the first position of the buffer. The first character position is always reserved for the printer carriage control character when the printer is used. The other positions may be used for output data. The spacing directives are:

	Character	*Comment*
	1X	default spacing (single spacing)
blank	'ƀ'	single spacing
zero	'0'	double spacing (before printing)
one	'1'	page eject (before printing)
plus	'+'	overprint previous line

Other directives may be available, depending on the setup of the printer. These directives must be used with formats for the PRINT statement and with formats for the WRITE statement when it is assigned a printer as an output device.

3.3.1 Integer Output (I specification)

The I specification for output has the same form as for input. With output, it is important to overspecify each field by providing space for extra characters, or to use the X format between items, otherwise the output will not be readable. Each digit of the value occupies one position in the output line. If the value is negative, the sign also occupies a position. Integer values are printed (or written) right justified in the output fields. This is shown in the following examples.

Given NUM = 3895, MCON = 785, KMIN = −831, ICOUNT = 75 and program segment

```
      PRINT 1000, NUM,MCON,KMIN,ICOUNT
1000  FORMAT(1X,I8,I7,I8,I7)
```

or

```
1000  FORMAT(1X,2(I8,I7))
```

or

```
      WRITE (*,1000) NUM,MCON,KMIN,ICOUNT
1000  FORMAT(1X,I8,I7,I8,I7)
```

or

```
1000  FORMAT(1X,2(I8,I7))
```

the output buffer is set up as:

ƀ|ƀ|ƀ|ƀ|ƀ|3|8|9|5|ƀ|ƀ|ƀ|ƀ|7|8|5|ƀ|ƀ|ƀ|ƀ|-|8|3|1|ƀ|ƀ|ƀ|ƀ|ƀ|ƀ|7|5|

The first position is specified as default (using 1X) in both the PRINT and WRITE statements. The actual output appears as:

ƀƀƀƀ3895ƀƀƀƀ785ƀƀƀƀ-831ƀƀƀƀƀ75

If the exact spacing of the numbers is to be specified, the format would be:

```
1000  FORMAT(5X,I4,4X,I3,4X,I4,5X,I2)
```

Because the programmer does not usually know the exact number of digits to be printed for each variable, a standard-size field should be used, one large enough to include the sign and a leading blank.

The rule for designing an I specification is:

let n   be the maximum number of digits
then Iw   is the specification where $w \geq n + 2$

Vertical Spacing of Output (/)

Using the slash as a format separator, several lines may be printed or written with a single output statement. A format for each line is included in the single FORMAT statement, with slashes separating them.

Given NUMC = 389, KVAL = 875, ICON = 32, MIN = −76538 and the program segment

```
        WRITE (*,1000) NUMC, KVAL, ICON, MIN
1000  FORMAT(1X,2I8/1X,2I8)
```

or

```
1000  FORMAT(I9,I8)
```

and the output buffer contains

ƀ|ƀ|ƀ|ƀ|ƀ|ƀ|3|8|9|ƀ|ƀ|ƀ|ƀ|ƀ|ƀ|8|7|5|

then

ƀ|ƀ|ƀ|ƀ|ƀ|ƀ|ƀ|3|2|ƀ|ƀ|-|7|6|5|3|8|

and the output is printed as:

```
 bbbbb389bbbbbb875
bbbbbb32bbb-76538
```

Notice that the spacing directive must be included in each of the two line descriptions of the format for the PRINT statement.

Given the same data and the statements

```
     WRITE (*,1000) NUMC, KVAL, ICON, MIN
1000 FORMAT(1X,2I8//1X,2I8)
```

or

```
1000 FORMAT(1X,2I8/'0',2I8)
```

the output is printed as:

```
bbbbb389bbbbbb875
          blank line
bbbbbb32bb-76538
```

By using slashes, vertical spacing can be controlled with either the PRINT or the WRITE statements.

3.3.2 Real Output (F, E, and G specifications)

Specifying output formats for real variables can be a problem because there is a wide range of possible values for the variables. For example, even if output is limited to seven significant digits, the location of the decimal point with respect to those digits can still be a problem. The choice of output specification depends on the programmer's knowledge of the expected output. The F, E, and G specifications are the most common with real numbers. The E specification is used if the numbers (usually very large or very small) are to be printed in exponential notation. This occurs frequently when processing scientific data. The F specification is used if exponential notation is not wanted. The G specification is used if the numbers are to be printed in exponential notation, only if they cannot be accurately printed in ordinary decimal notation.

Programming
Hint

> Accuracy: The programmer must limit the output to digits that are significant for the problem.

Output Using F Specification

Using F specification, a number is printed right justified in the output field with a decimal point and a sign. The field width should be overspecified so that there are leading blanks. The rule for designing the F specification is:

let   f   be the maximum number of whole digits
      d   be the desired number of fractional digits
    Fw.d   is the format where $w \geq f + d + 2$
    (the extra spaces are for sign and decimal point)

The following examples show the spacing:

Format	Spacing	Value	Output	
F6.1	xxxx.x	14.3	ƀƀ14.3	
F6.1		− 14.3	ƀ − 14.3	
F6.1		14	ƀƀ14.0	(padded)
F6.1		14.27	ƀƀ14.3	(rounded)
F6.1		14.21	ƀƀ14.2	(rounded)
F6.3		14.3	14.300	
F6.4		14.3	******	(error)
F6.3		− 14.3	******	(error)
F6.3		no value	UUUUUU	(error)

If the specification does not have space for all the fractional digits, the number is rounded. If it does not have space for all the whole digits, it is an error; however, the computer will fill the field with asterisks rather than stop processing. If you attempt to print a variable that has not been assigned a value (an undefined variable), the field will fill with U's.

The following examples show various ways to format real output for a PRINT or WRITE statement, using the F specification.

Given CONS = 56.756, VAL = − 7.325, BALNC = 543.15 and the program segment

```
      WRITE (*,1000) CONS,VAL,BALNC
1000  FORMAT(1X,F10.3,F10.3,F10.3)
```

or

```
1000  FORMAT(5X,F6.3,4X,F6.3,3X,F7.3)
```

or

```
1000  FORMAT(1X,3(3X,F7.3))
```

the output is:

ƀ	ƀ	ƀ	ƀ	5	6	.	7	5	6	ƀ	ƀ	ƀ	ƀ	ƀ	−	7	.	3	2	5	ƀ	ƀ	ƀ	5	4	3	.	1	5	0

Programming Hint

Debugging: When a row of asterisks appears in the output, increase the field width in the output specification and make sure that the variable type and the format specification match. When a row of U's appears, look for an undefined variable.

Output Using E Specification

E specification is used to produce output in scientific notation. It allows the programmer to indicate an exact number of significant digits for output. A number is printed right justified in the output field with a decimal point, a sign, and a signed exponent. The first significant digit of the value appears to the right of the decimal point. There is a zero on the left of the decimal point. This is the output specification to use to show a fixed number of significant digits, regardless of the size of the number. With seven significant digits, the output will have the form

$$0.\text{xxxxxxx}E \pm \text{xx} \quad \text{or} \quad -0.\text{xxxxxxx}E \pm \text{xx}$$

The field width should be overspecified so that there are leading blanks.

The rule for designing the E specification is:

> let   d   be the desired number of significant digits
> Ew.d   is the format where $w \geq d + 7$

The extra seven positions include the letter E, a signed two-digit exponent, a decimal point, a sign for the number, and a leading zero.

The following examples show the spacing:

Format	Spacing	Value	Output
E14.7	$\pm 0.\text{xxxxxxx}E \pm \text{xx}$	7654.385	␢0.7654385E + 04
E14.7		93895.3215	␢0.9389532E + 05 (rounded)
E14.7		− 93895.3215	− 0.9389532E + 05 (rounded)
E14.7		128.61	␢0.1286100E + 03 (filled)
E14.7		.20685	␢0.2068500E + 00 (filled)
E14.7		.091	␢0.9100000E − 01 (filled)

With the E format, it is always possible to display a real number. Spacing is provided by overspecification or by the X specification.

Given PVAL = 83.965, QCONS = − 1286.6378, SEQN = 13.7568 and the program segment

```
      PRINT 1000, PVAL, QCONS, SEQN
1000  FORMAT(1X,E10.3,E13.4,E11.2)
```

or

```
1000  FORMAT(2X,E9.3,2X,E11.4,2X,E9.2)
```

the output is:

```
|␢|0|.|8|4|0|E|+|0|2|␢|␢|-|0|.|1|2|8|7|E|+|0|4|␢|␢|␢|0|.|1|4|E|+|0|2|
```

Output Using G Specification

The G specification has the advantage of showing a specified number of significant digits regardless of the size of the number, using ordinary notation for numbers in the normal range. Given the specification

```
Gw.d
```

exactly d significant digits are shown in the output. The number is printed according to either the F or the E specification, depending on the value of the number and the field width specified. The four rightmost positions of the field are reserved for exponents. If the value will fit into the other positions using F format, that format will be used; otherwise E format is chosen.

The rule for designing a G specification is:

let   s   be the number of significant digits
use   Gw.d   where w ≥ s + 6
then if   exponent   < 0, the computer uses Ew.d
    if   exponent   > d, the computer uses Ew.d
    if 0 ≤ exponent ≤ d, the computer uses (Fw-4.0,4X) or (Fw-4.1,4X) . . . (Fw-4.s,4X) whichever is appropriate

The following examples show the spacing:

Format	Value	Output
G12.4	29870.	ƀƀ0.2987E + 05
G12.4	2987.	ƀƀƀ2987.ƀƀƀƀ
G12.4	298.7	ƀƀƀ298.7ƀƀƀƀ
G12.4	29.87	ƀƀƀ29.87ƀƀƀƀ
G12.4	2.987	ƀƀƀ2.987ƀƀƀƀ
G12.4	.2987	ƀƀƀ.2987ƀƀƀƀ
G12.4	.02987	ƀƀ0.2987E − 01
G9.4	29.87	29.87ƀƀƀƀ
G9.4	− 29.87	********* (error)
G10.4	29.87	ƀ29.87ƀƀƀƀ
G10.4	− 29.87	− 29.87ƀƀƀƀ

If the specification provides space for the significant digits but not for a minus sign, there is not enough space for Ew.d output. This is an error and the field will fill with asterisks.

The following example shows real values formatted for output using the G specification. Given AVAL = 714900, BVALUE = 0.07316, CON = 38.6200 and the program segment

```
      WRITE (*,1000) AVAL, BVALUE, CON
 1000  FORMAT(1X,3G10.4)
```

then the output is:

|0|.|7|1|4|9|E|+|0|6|0|.|7|3|1|6|E|−|0|1|ƀ|3|8|.|6|2|ƀ|ƀ|ƀ|ƀ|

3.3.3 Titling Output (alphanumeric literals)

FORTRAN recognizes alphanumeric strings enclosed in single quotation marks as character literals. These literals may be printed for use as titles and output labels, either in output statements or in formats. The following examples show literals printed with alphanumeric formats:

```
        PRINT 1000, 'WATERβQUALITYβREPORT'
1000    FORMAT(1X,A)
```

or

```
1000    FORMAT(1X,A20)
```

or

```
        WRITE (*,1000) 'WATER QUALITY REPORT'
1000    FORMAT(1X,A)
```

or

```
1000    FORMAT(1X,A20)
```

The output is:

```
|W|A|T|E|R|β|Q|U|A|L|I|T|Y|β|R|E|P|O|R|T|
```

If the literal appears in the output statement, the format must contain an A specification. The general form of the A specification is:

   A w

where w is the field width. This is used to print a character value right justified in the field. When the field specification is missing, the exact number of characters in the value is used. But when the field specification is given, characters are dropped from the left end or blanks are supplied to satisfy the field width. This is shown in the following examples:

Specification	*Value*	*Output*
A4	'ABCD'	ABCD
A4	'ABCDE'	BCDE
A4	'ABC'	βABC

**Programming
Hint**

> Efficiency: Specify titles and labels in format.
> Readability: Specify labels in output lines.
> Reliability: Never start character output in position 1, which is reserved for carriage control characters.

The character literal may be specified in the format instead of the output statement:

```
        WRITE (*,1000)
1000    FORMAT(1X,'WATER QUALITY REPORT')
```

The output is the same. When the character literal is specified in the format, an exact field width is provided.

Various data types may be mixed in an output statement. The following examples show output labeled for readability. Given AVG = 125.86 and the program segment

```
      PRINT 1000, 'AVERAGEb=',AVG
1000  FORMAT(1X,A,F8.2)
```

or

```
      PRINT 1000, AVG
1000  FORMAT(1X,'AVERAGEb=',F8.2)
```

the output is:

A	V	E	R	A	G	E	␢	=	␢	␢	1	2	5	.	8	6

Given L = 10, W = 5, H = 15 and the program segment

```
      INTEGER L,H,W
      . . .
      WRITE (*,1000) 'LENGTHb=',L,'WIDTHb=',
     1        W,'HEIGHTb=',H
1000  FORMAT(1X,3(A,I3,2X))
```

the output is:

L	E	N	G	T	H	␢	=	␢	1	0	␢	␢	W	I	D	T	H	␢	=	␢	␢	5	␢	␢	H	E	I	G	H	T	␢	=	␢	1	5

The following example shows column headings with two sets of output. Given the program segment

```
      INTEGER L,H,W
      . . .
      WRITE (*,1000)
1000  FORMAT(11X,'LENGTH',10X,'WIDTH',10X,'HEIGHT')
      . . .
      WRITE (*,2000) L,W,H
      . . .
      WRITE (*,2000) L,W,H
2000  FORMAT(1X,3(12X,I3))
```

then depending on the values of L, W, and H, the output might be:

	LENGTH	WIDTH	HEIGHT
	103	375	28
	45	20	15

3.3.4 Output Spacing Control

As we have seen, output values may be spaced apart either by overspecifying the field widths in the format statement or by using the X format. The T specification can also be used to space the data.

Horizontal Spacing (T specification)

The T specification sets tab postions in the output buffer. The form of the T specification is:

        Tp

where p is the character position from the left margin (including the printer directive position) where the next specification field is to begin. T1 is the position for the carriage control character. Only valid carriage control characters should be used in this tab position.

   Given CONS = 3856.7569, VAL = − 187.325, BALNC = 62543.15 and the program segment

```
        WRITE (*,1000) CONS, VAL, BALNC
   1000  FORMAT(4X,F7.2,5X,F6.1,5X,F6.0)
```

or

```
   1000  FORMAT(1X,T5,F7.2,T17,F6.1,T28,F6.0)
```

or

```
   1000  FORMAT(T5,F7.2,T17,F6.1,T28,F6.0)
```

then the output buffer contains:

```
0000000001111111111222222222233333
1234567890123456789012345678901234
 bbbb3856.7bbbbbb-187.3bbbbbb62543.
```

The output field for CONS starts in position 5 of the output buffer, the field for VAL starts in position 17, and that for BALNC in position 28. Using the T specification is particularly convenient when the output consists of columns of data.

   If data is to be printed in the following form:

GRADE REPORT

COURSE	GRADE
xxxx	xxx
xxxx	xxx
xxxx	xxx

then the following formats can be used:

```
1000  FORMAT ('1',T20,'GRADE REPORT')
1100  FORMAT ('+',T20,'_____  _____')
1200  FORMAT ('0',T13,'COURSE',T32,'GRADE')
1300  FORMAT ('+',T13,'_____',T32,'_____'/'0')
1400  FORMAT (T14,I4,T33,I3)
```

Format 1000 uses the printer directive '1' to force page ejection on the printer so that the title of the report starts at the top of a new page. Format 1100 uses the printer directive '+' to suppress a line advance. The character string in the format overprints the title, providing underlining. Format 1200 double spaces before printing the column headings. Format 1300 prints a second time on the line that has the column headings, which causes them to be underlined. Finally, format 1400 prints the data. Each x in the report design indicated a position to be used by a data digit.

3.3.5 Review Questions

1. Given the following integer variables,
   ICON = 78546, JMAX = 385, KCON = 7615, JVAL = −895932
   show the output for each of the following sets of statements:

   a.   WRITE (*,1000) ICON,JMAX,KCON,JVAL
   1000   FORMAT(1X,I5,I3,I7,I7)
   b.   WRITE (*,1000) ICON,JMAX,KCON,JVAL
   1000   FORMAT(1X,I5,5X,I3,5X,I4,5X,I7)
   c.   WRITE (*,1000) ICON,JMAX,KCON,JVAL
   1000   FORMAT(1X,I5,I8,I9,I12)
   d.   WRITE (*,1000) ICON,JMAX,KCON,JVAL
   1000   FORMAT(1X,4I10)
   e.   WRITE (*,1000) ICON,JMAX,KCON,JVAL
   1000   FORMAT(1X,I5,I3/I4,I7)
   f.   WRITE (*,1000) ICON,JMAX,KCON,JVAL
   1000   FORMAT(1X,2I10/1X,2I10)

2. Given the following real variables,
   W = 3697.12, X = 1756.3849, Y = −0.18954, Z = 24596.152
   show the output for each of the following sets of statements:

   a.   WRITE (*,1500) W,X,Y,Z
   1500   FORMAT(1X,F7.2,F9.4,F8.5,F9.3)
   b.   WRITE (*,1500) W,X,Y,Z
   1500   FORMAT(1X,F7.2,5X,F9.4,5X,F8.5,5X,F9.3)
   c.   WRITE (*,1500) W,X,Y,Z
   1500   FORMAT(1X,4F12.5)
   d.   WRITE (*,1500) W,X,Y,Z
   1500   FORMAT(1X,2F15.5/1X,2F15.5)
   e.   WRITE (*,1500) W,X,Y,Z
   1500   FORMAT(1X,F9.2,E15.4,G12.5,G12.5)

3. Write a FORMAT statement that could be used to print each of the following output lines:

a.

> ƀƀƀxxxxxxƀƀƀƀxxxƀƀƀxxxx.xxƀƀƀƀx.xxxx

b.

> ƀƀƀƀƀƀƀ0.xxxxxxExxxƀƀƀƀƀƀ0.xxxxxxExx

c.

> ƀƀƀƀƀTOTALƀ=ƀxxxxxxxxx

d.

> ƀƀƀ<u>NAME</u>:ƀƀƀƀƀƀƀƀƀƀƀƀ<u>DATE</u>:

4. Write a code segment to READ and print the numbers from each of the following input records:

a.

> |1|2|3| | |4|5|.|7|8| | | |9|8|7|.|E|−|0|5|

b.

> | | | |5| | |3| | |7| | |1|2|3|4|5| | |9|.|0|9|

c.

> |A|=|3| |S|U|M|=|1|4|.|7|

<hr>

3.4 Sample Programs Using Input/Output

The examples in this section show the use of formatted and unformatted input and output statements. These programs have been executed interactively on the Digital Equipment Corporation (DEC) computer model VAX 11/780. Some of the programs have been run using batch processing and others have been run interactively. The output of the interactive programs shows the input prompts and input as they would appear on a terminal screen.

3.4.1 Inventory Report Showing the Volume and Cost

Problem

Write a program to input the cost per cubic foot of steel rods and a set of data records containing the diameter in inches and the number and length of steel rods in feet. Compute the volume in cubic feet. Compute the cost of the rods, given values for the diameter and length. Also compute the total volume and total cost. The output is to be in the form of a table containing the diameter, number of rods of that diameter, length, volume of each rod, total volume, and total cost for the number of rods in each size. Print the accumulated totals at the end of the table.

Method

The program consists of four basic parts.

Pseudocode

```
Initialize values which will not be changed such as PI and initialize
    totals
Print the main heading and column headings
For each set of data
   read
   calculate
   print
End for
Print overall totals
Stop
```

Program

```
**************************************************************
*                                                            *
*    INVENTORY REPORT ON STEEL RODS                          *
*                                                            *
**************************************************************
*                                                            *
*    CONSTANTS:                                              *
*                                                            *
*      PI     = 3.14159                                      *
*                                                            *
*    INPUT VARIABLES:                                        *
*                                                            *
*      NUMROD - NUMBER OF RODS OF SAME SIZE AND              *
*               LENGTH                                       *
*      DIAROD - ROD DIAMETER (INCHES)                        *
*      RODLEN - LENGTH OF ROD (FEET)                         *
*      COST   - PRICE PER CUB. FT. OF STEEL ($XX.XX)         *
*                                                            *
*    OUTPUT VARIABLES:                                       *
*                                                            *
*      TVOL   - TOTAL VOLUME OF RODS OF SAME SIZE AND        *
*               LENGTH                                       *
*      TCOST  - TOTAL COST OF RODS OF SAME SIZE AND          *
*               LENGTH                                       *
*      TOTVOL - TOTAL VOLUME OF ALL OF THE RODS              *
*      TOTCOS - TOTAL COST OF ALL OF THE RODS                *
*                                                            *
**************************************************************
```

```
          REAL PI
          PARAMETER (PI=3.14159)
          INTEGER NUMROD
          REAL DIAROD, RODLEN, VOL, RADIUS
          REAL TVOL, TOTVOL, COST, TCOST, TOTCOS

          WRITE (*,900)
900       FORMAT(/1X,'INPUT COST PER POUND OF STEEL:')
          READ (*,1000) COST
1000      FORMAT(F5.2)
          WRITE (*,1005) COST
1005      FORMAT(/1X,'COST PER POUND OF STEEL =',F5.2)
          WRITE (*,1010)
1010      FORMAT(/1X,T25,'STEEL ROD INVENTORY REPORT')
          WRITE (*,1015)
1015      FORMAT('+',T25,'_____ ___ _____ _____')
          WRITE (*,1020)
1020      FORMAT(/1X,T20,'ITEM',T26,'NUMR',T35,'DIAM',
     1          T45,'LENGTH',T60,'VOLUME',T75,'COST')
          TOTVOL = 0.0
          TOTCOS = 0.0
          I = 0

*         DO CALCULATIONS FOR EACH SET OF DATA

          WRITE (*,1030)
1030      FORMAT(/1X,'INPUT DATA',/1X,'_____ ____')
   10     READ (*,1100,END=50) NUMROD, DIAROD, RODLEN
1100        FORMAT(I5,F5.2,F6.2)
            RADIUS = DIAROD / 24
            VOL = PI * RADIUS**2 * RODLEN
            TVOL = NUMROD * VOL
            TOTVOL = TOTVOL + TVOL
            TCOST = TVOL * COST
            TOTCOS = TOTCOS + TCOST
            I = I + 1
            WRITE (*,1200) I,NUMROD,DIAROD,RODLEN,
     1        TVOL,TCOST
1200        FORMAT(1X,T18,2I5,T33,F6.2,T44,F7.2,T54,
     1            F12.2,T68,F12.2)
          GO TO 10

*         ENDDO

   50     CONTINUE
          WRITE (*,1300) TOTVOL,TOTCOS
1300      FORMAT(/20X,'TOTAL VOLUME =',F12.2,5X,
     1            'TOTAL COST =',F12.2)
          STOP
          END
```

Output

```
INPUT COST PER POUND OF STEEL:
2.5

COST PER POUND OF STEEL = 2.50

                    STEEL ROD INVENTORY REPORT

          ITEM  NUMR    DIAM      LENGTH       VOLUME         COST

INPUT_DATA
1,12.,33.
            1     1    12.00      33.00        25.92         64.80
6,16.,13.
            2     6    16.00      13.00       108.91        272.27
4,22.,12.
            3     4    22.00      12.00       126.71        316.78
9,8.,8.
            4     9     8.00       8.00        25.13         62.83

          TOTAL VOLUME =       286.67    TOTAL COST =      716.68
```

Lines 10 through 50 contain the input calculations and printing for each set of input data. Notice that lines 10 and 50 are executable statements while the other numbered lines are formats. Two distinguishable sets of line numbers are used. Both sets are in increasing order and count at least by tens. This system makes it easy to find any numbered line and makes it possible to insert other numbered lines if the program is modified, without having to change any numbers.

> Maintainability: Number program lines in order by 10s or 100s.

All variables that represent totals must be initialized to zero before the data is read. Then if there is no data, they have the correct value.

3.4.2 The Sines of the Angles of a Triangle

Problem

Values for two angles A and B are to be read from the input. For each pair of values, A and B, calculate the value of the third angle C and print A, sin(A), B, sin(B), C, sin(C).

Method

Since a set of values is to be processed, the pseudocode must show how to process a single set of values and how to repeat the processing.

Pseudocode

Do for each pair of angles
    Input A and B
    Calculate the third angle (in degrees)
        C ← (180° − A − B)
    Calculate the sine of each angle
        sin(angle ∗ π / 180)
    Print the angles A, B, and C and their sines
End do
Stop

Program

```
**********************************************************
*                                                        *
*    TABLE OF ANGLES OF TRIANGLES AND SINE VALUES        *
*                                                        *
**********************************************************
*                                                        *
*    CONSTANTS:                                          *
*                                                        *
*       PI     = 3.14159                                 *
*                                                        *
*    INPUT VARIABLES:                                    *
*                                                        *
*       A        - ANGLE OF A TRIANGLE (DEGREES)         *
*       B        - ANGLE OF A TRIANGLE (DEGREES)         *
*                                                        *
*    OUTPUT VARIABLES:                                   *
*                                                        *
*       C        - ANGLE OF A TRIANGLE (DEGREES)         *
*                                                        *
**********************************************************

        REAL A, B, C, PI, CONST
        PARAMETER (PI=3.14159)

        WRITE (*,1010)
 1010   FORMAT('1',T31,'ANGLES OF TRIANGLES')
        WRITE (*,1015)
 1015   FORMAT('+',T31,'_____ __ _____')
        WRITE (*,1020)
 1020   FORMAT(/1X,T22,'A',T28,'SIN(A)',T39,'B',T45,
      1        'SIN(B)',T56,'C',T62,'SIN(C)'/)
        CONST = PI / 180.0

*       DO CALCULATIONS FOR ALL DATA

   10   READ (*,1100,END=50) A,B
 1100      FORMAT(2F5.3)
           C = (180 - A - B)
```

```
          WRITE (*,1200) A,SIN(A*CONST),B,
     1              SIN(B*CONST),C,SIN(C*CONST)
1200      FORMAT(/15X,3(4X,F5.2,3X,F5.2)//)
          GO TO 10

*      ENDDO

   50  CONTINUE
       STOP
       END
```

Output

		ANGLES OF TRIANGLES				
	A	SIN(A)	B	SIN(B)	C	SIN(C)
30.,60.						
	30.00	0.50	60.00	0.87	90.00	1.00
40.,50.						
	40.00	0.64	50.00	0.77	90.00	1.00
45.0,45.0						
	45.00	0.71	45.00	0.71	90.00	1.00
20.,70.						
	20.00	0.34	70.00	0.94	90.00	1.00
90.,60.						
	90.00	1.00	60.00	0.87	30.00	0.50

Notice that the structure of this program is the same as the structure of the problem in Section 3.4.1, except that the calculations are done in the output statement.

3.4.3 Value of a Polynomial

Problem

Read the coefficients of an equation $f(x) = ax^2 + bx + c$, along with a value for x. Print the equation and its value.

Program

```
*****************************************************************
*                                                               *
*   PRINT A QUADRATIC EQUATION AND ITS VALUE                    *
*                                                               *
*****************************************************************
*                                                               *
*   INPUT VARIABLES:                                            *
*                                                               *
*      A        - INTEGER COEFFICIENT                           *
*      B        - INTEGER COEFFICIENT                           *
*      C        - INTEGER COEFFICIENT                           *
*      X        - VARIABLE OF THE FUNCTION                      *
*                                                               *
*   OUTPUT VARIABLES:                                           *
*                                                               *
*      THE QUADRATIC EQUATION                                   *
*      Y        - THE VALUE OF THE POLYNOMIAL                   *
*                                                               *
*****************************************************************

        INTEGER A, B, C
        REAL X, Y

        WRITE (*,900)
900     FORMAT(1X,'INPUT VALUES FOR COEFFICIENTS',
     1          ' A,B,C AND FOR VARIABLE X')
        READ (*,1000) A,B,C,X
1000    FORMAT(3I5,F5.2)
        WRITE (*,1010)
1010    FORMAT(/1X,T9,'2')
        WRITE (*,1020)
1020    FORMAT(7X,'X   +     X +     = ')
        Y = X*(A*X + B) + C
        WRITE (*,1100) A,B,C,Y
1100    FORMAT('+',1X,I5,3X,I5,2X,I5,3X,F7.2)
        STOP
        END
```

Output from Two Runs

```
INPUT VALUES FOR COEFFICIENTS A,B,C AND FOR VARIABLE X
    1    1    1 2000

     1X² +   1X +   1=   421.00


INPUT VALUES FOR COEFFICIENTS A,B,C AND FOR VARIABLE X
    4    2    6  550

     4X² +   2X +   6=   138.00
```

If A = 1, B = 1, C = 1, X = 20.00, then the value of the quadratic polynomial is 421.00. If A = 4, B = 2, C = 6, X = 5.50, then the value of the quadratic polynomial is 138.00.

The main point of this program is to show output in a highly readable form. Note that overprinting is used to insert the coefficients and constant into the equation. This could be done without overprinting by including the literals and the numeric specifications in the same format statement. The assignment statement that calculates Y is partially factored. This is more efficient than writing it as Y = A * X ** 2 + B * X + C, because the computer has fewer arithmetic operations to perform.

3.4.4 Water Level File

Problem

Write a program to input water level measurements from a disk file. Write the water level measurements and the daily average level to another disk file.

Method

The input file 'RVRGAG' contains six measurements in each record. The measurements on each record give the water level on a particular day, at a particular location, at four-hour intervals. Write the measurements from a single record and their average to file 'RVRAVG' as a single record.

Program

```
************************************************************
*                                                          *
*    DAILY AVERAGE WATER LEVEL FROM RIVER GAUGE            *
*    MEASUREMENTS                                          *
*                                                          *
************************************************************
*                                                          *
*    FILES:                                                *
*                                                          *
*        RVRGAG - INPUT FILE, 6 MEASUREMENTS PER RECORD    *
*        RVRAVG - OUTPUT FILE, 6 MEASUREMENTS & AVERAGE    *
*                  PER RECORD.                             *
*                                                          *
*    INPUT VARIABLES:                                      *
*                                                          *
*        H1, H2, . . . , H6 - WATER LEVEL MEASUREMENTS     *
*                                                          *
*    OUTPUT VARIABLES:                                     *
*                                                          *
*        H1, H2, . . . , H6 - WATER LEVEL MEASUREMENTS     *
*        AVGH   - AVERAGE WATER LEVEL                      *
*                                                          *
************************************************************
```

```
            REAL H1, H2, H3, H4, H5, H6, AVGH

            OPEN (UNIT=12,FILE='RVRGAG',STATUS='OLD')
            OPEN (UNIT=13,FILE='RVRAVG',STATUS='NEW')

            WRITE (*,1000)
1000        FORMAT(/1X,T25,'OUTPUT TO FILE RVRAVG'/)

*           DO FOR EACH SET OF MEASUREMENTS

10          READ (12,*,END=50) H1,H2,H3,H4,H5,H6
              AVGH =(H1 + H2 + H3 + H4 + H5 + H6) /6.0
              WRITE (13,*) H1,H2,H3,H4,H5,H6,'AVGH=',AVGH
            GO TO 10

*           ENDDO

50          CONTINUE
            CLOSE (UNIT=12)
            CLOSE (UNIT=13)
            WRITE (*,*) 'RUN COMPLETED'
            STOP
            END
```

Input

```
100,110,120,130,140,160
50,75,100,125,150,175
11,22,33,44,55,66
81,84,86,88,90,91
120,125,128,131,133,135
201,213,218,220,225,227
```

Output to File

```
100.0000      110.0000      120.0000 130.0000 140.0000
160.0000 AVGH =    126.6667
50.00000       75.00000     100.0000 125.0000 150.0000
175.0000 AVGH =    112.5000
11.00000       22.00000      33.00000 44.00000 55.00000
66.00000 AVGH =    38.50000
81.00000       84.00000      86.00000 88.00000 90.00000
91.00000 AVGH =    86.66666
120.0000      125.0000      128.0000 131.0000 133.0000
135.0000 AVGH =    128.6667
201.0000      213.0000      218.0000 220.0000 225.0000
227.0000 AVGH =    217.3333
```

Output to Printer or Terminal

```
OUTPUT TO FILE RVRAVG

RUN COMPLETED
```

   Because the output from this program was sent to a file rather than a printer
or terminal, a WRITE(*,*) statement was placed at the beginning of the program
to identify the output. Another WRITE(*,*) statement was placed at the end of the
program to advise the user that the program ran correctly.

*Programming
Hint*

> When all significant output from a program is written to a storage device, the
> program should print messages indicating the progress of the execution and the
> number of records written to the device.

3.4.5 Average Value

Problem

Write a program to read a set of data values and calculate their average.

Method

Two intermediate variables are needed, one to accumulate the total of the data
values, the other to count the data values. Both should be initialized to zero in
order to be correct if there are no data values in the input file.

Program

```
*****************************************************************
*                                                               *
*    AVERAGE OF A SET OF DATA VALUES                            *
*                                                               *
*****************************************************************
*                                                               *
*    INPUT VARIABLES:                                           *
*                                                               *
*       X        - DATA VALUE                                   *
*                                                               *
*    OUTPUT VARIABLES:                                          *
*                                                               *
*       AVG      - AVERAGE DATA VALUE                           *
*                                                               *
*****************************************************************

        REAL X, AVG, TOTAL
        INTEGER CNT
```

```
             TOTAL = 0.0
             CNT = 0

*       DO FOR EACH DATA VALUE

         WRITE (*,*) 'INPUT NUMBER OR CONTROL-Z ',
       1              'TO END INPUT:'
10       READ (*,*,END=50) X
            TOTAL = TOTAL + X
            CNT = CNT + 1
         GO TO 10

*       ENDDO

50       CONTINUE
         AVG = TOTAL / CNT
         WRITE (*,*)
         WRITE (*,*)'AVERAGE =',AVG
         STOP
         END
```

Output

```
INPUT NUMBER OR CONTROL-Z TO END INPUT:
5
45
20
70
100

AVERAGE =    48.00000
```

Note that if there is no input data, this program will terminate abnormally because of attempted division by zero.

3.4.6 Computer Sales Report

Problem

A computer store carries two different models of computer. Given the number of computers of each model sold during the week, and the unit cost and sales price of each model, calculate the net sales for the week.

Method

The input consists of three records containing

1. the number of computers of each model sold
2. the unit cost of each model computer
3. the sales price of each model

Calculate and print the total cost of each model computer, the total price of each model, the net sales per unit for each model, and the total net sales.

Pseudocode

    Input MODEL1,MODEL2
    Input COST1,COST2
    Input PRICE1,PRICE2
    Calculate total cost per model
    Print total costs
    Calculate total price per model
    Print total prices
    Calculate net sales per model
    Print net sales
    Calculate overall total cost, total price, total net sales
    Print totals
    Stop

Program

```
****************************************************************
*                                                              *
*   COMPUTER SALES REPORT                                      *
*                                                              *
****************************************************************
*                                                              *
*   INPUT VARIABLES:                                           *
*                                                              *
*      NUMDL1 - NUMBER OF COMPUTERS SOLD (MODEL 1)             *
*      NUMDL2 - NUMBER OF COMPUTERS SOLD (MODEL 2)             *
*      CSMDL1 - UNIT COST OF COMPUTERS (MODEL 1)               *
*      CSMDL2 - UNIT COST OF COMPUTERS (MODEL 2)               *
*      PRMDL1 - SALES PRICE OF COMPUTERS (MODEL 1)             *
*      PRMDL2 - SALES PRICE OF COMPUTERS (MODEL 2)             *
*                                                              *
*   OUTPUT VARIABLES:                                          *
*                                                              *
*      TCSMD1 - TOTAL COST OF COMPUTERS (MODEL 1)              *
*      TCSMD2 - TOTAL COST OF COMPUTERS (MODEL 2)              *
*      TPRMD1 - TOTAL PRICE OF COMPUTERS (MODEL 1)             *
*      TPRMD2 - TOTAL PRICE OF COMPUTERS (MODEL 2)             *
*      TNET1  - TOTAL NET SALES OF COMPUTERS (MODEL 1)*
*      TNET2  - TOTAL NET SALES OF COMPUTERS (MODEL 2)*
*      TOTCST - TOTAL COST OF ALL COMPUTERS SOLD              *
*      TOTPRI - TOTAL SALES PRICE OF ALL COMPUTERS            *
*               SOLD                                           *
*      TOTNET - TOTAL NET SALES                               *
*                                                              *
****************************************************************
```

```
            REAL CSMDL1,CSMDL2,PRMDL1,PRMDL2
            REAL TCSMD1,TCSMD2,TPRMD1,TPRMD2,TNET1,TNET2
            REAL TOTCST,TOTPRI,TOTNET
            INTEGER NUMDL1,NUMDL2

     *   INPUT SALES FIGURES

            PRINT*, 'INPUT THE NUMBER SOLD FOR MODEL 1',
           1          ' AND MODEL 2'
            READ (*,1000) NUMDL1,NUMDL2
     1000   FORMAT(2I5)
            PRINT*
            PRINT*, 'INPUT THE UNIT COST OF MODEL 1',
           1          ' AND MODEL 2'
            READ (*,1100) CSMDL1,CSMDL2
     1100   FORMAT(2F10.0)
            PRINT*
            PRINT*, 'INPUT THE SALES PRICE OF MODEL 1',
           1          ' AND MODEL 2'
            READ (*,1200) PRMDL1,PRMDL2
     1200   FORMAT(2F10.0)

     *   CALCULATE TOTALS AND PROFIT

            TCSMD1 = NUMDL1 * CSMDL1
            TCSMD2 = NUMDL2 * CSMDL2
            TPRMD1 = NUMDL1 * PRMDL1
            TPRMD2 = NUMDL2 * PRMDL2
            TNET1 = TPRMD1 - TCSMD1
            TNET2 = TPRMD2 - TCSMD2
            TOTCST = TCSMD1 + TCSMD2
            TOTPRI = TPRMD1 + TPRMD2
            TOTNET = TNET1 + TNET2

     *   OUTPUT REPORT

            WRITE (*,2000)
     2000   FORMAT(//18X,'SALES REPORT')
            WRITE (*,2100) 1,2
     2100   FORMAT(/12X'MODEL',I2,11X,'MODEL',I2)
            WRITE (*,2200) TCSMD1,TCSMD2
     2200   FORMAT(4X,'COST ',F10.2,8X,F10.2)
            WRITE (*,2300) TPRMD1,TPRMD2
     2300   FORMAT(4X,'PRICE',F10.2,8X,F10.2)
            WRITE (*,2400)TNET1,TNET2
     2400   FORMAT(4X,'NET  ',F10.2,8X,F10.2)
            WRITE (*,2500) TOTCST,TOTPRI,TOTNET
     2500   FORMAT(/1X,'TOTAL COST =',F10.2,4X,'TOTAL',
           1          ' PRICE =', F10.2/1X,'NET PROFIT =',
           2          F10.2)
            STOP
            END
```

Output

```
INPUT THE NUMBER SOLD FOR MODEL 1 AND MODEL 2
     5    6

INPUT THE UNIT COST OF MODEL 1 AND MODEL 2
2500.0    2650.0

INPUT THE SALES PRICE OF MODEL 1 AND MODEL 2
2800.0    3150.0


                    SALES REPORT

              MODEL 1            MODEL 2

     COST    12500.00           15900.00
     PRICE   14000.00           18900.00
     NET      1500.00            3000.00

TOTAL COST =  28400.00   TOTAL PRICE =   32900.00
NET PROFIT =   4500.00
```

Chapter Summary

There are two methods of input/output in FORTRAN 77. First, in list-directed input/output, a default format is used and the programmer has little or no control over the spacing. However, the person entering data at a terminal may use free spacing. List-directed output is convenient for debugging programs. The general forms of the list-directed statements are:

```
READ *,var1,var2,...,varn
READ (*,*,END=n) var1,var2,...,varn
PRINT *, expr1,expr2,...,exprn
WRITE (*,*) expr1,expr2,...,exprn
```

The input list contains only variables; the output list may contain variables, literals, and expressions. The asterisk directs the computer to use a default value. In the first READ statement above and the PRINT statement this refers to a default format. In the second READ statement and the WRITE statement, default logical unit numbers are also specified.

In list-directed input, data values may be separated by blanks, commas, or a combination of the two. In list-directed output, numbers are placed right justified in predetermined fields.

Second, formatted input/output gives the programmer control over the spacing of the data, making it possible to design attractive and readable output. The general forms of the formatted input/output statements are:

```
READ fmt,var1,var2,...,varn
READ (lun,fmt,END=n,ERR=m) var1,var2,...,varn
PRINT fmt, expr1,expr2,...,exprn
WRITE (lun,fmt) expr1,expr2,...,exprn
```

where lun is a logical unit number, fmt is the format number and n and m are program line numbers.

The format statement has the general form

```
FORMAT (ct1,spec1,spec2,...,specn)
```

These format specifications include:

Iw	for integer data
Ew.d, Fw.d, Gw.d	for real data
wX, Tc	to indicate horizontal spacing
/ and control directives	to indicate vertical spacing

The printer control directives are:

' '	single spacing
'0'	double spacing
'+'	overprinting
'1'	paging

Every output format must start with a printer control directive. Numeric data is right justified in the specified field; alphanumeric data is left justified.

Input may be obtained from permanent data files by connecting the file with the program and assigning a logical unit number through an OPEN statement. Output may be written to a permanent data file by connecting the file with the program in the same way. If a file is explicitly opened by the program, it should also be explicitly closed. The basic forms of the OPEN and CLOSE statements are:

OPEN (UNIT = lun,FILE = extname,STATUS = 'OLD') for an input file
OPEN (UNIT = lun,FILE = extname,STATUS = 'NEW') for an output file
CLOSE (UNIT = lun)

Exercises

1. Write a program to generate the Cartesian coordinates of points (x,y) on the perimeter of a circle of radius 1. Print a table of values θ, x, y for the values of θ in the input. The coordinates are given by:

    $x = \cos(\theta)$
    $y = \sin(\theta)$

    Title and label the output.

2. Write a program to input readings of daily weather: time of day, temperature, humidity, wind strength, and barometric pressure. Print the data and the maximum, minimum, and average temperature, humidity, wind velocity, and barometric pressure. Title and label the output.

3. Each of a set of input records contains an item number, quantity, and unit price for a particular size of widget. Print a report showing the input data and total price for each record, overall total quantity, and overall total price. Title and label the output.

4. Write a program to compute the sizes of a series of water tanks that hold w cubic feet of water for all w in the input file 'TANK'. The height of the tank must be twice the diameter of the tank. Print a table with title and labels as follows:

WATER TANK SIZES

CAPACITY (IN 1000S)	DIAMETER	HEIGHT
100	. . .	
200	. . .	
. . .	. . .	

5. Write a program to compute the diameter in meters of a steel rod, an aluminum rod, and a copper rod, which withstand a tensile load of 100,000 lbs. The allowable tensile stress of steel, aluminum, and copper is 25,000 lbs/m², 15,000 lbs/m², and 20,000 lbs/m² respectively.

$$\text{area of rod} = \frac{\text{tensile load}}{\text{allowable tensile stress}}$$
$$\text{area} = \pi r^2 \quad \text{where diameter } d = 2r$$

Print the type of material, load, allowable stress, and diameter. Use formatted output.

6. Write a program to compute the range of a projectile given the velocity and the angle at which the projectile is fired. The range is computed from the equation
   $$R = v^2 \sin(2\theta)/g$$
where $g = 32.2$ is the gravitational constant. Compute the range for a velocity of 1000 at angle θ (degrees) for values of θ found in an input file. Print the velocity V, the angle θ in degrees, and the range R. Title and label the output.

7. Write a program to input a student record containing a six-digit student ID, a 30-character student name, and five test scores of three digits each from a file 'ROSTER'. For each student, write the ID, the name, the scores, and the average score to a file 'GRADES'. Print a class average for each test and an overall class average.

8. Write a program to estimate the cost of building an industrial plant. Input the number of square feet in each of three buildings in the plant complex. Input the price per square foot of each building. Input the cost of equipment for each building. Calculate and print the total cost of building the plant.

9. Write a program to print the weekly sales of a travelling salesman for a steel company. The input consists of the number of tons of steel sold each of five working days. The steel sells for $500.00 per ton which includes an 8% commission. Print the total amount of steel sold, the total cost of the steel, and the total amount of the commission.

4 Control Structures

A program consisting of just assignment and input/output statements is executed one statement after another, in sequence. Because each statement is executed only once, one set of data can be processed (unless the code is duplicated). This normal order of execution can be changed by using control structures other than the sequence. Selection and repetition structures make it possible to process more than one set of data and to vary the processing to take into account variations in the data.

One standard selection structure, which is not fully available in standard FORTRAN 77, is the case structure. It offers more than two choices and asks questions with a wider range of possible answers than just true and false. Several standard types of repetition structures are not available in standard FORTRAN 77. Some versions of FORTRAN 77 offer these structures as extensions. When they are not available, they can be simulated by using other control structures. The most important of these structures are included in this text, but they are identified as being nonstandard.

A *sequence structure* is one in which the statements are executed one after the other, in order, during the execution of the program. An entire program is usually a sequence of structures. Sequence structures can also be nested in other structures. The body of a repetition structure and the choices of a selection structure are usually themselves sequences.

A *selection structure* is one in which there are two or more possible sequences of execution. The computer must decide which sequence to execute, based on the state of the processing or the details of the data. The simple selection structure contains only two possible sequences. It is controlled by a decision based on a true or false answer to a question.

A *repetition structure* controls the execution of a sequence that may be executed more than once. This allows the processing of many sets of data, or the repetitive processing of a single set of data. Repetition structures are informally called looping structures.

4.1 Sequence and Selection Control

Two of the three basic control structures can be directly implemented in FORTRAN as blocks of code with a single entrance at the top, a single exit at the bottom, and top to bottom control flow.

4.1.1 Sequence Structure

The sequence of statements is the basic building block of a FORTRAN program. Consecutive program statements are executed in sequence as they are written, provided that the computer is not directed to leave the sequence. The elements of a sequence may be simple statements or control structures, as shown in Fig. 4.1. The pseudocode for Fig. 4.1 is:

stmt 1	stmt 1	stmt 1
stmt 2	selection structure	repetition structure
stmt 3	stmt 2	stmt 2
stmt 4		

Notice that the selection and repetition structures may be embedded in a sequence structure without changing the basic top-down flow of control. Sequence,

Figure 4.1

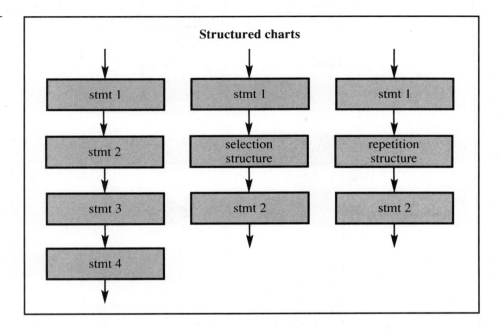

selection, and repetition structures may be nested inside each other provided that the basic sequential flow is maintained.

The structured flowchart of Fig. 4.2 shows complex nesting of sequence, selection, and repetition structures. Notice that the top-down flow is maintained with proper entries at the top and exits at the bottom. The pseudocode is:

```
stmt 1
stmt 2
DO WHILE (condition)
    stmt 3
    IF (condition) THEN
        stmt 6
        stmt 7
    ELSE
        stmt 4
        stmt 5
    ENDIF
    stmt 8
ENDDO
stmt 9
stmt 10
```

Figure 4.2

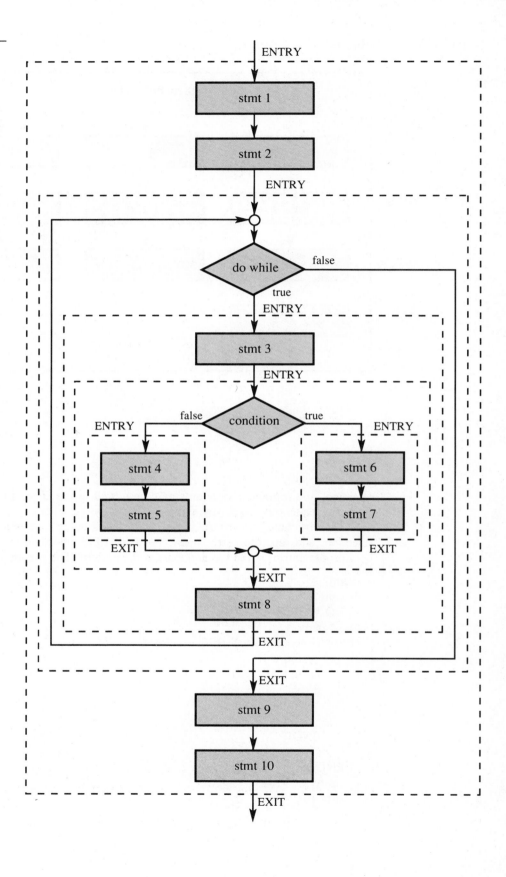

4.1.2 Relational Operators and Relational Expressions

The standard mathematical symbols for numeric comparisons cannot be used in FORTRAN. Instead the following abbreviated keywords are used to compare both numeric data and character data.

Mathematical symbol	*FORTRAN symbol*	*Meaning*
$=$	.EQ.	equal to
$>$	.GT.	greater than
$\geq$	.GE.	greater than or equal to
$<$	.LT.	less than
$\leq$	.LE.	less than or equal to
$\neq$	.NE.	not equal to

Periods are required on both sides of the FORTRAN abbreviated words. No embedded blank spaces are allowed.

Relational Expressions

Relational expressions may be used to compare variables, constants, and expressions, as in the following examples:

```
A = 8.5
B = 10.5
IF (A + 10.0 .GT. B + 6.0) THEN          true

L = 5
K = 11
IF (L .GE. K/2) THEN                      true
   IF (REAL(L) .GE. REAL(K)/2.0) THEN     false

X = .8
Y = 20.0
IF (X*Y .EQ. 16.0) THEN                   probably false
   IF (ABS(X*Y-16.0) .LT. .0001) THEN     true

IF (SQRT(6.25) .EQ. 2.5) THEN             true
```

Using these relational expressions, you can instruct the computer to vary the processing, and to select a sequence of instructions appropriate for the data.

4.1.3 Simple and Nested Blocks (IF–THEN–ENDIF and IF–THEN–ELSE–ENDIF)

A selection structure is a two-way branch structure. Control flow passes through one of the two possible paths based on a condition with a true or false answer. This condition generally has the form of a relational expression. Figs. 4.3 and 4.4 show the structured chart for this structure and the corresponding FORTRAN structure. The structure may take the form of either a single-branch IF statement or a two-branch IF statement.

Fig. 4.3 shows the structure when one of the branches is not needed. Here,

Figure 4.3

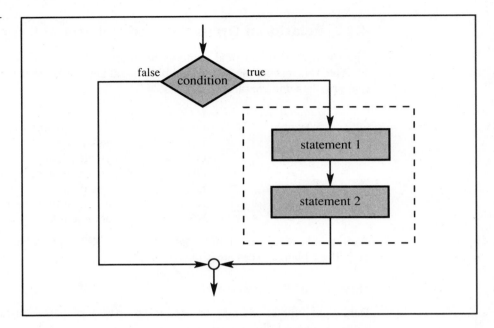

Figure 4.4

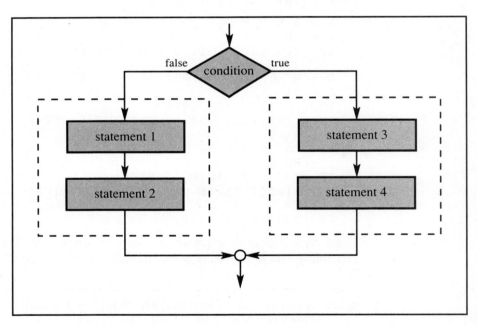

instead of a choice of two actions, the choice is whether to do the processing or omit it.

FORTRAN structure

```
IF (condition) THEN        IF (condition) THEN
   sequence                   statement 1
ENDIF                         statement 2
                           ENDIF
```

Notice that the flowchart uses different symbols for decisions and for executable statements. The rectangular boxes of executable statements are called *process boxes*. The diamond-shaped box represents two-way decisions. Arrows on the flowlines indicate the direction of control. One of the two directions of control is selected, based on the decision. The arrows into the small circle, called a *collector,* bring the selection structure to a close.

FORTRAN structure

```
IF (condition) THEN        IF (condition) THEN
   sequence                   statement 3
ELSE                          statement 4
   sequence                ELSE
ENDIF                         statement 1
                              statement 2
                           ENDIF
```

The words IF, THEN, ELSE, and ENDIF are keywords in FORTRAN, only used in these selection structures. In both forms of the structure, the sequence of statements after the keyword THEN is only executed when the condition is true. If there is an ELSE clause, its sequence of statements is only executed when the condition is false.

Programming Hint

> Indent embedded sequences for readability.

```
IF ( condition ) THEN      IF (K .LT. 0) THEN
   statement 1                K = - K
   statement 2                WRITE (*,*)'NEGATIVE K'
ENDIF                      ENDIF
statement 3               WRITE (*,*) K
```

The example above shows one statement after the close of the selection structure. That statement will be executed no matter which choice is made. The sequence inside the structure is either executed or omitted, but statement 3 is always executed. Fig. 4.5 shows the flowchart for this example.

The two-branch structure is shown in the following example:

```
IF ( condition ) THEN      IF (X .GE. 0) THEN
   statement 1                CUBRT = X ** (1.0/3.0)
ELSE                       ELSE
   statement 2                CUBRT = -(-X)** (1.0/3.0)
ENDIF                      ENDIF
statement 3               WRITE (*,*) CUBRT
```

The diagram for the two-branched structure is shown in Fig. 4.6. Here, the computer executes either the statements between the THEN and the ELSE, or between the ELSE and the ENDIF. Each of these sequences of one or more statements is called a *block*.

The following examples show both one- and two-branch selection structures:

Figure 4.5

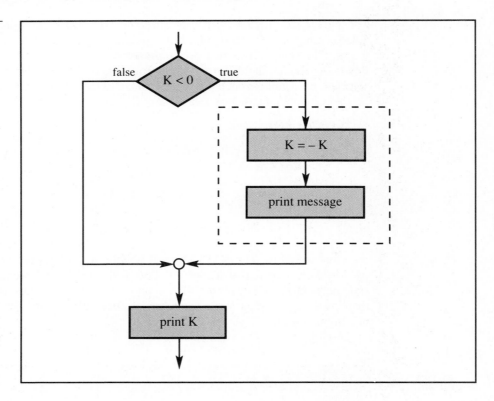

Figure 4.6

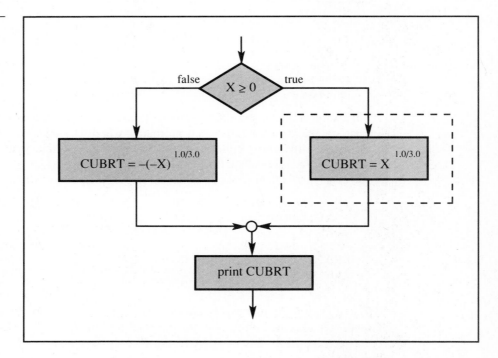

```
IF (X .LT. 0.0) THEN     IF (A .LE. B) THEN
   X = -X                    XMAX = B
ENDIF                     ELSE
                             XMAX = A
IF (X .LE. XMAX) THEN     ENDIF
ELSE
   XMAX = X
ENDIF
```

Scientific programming frequently uses a small variety of this type of structure:

Questions	*FORTRAN structure*

Are two integers equal?	IF (K .EQ. N) THEN
	   they are equal
	ELSE
	   they are not equal
	ENDIF

Is an integer positive?	IF (K .GT. 0) THEN
	   it is positive and greater than 0
	ELSE
	   it is negative or 0
	ENDIF

Are two real numbers equal?	IF (ABS(X-Y) .LT. .00001) THEN
	   they are equal to 5 decimal places
	ELSE
	   they are not equal
	ENDIF

Are two real numbers equal to within a given relative error?	IF (ABS(X-Y) .LT. .00001*ABS(X)) THEN
	   they agree in the first 5 digits
	ELSE
	   they are not equal
	ENDIF

Is a real number equal to zero?	IF (ABS(X) .LT. .00001) THEN
	   it is approximately equal to zero
	ELSE
	   it is not equal to zero
	ENDIF

Programming Hint

> Compare real numbers for equality by setting a tolerance within which they are approximately equal.

4.1.4 Nested Blocks (IF–THEN–ELSEIF–THEN–ENDIF)

There are two ways of nesting selection structures: either in the true branch of another structure or in the false branch. When one block IF structure is to be nested

Figure 4.7

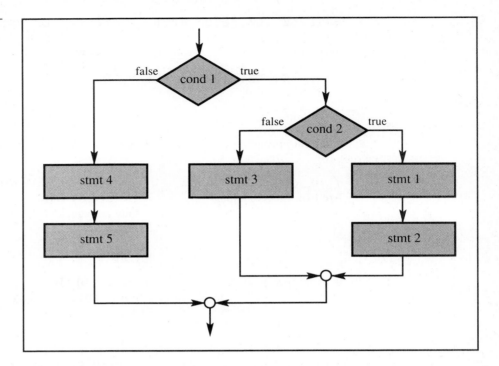

inside another and the inner block is on the true branch of the main selection structure, there is no change in notation. This is shown in the following example and in Fig. 4.7.

```
IF (condition) THEN
  IF (condition) THEN
    sequence
  ELSE                                    inner IF-THEN-ELSE-ENDIF block
    sequence
  ENDIF
ELSE
  sequence
ENDIF
```

The code corresponding to Fig. 4.7 is:

```
IF (condition 1) THEN
  IF (condition 2) THEN
    stmt 1
    stmt 2
  ELSE
    stmt 3
  ENDIF
ELSE
  stmt 4
  stmt 5
ENDIF
```

Two decisions are needed to separate the three cases.

If the nested block IF is part of the ELSE branch of the main selection structure, the keyword ELSEIF replaces the ELSE and the following IF. No ENDIF is needed for the nested block. The general form for this type of nesting is:

```
IF . . . THEN . . . ELSEIF . . . THEN . . . ELSEIF
. . . THEN . . . ELSE . . . ENDIF
```

The ELSEIF clauses may be aligned, reducing the amount of indentation needed to make the code readable. The diagram for the following example is shown in Fig. 4.8.

```
IF (condition 1) THEN
   sequence
ELSEIF (condition 2) THEN
   sequence
ELSEIF (condition 3) THEN
   sequence
ELSE
   sequence
ENDIF
```

Scientific programming frequently uses a small variety of this structure:

Figure 4.8

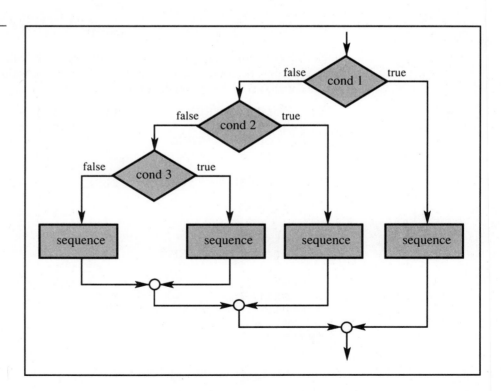

Questions	*FORTRAN structure*

Which of two integers is larger?	IF (K .GT. N) THEN
	  K is the larger
	ELSEIF (N .GT. K) THEN
	  N is the larger
	ELSE
	  they are equal
	ENDIF

Which of two real numbers is larger?	IF (X .GT. Y) THEN
	  X is the larger
	ELSEIF (Y .GT. X) THEN
	  Y is the larger value
	ELSE
	  they are exactly equal
	ENDIF

Which of three numbers is the largest?	IF (A .GT. B) THEN
	  IF (A .GT. C) THEN
	    A is the larger
	  ELSE
	    C is the largest value
	  ENDIF
	ELSEIF (B .GT. C) THEN
	  B is the largest value
	ELSE
	  C is the largest value
	ENDIF

Block IF structures may be nested in any way that will implement the algorithm. They may be embedded in sequences within the selections. Some of the possibilities are shown in the following examples:

```
IF (cond 1) THEN            IF (cond 1) THEN
  stmt 1                      IF (cond 2) THEN
  IF (cond 2) THEN              stmt 1
    stmt 2                      stmt 2
  ELSE                        ENDIF
    stmt 3                   ELSE
  ENDIF                       IF (cond 3) THEN
  stmt 4                        stmt 3
ELSE                          ELSE
  stmt 5                        stmt 4
  IF (cond 3) THEN            ENDIF
    stmt 6                    stmt 5
  ELSE                        stmt 6
    stmt 7                  ENDIF
  ENDIF
  stmt 8
ENDIF
stmt 9
```

```
IF (cond 1) THEN
   stmt 1
ELSEIF (cond 2) THEN
   stmt 2
ELSEIF (cond 3) THEN
   stmt 3
ELSEIF (cond 4) THEN
   stmt 4
ELSEIF (cond 5) THEN
   stmt 5
ELSE
   stmt 6
ENDIF
```

Notice that every block starting with an IF must end with an ENDIF. The block starting with the keyword ELSEIF, however, does not need a matching ENDIF. Notice also that an ELSE may be followed by a block starting with an IF, as in the second example. This occurs when an ENDIF is to be used so that statements may be placed between the two ENDIFs.

The third of these examples shows the FORTRAN method of implementing a case structure. There are five different cases to be identified and a sixth possibility if none of the others is true. An example of this is:

Print the grade earned if the grading scale is:

90–100	A
80–89	B
70–79	C
60–69	D
0–59	F

Any other grade is in error.

The code for this is:

```
IF (GRADE .LT. 60) THEN
   WRITE (*,*) 'F'
ELSEIF (GRADE .LT. 70) THEN
   WRITE (*,*) 'D'
ELSEIF (GRADE .LT. 80) THEN
   WRITE (*,*) 'C'
ELSEIF (GRADE .LT. 90) THEN
   WRITE (*,*) 'B'
ELSEIF (GRADE .LE. 100) THEN
   WRITE (*,*) 'A'
ELSE
   WRITE (*,*) 'ERROR IN GRADE'
ENDIF
```

The flowchart of a case structure corresponding to the third example is shown in Fig. 4.9.

Figure 4.9

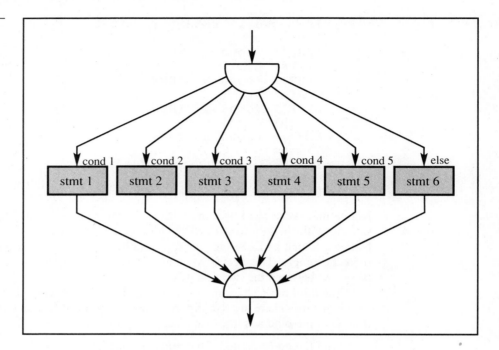

4.1.5 Review Questions

1. Draw the structured flowcharts for the examples on pages 154 and 155.

2. Write the selection structures for the following:

   a. If A is greater than 10, set A to 25.
   b. If W is greater than Y, increment Y by 5.
   c. If P is less than Q, set P equal to Q.
   d. If K is 0, read the values for W, X, Y, and Z.
   e. If I is greater than K, set the value of K to I.

3. Write the block transfer statements for the following:

   a. If A is greater than B, execute the following statements:

   ```
   READ*, W,X,Y
   Z = W * X + Y
   R = Z + 10.5
   ```

   b. If the weekly sales of a machine part are greater than $2000, compute the net income based on a 15% markup of the sale price over the cost and print the sales, cost, and net.
   c. If the monthly salary of an employee exceeds $5000, withhold federal tax of 25% and state tax of 8%. But if the salary is less than or equal to $5000, withhold 20% federal tax and 6% state tax.
   d. Print a statement indicating whether the day's rainfall was light, moderate, or heavy depending on whether it was less than 1 in., between 1 and 2 in., or more than 2 in.
   e. If the temperature in the computer room is higher than 60°F and lower than 100°F, print the temperature; otherwise print a warning that the computer should not be used.

4. Write the block transfer statements for the following:

   a. If a salesman sells $20,000 or more, his commission is 20%. If he sells less than $20,000, his commission is 10%. Print the amount of sales and the commission.
   b. The computed roots of a quadratic equation $AX^2 + BX + C = 0$ are given by the formulas

$$X_1 = \frac{-B + \sqrt{B^2 - 4AC}}{2A} \qquad X_2 = \frac{-B - \sqrt{B^2 - 4AC}}{2A}$$

   These formulas cannot be used if the value of A is 0, and the answers are complex if the value of $B^2 - 4AC$ is negative. Print the two real roots if they exist; otherwise print appropriate messages.
   c. The formula for the area of a triangle is:

$$Area = \frac{1}{2} b\, h \qquad \text{for a right triangle}$$

$$Area = \sqrt{s(s-a)(s-b)(s-c)} \qquad \text{for other triangles}$$

$$\text{where } s = \frac{a+b+c}{2}$$

   Given the sides a, b, and c of a triangle, determine whether it is a right triangle. Print the sides and the area.

5. Write the block IF statements for the following:

   a. If a salary figure is less than or equal to $50.00, it is an hourly wage. If it is greater than $50.00 and less than or equal to $5000.00, it is a monthly wage. Otherwise it is an annual wage. Compute the monthly salary based on the amount of the salary and a 40-hour work week.
   b. Print the length of the longest side of a triangle having sides a, b, and c.
   c. If a boiler temperature is lower than 40°, print LOW. If it is between 40° and 80°, print AVERAGE. If it is higher than or equal to 80°, print HIGH. If it is over 80°, print a warning.

4.2 Loop Control

A repetition structure should be used when a set of instructions is to be executed more than two or three times, or an unknown number of times. There are several types of loop constructs to cover a variety of needs. One type of repetition structure, a DO WHILE loop, executes a sequence of instructions while some particular condition is true. If it is false to begin with, however, the sequence of instructions that form the body of the loop is omitted entirely. A second type of repetition structure, a REPEAT UNTIL loop, contains a sequence of instructions that are executed one or more times until some particular condition is true. In a REPEAT UNTIL loop, the condition is tested at the end of the loop; therefore the instructions in the loop are executed at least once. If it is executed a fixed number of times, it is known as an iterative DO loop.

Standard FORTRAN 77 does not have all these constructs, but they are available in many systems as extensions. Because they are standard control structures for structured programming, there are correct ways to implement them in

FORTRAN. The following sections present these structures and their variations both as simulated in FORTRAN and as language extensions.

4.2.1 Conditional Loops (DO WHILE and REPEAT UNTIL)

These types of loops are controlled by explicit conditions, which may be comparisons of data values, e.g., (ID .EQ. ITEMID); identification of a trailer value in the input, e.g., (INPUT .NE. 99999); or the use of a programmer-defined counter, e.g., (COUNT .LT. 100). The conditions are explicit in that they form the main part of the control statements defining the structure.

In general, the DO WHILE loop is the most useful when many values are being processed. The REPEAT UNTIL loop is most useful when searching for a particular value.

DO WHILE Loop

Fig. 4.10 shows the structure of a DO WHILE loop. Notice that the execution starts by deciding whether the loop body should be executed at all. As pseudocode or as a FORTRAN extension, this structure can be written in two ways. Check a programming manual for the exact syntax available.

Figure 4.10

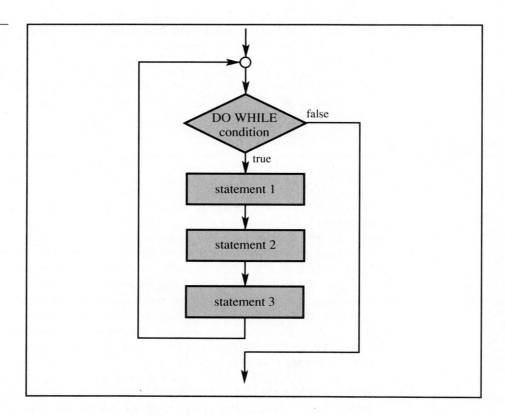

```
DO WHILE (condition)        WHILE (condition) DO
   statement 1                 statement 1
   statement 2                 statement 2
   statement 3                 statement 3
ENDDO                       END WHILE
```

Throughout this text, we use the form DO WHILE . . . ENDDO. The instructions that form the body of the loop are executed as long as the condition remains true. If the condition becomes false during the execution of the loop body, the entire sequence of instructions is completed before the loop is exited. Instructions with this type of loop control may be executed many times or not at all.

The body of this repetition structure is a nested sequence. Repetition structures may themselves be nested, in sequences, in selection structures, or in other repetition structures. The following pseudocode shows a repetition structure as part of a sequence. It calculates the sum and the average of the odd numbers from 1 through 99. (Note that there are formulas to do this more efficiently; we present it simply as an example to show the structure.)

```
NSUM = 0
ICNT = 0
NUM = 1
DO WHILE (NUM .LE. 99)
  NSUM = NSUM + NUM
  ICNT = ICNT + 1
  NUM = NUM + 2
ENDDO
AVG = REAL(NSUM)/ ICNT
```

The flowchart for this code is shown in Fig. 4.11. In the flowchart, sequences of assignment statements are included in the same process box to save space.

Programming Hint

> Use the simulated DO WHILE if your system does not have the DO WHILE extension to FORTRAN 77.

When the DO WHILE instruction is unavailable, you can simulate the structure, as in the following code:

```
        NSUM = 0
        ICNT = 0
        NUM = 1

*       DO WHILE (NUM .LE. 99)

10      IF (NUM .LE. 99) THEN
           NSUM = NSUM + NUM
           ICNT = ICNT + 1
           NUM = NUM + 2
           GO TO 10
        ENDIF
```

```
*      ENDDO

       AVG = REAL(NSUM)/ ICNT
```

Notice that the last statement in the block is a GO TO, which takes control back to statement 10, the IF statement. This forms a looping structure that repeats as long as the condition is true. When the condition is false, control leaves the loop and the value of AVG is calculated.

Programming Warning

> Do not use the GO TO statement except to simulate the DO WHILE and REPEAT UNTIL loops.

The following example shows data values that are input rather than generated. If the range of data values is known, a number (trailer value) outside the range, such as 9999, can be used to indicate the end of the data and, in the program, to

Figure 4.11

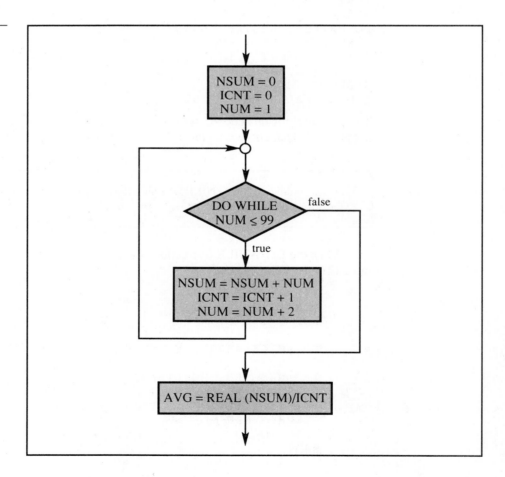

terminate the loop. This example has the DO WHILE extension and a simulated DO WHILE loop.

```
ICNT = 0
NSUM = 0
READ (*,*) NUM
DO WHILE (NUM .NE. 9999)
   NSUM = NSUM + NUM
   ICNT = ICNT + 1
   READ (*,*) NUM
ENDDO
AVG = REAL(NSUM)/ICNT
```

```
        ICNT = 0
        NSUM = 0
        READ (*,*) NUM

*       DO WHILE (NUM .NE. 9999)

10      IF (NUM .NE. 9999) THEN
           NSUM = NSUM + NUM
           ICNT = ICNT + 1
           READ (*,*) NUM
        GO TO 10
        ENDIF

*       ENDDO

        AVG = REAL(NSUM)/ICNT
```

Notice that when the numbers are generated, NUM is initialized ahead of the loop, along with ICNT and NSUM. When the numbers are obtained from the input, NUM is initialized through the input statement ahead of the loop. This is known as a *priming READ*. The loop control variable must always be initialized ahead of the control statement of a DO WHILE loop. When the numbers were being generated, the last statement of the loop body was NUM = NUM + 2, which generated the next odd value of NUM. When the numbers are input, the last statement of the loop body before the ENDDO or GO TO is a READ statement, which obtains the next value of NUM.

END Controlled Loop

When data is obtained from input, the END= option of the READ statement may be used to control the repetition. This is a variation of the DO WHILE structure:

```
        ICNT = 0
        NSUM = 0

*       DO WHILE NOT END OF INPUT DATA

10      READ (5,2000,END=50) NUM
```

```
2000    FORMAT(I5)
        NSUM = NSUM + NUM
        ICNT = ICNT + 1
        GO TO 10

*       ENDDO

50      AVG = REAL(NSUM)/ICNT
```

The two READ statements of the previous example have been merged into the loop control statement. This is still a DO WHILE loop because the test for completion precedes the body of the loop. If there is no data, the body of the loop is skipped. Both this and the previous version of the example are not robust; the execution will stop on the division with an error condition if there is no data. Note, however, that the value of ICNT is accurate. It would be wrong to initialize it to something other than zero.

If a trailer value such as 9999 is expected but an END= option is used for safety, the code is as follows:

```
        ICNT = 0
        NSUM = 0
        AVG = 0
        READ (*,END=50) NUM
        DO WHILE (NUM .NE. 9999)
          NSUM = NSUM + NUM
          ICNT = ICNT + 1
          READ (*,END=40) NUM
        ENDDO
40      AVG = REAL(NSUM)/ICNT
50      CONTINUE
```

Different labels are used for each END= so that the division used in the calculation of the average will not take place if ICNT is zero. In this case the average is zero also, so AVG is given an initial value. CONTINUE allows the control flow to continue to the next statement. A CONTINUE statement is not executed. Instead, it is used with a line number to mark a place in the program.

REPEAT UNTIL Structure

Occasionally it is necessary to write a loop that is executed at least once. The REPEAT UNTIL structure is used for this, although it is rarely found in FORTRAN extensions. (When it is available, details will be found in the computer's FORTRAN manual.) You can simulate this type of loop by placing the condition after the loop body as in the following example, which calculates the average of the odd numbers from 1 through 99:

```
label       statement 1
            statement 2
            statement 3
            IF(.NOT. (condition))GO TO label
```

Figure 4.12

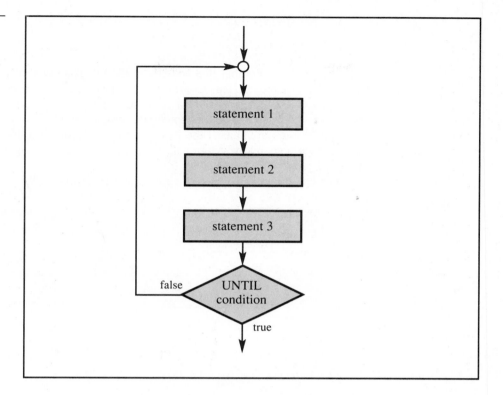

```
      NSUM = 0
      ICNT = 0
      NUM = 1

*     REPEAT UNTIL (NUM .GT. 100)

10    NSUM = NSUM + NUM
        ICNT = ICNT + 1
        NUM = NUM + 2
      IF (.NOT. (NUM .GT. 100))GO TO 10

*     END REPEAT

      AVG = REAL(NSUM) / ICNT
```

Notice that the condition NUM .GT. 100 is false until NUM is 101. Then the condition becomes true and control exits from the loop to the calculation of the average. The flowchart for this example is given in Fig. 4.12.

4.2.2 Counting Loops (DO . . . CONTINUE)

FORTRAN has one standard repetition structure, called a DO-loop, which is controlled by counting. The DO-loop is similar in execution to a DO WHILE loop, but different in appearance. It has the general form

```
         DO label variable = v1,v2,v3
            statement sequence
label CONTINUE
```

The label is a line number that appears in the DO statement as a reference to the CONTINUE statement. This identifies the range of the loop. The variable is known as the *index variable*. It is used for counting and may be either integer or real. The values, v1, v2, and v3 are either constants, simple variables, or expressions. Value v1 means the initial value of the index variable; v2 refers to the limit of range of the index variable; and v3 (optional) is the step size for counting. The default value of v3 is 1.

The DO-loop can be used to count either up or down. When v3 is positive, it counts up; when v3 is negative, it counts down. That is, if step v3 is positive, the loop counts up if v2 ≥ v1; if step v3 is negative, the loop counts down if v2 ≤ v1.

Programming Hint

> Readability and consistency: Use a CONTINUE statement to terminate a DO-loop.

In this example:

```
      DO 50 I = 1, 10
         WRITE (*,*) I, I*5
50       CONTINUE
```

the variable I is assigned a value of 1; then the check is made for termination. Because I does not exceed 10, the WRITE statement executes, the value of I increments to 2, and the sequence repeats starting with the comparison of I and 10. The output is:

```
       1        5
       2       10
       3       15
       4       20
       5       25
       6       30
       7       35
       8       40
       9       45
      10       50
```

After the last values are printed, I becomes 11, the loop terminates, and control transfers to the statement following the loop.

If the DO-loop is

```
      DO 50 I = 10, 1, −1
         WRITE (*,*) I, I*5
50       CONTINUE
```

the variable I is assigned a value of 10; then the check is made for termination. Because I is not less than 1, the WRITE statement executes, the value of I decrements to 9, and the loop repeats. The output is:

```
      10        50
       9        45
       8        40
       7        35
       6        30
       5        25
       4        20
       3        15
       2        10
       1         5
```

The DO loop can be used to sum a set of input values if the number of values in the input set is known. The following example reads 25 numbers, prints the numbers, and prints their sum:

```
      SUM = 0.0
      DO 10 I = 1, 25
         READ (*,*) X
         SUM = SUM + X
         WRITE (*,*) X
10    CONTINUE
      WRITE (*,*) 'SUM=',SUM
```

We assume that there are exactly 25 numbers to read. The index variable takes on the values 1 through 25, counting the numbers as they are read. Then it becomes 26 and the loop is exited to the line following the CONTINUE statement, which is the WRITE statement.

If the step size of a DO-loop is not 1 or -1, the limiting value may not be one of the values used. For example:

```
      DO 10 K = 1, 10, 2
         WRITE (*,*) K
10    CONTINUE
```

prints

```
1
3
5
7
9
```

The final value printed is 9. The index variable increments to 11 and the loop terminates.

```
      DO 10 K = 0, -10, -2
         WRITE (*,*) K
10    CONTINUE
```

prints

```
 0
-2
-4
-6
-8
-10
```

A DO-loop should be controlled with integer variables when possible. Real variables can be used, but because of the internal binary representation of numbers, they must be used cautiously. When a real variable is used as the index variable of a DO-loop, it should only take on integer values, as in Section 4.4.1, or have fractional parts that are powers of two.

Programming Hint

Use an integer variable for counting and as a loop index.

Here are two more examples:

```
      DO 10 A = 1.0, 3.0, 0.5
         WRITE (*,*) A
10       CONTINUE
```

prints

```
1.0
1.5
2.0
2.5
3.0
```

```
      DO 10 A = 1.0, 3.0, 2.0/3.0
         WRITE (*,*) A
10       CONTINUE
```

prints

```
1.0
1.6667
2.3334
```

In the first of these the step size is 2^{-1}, thus the final index value is exactly 3.0. In the second, the step size is not a power of two. Algebraically, $1.0 + 3*(2.0/3.0)$ should be exactly 3.0, but to most computers it is greater than 3.0, so the loop terminates.

If variables or expressions are used in the loop control, as in

```
      M = 2
      N = 12
      DO 10 I = M, N, M+1
         WRITE (*,*) I
10       CONTINUE
```

which prints

```
2
5
8
11
```

take care not to change the values of M or N in the loop.

The following examples show legal and illegal DO statements:

how many steps

DO-loop statement	Index values	Comment
DO 2 I = 1, 100,2	1, 3, 5, ..., 99	legal
DO 10 A = 1.0, 10.0, 0.5	1.0, 1.5, 2.0,...,10.0	legal
DO 10 K = 10, 2, 2	does not count down	null loop
DO 100 M = 10, 0, -1	10, 9, 8,...,0	legal
DO 100 X = 20.0, 0.0, -1.0	20.0,19.0,...,0.0	legal
DO 200 N = M, K	M,M + 1,...,K	legal if K$\geq$M
DO 300 L = 2*I,J*K,N	2*I,2*I + N,...,J*K	depends on I, J, K, N
DO 50 B = A, C, B	dual use of B	illegal
DO 10 J = 1, 10, 0	does not count up	illegal

Almost any expressions may be used to determine the initial value of the index variable, the limiting value, and the step size. However, the index variable may not be referenced in the control, and the step size must be such that the limiting value can be reached.

There are some restrictions on the use of the DO-loop in a program. There must be no transfers of control from outside the DO-loop to inside the loop.

Programming Rule

> Do not transfer control from outside a loop to inside.

When a program is built for reliability, every READ statement should have an END= option. In the following example, we assume that there are 25 numbers to read, but the END= option guards against the input error of having fewer than 25 numbers.

```
      SUM = 0.0
      DO 10 I = 1, 25
         READ (*,*,END=20) X
         SUM = SUM + X
         WRITE (*,*) X
10       CONTINUE
20       PRINT*, 'SUM=',SUM
```

In this example, if there are exactly 25 numbers read, the index variable takes on the values 1 through 25, then becomes 26, and the loop is exited to line 20. If there are fewer than 25 values, the exit is forced when no input value is found. In this case, the exit is forced by a transfer of control to line 20, and the sum is printed. In general, transfer of control should not be made out of DO-loops and index variables should not be altered inside DO-loops. However, this example shows an exception to these rules, as the loop must be exited immediately when there is no input data. The forced exit transfers control to the next statement after the loop. This can be considered a single entry–single exit loop structure if 20 PRINT*, 'SUM = ', SUM is understood as the exit.

Programming Hint

> Maintainability: Abnormal loop exits should always continue at the same location as normal loop exits.

4.2.3 Nested Loops

Do-loops are frequently nested in FORTRAN applications. The following example shows one DO-loop nested inside another:

```
      DO 20 I = 1, 3
         DO 10 J = 1, 5
            WRITE (*,*) I, J
10          CONTINUE
20       CONTINUE
```

FORTRAN permits nested loops to have a common last statement, but programs are easier to maintain if each loop has its own CONTINUE statement. The loops must be completely nested. It is an error if they simply overlap.

Programming Warning

> DO-loops may not overlap. They must be either completely separate or completely nested.

The I index value of the outer loop is available inside the inner loop, but the J index value of the inner loop is not available in the outer loop. Execution of the code follows these steps:

1. Initialize I to 1.
2. If I ≤ 3, step 3; otherwise step 8.
3. Initialize J to 1.
4. If J ≤ 5, step 5; otherwise step 7.
5. Print I and J.
6. Increment J by 1, go to step 4.
7. Increment I by 1, go to step 2.
8. Continue.

The flowchart is shown in Fig. 4.13.

When I is > 3 and J is > 5, the nested loops terminate. The values printed are:

```
        1       1
        1       2
        1       3           I = 1   J = 1,2,3,4,5
        1       4
        1       5
        ─────────────────   inner loop terminates
        2       1
        2       2
        2       3           I = 2   J = 1,2,3,4,5
        2       4
        2       5
        ─────────────────   inner loop terminates
        3       1
        3       2
        3       3           I = 3   J = 1,2,3,4,5
```

                                    ∃   4
                                    ∃   5   both inner and outer
                                                        loops terminate

Notice that the inner index varies faster than the outer index. The inner loop is
executed five times for each execution of the outer loop. The WRITE statement is
executed $3 \times 5 = 15$ times. Because both index variables are available in the
inner loop, they must be different variables.

Figure 4.13

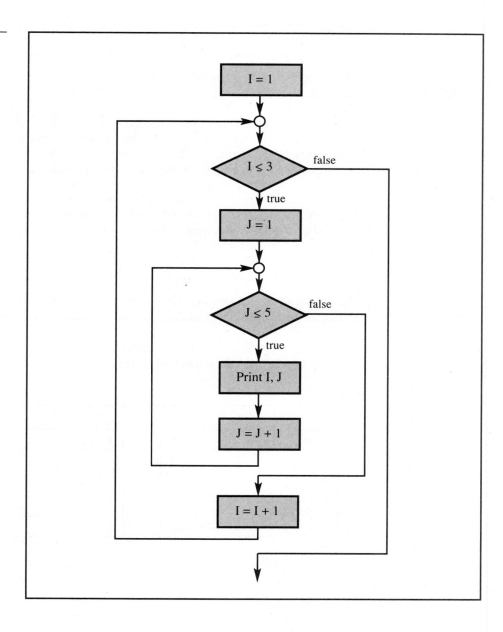

The following examples show proper and improper nesting of DO-loops:

```
           Correct                        Incorrect
      DO 40 I = 1, 10                 DO 30 K = 1, 10
         DO 20 J = 1, 20                 DO 20 J = 1, 20
            DO 10 K = 1, 5                  DO 10 K = 1,5
                 ...                             ...
10          CONTINUE              10          CONTINUE
20       CONTINUE                 20       CONTINUE
         DO 30 J = 1, 10                 DO 40 J = 1, 10
              ...                             ...
30       CONTINUE                 30       CONTINUE
40    CONTINUE                    40    CONTINUE
```

Program Warning

> Index variables may not be reused within nested loops.

Notice that in the correct program above, the index variable J is used twice, but in completely separate DO-loops. In the incorrect program, the index variable K is used twice in nested loops. This is incorrect because a single variable cannot be used to do two things, to count through two sequences, at the same time.

In the correct program, the second J loop is nested correctly in the outer loop. In the incorrect program, the outer loop and the second J loop overlap rather than being correctly nested. The indented form in the incorrect example looks correct, but the use of line labels shows that it is not. The logical structure of these examples is shown in Fig. 4.14.

Programming Hint

> Use indentation for readability. The computer ignores the indentation of code.

DO-loops may be nested to any depth or may follow each other sequentially. They may also be nested in selection structures, and selection structures may be

Figure 4.14

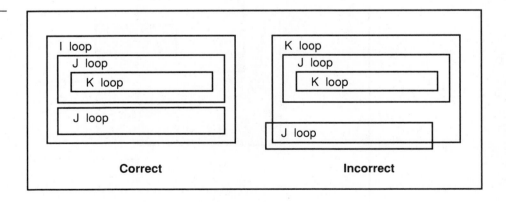

nested in DO-loops. Remember, however, that the more complex the program structure, the more difficult it is to understand the program.

4.2.4 Review Questions

1. Show the output of the following DO WHILE loops. Show the FORTRAN code equivalent using the GOTO and IF statements.

    a. I = 1
       DO WHILE (I .LT. 10)
          WRITE (*,*) I, 2*I
          I = I + 1
       ENDDO

    b. I = 1
       DO WHILE (I .LE. 10)
          WRITE (*,*) I, 2*I
          I = I + 1
       ENDDO

    c. I = 5
       DO WHILE (I .LE. 10)
          WRITE (*,*) I, 2*I
          I = I + 2
       ENDDO

2. Show the output of the following code segments. Rewrite each as a DO WHILE structure.

    a.   I = 1
       10   IF (I .LT. 5) THEN
                WRITE (*,*) I
                I = I + 1
             GO TO 10
             ENDIF

    b.   I = 0
       10   IF (I .LE. 5) THEN
                WRITE (*,*) I, 2*I
                I = I + 1
             GO TO 10
             ENDIF

3. Show the output for each of the following REPEAT UNTIL code segments.

    a.   I = 1
       10   WRITE (*,*) I,I+2
                I = I + 1
             IF (.NOT. (I .GT. 10)) GO TO 10

    b.   I = 0
       10   WRITE (*,*) I,2*I
                I = I + 1
             IF (.NOT. (I .GE. 10)) GO TO 10

   c.   I = 5
     10   WRITE (*,*) I,2*I
          I = I + 1
          IF (.NOT. (I .EQ. 10)) GO TO 10

4. For each of the following DO statements, indicate the initial value assigned to the index variable and the final value available inside the loop before termination. Indicate how many times the body of the loop would be executed.

  a. DO 10 I = 2, 15, 2
  b. DO 10 K = 12, 4, − 1
  c. DO 10 L = − 15, 10,2
  d. DO 30 N = − 12, − 15, − 1
  e. DO 30 J = − 5, 14
  f. DO 30 I = 0, 10
  g. DO 40 M = N,L   where N = 10 and L = 120
  h. DO 40 I = 2*M, 3*L, K   where M = 2, L = 10, K = 4

5. Which of the following DO statements are incorrect? Why?

  a. DO   I = 5, 10
  b. DO 7 J = 5, 15, − 1
  c. DO 8   K = 15, 5
  d. DO 10   L = − 5, − 20
  e. DO − 1 M = 10,50,2
  f. DO 10   A = 50.0, 10.0, 2
  g. DO 10   B = 5.0, 12.0, 0.5

6. Which of the following nested DO-loops are incorrect? Why?

  a.   DO 10 I = 1, 10
           DO 20 J = 1, 20

           ...
    10   CONTINUE
    20 CONTINUE

  b.   DO 20 I = 1, 10
           DO 40 J = 1, 20
              DO 10 I = 1, 5

              ...
    10   CONTINUE
    20   CONTINUE
    40 CONTINUE

  c.   DO 50 I = 1, 10
           DO 20 J = 1, 20
              DO 10 K = 1, 5

              ...
    10   CONTINUE
    20   CONTINUE
           DO 40 J = 1, 20
              DO 30 K = 1, 5

              ...
    30   CONTINUE
    40   CONTINUE
    50 CONTINUE

```
      d.      DO 50 I = 1, 10
                 DO 10 J = 1, 20
                    DO 20 K = 1, 5
                 ...
      10           CONTINUE
      20        CONTINUE
                 DO 30 J = 1, 20
                 ...
      30        CONTINUE
      50     CONTINUE

      e.      DO 20 I = 1, 10
                 DO 10 J = 1, 20
                 ...
      10        CONTINUE
                 DO 30 J = 1, 20
                 ...
      20        CONTINUE
      30     CONTINUE
```

4.3 Logical Data Manipulation

A logical expression consists of logical variables and logical operators. A logical variable must be explicitly declared LOGICAL. It may have a logical data value of either .TRUE. or .FALSE. A logical operator implements an English connective such as "and" or "or." Logical expressions in FORTRAN are used in the conditions that control branching and DO WHILE loops. Two types of operators are used, relational and logical. The relational operators, which we discussed in Section 4.1.2, compare the values of two numbers or two character strings. They produce a logical value of .TRUE. or .FALSE.

4.3.1 Declaration and Use of LOGICAL Data

Logical values may be assigned to variables that are declared to be LOGICAL. The general form of the declaration is:

```
LOGICAL var1,var2,....,varn
```

These variables may be assigned only the values of true and false. The logical constants are .TRUE. and .FALSE. These may be assigned to logical variables, or relational expressions may be assigned, as shown in the following examples:

```
LOGICAL P,Q,R,W,X,Y
...
P = .TRUE.                      P has the value "true"
Q = 10.5 .GT. 14.0             Q has the value "false"
R = 10.5 * 2 .LT. 12.8         R has the value "false"
X = K .NE. N                   if K = N then X is "false"
                                   else X is "true"
```

In the following example, a senior student is eligible for a scholarship if he or she has a grade point average of 3.5 or better. A code of 4 indicates that a student is a senior.

```
      INTEGER CODE, STUDID
      REAL GPA
      LOGICAL SENIOR, BPLUS

      READ (*,*) STUDID,CODE,GPA
      SENIOR = CODE .EQ. 4
      BPLUS = GPA .GE. 3.5
      IF (SENIOR .AND. BPLUS) THEN
         PRINT 1000, STUDID
1000     FORMAT(1X,'STUDENT =',I5,' IS ELIGIBLE FOR',
     1           ' A SCHOLARSHIP')
      ENDIF
```

If logical variables were not used, the condition would be written as:

```
      (CODE .EQ. 4 .AND. GPA .GE. 3.5)
```

Logical variables may be used anywhere logical expressions may be used. In the following example, each logical variable must be assigned a value before it is used:

```
      LOGICAL W,X,Y
      . . .
      DO WHILE (X)
      . . .
      ENDDO

      IF (W) THEN
      . . .
      ENDIF

      IF (Y) THEN
      . . .
      ELSEIF (W) THEN
      . . .
      ELSE
      . . .
      ENDIF
```

Logical variables may be used as flags in subroutine calls to indicate normal or abnormal processing. In the following example, the subroutine is expected to return the average of the data values. If there is no data, it returns an error flag. Subroutines are presented in chapter five.

```
      SUBROUTINE AVGDAT(AVG,NODATA)
      REAL AVG,SUM
      LOGICAL NODATA
      INTEGER KNT

      NODATA = .TRUE.
      SUM = 0.0
      KNT = 0
```

```
*        DO WHILE (MORE DATA)

10       READ (*,*,END=20) X
            SUM = SUM + X
            KNT = KNT + 1
         GO TO 10

*        ENDDO

20       IF (KNT .GT. 0) THEN
            NODATA = .FALSE.
            AVG = SUM / KNT
         ENDIF
         RETURN
         END
```

4.3.2 Logical Operators and Logical Expressions

FORTRAN does not use the common mathematical, logic, or engineering symbols for the logical operators. Instead, abbreviations are used.

order

FORTRAN symbol	Meaning
2 .AND.	and
3 .OR.	inclusive or
1 .NOT.	not
.EQV.	equivalent
4 .NEQV.	exclusive or

The following tables show the results obtained from using these operators (T means true; F means false):

.NOT. operator

A	.NOT. A
F	T
T	F

.AND. operator

A	B	A .AND. B
F	F	F
F	T	F
T	F	F
T	T	T

.OR. operator

A	B	A .OR. B
F	F	F
F	T	T
T	F	T
T	T	T

.EQV. operator

A	B	A .EQV. B
F	F	T
F	T	F
T	F	F
T	T	T

.NEQV. operator

A	B	A .NEQV. B
F	F	F
F	T	T
T	F	T
T	T	F

Given A = .TRUE., B = .FALSE., and C = .TRUE., then

A .AND. B	is false
A .OR. B	is true
A .OR. B .OR. C	is true

.NOT. A	is false
.NOT. (B .AND. C)	is true
.NOT. (A .OR. B)	is false
A .AND. (B .OR. C)	is true

When parentheses are used in an expression, the innermost parentheses are evaluated first, just as with arithmetical operators. When parentheses are not used, the order of precedence of the logical operators is:

highest	.NOT.
	.AND.
	.OR.
lowest	.EQV., .NEQV.

The following pairs of expressions are equivalent:

A .OR. (B .AND. C)	and	A .OR. B .AND. C
(A .AND. B) .OR. C	and	A .AND. B .OR. C
A .OR. (.NOT. B)	and	A .OR. .NOT. B
(.NOT. A) .OR. B	and	.NOT. A .OR. B
A .AND. (.NOT. B)	and	A .AND. .NOT. B
(.NOT. A) .AND. B	and	.NOT. A .AND. B
A .OR. .NOT. B .AND. C	and	A .OR. ((.NOT. B) .AND. C)

In the following examples, parentheses are used to change the order of evaluation:

A .AND. (B .OR. C)
.NOT. (A .AND. B)
.NOT. (A .OR. B .OR. C)
(A .OR. B) .AND. C

Given W = .TRUE., X = .TRUE., Y = .FALSE., and Z = .TRUE., then

.NOT. (W .OR. X .AND. (Y .OR. Z)) is evaluated as:
.NOT. (W .OR. X .AND.   .TRUE.)
.NOT. (W .OR.   .TRUE.)
.NOT. (.TRUE.)
.FALSE.

Programming Hint

Clarity: Use parentheses in logical expressions to avoid confusion and ambiguity.

The order of precedence of the operators in a logical expression containing arithmetic, relational, and logical operators is:

highest	parenthesized expressions
	arithmetic operations
	relational operations
	logical operations
lowest	assignment

Given A = 10.5, B = 18.6, C = 2.0, D = 4.0, and E = 6.2, then

.NOT.	A ∗ C .GT. B	.AND.	D ∗ C	.LT. B	is evaluated as:
.NOT.	21.0 .GT. B	.AND.	8.0	.LT. B	(arithmetic)
.NOT.	.TRUE.	.AND.		.TRUE.	(relational)
.FALSE.		.AND.		.TRUE.	(logical)
		.FALSE.			(logical)

4.3.3 Compound Conditions

When more than one question is to be asked, the questions may often be combined into a compound condition. For example:

```
IF (cond 1) THEN
  IF (cond 2) THEN
    stmt 1
    stmt 2
  ENDIF
ENDIF
```

is equivalent to

```
IF (cond 1 .AND. cond 2) THEN
  stmt 1
  stmt 2
ENDIF
```

Stmt 1 and stmt 2 are to be executed only when both cond 1 and cond 2 are true. The flowchart for this is shown in Fig. 4.15.

In the next example:

```
IF (cond 1) THEN
  stmt 1
  stmt 2
ENDIF
ELSEIF (cond 2) THEN
  stmt 1
  stmt 2
ENDIF
```

is equivalent to

```
IF (cond 1 .OR. cond 2) THEN
  stmt 1
  stmt 2
ENDIF
```

Stmt 1 and stmt 2 are to be executed if either of the conditions are true. The flowchart is shown in Fig. 4.16.

In the following example, a senior student is eligible for a scholarship if he or she has a grade point average of at least 3.5. The same scholarship can be awarded to a junior student who has a grade point average of at least 3.75.

Figure 4.15

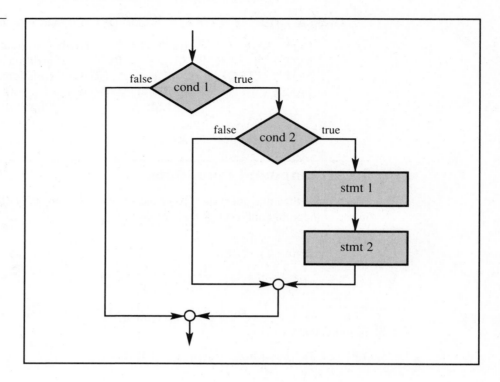

Figure 4.16

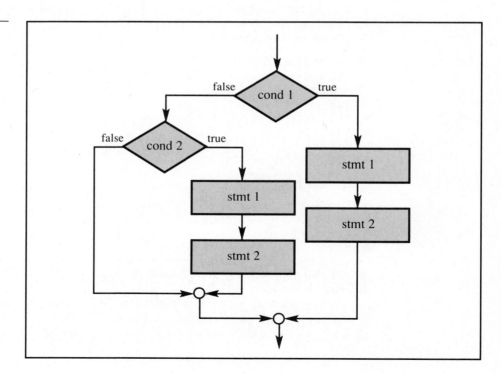

```
      INTEGER
      INTEGER CODE, STUDID
      REAL GPA
      LOGICAL JUNIOR, SENIOR, BPLUS, AMINUS

      READ (*,*) STUDID,CODE,GPA
      JUNIOR = CODE .EQ. 3
      SENIOR = CODE .EQ. 4
      BPLUS = GPA .GE. 3.5
      AMINUS = GPA .GE. 3.75
      IF (SENIOR .AND. BPLUS .OR. JUNIOR .AND.
     1    AMINUS) THEN
         PRINT 1000, STUDID
1000     FORMAT(1X,'STUDENT =',I5,' IS ELIGIBLE FOR',
     1              ' A SCHOLARSHIP')
      ENDIF
```

4.3.4 Review Questions

1. Given the values of the following variables, evaluate the following relational expressions:
   A = 5.0, B = 10.2, C = 12.5, D = 18.0

   a. A + B .GT. C
   b. A ∗ B − C .LT. D ∗∗ 2
   c. A + B ∗ 5 .LE. D ∗ C

2. Given the logical values for the following variables, evaluate the following expressions:
   P = .TRUE., Q = .FALSE., R = .TRUE., T = .FALSE.

   a. P .OR. Q .OR. T .AND. R
   b. P .AND. Q .OR. R
   c. P .AND. (Q .OR. R)
   d. .NOT. (P .OR. R)
   e. Q .AND. .NOT. (R .OR. T)
   f. (P .AND. R) .AND. .NOT. (R .OR. T)

3. Given the values of the following variables, evaluate the following expressions:
   I = 7, J = 10, K = 3, L = 18, M = 9, N = 6

   a. I .LT. K .AND. L .EQ. M + N
   b. .NOT. (J .GT. L − N)
   c. L − 5 .GT. N + M .OR. I .NE. J
   d. I + J .GT. K ∗ 5 .AND. L∗ 2 .GT. M
   e. .NOT. (I ∗ J .LT. K) .AND. (L ∗ M .GT. N ∗ K)

4.4 Sample Programs Using Control Structures

These program examples show the use of the various control structures. These programs have been executed interactively on the Digital Equipment Corporation (DEC) computer model VAX 11/780. In some cases, the output includes the screen input data; where it is included, it is identified.

4.4.1 Table of Torsion Shear Stresses for Rods

Problem

Write a program to print a table of torsion shear stresses for rods having various torsion loads at various offsets.

Let D = diameter of rod   D = 2, 3
     P = torsion load in pounds   P = 1000, 2000
     L = offset   L = 10, 20, 30

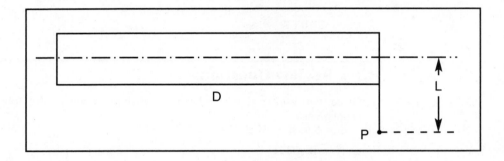

The torsion shear stress is given by the formula

$$T_s = \frac{16\ P\ L}{\pi\ D^3}$$

Pseudocode

```
For each rod diameters
   output the rod diameter
   For each load
      output the load
      For each offset length
         calculate the shear stress
         output offset length and shear stress
      end for
   end for
end for
Stop
```

Program

```
***********************************************************
*                                                         *
*   PRINT A TABLE OF TORSION SHEAR STRESSES               *
*                                                         *
***********************************************************
*                                                         *
*   CONSTANT:                                             *
*                                                         *
*      PI = 3.14159                                       *
*                                                         *
*   INPUT VARIABLES:                                      *
*                                                         *
*      D       - DIAMETER OF THE ROD                      *
*      P       - TORSION LOAD APPLIED (POUNDS)            *
*      L       - LOAD OFFSET LENGTH (INCHES)             *
*                                                         *
*   OUTPUT VARIABLES:                                     *
*                                                         *
*      SHRSTR - COMPUTED SHEAR STRESS (LBS/SQ IN)        *
*                           16*P*L                        *
*                 SHRSTR = --------                       *
*                          PI*D**3                        *
***********************************************************
        REAL D,P,L,SHRSTR,PI
        PARAMETER (PI=3.14159)

        DO 30 D = 2.0,3.0
           WRITE (*,1000) D
1000       FORMAT('1',20X,'DIAMETER OF ROD =',F3.0)
           WRITE (*,1500)
1500       FORMAT('+',20X,'_____ __ ____')
           DO 20 P = 1000.0,2000.0,1000.0
              WRITE (*,2000) P
2000          FORMAT(//1X,'TORSION LOAD IS =',F8.0)
              WRITE (*,3000)
3000          FORMAT(/10X,'OFFSET LENGTH',4X,'TORSION ',
      1              'SHEAR STRESS')
              WRITE (*,3500)
3500          FORMAT('+',9X,'_____ _____',4X,'_____ ',
      1              '_____ _____')

*          COMPUTE TORSION SHEAR STRESS

              DO 10 L = 10.0,30.0,10.0
                 SHRSTR = (16*P*L)/(PI*D**3)
                 WRITE (*,4000) L,SHRSTR
4000             FORMAT(13X,F5.0,9X,F13.2)
10            CONTINUE
20         CONTINUE
30      CONTINUE
        STOP
        END
```

Output

```
                         DIAMETER OF ROD = 2.


TORSION LOAD IS =    1000.

           OFFSET LENGTH        TORSION SHEAR STRESS
               10.                   6366.20
               20.                  12732.41
               30.                  19098.61


TORSION LOAD IS =    2000.

           OFFSET LENGTH        TORSION SHEAR STRESS
               10.                  12732.41
               20.                  25464.81
               30.                  38197.22



                         DIAMETER OF ROD = 3.


TORSION LOAD IS =    1000.

           OFFSET LENGTH        TORSION SHEAR STRESS
               10.                   1886.28
               20.                   3772.56
               30.                   5658.85


TORSION LOAD IS =    2000.

           OFFSET LENGTH        TORSION SHEAR STRESS
               10.                   3772.56
               20.                   7545.13
               30.                  11317.69
```

Notice that this program contains three nested iterative DO-loops. It will print three values of offset lengths and torsion shear stresses for each torsion load, and will process two different torsion loads for each rod diameter. In all, twelve torsion shear stresses will be calculated and printed. For each rod size, several different loads are printed. For each load, several different offset lengths are used and several shear stresses are computed and printed.

Placing the formats next to the input/output statements that use them makes the program easier to debug.

4.4.2 Table of Pendulum Periods

Problem

Write a program to compute the period of a simple pendulum for arm lengths starting at 1 foot and reaching a period of 4 seconds. The formula is:

$$T = 2\pi\sqrt{\frac{L}{g}} \qquad \text{where } g = 32 \text{ ft/sec}^2$$

Pseudocode

```
L ← 1
Calculate pendulum period
Do while period ≤ 4
   output length L and period
   L ← L + 1
   calculate pendulum period
End do
Stop
```

Program

```
*****************************************************************
*                                                               *
*    PRINT A TABLE OF PENDULUM PERIODS                          *
*                                                               *
*****************************************************************
*                                                               *
*    CONSTANTS:                                                 *
*                                                               *
*      PI = 3.14159                                             *
*      G  = 32.0 FT/SEC*SEC GRAVITATIONAL ACCELERATION*
*                                                               *
*    INPUT VARIABLES:                                          *
*                                                               *
*      L     - LENGTH OF THE PENDULUM ARM (FEET)               *
*                                                               *
*    OUTPUT VARIABLES:                                         *
*                                                               *
*      PERIOD - COMPUTED PERIOD (SECONDS)                      *
*               PERIOD = 2*PI*SQRT(L/G)                        *
*                                                               *
*****************************************************************

      REAL L,T,G,PERIOD,PI
      PARAMETER (G=32.0,PI=3.14159)

      L = 1.0
      PERIOD = 2.0 * PI * SQRT(L/G)
```

```
        WRITE (*,1000)
1000    FORMAT('1',T19,'OUTPUT')
        WRITE (*,1100)
1100    FORMAT('+',T19,'_____')
        WRITE (*,1200)
1200    FORMAT(/T12,'LENGTH',T26,'PERIOD')
        WRITE (*,1300)
1300    FORMAT('+',T12,'_____',T26,'_____'/)

*       DO WHILE (PERIOD .LE. 4.0)

5       IF (PERIOD .LE. 4.0) THEN
          WRITE (*,2000) L,PERIOD
2000      FORMAT(10X,F5.0,5X,F10.2)
          L = L + 1.0
          PERIOD = 2.0 * PI * SQRT(L/G)
          GO TO 5
        ENDIF

*       ENDDO

        STOP
        END
```

Output

```
                          OUTPUT

              LENGTH           PERIOD

                 1.             1.11
                 2.             1.57
                 3.             1.92
                 4.             2.21
                 5.             2.48
                 6.             2.71
                 7.             2.93
                 8.             3.13
                 9.             3.32
                10.             3.50
                11.             3.67
                12.             3.84
                13.             3.99
```

Note that both constants are initialized as parameters for the program. This is a DO WHILE loop. Because the value being tested is not the value being incremented, PERIOD must be calculated just before the beginning of the loop and just before the end of the loop.

4.4.3 Comparison of Experimental Results

Problem

Write a program that reads sets of three experimental results, determines whether at least two of the three are approximately the same, and prints the value.

Pseudocode

        For each set of values
            Input the values X, Y, and Z
            If X   Y   Z (all values approximately equal) then
                True value = (X + Y + Z)/ 3.0
            If X   Y (two values approximately equal) then
                True value = (X + Y) / 2.0
            If Y   Z (two values approximately equal) then
                True value = (Y + Z) / 2.0
            If X   Z (two values approximately equal) then
                True value = (X + Z) / 2.0
            Print True value
        End for

If only two of the measurements agree, the average of those two is printed. If all three agree, the average of the three is printed.

Program

```
***********************************************************
*                                                         *
*    COMPARISON OF EXPERIMENTAL RESULTS                   *
*                                                         *
***********************************************************
*                                                         *
*    INPUT VARIABLES:                                     *
*                                                         *
*      X,Y,Z - EXPERIMENTAL VALUES                        *
*                                                         *
*    OUTPUT VARIABLES:                                    *
*                                                         *
*      X,Y,Z - INPUT VALUES                               *
*      W     - AVERAGE OF THOSE INPUT VALUES WHICH        *
*              ARE APPROXIMATELY THE SAME                 *
*                                                         *
***********************************************************

        REAL W,X,Y,Z

        WRITE (*,500)
500     FORMAT(/1X,'INPUT',35X,'OUTPUT')
```

```
*        DO WHILE MORE DATA

10       READ (*,1000,END=20) X,Y,Z
1000     FORMAT(3(F5.3))
           IF (ABS(X-Y) .LE. .01) THEN
             W = (X+Y)/2.0
             IF (ABS(X-Z) .LE. .01 .OR. ABS(Y-Z) .LE.
     1           .01) THEN
               W = (X+Y+Z)/3.0
             ENDIF
           ELSEIF (ABS(X-Z) .LE. .01) THEN
             W = (X+Z)/2.0
           ELSEIF (ABS(Y-Z) .LE. .01) THEN
             W = (Y+Z)/2.0
           ENDIF
           WRITE (*,2000) X,Y,Z,W
2000     FORMAT(/26X,4(F5.3,5X))
           W = 0.0
         GO TO 10

*        ENDDO

20       CONTINUE
         STOP
         END
```

Output

INPUT		OUTPUT		
.556 .557 .558				
	0.556	0.557	0.558	0.557
.462 .465 .467				
	0.462	0.465	0.467	0.465
.662 .666 .777				
	0.662	0.666	0.777	0.664
.662 .775 .777				
	0.662	0.775	0.777	0.776

The DO WHILE loop in this program contains a case statement with a nested IF statement.

4.4.4 Impedance and Inductance of an Electrical Coil

Problem

Write a program to compute the impedance Z and the inductance L of an electrical coil, given voltage V, current I (amps), and resistance R (ohms) for five different circuits. The coil is in the following AC circuit:

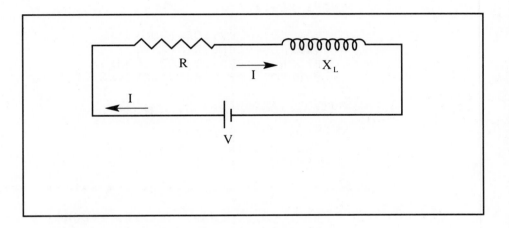

Method

$$\text{Impedance} = \frac{\text{voltage}}{\text{current}}$$

$$Z = \frac{V}{I}$$

$$\text{Impedance}^2 = \text{resistance}^2 + \text{reactance}^2$$

$$X_L = \sqrt{Z^2 - R^2}$$

$$\text{Reactance } X_L = 2\,\pi\,f\,L$$

$$L = \frac{X_L}{2\,\pi\,f}$$

where L is the inductance of the coil

Program

```
*************************************************************
*                                                           *
*   INDUCTANCE OF A COIL IN A RESISTANCE AND                *
*   REACTANCE AC SERIES CIRCUIT FOR FIVE SETS OF            *
*   VALUES                                                   *
*                                                           *
*************************************************************
*                                                           *
*   INPUT VARIABLES:                                        *
*                                                           *
*       VOLT   - VOLTAGE (VOLTS)                            *
*       IAMP   - CURRENT (AMPS)                             *
*       RESTNC - RESISTANCE (OHMS)                          *
*       FREQNC - FREQUENCY (CYCLES/SECOND)                  *
*                                                           *
*   OUTPUT VARIABLES:                                       *
*                                                           *
*       IMPDNC - IMPEDANCE                                   *
*       INDCTN - INDUCTANCE                                  *
*       RECTNC - REACTANCE                                   *
*                                                           *
*************************************************************

        REAL VOLT, IAMP, RESTNC, FREQNC, PI
        REAL IMPDNC, INDCTN, RECTNC
        PARAMETER (PI=3.14159)

        WRITE (*,500)
500     FORMAT(/5X,'INPUT',35X,'OUTPUT')

*       FIVE SETS OF VALUES

        DO 10 I= 1,5
          READ (*,1000) VOLT, IAMP, RESTNC, FREQNC
1000      FORMAT(4F5.0)
          IMPDNC = VOLT/IAMP
          INDCTN = SQRT(IMPDNC**2 - RESTNC**2)
          RECTNC = INDCTN/(2.0 * PI * FREQNC)
          WRITE (*,2000) VOLT, IAMP, INDCTN, RECTNC
2000      FORMAT(25X,4(5X,F6.2))
10      CONTINUE
        STOP
        END
```

Output

```
    INPUT                                        OUTPUT
 120.  12.   6.    50.
                            120.00      12.00       8.00      0.03
 220.  10.   8.    50.
                            220.00      10.00      20.49      0.07
 150.  15.   9.    50.
                            150.00      15.00       4.36      0.01
 120.  10.   8.    60.
                            120.00      10.00       8.94      0.02
 220.  12.   6.    60.
                            220.00      12.00      17.32      0.05
```

4.4.5 Engineering Sales Commission

Problem

Write a program to compute the commission for the salespersons selling scientific equipment in an engineering firm. The commission rate is as follows:

Commission	Sales
10%	$10,000–$20,000
15%	$20,000–$30,000
20%	over $30,000

Method

The input for each salesperson consists of the salesperson's ID and the total sales for the week. Print the ID, week's sales, and commission for each salesperson. Also print the total sales and total commission.

Pseudocode

```
Initialize totals
For each salesperson
    Input ID, SALES
    add to total sales
    calculate commission
    add to total commissions
    Output ID, SALES, COMMSN
End for
Output totalsales, total commissions
Stop
```

Program

```
****************************************************
*                                                  *
*   SALES REPORT OF AN XYZ ENGINEERING CORP.        *
*                                                  *
****************************************************
*                                                  *
*   INPUT VARIABLES:                                *
*                                                  *
*      ID      - SALES PERSON ID                    *
*      SALES   - SALES FOR CURRENT WEEK             *
*                                                  *
*   OUTPUT VARIABLES:                               *
*                                                  *
*      COMMSN - COMMISSION FOR CASH SALES           *
*      TOTSAL - TOTAL SALES FOR CURRENT WEEK        *
*      TOTCOM - TOTAL COMMISSION FOR CURRENT WEEK   *
*                                                  *
****************************************************


        INTEGER ID
        REAL SALES, TOTSAL, TOTCOM, COMMSN

        TOTSAL = 0.0
        TOTCOM = 0.0
        WRITE (*,500)
500     FORMAT(/1X,'INPUT',30X,'OUTPUT'/)

*       DO WHILE (MORE DATA)

10      READ (*,1000,END=20) ID,SALES
1000    FORMAT(I5,F7.2)
          TOTSAL = TOTSAL + SALES
          IF (SALES .GE. 30000.00) THEN
            COMMSN = SALES * 0.20
          ELSEIF (SALES .GE. 20000.00) THEN
            COMMSN = SALES * 0.15
          ELSEIF (SALES .GE. 10000.00) THEN
            COMMSN = SALES * 0.10
          ELSE
            COMMSN = 0.0
          ENDIF
          TOTCOM = TOTCOM + COMMSN
          WRITE (*,2000) ID,SALES, COMMSN
2000      FORMAT(20X,I5,5X,F8.2,5X,F8.2)
        GO TO 10

*       END DO

20      CONTINUE
        WRITE (*,4000) TOTSAL, TOTCOM
```

```
4000   FORMAT(/28X,F10.2,5X,F8.2)
       STOP
       END
```

Output

INPUT		OUTPUT	
235000.	2	35000.00	7000.00
330000.	3	30000.00	6000.00
525000.	5	25000.00	3750.00
720000.	7	20000.00	3000.00
1015000.	10	15000.00	1500.00
118000.	11	8000.00	0.00
		133000.00	21250.00

Chapter Summary

FORTRAN provides a variety of control structures. The ones introduced in this chapter are the most important, and you should use them to write FORTRAN programs. They include sequence structure, selection structure, and repetition structure.

A variety of selection structures are available:

IF–THEN–ENDIF
IF–THEN–ELSE–ENDIF
IF–THEN–ELSEIF–THEN–ENDIF

Most of these are conditional, depending on the evaluation of a relational or a logical condition. The case structure can be implemented using the IF–THEN–ELSEIF–THEN–ELSE–ENDIF.

There are also several repetition (looping) constructs:

DO WHILE	implemented as	n	IF (cond) THEN
statements			statements
ENDDO			GO TO n
			ENDIF
iterative DO	written as		DO n I = V1,V2,V3
			statements
		n	CONTINUE

These constructs may all be nested inside one another. But it is important for program maintenance and readability to structure nested constructs carefully.

Logical variables can be used to avoid having to reevaluate logical expressions that are used in several places. Relational and logical operators make it possible to ask complex questions, but they must be used with care.

Exercises

1. A 20 kg projectile is fired vertically upward from the ground to a height of s_0 meters with an initial velocity of v_0 meters/sec. Write a program to determine the maximum height it will reach if atmospheric resistance is ignored, for five input values of v_0. Given the initial conditions

$$s_0 = 0 \quad v_0 = 80$$

and the final conditions

$$s_t = h \quad v_t = 0$$

(height and velocity at time t)

you will need to solve the formula

$$v_t^2 = v_0^2 + 2a_c(s_t - s_0)$$

for h where $a_c = -9.81 \text{ m/sec}^2$

2. An 800-kg car traveling on a road at 60 m/sec requires a force of $F = ma$ to stop, where $a = (v_t^2 - v_0^2)/(2 d)$. Write a program to calculate the retarding force needed to stop the car 50, 60, 70, . . . 100 m.

3. Write a program to calculate the pressure of water at depths of 100, 200, . . . 1000 ft. The density D of water is 62.4 lb/ft³. The pressure is given by $p = hD$ at depth h.

4. A lens has a convex surface of radius $r_1$cm and a concave surface of radius $r_2$cm. It is made of glass having a refraction index of n. Compute the focal length of the lens. Determine whether the lens is convergent or divergent for each set of input values. The input consists of values of r_1, r_2, and n. The formula for the focal length is:

$$f = \frac{1}{n-1} \times \frac{r_1 r_2}{r_1 + r_2}$$

The lens is convergent if $f > 0$, divergent if $f < 0$.

5. Write a program to compute the resultant focal length f of two thin lenses of focal lengths f_1 and f_2 placed in contact. The formula is:

$$f = \frac{f_1 + f_2}{f_1 f_2}$$

Do this for all combinations of focal lengths:

$f_1 = -50, -40, . . . 30, 40, 50$
$f_2 = -50, -40, . . . 30, 40, 50$

6. Write a program to calculate the average depth of the water table measured in a number of wells in a community. The input consists of the measurements. In addition, if the depth is less than 100 ft, print 'HIGH'; if it is 100 to 1000 ft, print 'MEDIUM'; if it is over 1000 ft, print 'LOW'.

7. Write a program to compute the discharge rate of water through a Venturi meter having a pipe radius of $r_2$cm and a throat radius of $r_1$cm. The difference of the liquid heights h in the monometer tube is 6 cm. The formulas are:

$$A_a = \pi \, r_2^2 \quad \text{and } A_b = \pi \, r_1^2$$

$$\text{Ratio} = \frac{A_a^2}{A_b^2} \quad \text{Discharge rate Q} = 25 \, \pi \, \sqrt{\frac{1960h}{\text{Ratio} - 1}}$$

5

Modular Design and Subprograms

Objective: To subdivide a project into modular, functional, and manageable units of code.

*W*e presented hierarchy charts in Chapters 1 and 2 as a way to identify and represent the various functional units of a program. We have also used pseudocode to show the steps of solving a problem. When a problem is large and complex, it is best to divide it into sections or modules and write separate programs to handle them, because it is too hard to debug and maintain a large program as a single program. Top-down design, hierarchy charts, flowcharts, and pseudocode make it possible to divide a program into functional units before the actual programming begins. FORTRAN 77 supports several kinds of subprograms to implement modules of a large project.

5.1 Concepts of Modular Programming

Many present-day engineering and scientific projects are too large to be implemented by a single programmer. Other projects are too complex for a programmer to remember all the details at one time. Still others require more code than can be conveniently viewed on a screen, or contain calculations that are used in more than one place and that require duplicate code. You can see that projects are more easily managed if they are broken into tasks along logical lines, and the tasks further broken into subtasks until their solutions can be easily understood and programmed. We speak about breaking a project into tasks rather than a program because the definition of the tasks comes at the design stage of program development. Tasks and subtasks are defined on a functional basis. A task is properly defined if its function can be described in a single sentence using a single verb. If one of the conjunctions "and" or "or" must be used, two modules should be defined rather than one.

Modular programs have the following advantages:

- Small modules are easier to understand and maintain than lengthy programs.
- Modules can be tested independently and incrementally integrated before the entire program has been written.
- Modules can be written independently by different programmers.
- Modules can be relatively independent, making debugging easier.
- Modules can be modified or replaced in order to tune a program to the needs of specific applications without affecting the entire program.
- Code repetitions can be avoided.
- The overall program is simpler and easier to read.

5.1.1 Design of Modular Programs

It should be possible to give an overall functional description of a program. For example, if we had a Handy Home Robot to do mechanical chores, one program description might be:

Assemble the bicycle

If the robot was not specifically designed for this, the instruction could be functionally decomposed into four steps:

> Get tools
> Check parts list
> Assemble parts
> Put tools away

Assembly of the parts could be further decomposed into:

> Assemble frame
> Assemble gears
> Assemble wheels

The relationships between these various instructions could be shown diagrammatically as in the hierarchy chart of Fig. 5.1. A further level with more details might consist of the numbered instructions from the assembly manual. At the bottom level would be the small programs that directed the robot to move its arms and alter its grasp. Notice that the diagram in Fig. 5.1 is hierarchical in that the most general instructions are at the top and the most specific at the bottom. Each instruction that is divided into units is a general description of the functional result of all of the units. A particular tool or bicycle part may be needed to carry out more than one instruction. Nevertheless, the instructions have been made as independent as possible, grouping smaller tasks along logical lines.

There are two common approaches to the implementation of modular programs. The *top-down* approach has been illustrated in developing the chart in Fig. 5.1. It consists of designing and implementing the overall program before tackling the details. For example, it would be possible to write a program instructing the robot how to check a list of parts against actual parts at a logical level that does not include instructions on positioning the arm and hand. The *bottom-up* approach would be to start with the little details such as moving the arm to locate

Figure 5.1

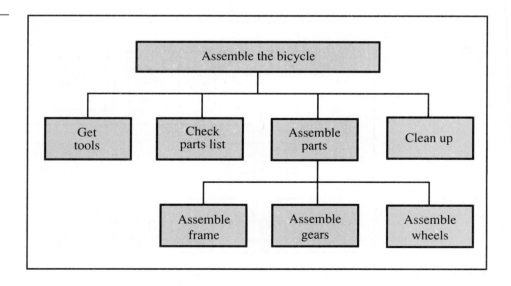

and orient a nonspecific part. Then this would be integrated with other basic modules to check the parts list or to assemble parts.

The modular design procedure consists of the following steps:

- Define the problem clearly.
- Select the simplest and most efficient solution procedure.
- Identify the subprocedures or tasks to be performed to as many levels as necessary.
- Draw charts to show the relationships between the procedures and subprocedures.
- Study the design for accuracy and completeness and refine it as necessary.

Each procedure and subprocedure of the diagram is implemented by a program or subprogram for computer execution.

Figure 5.2

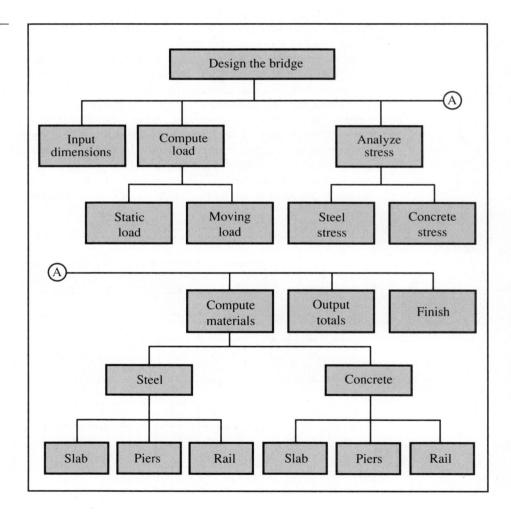

When dividing a problem into functional parts, the programmer should

identify the way the data is obtained and stored
identify any formulas needed to process the data
identify any processing and output of answers

Most programs can be divided into at least three parts, the input processing, the calculations, and the output processing. If any of these parts are complex, they can be written and tested separately. Any calculation that would be convenient to have in a function library can be written separately. Not all modules and submodules of a hierarchy chart need to be coded separately, but major ones should be, to keep the programming task down to a manageable size. Fig. 5.2 shows a hierarchy chart for a complex programming project.

Function subprograms are used when a library program would be useful, when a single value is being calculated from data that can be passed as arguments. Subroutine subprograms are used when there are large amounts of input or output or when more than one value is being calculated from data. For example, a function subprogram would be used to find the average value of a set of input data values. A subroutine subprogram would be used to find the maximum, minimum, and average. A function subprogram would be used to convert an input value from degrees Fahrenheit to degrees Celsius. A subroutine subprogram would be used to convert an output value from degrees Fahrenheit to degrees Celsius and then print it. In the latter case, there would be no value to return. A function or subroutine subprogram would also be written if the same code was needed several places in a program.

5.1.2 Review Questions

1. What does a module in a hierarchy chart represent?

2. What is the relationship between lower-level and upper-level modules in a hierarchy chart?

3. What is meant by modular design?

4. What feature of FORTRAN 77 makes it possible to write modular programs?

5. What are function subprograms used for?

6. What are subroutine subprograms used for?

5.2 Statement Functions

A statement function provides a shorthand notation for writing an expression. For example, the polynomial $ax^3 + bx^2 + cx + d$ might be given the name POLY(X). Then POLY(X) could be used in the program anywhere that the polynomial was needed. Thus a statement function can be used whenever a function is described mathematically by a single formula. If different formulas are needed for different variable domains, a statement function cannot be used.

5.2.1 User-Defined Functions

A statement function is written in the form of an assignment statement. On the left side of the equal sign is the general form by which the function is to be referenced; on the right side is the expression that implements the function. The general form is:

```
func(arg1,arg2,...) = expr
```

Examples of this are:

```
POLY(X) = ((A*X + B)*X + C)*X+ D
CBRT(X) = X**(1.0/3.0)
AVG(X,Y) = (X + Y)/2.0
```

The function name follows the rules for variable names or identifiers. For example:

```
REAL X

CBRT(X) = X**(1.0/3.0)
IROND(X) = X + 0.5 * SIGN(X)
```

The general argument X represents a real number. Since CBRT is real by default, a real value for the cube root will be used wherever CBRT is used. Since IROND is integer by default, wherever it is used an integer will be produced which is the value of X rounded to the nearest whole number. A statement function may refer to another function, but it may not refer to itself directly or indirectly.

Although the statement function resembles an assignment statement, it is a definition rather than an executable statement. Therefore it is placed at the beginning of the program, after the type declarations but before the executable statements. The computer uses the definition by effectively replacing all executable references to the function with the equivalent expression. The arguments in the function definition are dummy arguments. When the function is used, the dummy arguments are effectively replaced by the actual arguments.

```
WRITE (*,*) POLY(3.5)
```

is executed as:

```
WRITE (*,*) ((A*3.5 + B)*3.5 + C)*3.5 + D

W = POLY(Y+Z)
```

is executed as:

```
ARG = Y + Z
W = POLY(ARG)
W = ((A * ARG + B) * ARG + C) * ARG + D
```

If real arguments 3.5 and Y+Z are used, the dummy argument must be declared as real also. If the value to be calculated is real, then the function name must be implicitly real. Since POLY has one dummy argument, it must be given one argument each time it is used. The values A, B, C, and D are not arguments but actual variables of the program. A statement function may be defined with a combination of actual variables and dummy arguments.

5.2.2 Argument Passing

A statement function can be referenced wherever an expression can be used. Its dummy arguments may be simple variables or function names. Its real arguments may be constants, variables, expressions, or names of actual functions, including the name of a statement function. The actual arguments must match the dummy arguments as to number, order, and type. When the function is called, the expression that is evaluated may contain constants, dummy arguments, and ordinary variables. This is shown in the following examples:

	Declarations	*References*
REAL	F, W, X, Y	
REAL	A, B, C	

DIFF(W,X,Y) = W*(X + Y) + Y*W	DIFF(A,SQRT(B), -3.9)
CONS(F,X) = X $-$ F(X) + .5	CONS(SQRT,Y)
AVG(X,Y) = (X + Y)/ 2.0	AVG(1.0,4.0)
MID(A,B) = (A + B) / 2.0	MID(1.0,4.0)

In the reference to the function DIFF,

> A replaces W
> SQRT(B) replaces X
> -3.9 replaces Y

giving

```
DIFF(A,SQRT(B),-3.9) = A*(SQRT(B) + (-3.9))
                       + (-3.9) * A
```

In the reference to the function CONS,

> SQRT replaces F
> Y replaces X

giving

```
CONS(SQRT,Y) = Y - SQRT(Y) + .5
```

In the reference to the function AVG the average of the values 1.0 and 4.0 is calculated and 2.5 is assigned as the value of the function:

```
AVG(1.0,4.0) = (1.0 + 4.0)/ 2.0
```

which is 2.5.

In the reference to the function MID, the same average is calculated, but the function is integer by default. Therefore the expression is evaluated as

```
MID(1.0,4.0) = (1.0 + 4.0) / 2.0
```

which is 2.

Fig. 5.3 shows this program segment as a box that contains smaller boxes, which are the statement functions as well as storage locations for variables.

As shown in these examples, the function name may have a different type than the expression being assigned to it. If the expression is real and the function is integer, the calculated value of the expression will be truncated to an integer

Figure 5.3

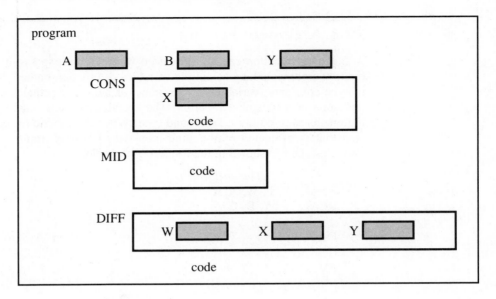

during execution. The function definition may include variables that are not dummy parameters. These are ordinary variables of the program. Actual arguments that are expressions are evaluated before the function is evaluated. For example,

```
A = 2.0
B = 1.44
C = DIFF(1.4*A,SQRT(B),-3.9)
```

    1.4*A   is evaluated as   2.8
    SQRT (B)   "   1.2

then

```
    C = DIFF(2.8,1.2,-3.9)
```

When evaluating a reference to a statement function:

1. Evaluate the arguments.
2. Replace the dummy arguments with the values of the actual arguments.
3. Evaluate the expression in the statement function.
4. Return the value of the statement function to the place where it was referenced.

If a variable that is used in other places in a program is used as a dummy argument, the situation is confusing. To the computer, they are two different variables. In the following example,

```
REAL X, Y
FUNC(X) = 1.0 / X

X = 5.0
Y = X - FUNC(X - 5.5)
```

the order of evaluation is:

Figure 5.4

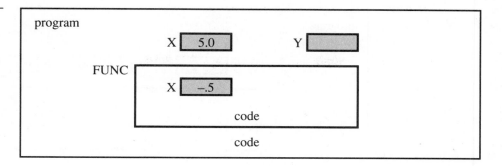

step 1	Y = 5.0 − FUNC(5.0 − 5.5)
step 2	Y = 5.0 − FUNC(− .5)
step 3	Y = 5.0 − (1.0 / − .5)
step 4	Y = 5.0 − (− 2.0)
step 5	Y = 5.0 + 2.0
step 6	Y = 7.0

The X that is the dummy variable has the value − .5; the actual variable X has the value 5.0. Outside the function statement, the actual variable is used. Inside the function statement, the dummy variable is used. This is shown in Fig. 5.4. The X that is the dummy variable cannot be accessed outside the statement function; it is *local* to it. The X that is the actual variable cannot be accessed inside the statement function because the name is reused. Any other actual variable, such as Y, could be accessed both inside and outside the statement function, provided it is given a value. It is *global* to the statement function.

Programming Hint

> Do not use names of dummy arguments for actual variables since this could lead to confusion.

In FORTRAN 77, when an argument is passed to a statement function, the effect is to rename the variable being passed.

```
REAL X,Y,Z,T,W,P,S
VALUE(X,Y,Z) = 5 * X - 3 * Y + 4 * Z - 5.0
P = 2.0
W = 1.5
T = 3.6
S = VALUE(T,W,P)
```

Fig. 5.5 shows the values of T, W, and P being passed to the function VALUE. The result of evaluating the function is passed back and stored in the variable S of the program.

When an intrinsic function is invoked, the computed value is passed to it in the same way. However, intrinsic functions reside outside the user's program in the FORTRAN library. Fig. 5.6 shows the value of C being passed to the function

Figure 5.5

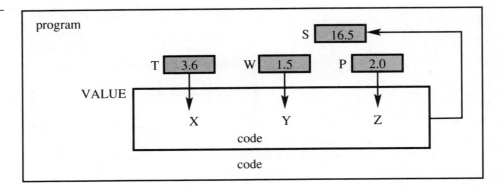

Figure 5.6

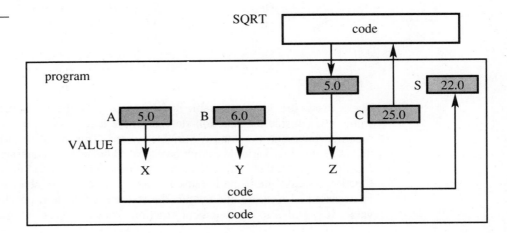

SQRT, the result being passed back, and then passed on with the values of A and B to the statement function.

```
REAL X,Y,Z,A,B,C,S
VALUE(X,Y,Z) = 5 * X - 3 * Y + 4 * Z - 5.0

A = 5.0
B = 6.0
C = 25.0
S = VALUE(A,B,SQRT(C))
```

The value of the square root is returned from the library function and temporarily stored in an unnamed location in the program. From there it is passed to the statement function along with the values of A and B.

Programming Warning

> Actual arguments and dummy arguments must match in number, order, and type.

Figure 5.7

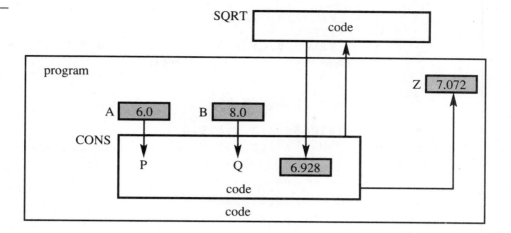

Fig. 5.7 shows the use of an intrinsic library function in the statement function itself.

```
REAL P,Q,Z,A,B
CONS(P,Q) = P + Q - SQRT(P*Q)

A = 6.0
B = 8.0
Z = CONS(A,B)
```

In this example, the square root routine is invoked by the statement function and the value $P * Q = 48.0$ is sent to it. The value of the square root is returned to the statement function. The evaluation of the statement function expression is completed and returned to the main program.

5.2.3 Review Questions

1. Write the following algebraic functions as statement functions using Horner's method whenever possible.

   a. $f(x,y) = x^3 + y^3 + x^2 + y^2 + 2xy + 18$
   b. $f(x) = ax^2 + bx + c$ where a, b, and c are constants
   c. $f(p,q,r) = p^2 + |q-r| + \sqrt{2r}$

2. Given the following program segments, show the value of S after execution.

   a.
   ```
   REAL X,Y,Z,P,C,D,S
   FUNC(X,Y,Z) = ABS(X-Y) + SQRT(Z) * 2.0
   P = 3.5
   C = 7.8
   D = .81
   S = FUNC(P,C,D)
   ```

```
b. REAL A,B,C,W,X,Y
   INTEGER S
   IVAL(A,B,C) = A * B - C / 2.0 + 6.0
   W = 4.0
   X = 16.0
   Y = 6.8
   S = IVAL(W,X,Y)

c. INTEGER A,B,C,S,P,Q
   PLUS(P,Q) = P + Q + C
   A = 3
   B = 5
   C = -7
   S = PLUS(A+B,A-B)

d. REAL X,S
   DOUB(X) = 2*X + 1
   X = 3.0
   S = DOUB(DOUB(X))
```

5.3 Function Subprograms

A function subprogram, like a library function, is located outside the program that invokes it, but it is written by the programmer. These programmer-defined function subprograms are usually mathematical. They implement and give a name to a particular mathematical function of one or more arguments. When they are used in a mathematical expression, values are provided for the variables and the code associated by the user with the function name is executed, returning a single value. For instance, FORTRAN 77 does not contain a library function for the cube root. The programmer could define such a function and name it CBRT. The function could be used by providing it with values such as:

```
CBRT(27.0)
CBRT(-1.25)
CBRT(X)
CBRT(2.3*X - 7.0)
```

It could then be used in the same way as a library function:

Y = CBRT(X) − 14.2	assignment statement
WRITE (*,*) CBRT(X − Y)	output statement
IF (CBRT(X) .LT. 5.0)THEN	comparison

The cube root could be defined briefly for nonnegative arguments:

```
CBRT(X)
```

is the same as

```
X**(1.0/3.0)
```

or for both positive and negative arguments:

```
   CBRT(X)
```

is the same as the value calculated by

```
IF (X .GE. 0.0) THEN
   CBRT = X**(1.0/3.0)
ELSE
   CBRT = -(-X) ** (1.0/3.0)
ENDIF
```

A function name follows the rules for data names. The name should be explicitly typed according to the type of the value that it represents. For example:

```
REAL Y
INTEGER K
REAL CBRT
INTEGER ROUND

Y = CBRT(3.7)
K = ROUND(Y)
```

Since CBRT is real, a real value for the cube root will be used wherever CBRT is used. ROUND is integer, so wherever it is used, an integer that is the value of Y rounded to the nearest whole number will be produced. The function name's type need not match the type of the arguments passed to it. The type of the function name is the type of value returned by the function.

Function subprograms have the following properties:

- They are invoked by name.
- They must have at least one argument.
- They always return a single value, assigned to the function name before returning to the invoking program.
- The value returned is of the same type as the function name.
- The function type should be explicitly declared for readability.

5.3.1 Definition and Control

The general form of a function subprogram is:

```
type FUNCTION funcname(arg1,arg2,...)
        declarations
   .
   .        body of the function
   .
funcname = ...
RETURN
END
```

The subprogram starts with a FUNCTION statement containing a prototype of the function call, consisting of the function name and dummy arguments. The function should be explicitly typed. It must contain one or more RETURN statements, one of which is the last executable statement before the END statement. Control returns to the program that invokes the function through the execution of a

RETURN statement. Immediately before the return, a value must be assigned to the function name—this is the value being returned.

> User function names should be explicitly typed in both the function subprogram and the calling program.

The following example of a function subprogram returns the sum of its arguments:

```
REAL FUNCTION FSUM(W,X,Y,Z)
REAL W,X,Y,Z

FSUM = W + X + Y + Z
RETURN
END
```

When writing a function subprogram, it is important to handle all values of the arguments correctly. For example, in writing a cube root routine that computes the cube roots of nonnegative numbers, it would be important to indicate an error if a negative argument is used.

```
*   CALCULATE CUBE ROOT OF A NONNEGATIVE NUMBER

    REAL FUNCTION CBRT(X)
    REAL X

    IF (X .LT. 0.0) THEN
       PRINT*, 'ERROR - NEGATIVE ARGUMENT'
       STOP
    ELSE
       CBRT = X **(1.0/3.0)
    ENDIF
    RETURN
    END
```

The STOP statement is used in subprograms only when the processing must be stopped because an error has occurred. The last statement of each subprogram is an END statement; it marks the end for compilation purposes. The normal way of terminating processing of a subprogram is by a RETURN to the program that invokes it.

Another way of indicating an error is to use the function itself as the error flag and return the value of the cube root through the arguments, as in the following example:

```
*   CALCULATE CUBE ROOT OF A NONNEGATIVE NUMBER

    LOGICAL FUNCTION CBRT(X,XCBRT)
    REAL X,XCBRT

    CBRT = .FALSE.
    IF (X .GE. 0.0) THEN
```

```
      XCBRT = X **(1.0/3.0)
      CBRT = .TRUE.
   ENDIF
   RETURN
   END
```

A function that returns an error flag is used to check whether the value of the function is .TRUE. before using the values returned through the arguments. This cube root function would be used as follows:

```
      IF (CBRT(Y,YCBRT)) THEN
         WRITE (*,1000) Y,YCBRT
1000     FORMAT(1X,'THE CUBE ROOT OF',F8.5,' IS',F8.5)
      ENDIF
```

The following example correctly calculates cube roots of both positive and negative numbers:

```
*   CALCULATE CUBE ROOT OF ANY NUMBER

      REAL FUNCTION CBRT(X)
      REAL X

      IF (X .LT. 0.0) THEN
         CBRT = - (-X) **(1.0/3.0)
      ELSE
         CBRT = X **(1.0/3.0)
      ENDIF
      RETURN
      END
```

To be correctly structured, program modules must have only one entry point and one exit. This requirement is satisfied by function subprograms even when there are several return statements. Whichever return is used, it returns to the same place in the program that invokes it.

The following example shows the placement of a function subprogram outside the main program:

```
      REAL FSUM,SUM,AVERG,A,B,C,D
      READ (*,1000) A,B,C,D
1000  FORMAT(4F5.0)
      SUM = FSUM(A,B,C,D)
      AVERG = SUM / 4.0
      WRITE (*,2000) A,B,C,D
2000  FORMAT(1X,4F6.2)
      WRITE (*,3000) SUM,AVERG
3000  FORMAT(1X,2F8.2)
      STOP
      END

      REAL FUNCTION FSUM(W,X,Y,Z)
      REAL W,X,Y,Z
      FSUM = W + X + Y + Z
      RETURN
      END
```

Notice that the sum is assigned to the function name FSUM ahead of the return statement.

When the main program passes the actual arguments to the subprogram, control of the processor also passes to the subprogram. The main program is in suspension until the value of the function is computed and control of the processor passes back to the main program. Then the main program resumes processing at the point where it was suspended, generally in the middle of the execution of a FORTRAN statement. In the example above, processing resumes with the storing of the value of FSUM in the variable SUM.

The following example shows a function that is invoked three times to calculate the surface area of a rectangular solid of sides L1, L2, and L3. Each time the function is invoked, a different set of values is passed as arguments.

```
REAL L1,L2,L3,A1,A2,A3,A
REAL AREA
READ (*,*) L1,L2,L3
A1 = AREA(L1,L2)
A2 = AREA(L2,L3)
A3 = AREA(L1,L3)
A = 2*(A1 + A2 + A3)
WRITE (*,*) L1,L2,L3,A
STOP
END

REAL FUNCTION AREA(X,Y)
REAL X,Y
AREA = X * Y
RETURN
END
```

Fig. 5.8 shows the passing of the arguments and the values returned.

Figure 5.8

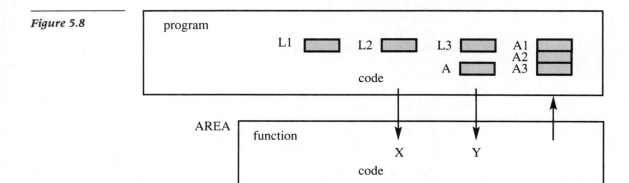

Figure 5.9

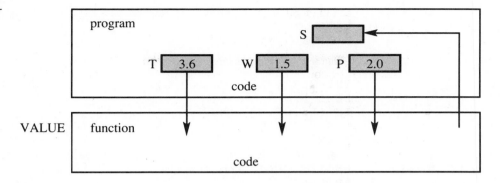

5.3.2 Argument and Parameter Passing

In FORTRAN 77, when arguments are passed to a function, it computes the result and returns it to the calling program. Fig. 5.9 shows the transmission of the arguments and the result of the function in the following example:

```
REAL VALUE,T,W,P,S

P = 2.0
W = 1.5
T = 3.6
S = VALUE(T,W,P)
```

The name of the function is shown outside the function itself, because the name is available to the main program, although the data storage and code inside the function are not.

Programming Warning

Actual arguments and dummy arguments must match in number, order, and type.

5.3.3 Review Questions

1. Given the function subprogram

```
REAL FUNCTION F(A,B,K)
REAL A,B
INTEGER K

    . . . .

RETURN
END
```

and a main program with the values X = 1.7, Y = −13.5, N = 9, what is the value of each dummy argument for each of the following invocations of the function?

a. F(X,Y,N)
b. F(Y,2.0*Y,N − 7)
c. F(SQRT(1.0*N),X + Y,5)

2. Given the following function subprogram,

```
INTEGER FUNCTION H(P,Q)
REAL P,Q
IF (P .GT. Q) THEN
   H = P - Q
ELSE
   H = Q - P
ENDIF
RETURN
END
```

What value is returned for each of the following invocations of the function?

a. A = 23.7
   B = −18.0
   C = H(A,B)

b. A = 0.0
   B = 4.6
   C = H(A+B,B)

c. A = 4.0
   B = 3.0
   C = H(SQRT(A*A+B*B),A+B)

3. Write a function subprogram SLOPE(X1,Y1,X2,Y2) that returns the slope of the line segment between the points (x1,y1) and (x2,y2).

4. Write a function subprogram HYPOT(A,B) that returns the length of the hypotenuse of a right triangle having legs of length A and B.

5. Write a function subprogram to calculate the highest point reached by a projectile fired directly upward from a height h_0 with an initial velocity of v_0. The maximum height occurs when the velocity $v = at + v_0 = 0$. The height is given by

$$h = h_0 + v_0 t + \frac{1}{2} a t^2$$

$$a = 32 \text{ ft/sec}^2$$

5.4 Subroutine Subprograms

A subroutine is a separate, independently compilable program module that cannot be run by itself, but must be executed under the control of a main program or another subprogram. It differs from a main program in that it may have arguments. It differs from a function subprogram in that it is invoked differently and does not return a result through its name. It also has a different purpose. Subroutine subprograms are intended to have side effects. They are used to control input or output, including validation of data, and to manipulate data. The arguments are used to receive and return values. When more than one value is to be returned by a subprogram, a subroutine should be used rather than a function. As with function subprograms, a subroutine can be called by any other routine, but it cannot be called by itself directly or indirectly.

5.4.1 Definition and Control

The subroutine subprogram starts with a header statement, which includes a prototype of the reference used in the call. The general form of the subroutine statement is:

```
SUBROUTINE subname(arg1,arg2,...)
```

The subroutine name follows the rules for the construction of FORTRAN names. However, as it is not used to return a value, it does not have a type. The subroutine name cannot be assigned a value or be referenced within the same subprogram. Dummy arguments may be variable names, array names, or dummy subprogram names. Corresponding actual arguments may be constants, variables, expressions, array names, or actual function or subroutine names. The names of statement functions may not be used as actual arguments when invoking a subprogram.

The structure of the subroutine subprogram is as follows:

```
SUBROUTINE subname (par1,par2,...,parn)
    declarations
        .
        .
    body of the subroutine
        .
RETURN
END
```

When the calling program invokes a subroutine, the values of the actual arguments are indirectly passed to the dummy arguments of the subroutine and control passes to the first executable statement of the subroutine. While the subroutine, the called program, is executing, the execution of the calling program is suspended. When the RETURN statement executes, the execution of the subroutine is terminated and control returns to the calling program. Processing resumes in the calling program at the first statement after the call.

A subroutine is invoked by a CALL statement, which has the general forms

```
CALL subname(arg1,arg2,...,argn)
```

or

```
CALL subname
```

Subroutines may have zero or more arguments.

Programming
Rule

> Subroutine arguments must match the actual arguments in number, order, and type.

The following example shows a call to a subroutine:

```
      REAL A,B,C,D,SUM,AVG

      READ (*,1000) A,B,C,D
1000  FORMAT(4F5.0)

      CALL SUMAVG(A,B,C,D,SUM,AVG)

      WRITE (*,1100) A,B,C,D
1100  FORMAT(1X,4F8.2)
      WRITE (*,1200) SUM,AVG
1200  FORMAT(1X,'SUM =',F10.2,'AVG =',F10.2)
      STOP
      END


*************************************************************
*                                                           *
*    CALCULATE SUM AND AVERAGE OF FOUR NUMBERS              *
*                                                           *
*    DUMMY ARGUMENTS:                                       *
*                                                           *
*       INPUT          W, X, Y, Z                           *
*                                                           *
*       OUTPUT         SUM, AVRG                            *
*                                                           *
*************************************************************

      SUBROUTINE SUMAVG(W,X,Y,Z,SUM,AVRG)
      REAL W,X,Y,Z,SUM,AVRG

      SUM = W + X + Y + Z
      AVRG = SUM / 4.0
      RETURN
      END
```

Notice that when the CALL statement executes and control passes to the subroutine, only four (A, B, C, D) of the six actual arguments have values. These four

Figure 5.10

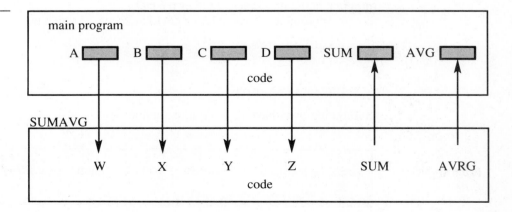

are used as input parameters to the subroutine. The other two (SUM, AVG) are output parameters from the subroutine. Subroutine documentation should include the use of parameters for input, output, or both. Fig. 5.10 shows the passing of arguments.

5.4.2 Argument and Parameter Passing

Arguments are passed to subroutines in the same way they are passed to functions. This is shown in the following example and in Fig. 5.11.

```
REAL W,X,Y,Z
READ*, W,X,Y,Z
 .
 .
 .
CALL SUB(W,X,Y,Z)
 .
 .
 .
STOP
END

SUBROUTINE SUB(P,Q,R,S)
REAL P,Q,R,S,T,U
T = P + Q * R
U = T * S
WRITE (*,*) T,U
P = T
Q = U
RETURN
END
```

The variables W, X, Y, and Z are declared in the main program which, after reading values for them, calls the subroutine SUB. When control transfers to SUB, the values of W, X, Y, and Z become the values of P, Q, R, and S, dummy variables of the routine SUB. Since the subroutine changes the values of P and Q,

Figure 5.11

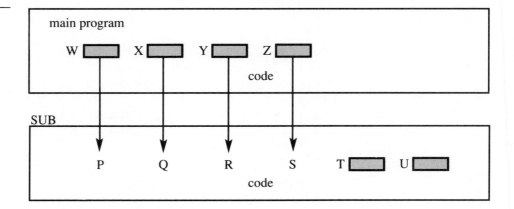

Figure 5.12

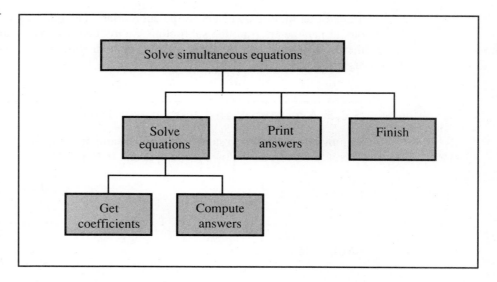

when control returns to the calling program (main), the values of W and X will have been changed. The names P and W refer to the same data object and the names Q and X refer to the same data object, as do the names R and Y, S and Z.

Programming Warning

> Changing the value of a dummy argument changes the value of the associated actual argument.

The following example shows several layers of subroutine calls. The structure of the program is shown in Fig. 5.12. Some of the boxes of the hierarchy chart are implemented as subroutines, others are not.

```
      REAL X,Y
      CALL SOLVE(X,Y)
      WRITE (*,1000) X,Y
1000  FORMAT(1X,'X =',F5.2/1X,'Y =',F5.2)
      STOP
      END

      SUBROUTINE SOLVE (P,Q)
      REAL P,Q,A,B,C,D,E,F,DEN
      CALL COEFFS (A,B,C,D,E,F)
      DEN = A * E - B * D
      P = (C * E - B * F) / DEN
      Q = (A * F - C * D) / DEN
      RETURN
      END

      SUBROUTINE COEFFS (S,T,U,V,W,Z)
      REAL S,T,U,V,W,Z
```

```
READ (*,*) S,T,U,V,W,Z
RETURN
END
```

Notice that the main program calls the subroutine SOLVE, which in turn calls the subroutine COEFFS. Since the main program does not need to know the values of the coefficients, the input routine is called from the calculation routine.

*Programming
Hint*

> Maintainability: Input should be obtained by the routine that uses it or by a lower-level routine.

5.4.3 Subprogram Activation

A main program remains active until a STOP statement has been executed. A subroutine or function remains active until one of its return statements is executed. Fig. 5.13 shows a hierarchy chart of a main program and four subprograms. Several of the subroutine names appear twice because they are called by more than one routine. Each routine is active while it is executing and while the routines below it are executing. It is still in the computer's memory, but it is temporarily suspended while the routines below it are executing. When it is no longer active, it vanishes from the computer's memory, to be reloaded when it is called again.

Fig. 5.14 shows the periods of activity and suspension of these routines. The main program MP calls SUB1, at which point both the main program and SUB1 are active and in memory. SUB1 calls SUBA, adding it to the working set of active routines in memory. SUBA calls SUBB. This is the greatest nesting of routines. SUBB can access through argument/parameter lists any variables that may have been passed down the line to it from the main program, SUB1 or SUBA. Values

Figure 5.13

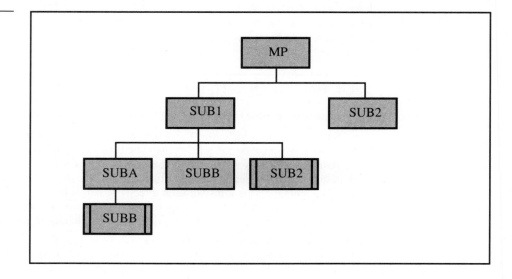

Figure 5.14

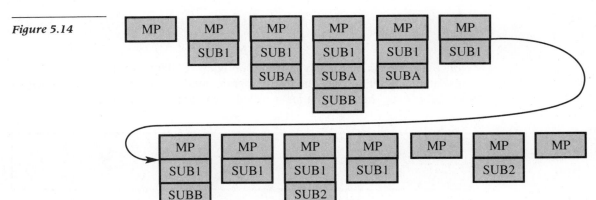

can only be passed to subprograms from other routines that are active and in memory at the same time. When SUBB has finished executing, control returns to SUBA, which finishes, returning control to SUB1. Both SUBB and SUBA, no longer active, are released from memory. SUB1 calls SUBB, the second time it is called. It is loaded into memory again from secondary storage. When SUBB finishes executing, control returns to SUB1 and SUBB is replaced in memory by SUB2, called by SUB1. When SUB2 finishes executing, control returns to SUB1, which finishes, returning control to the main program. The memory occupied by SUB2 is released, then the memory occupied by SUB1. When the main program calls SUB2 directly, it is loaded into memory again. Then the call to SUB2 by main finishes executing, returns control to the main program, and the main program finishes executing.

Each subprogram has its own local variables and dummy arguments. Except for variables in a COMMON block, which will be discussed in Section 5.5, these are the only variables available when a subprogram is executing. When the subprogram finishes executing, the local variables and dummy arguments are no longer available. If the subprogram is called a second time, the call must provide new values for the dummy arguments. In the subprogram, new values must be supplied for the local variables.

5.4.4 Review Questions

1. Indicate whether each of the following statements is true or false.

   a. Subroutines are usually used to implement modules in modular programming.
   b. Subroutines must be compiled at the same time as a main program.
   c. A subroutine is invoked by using its name in an expression.
   d. Values can be passed between any two routines by using an argument/parameter list.
   e. A subroutine must not invoke itself directly or indirectly.
   f. A subroutine may not be called more than once by any one subprogram.
   g. Subroutines should not change the values of their dummy arguments.

2. Each of the following program segments is valid in FORTRAN, but may cause problems. Identify what should not be done, and what might happen.

a.
```
REAL X
CALL SUB(X,X)
 . . .
STOP
END

SUBROUTINE SUB(A,B)
REAL A,B
A = 2.0
 . . .
RETURN
END
```

b.
```
CALL S(2)
 . . .
STOP
END

SUBROUTINE S(K)
INTEGER K
K = 7
 . . .
RETURN
END
```

c.
```
REAL Z
CALL A(3.2*SQRT(Z))
 . . .
STOP
END

SUBROUTINE A(X)
REAL X
READ *, X
 . . .
RETURN
END
```

d.
```
REAL A,B,C,D
CALL PART(A,B,C,D)
 . . .
STOP
END

SUBROUTINE PART(X,Y,Z)
REAL X,Y,Z
 . . .
RETURN
END
```

e.
```
REAL A,B,C
CALL NEXT(A,B,C)
 . . .
```

```
      STOP
      END

      SUBROUTINE NEXT(X,Y,Z,W)
      REAL X,Y,Z,W
       . . .
      RETURN
      END
```

f.
```
      REAL X
      CALL S(X)
       . . .
      STOP
      END

      SUBROUTINE S(X)
      INTEGER X
       . . .
      RETURN
      END
```

3. Given the lengths of the three sides of a triangle, the angles of the triangle may be calculated from the formula

$$\cos A = \frac{b^2 + c^2 - a^2}{2\,b\,c}$$

Write a subroutine ANGLE(SIDEA,SIDEB,SIDEC,ANGLEA,ANGLEB,ANGLEC) that calls a function to calculate each angle, and write the function.

5.5 Shared Variables and Constants

When large amounts of data are to be shared between the main program and external subprograms or between external subprograms, the COMMON statement can be used. This statement sets aside a storage area in memory that is directly accessible to just those routines that need the data. Therefore, details of the data storage are hidden from those modules that do not need to know them. The allocated memory functions as a database or internal file, but data stored in it is accessed as ordinary variables. The allocated section of memory is only available to those routines that contain the COMMON statement.

We present the COMMON statement in this section, however, for historical reasons only. Unless its use is documented very thoroughly, it can lead to maintenance problems.

Programming Warning

Maintenance and reliability: Avoid using the COMMON statement. Use argument lists to pass values between routines.

5.5.1 COMMON Statements

If only one shared section of memory is needed, an unnamed COMMON block should be used. This block of data may contain simple variables or arrays of any type. The general form of the COMMON statement is:

```
COMMON var1,var2,var3,...,varn
```

For example:

```
COMMON W,X,Y,Z1,Z2,Z3,Z4,Z5,N,M
REAL W,X,Y,Z
INTEGER N,M
```

Arrays may be declared either in the COMMON statement or in the type statement. For documentation purposes, it is advisable to declare them in the COMMON statement.

Variables in common are stored contiguously in the memory reserved for them, as in the following example:

```
COMMON W,X,Y,Z1,Z2,Z3,Z4,Z5,N,M
```

W	
X	
Y	
Z1	
Z2	
Z3	
Z4	
Z5	
N	
M	

Although the same section of memory is accessible by all routines that contain the COMMON statement, the storage locations may be known by different names in different routines, as in the following example:

```
*      MAIN PROGRAM
       . . .
       END

       SUBROUTINE SUB(A,K)
       COMMON W,X,Y,N,M
       . . .
       END

       REAL FUNCTION F(X)
       COMMON A1,A2,A3,K,L
       . . .
       END
```

SUB		F
W		A1
X		A2
Y		A3
N		K
M		L

Each of the routines SUB and F has a list of data names corresponding to the space allocated for common data. The names do not have to be the same. In fact, values that belong to an array in one routine may be given separate variable names in another. But the types of the data names must match. If a stored value is REAL, it should always be referred to by a real name; if it is INTEGER, it should always have an integer name. Unless for some reason it is necessary to give common data different names in different routines, a program is easier to debug if the names are the same. In this example, the main program does not contain a COMMON statement. Therefore these data values cannot be accessed from the main program. The X that is an argument of F is not the same variable as the X that is part of the COMMON statement of SUB.

Programming Warning

> Do not pass common data as arguments.

Variables listed in a COMMON statement should not be passed as arguments to another routine, as this can result in errors that are hard to detect. Errors involving common data are harder to find than errors involving arguments. The use of the COMMON should be included in the general documentation of the program. One way to do this is with an HIPO chart, as shown in Fig. 5.15. LUN 5 stands for logical unit 5, the standard input device on some systems. LUN 6 stands for logical unit 6, the standard output device on some systems.

Figure 5.15

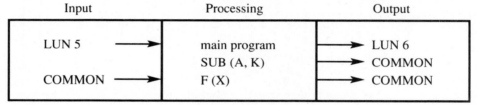

Figure 5.16

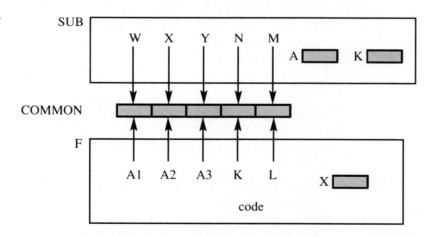

The center column of the chart in the figure lists the processing routines of the program. The input column indicates which routines have input and its source; the output column indicates which routines have output and its destination. The main program controls reading and printing. Subroutine SUB stores values in COMMON, but does not assume that values are already there. Function F uses values already in COMMON and changes some of them. If more detail were wanted, the contents of the files could be described in this diagram, COMMON data could be described, and the particular items used could be given. The user area of the computer memory would be as shown in Fig. 5.16.

In the figure, two different sets of names are associated with this COMMON area, but each set is local to a single routine. The use of the same name in a different routine does not refer to the same common data unless it is used the same way in a COMMON statement.

5.5.2 Block or Named COMMON Statements

When several distinct sets of data are shared by various routines, several common blocks can be allocated in different parts of the program, to be shared by different sets of routines. For example, several routines may share a set of scientific tables. Several other routines may share a set of empirical data. The different common areas may be given appropriate names. The general form of the COMMON statement for named common blocks is:

```
COMMON /name1/var1,var2,...,varn/name2/var1,
       var2,...,vark
```

In general, it is better to use a separate COMMON statement for each named area. For example:

```
COMMON /name1/var1,var2,...,varn
COMMON /name2/var1,var2,...,vark
```

An example of this would be:

```
COMMON /EDATA/X,Y,Z,N
COMMON /VALUES/A,B,C,K
```

The storage allocated would be arranged as follows:

```
                            X  ┌──────────┐
                            Y  ├──────────┤
EDATA                       Z  ├──────────┤
─ ─ ─ ─ ─ ─ ─ ─ ─ ─ ─ ─ ─ ─ N ─├──────────┤
                            A  ├──────────┤
                            B  ├──────────┤
VALUES                      C  ├──────────┤
                            K  └──────────┘
```

Named areas of COMMON can be used either together or separately, as in the following example:

```
COMMON /BLOCK1/A,B,C/BLOCK2/W,X,Y/BLOCK3/Z,P
```

```
      REAL A,B,C,W,X,Y,Z
      INTEGER P
      . . .
      CALL SUB1
      . . .
      CALL SUB2
      . . .
      CALL SUB3
      . . .
      CALL SUB4
      . . .
      STOP
      END

      SUBROUTINE SUB1
      COMMON /BLOCK1/A,B,C
      REAL A,B,C
      . . .
      RETURN
      END

      SUBROUTINE SUB2
      COMMON /BLOCK2/W,X,Y
      REAL W,X,Y
      . . .
      RETURN
      END

      SUBROUTINE SUB3
      COMMON /BLOCK1/A,B,C/BLOCK3/P,Q
      REAL A,B,C,P
      INTEGER Q
      . . .
      RETURN
      END

      SUBROUTINE SUB4
      COMMON /BLOCK1/A,B,C/BLOCK2/W,X,Y
      REAL A,B,C,W,X,Y
      . . .
      RETURN
      END
```

The documentation for this program should show that:

> BLOCK1 is accessible to the main program, SUB1, SUB3, and SUB4
> BLOCK2   "   main program, SUB2, and SUB4
> BLOCK3   "   main program and SUB3

COMMON is used for shared variables. They must be initialized by one of the subprograms or by assignment statements in the main program during execution time. DATA and PARAMETER statements cannot be used with shared variables. The values remain in memory while the program is executing, but they are only accessible to routines that contain the proper COMMON statements.

5.5.3 SAVE Statement

Occasionally it is necessary for a function or subroutine to save a value from one of its activations to the next. For example, if a subroutine is to count the number of times it is called, the count must be preinitialized to zero and one must be added to it on each call. The counter variable cannot be an ordinary variable or it would have the same initial value of zero every time the routine is loaded and becomes active. Instead, the SAVE statement can be used. The general form of this statement is:

```
SAVE name1,name2,...,namen
```

or

```
SAVE
```

where the names in the SAVE statement are names of simple variables, arrays, or common blocks. If the list of names is missing, all the local variables of the routine are saved. The SAVE statement is inefficient, so it should be used only when a routine must keep a record of its own behavior, as in the following example:

```
*   MAIN PROGRAM
      . . .
      DO WHILE (...)
        CALL A
      ENDDO
      CALL B
      STOP
      END

      SUBROUTINE A
      INTEGER KNT
      SAVE KNT
      DATA KNT/0/
      . . .
      KNT = KNT + 1
      . . .
      RETURN
      END

      SUBROUTINE B
      . . .
      DO WHILE (...)
        CALL A
      . . .
      ENDDO
      RETURN
      END
```

In this example, neither the main program nor subroutine B can count the number of calls to subroutine A. By making KNT a saved variable, subroutine A can count its own activations. The initial value of KNT is zero. The first time A is called, KNT becomes one. The second time A is called, KNT becomes two, and so forth.

5.5.4 Review Questions

1. Indicate whether the following statements are true or false.

    a. The variables specified in a COMMON statement are assigned a block of storage.
    b. All variables needed in subprograms must be specified in COMMON statements in the main program.
    c. The variables in a subroutine COMMON statement may be dummy variables.
    d. Shared data area can be initialized using an assignment statement.

2. Diagram the storage allocation for the following COMMON statements:

    a. COMMON AVAL,CONST,VALUE,PACE
    b. COMMON ACON,BMAX,CON,VAL
    c. COMMON BLK1/A,B,C/BLK2/F,G
    d. COMMON ABLK/X,Y,Z/BLK2/G,H

3. Write a subroutine CNTR. When it is called, it prints 1 the first time, 2 the second time, 3 the third time, and so forth.

5.6 Sample Programs Using Subprograms

These examples are designed to illustrate the use of main driver routines to test statement functions and function and subroutine subprograms. These programs have been executed interactively on the Digital Equipment Corporation (DEC) computer model VAX 11/780. In some cases, the output includes the screen input data; where it is included, it is identified.

5.6.1 Square Root Routine

Problem

Write a square root routine that does not stop the processing when a negative argument is passed to it. Write a driver to test the routine.

Method

Use the Newton-Raphson method of calculating the square root. If the argument is negative, return an error flag. The algorithm was presented in Chapter 1, section 1.5.3.

Program

```
***********************************************************
*                                                         *
*   MAIN PROGRAM DRIVER FOR CALCULATING SQUARE ROOT       *
*                                                         *
***********************************************************
```

```
        REAL X,SQR
        LOGICAL XSQRT

        WRITE (*,1000)
1000    FORMAT (1X,'INPUT DATA',T33,'NUMBER',15X,
     1          'SQUARE ROOT'/)

*       DO WHILE (MORE DATA)

10      READ (*,*,END=50) X
          IF (XSQRT(X,SQR)) THEN
            WRITE (*,2000) X,SQR
2000        FORMAT(T30,F10.3,13X,F10.3)
          ELSE
            WRITE (*,3000) X
3000        FORMAT(T30,F10.3,' IS A NEGATIVE ARGUMENT,'
     1             /T41,'NO SQUARE ROOT')
          ENDIF
        GO TO 10

*       ENDDO

50      CONTINUE
        STOP
        END


******************************************************
*                                                    *
*   SQUARE ROOT CALCULATION USING NEWTON-RAPHSON     *
*   METHOD                                           *
*                                                    *
******************************************************
*                                                    *
*   ARGUMENTS:                                       *
*                                                    *
*      INPUT:                                        *
*                                                    *
*         X   - REAL NUMBER WHOSE SQUARE ROOT IS     *
*               REQUIRED                             *
*                                                    *
*      OUTPUT:                                       *
*                                                    *
*         S   - SQUARE ROOT OF X IF FUNCTION .TRUE.  *
*               UNDEFINED IF FUNCTION .FALSE.        *
*                                                    *
******************************************************

        LOGICAL FUNCTION XSQRT(X,S)
        REAL X,S,S0,ERR

        IF (X .LT. 0.0) THEN
          XSQRT = .FALSE.
          RETURN
```

```
          ENDIF
          XSQRT = .TRUE.
          IF (X .EQ. 0.0) THEN
             S = 0.0
             RETURN
          ENDIF
          S0 = X / 2.0
          ERR = .0001 * X

*         REPEAT UNTIL (ABS(S0-S) .LT. ERR)

10        S = (S0 + X/S0) / 2.0
          IF (.NOT.(ABS(S-S0) .LT. ERR) THEN
             S0 = S
             GO TO 10
          ENDIF

*         END REPEAT

          RETURN
          END
```

Output

```
┌─────────────────────────────────────────────────────────────────────────────
│  INPUT DATA                      NUMBER                   SQUARE ROOT
│
│  25
│                                  25.000                      5.000
│  677
│                                  677.000                    26.019
│  -16
│                                  -16.000 IS A NEGATIVE ARGUMENT,
│                                          NO SQUARE ROOT
│  625
│                                  625.000                     25.000
│  0
│                                  0.000                        0.000
└─────────────────────────────────────────────────────────────────────────────
```

This program uses a function rather than a subroutine even though there are two values to return: the value of the square root, if there is one, and the flag indicating whether or not there is a valid square root. The function itself returns the flag, and the square root is returned through the argument list. A function should return values through its argument list only if the function itself has the role of error flag. The DO WHILE loop control in the driver has been set up so that any number of test values can be used.

5.6.2 Thrust of Rocket Engines

Problem

Write a program to calculate the average thrust of a rocket engine, given the weight of the rocket and its velocity at time t during the burning of the first stage.

Pseudocode

Input the weight in pounds, velocity, and time.
Calculate the force due to thrust using the formula

$$F = \frac{w\,v}{gt}$$

for w = 5000.00 lbs
    v = 2000 ft/sec
    t = 10.0 sec.

Calculate the total thrust using the formula

$$T = w + F$$

Print the values of w, v, t, F, and T.

Program

```
***************************************************************
*                                                             *
*    PRINT THE THRUST OF A ROCKET UNDER GRAVITATION           *
*    AND ACCELERATION                                         *
*                                                             *
***************************************************************
*                                                             *
*    INPUT VARIABLES:                                         *
*                                                             *
*       WT      - WEIGHT OF THE ROCKET (POUNDS)               *
*       VEL     - VELOCITY OF THE ROCKET (FEET/SECOND)*
*       TIME    - DURATION OF THRUST (SECONDS)                *
*                                                             *
*    OUTPUT VARIABLES:                                        *
*                                                             *
*       FORCE   - FORCE DUE TO ACCELERATION (POUNDS)          *
*                                                             *
*    STATEMENT FUNCTIONS:                                     *
*                                                             *
*       TOTFRC - TOTAL FORCE DUE TO THRUST (POUNDS)           *
*       TOTHR  - TOTAL THRUST DUE TO ACCELERATION AND         *
*                WEIGHT (POUNDS)                              *
*                                                             *
***************************************************************
```

```
        REAL WT,VEL,TIME,G,FORCE,W,V,T,F
        PARAMETER (G=32.0)

        TOTFRC(W,V,T) = (W * V) / (G * T)
        TOTHR(W,F) = W + F

        WRITE (*,*) 'INPUT DATA'
        READ (*,1000) WT,VEL,TIME
1000    FORMAT(3F6.0)
        FORCE = TOTFRC(WT,VEL,TIME)
        WRITE (*,1200) WT,VEL,TIME,FORCE
1200    FORMAT(//7X,'OUTPUT DATA'
     1          //1X,'WEIGHT =',F10.2
     2          /1X,'VELOCITY =',F10.2
     3          /1X,'TIME =',F10.2
     4          /1X,'FORCE DUE TO ACCELERATION ='
     5          ,F10.2)
        WRITE (*,1500) TOTHR(WT,FORCE)
1500    FORMAT(1X,'TOTAL THRUST DUE TO ACCELERATION ='
     1          ,F12.2)
        STOP
        END
```

Output

```
INPUT DATA
5000. 2000. 10.


        OUTPUT DATA

WEIGHT =    5000.00
VELOCITY =  2000.00
TIME =       10.00
FORCE DUE TO ACCELERATION =  31250.00
TOTAL THRUST DUE TO ACCELERATION =    36250.00
```

Statement functions are used in this program because of the simplicity of the formulas. The constant G is accessed directly rather than being passed as an argument, simply because it is a constant element of the formula.

5.6.3 Rocket Acceleration

Problem

Write a function to calculate the acceleration of a rocket, given the weight of the rocket in pounds, the thrust of the engine in pounds, and the velocity of the exhaust gases in ft/sec.

Pseudocode

Input the weight, thrust, and velocity.
Compute the time rate of change of momentum using the formulas

$$\frac{F}{-V_g} = \frac{m}{t} \qquad\qquad V_g = \frac{Ft}{-m}$$

where V_g is the velocity of the exhaust gases from the engine
        F is the total thrust of the engines
      $\dfrac{m}{t}$ is the ratio of loss of mass m in time t

Compute the mass lost after t seconds.

$$m_{loss} = t\,\frac{m}{t} \quad = t\,\frac{F}{-V_g}$$

Compute the net mass remaining after t seconds.

$$m_{t\ remaining} = \frac{w}{g} - m_{loss} \quad = \frac{w}{g} - \left(\frac{F}{-V_g}\,t\right)$$

Compute the weight at w_t.

$$w_t = m_{t\ remaining}\, g$$

Compute the unbalanced force that causes acceleration.

$$F_t = thrust - w_t$$

Compute the acceleration

$$a = F_t\,/\,m_t$$

Print the results
Stop

Program

```
*********************************************************
*                                                       *
*   MAIN DRIVER PROGRAM : COMPUTE THE ROCKET            *
*                         ACCELERATION                  *
*                                                       *
*********************************************************

      REAL WEIGHT,THRUST,VELGAS,TIME
      REAL SUBACL

      WRITE (*,*) 'INPUT DATA'
      READ (*,*) WEIGHT,THRUST,VELGAS,TIME
      WRITE (*,1000) WEIGHT,THRUST,VELGAS
1000  FORMAT(/35X,'OUTPUT DATA'
     1       //25X,'WEIGHT OF ROCKET:',F10.2,' LBS'
```

```
   2          /25X,'THRUST OF ENGINES:',F10.2,' LBS'
   3          /25X,'VELOCITY OF EXHAUST:',F10.2,
   4          ' FT/SEC')
     WRITE (*,1500) SUBACL(WEIGHT,THRUST,VELGAS,
   1          TIME)
1500 FORMAT(25X,'ACCELERATION OF THE VEHICLE:'
   1          ,F10.2,' FT/SEC*SEC')
     STOP
     END


*****************************************************
*                                                   *
*   CALCULATION OF ROCKET ACCELERATION              *
*                                                   *
*****************************************************
*                                                   *
*    ARGUMENTS:                                      *
*                                                   *
*        WT      - WEIGHT OF ROCKET (POUNDS)        *
*        THR     - THRUST OF THE ENGINES (POUNDS)   *
*        VGAS    - VELOCITY OF EXHAUST GAS (FEET/   *
*                  SECOND)                          *
*        TIME    - DURATION OF THRUST (SECONDS)     *
*                                                   *
*        RETURNS ACCELERATION (FEET/SECOND SECOND)  *
*                                                   *
*****************************************************

     REAL FUNCTION SUBACL(WT,THR,VGAS,TIME)
     REAL WT,THR,VGAS,G,TIME,FTUNB,MT,UBWT
     PARAMETER(G=32.0)

     FUNFOR(THR,VGAS) = THR /(- VGAS)
     FUNACL(FTUNB,MT) = FTUNB / MT

     MT = WT / G - FUNFOR(THR,VGAS) * TIME
     UBWT = MT * G
     FTUNB = THR - UBWT
     SUBACL = FUNACL(FTUNB,MT)
     RETURN
     END
```

This example uses a function subprogram to compute and return a value. The function contains several statement functions.

Output for three sets of input data

```
INPUT DATA
10000.,80000.,50000.,15.
                              OUTPUT DATA

                         WEIGHT OF ROCKET: 10000.00 LBS
                         THRUST OF ENGINES: 80000.00 LBS
                         VELOCITY OF EXHAUST: 50000.00 FT/SEC
                         ACCELERATION OF THE VEHICLE: 205.74 FT/SEC*SEC


   INPUT DATA
   5000.,80000.,100000.,15.

                              OUTPUT DATA

                         WEIGHT OF ROCKET: 5000.00 LBS
                         THRUST OF ENGINES: 80000.00 LBS
                         VELOCITY OF EXHAUST: 100000.00 FT/SEC
                         ACCELERATION OF THE VEHICLE: 443.48 FT/SEC*SEC


   INPUT DATA
   10000.,80000.,50000.,900.

                              OUTPUT DATA

                         WEIGHT OF ROCKET: 10000.00 LBS
                         THRUST OF ENGINES: 80000.00 LBS
                         VELOCITY OF EXHAUST: 50000.00 FT/SEC
                         ACCELERATION OF THE VEHICLE: 13.65 FT/SEC*SEC
```

5.6.4 Oil Production

Problem

Compute the amount of oil produced by five wells. At 100% production, each well produces 50 barrels per day. Normally each well produces at a rate less than 100%. Given the percent production for each well, compute the total monthly production for each well and the overall total monthly production.

Method

Assume the input consists of one record for each day of the month. Use a function to input the data and a subroutine to compute the total monthly production for each well. Also compute total monthly production from all wells.

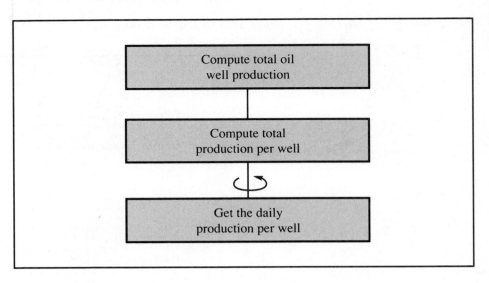

Program

```
************************************************************
*                                                          *
*    COMPUTE THE TOTAL MONTHLY OIL PRODUCTION FOR          *
*    FIVE WELLS                                            *
*                                                          *
************************************************************
*                                                          *
*    OUTPUT VARIABLES:                                     *
*                                                          *
*       TOTAL - TOTAL MONTHLY PRODUCTION OF ALL WELLS*
*                                                          *
*    SUBPROGRAMS:                                          *
*                                                          *
*       WELLS - INPUT SUBROUTINE                           *
*                                                          *
************************************************************

       REAL T1,T2,T3,T4,T5,TOTAL
       DATA T1,T2,T3,T4,T5/0.0,0.0,0.0,0.0,0.0/

       CALL WELLS(T1,T2,T3,T4,T5)
       WRITE (*,500)
500    FORMAT(/30X,'OUTPUT DATA')
       WRITE (*,1000) 1,T1,2,T2,3,T3,4,T4,5,T5
1000   FORMAT(5(/28X,'WELL',I2,' =',F7.2))
       TOTAL = T1 + T2 + T3 + T4 + T5
       WRITE (*,1100) TOTAL
```

```
1100    FORMAT(/28X,'TOTAL PRODUCTION =',F8.2)
        STOP
        END


********************************************************
*                                                      *
*    COMPUTE THE TOTAL MONTHLY OIL PRODUCTION FOR       *
*    EACH WELL                                          *
*                                                      *
********************************************************
*                                                      *
*    OUTPUT VARIABLES:                                  *
*                                                      *
*        T1, T2, T3, T4, T5 - TOTAL MONTHLY PRODUCTION *
*                             PER WELL                  *
*                                                      *
*    SUBPROGRAMS:                                       *
*                                                      *
*        GET     - LOGICAL FUNCTION TO INPUT PRODUCTION *
*                  RATES                                *
*                                                      *
********************************************************

        SUBROUTINE WELLS(T1,T2,T3,T4,T5)
        REAL T1,T2,T3,T4,T5
        REAL W1,W2,W3,W4,W5
        LOGICAL GET

        WRITE (*,1000)
1000    FORMAT(5X,'INPUT DATA')

*       DO WHILE(MORE DATA)

10      IF(GET(W1,W2,W3,W4,W5)) THEN
            T1 = T1 + W1 * 50.0
            T2 = T2 + W2 * 50.0
            T3 = T3 + W3 * 50.0
            T4 = T4 + W4 * 50.0
            T5 = T5 + W5 * 50.0
            GO TO 10
        ENDIF

*       ENDDO

        RETURN
        END
```

```
      ********************************************************
      *                                                      *
      *    GET THE DAILY PRODUCTION FOR EACH WELL            *
      *                                                      *
      ********************************************************
      *                                                      *
      *    OUTPUT VARIABLES:                                 *
      *                                                      *
      *      W1, W2, W3, W4, W5 - PERCENT PRODUCTION PER     *
      *                          DAY                         *
      *                                                      *
      *      RETURNS .TRUE. IF DATA FOUND, .FALSE. IF END    *
      *      OF FILE                                         *
      *                                                      *
      ********************************************************

            LOGICAL FUNCTION GET(W1,W2,W3,W4,W5)
            REAL W1,W2,W3,W4,W5,W
            INTEGER ID

            READ (*,1000,END=50) W1,W2,W3,W4,W5
      1000  FORMAT(5F5.2)
            GET = .TRUE.
            RETURN
      50    CONTINUE
            GET = .FALSE.
            RETURN
            END
```

Output

```
      INPUT DATA
  .3    .4    .5    .6    .7
  .3    .0    .5    .6    .7
  .1    .3    .5    .8    .9
  .4    .6    .0    .7    .6



            OUTPUT DATA

      WELL 1 =   55.00
      WELL 2 =   65.00
      WELL 3 =   75.00
      WELL 4 =  135.00
      WELL 5 =  145.00

      TOTAL PRODUCTION =   475.00
```

5.6.5 Heat Flow

Problem

Write a program to compute the heat conduction through the four walls of a room that has an insulated floor and ceiling.

Method

Input values for the thickness of the walls, the dimensions of the walls, the thermal conductivity of the material used in the walls, and the temperatures inside and outside the room. Use an input subroutine, a function to compute the heat loss, and an output subroutine.

Given   w1, w2   the dimensions of the room
           h   the height of the walls
           l   the thickness of the walls
           k   the thermal coefficient of the wall material
           t_i, t_o the temperatures inside and outside

Pseudocode

Input the data w1,w2,h,l,k,t_i,t_o
Compute the area
   area = 2 (w1 + w2) h
Compute the heat loss
   htloss = k · area (t_i − t_o) / l
Stop

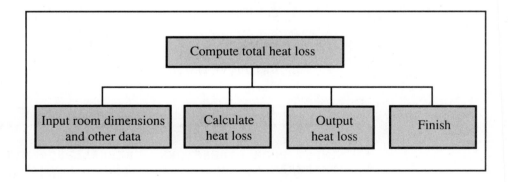

Program

```
*************************************************************
*                                                           *
*    COMPUTE THE HEAT LOSS THROUGH THE WALLS OF              *
*    A ROOM                                                  *
*                                                           *
*************************************************************
*                                                           *
*    INPUT VARIABLES:                                        *
*                                                           *
*       W1, W2     - DIMENSIONS OF THE ROOM                  *
*       H          - HEIGHT OF THE WALLS                     *
*       TH         - THICKNESS OF THE WALLS                  *
*       K          - THERMAL COEFFICIENT OF THE WALL         *
*                    MATERIAL                                *
*       TO         - OUTSIDE TEMPERATURE                     *
*       TI         - INSIDE TEMPERATURE                      *
*                                                           *
*    OUTPUT VARIABLES:                                       *
*                                                           *
*       HTLOSS     - HEAT LOSS THROUGH THE WALLS (BTU)       *
*                                                           *
*    SUBPROGRAMS:                                            *
*                                                           *
*       DATAIN     - SUBROUTINE TO READ VALUES INTO          *
*                    COMMON                                  *
*       CALHET     - FUNCTION TO CALCULATE HEAT LOSS         *
*       DATOUT     - OUTPUT SUBROUTINE                       *
*                                                           *
*************************************************************

      COMMON W1,W2,H,TI,TO,K,TH
      REAL W1,W2,H,TI,TO,K,TH
      REAL HTLOSS
      REAL CALHET

      CALL DATAIN
      HTLOSS = CALHET()
      CALL DATOUT(HTLOSS)
      STOP
      END


*************************************************************
*                                                           *
*    INPUT ROOM DIMENSIONS, THERMAL PROPERTY AND            *
*    TEMPERATURE                                             *
*                                                           *
*************************************************************

      SUBROUTINE DATAIN
      COMMON W1,W2,H,TI,TO,K,TH
      REAL W1,W2,H,TI,TO,K,TH
```

```
       WRITE (*,*) 'INPUT DATA'
       READ (*,1000) W1,W2,H,TH,K,TI,TO
1000   FORMAT(5F5.2,2F7.2)
       RETURN
       END


***********************************************************
*                                                         *
*    CALCULATE HEAT LOSS                                  *
*                                                         *
***********************************************************

       REAL FUNCTION CALHET()
       COMMON L1,L2,H,TI,TO,K,TH
       REAL L1,L2,H,TI,TO,K,TH

       AREA = 2 * (L1 + L2) * H
       CALHET = K * AREA * (TI - TO)/TH
       RETURN
       END


***********************************************************
*                                                         *
*    OUTPUT INPUT VALUES AND HEAT LOSS                    *
*                                                         *
***********************************************************

       SUBROUTINE DATOUT (HTLOSS)
       COMMON W1,W2,H,TI,TO,K,TH
       REAL W1,W2,H,TI,TO,K,TH
       REAL HTLOSS

       WRITE (*,1000) W1,W2,H,TH,K,TI,TO,HTLOSS
1000   FORMAT(/42X,'OUTPUT DATA'
      1        //38X,'ROOM LENGTH = ', F5.2
      2        /38X,'ROOM WIDTH = ',F5.2
      3        /38X,'WALL HEIGHT = ',F5.2
      4        /38X,'WALL THICKNESS = ',F5.2
      5        /38X,'THERMAL CONDUCTIVITY =',F5.2
      6        /38X,'INSIDE TEMP =',F7.2
      7        /38X,'OUTSIDE TEMP =',F7.2
      8        /38X,'HEATLOSS = ',F8.2)
       RETURN
       END
```

Output

```
INPUT DATA
12.  12.  8.   1.   .3  85.   30.

                        OUTPUT DATA

                        ROOM LENGTH = 12.00
                        ROOM WIDTH = 12.00
                        WALL HEIGHT =  8.00
                        WALL THICKNESS =  1.00
                        THERMAL CONDUCTIVITY = 0.30
                        INSIDE TEMP =  85.00
                        OUTSIDE TEMP =  30.00
                        HEATLOSS =  6336.00
```

5.6.6 Approximating the Area under a Curve

Problem

Write a program that will find the approximate value of the area under the curve
f(t) for $0 \le t \le T$ where f(t) is any library or user function.

Method

Use the trapezoidal rule:

$$\text{area} = (f(t_0)/2 + f(t_1) + f(t_2) + \ldots + f(t_{n-1}) + f(t_n)/2)dx$$

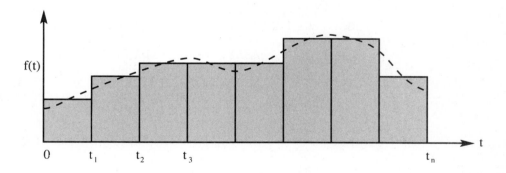

Pseudocode

Compute the value of the function at $t_0, t_1, t_2, \ldots t_n$
Compute the area by the trapezoidal formula

By increasing the value of n to be n = 10, 20, 40, . . . and recalculating the
approximation, eventually two approximations will be found that are approximately equal. These are assumed to be an accurate value for the area.

Program

```
***********************************************************
*                                                         *
*  CALCULATE THE AREA UNDER THE CURVE F(T) USING THE*
*  TRAPEZOIDAL RULE AND THE INTEGRAL, FOR COMPARISON*
*                                                         *
***********************************************************
*                                                         *
*  INPUT VARIABLES:                                       *
*                                                         *
*    LLIMIT - LOWER LIMIT OF THE FUNCTION                 *
*    ULIMIT - UPPER LIMIT OF THE FUNCTION                 *
*    X      - INDEPENDENT VARIABLE                        *
*                                                         *
*  OUTPUT VARIABLES:                                      *
*                                                         *
*    AREAN  - AREA COMPUTED BY THE TRAPEZOIDAL RULE *
*    AREAI  - AREA COMPUTED BY THE INTEGRAL               *
*                                                         *
***********************************************************

        REAL T,LLIMIT,ULIMIT,Y,DT,X,AREAO,AREAN,AREAI
        INTEGER N

*       THE SAMPLE FUNCTION

        F(X) = X*X + 4.0

*       THE INTEGRAL OF THE SAMPLE FUNCTION

        FP(X) = (1.0/3.0) * (X**3) + 4.0*X

        WRITE (*,1000)
1000    FORMAT('1','INPUT THE LOWER LIMIT AND UPPER
     1         'LIMIT OF THE FUNCTION')
        READ (*,*) LLIMIT,ULIMIT
        N = 10
        DT = (ULIMIT - LLIMIT) / N
        AREAN = (ULIMIT - LLIMIT) * (F(LLIMIT) +
     1            F(ULIMIT))/2.0

*       REPEAT UNTIL (ABS(AREAN-AREAO) .LT. 0.01)

10      AREAO = AREAN
        T = LLIMIT
        Y = F(LLIMIT)/2.0

*       CALCULATE F(LLIMIT)/2 + F(DT) + F(2*DT)
*           + . . . + F(N*DT)/2

        DO 20 K = 1,N-1
          T = T + DT
          Y = Y + F(T)
```

```
 20        CONTINUE
           T = T + DT
           Y = Y + F(T)/2.0

 *         AREA COMPUTED UNDER THE CURVE

           AREAN = Y * DT

 *         THE NUMBER OF STEPS IS DOUBLED TO INCREASE
 *             ACCURACY

           DT = DT/2.0
           N = N * 2
           IF (.NOT. (ABS(AREAN-AREAO) .LT. 0.01)) THEN
              GO TO 10
           ENDIF

 *     END REPEAT

       WRITE (*,1100) LLIMIT, ULIMIT
 1100  FORMAT(/1X,'LOWER LIMIT =',F5.2,5X,'UPPER ',
      1        'LIMIT =',F5.2/)
       WRITE (*,*) 'FOR COMPARISON:'
       WRITE (*,1200) AREAN
 1200  FORMAT(/1X,'AREA COMPUTED BY TRAPEZOIDAL ',
      1        'RULE =',F8.2)
        AREAI = FP(ULIMIT) - FP(LLIMIT)
       WRITE (*,1300) AREAI
 1300  FORMAT(1X,'AREA COMPUTED BY INTEGRAL ='
      1        ,F8.2)
        STOP
        END
```

Output

```
 INPUT THE LOWER LIMIT AND UPPER LIMIT OF THE FUNCTION
 0.0,8.0

 LOWER LIMIT = 0.00     UPPER LIMIT = 8.00

 FOR COMPARISON:

 AREA COMPUTED BY TRAPEZOIDAL RULE =  202.67
 AREA COMPUTED BY INTEGRAL =  202.67
```

This program calculates the integral accurate to two decimal places. A sample function is included in the program. For comparison, the area is also computed from the integral.

5.6.7 Current in Parallel Circuits

Program

Write a program to compute the current and effective resistance of each branch of a parallel circuit.

Method

Input the voltage V and resistances R1, R2, and R3 for the parallel circuit. Use a function to compute the current in each parallel branch, a statement function to compute the effective resistance, and a function to compute the total power loss in the AC circuit. Write a subroutine to output the results. The formulas are as follows:

$$V = VR1 = VR2 = VR3 \quad \text{equal voltage on all branches}$$

$$IR1 = \frac{V}{R1} \quad \text{current on branch of circuit}$$

$$IR2 = \frac{V}{R2}$$

$$IR3 = \frac{V}{R3}$$

total current $I = IR1 + IR2 + IR3$ (amps)

effective resistance $R = \dfrac{V}{I}$ (ohms)

power $= V\,I\,\cos(A)$

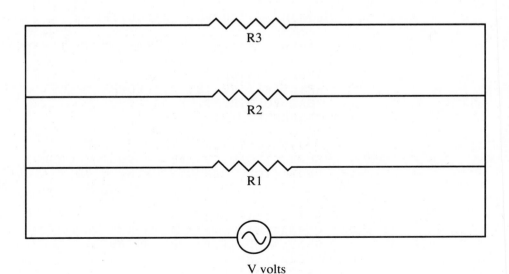

V volts

Pseudocode

Input the voltage V, resistance R1, R2, and R3
Compute the current in each branch of the circuit
Compute the total current
Compute the effective resistance
Compute the power drop across the circuit
Output the branch currents, total current, effective resistance and power
    drop
Stop

Program

```
**********************************************************
*                                                        *
*   COMPUTE THE CURRENT, RESISTANCE AND POWER DROP IN*
*   A PARALLEL AC CIRCUIT                                *
*                                                        *
**********************************************************
*                                                        *
*   INPUT VARIABLES:                                     *
*                                                        *
*     V           - VOLTAGE OF CIRCUIT (VOLTS)           *
*     R1,R2,R3 - RESISTANCES IN PARALLEL (OHMS)          *
*     THETA       - PHASE ANGLE (DEGREES)                *
*                                                        *
*   STATEMENT FUNCTIONS:                                 *
*                                                        *
*     CFUNR       - CURRENT IN BRANCH OF CIRCUIT (AMPS)  *
*     REFUNC      - EFFECTIVE RESISTANCE (OHMS)          *
*     PFUNC       - POWER DROP ACROSS CIRCUIT (VOLTS)    *
*                                                        *
*   SUBPROGRAMS:                                         *
*                                                        *
*     OUTSUB      - OUTPUT SUBROUTINE                    *
*                                                        *
**********************************************************

         REAL V,R1,R2,R3
         REAL IR1,IR2,IR3,R,I,POWER
         REAL VOLT,REST,THETA,PI
         PARAMETER (PI=3.14159)

         CFUNR(VOLT,REST) = VOLT / REST
         REFUNC(VOLT,CURENT) = VOLT / CURENT
         PFUNC(VOLT,CURENT,THETA) = VOLT * CURENT *
        1            COS(PI/180.0*THETA)

         WRITE (*,1000)
1000     FORMAT(1X,'INPUT DATA')
         READ 1500, V,R1,R2,R3,THETA
1500     FORMAT(5F5.0)
         WRITE (*,1600)
```

```
1600    FORMAT(/13X,'OUTPUT DATA')
        IR1 = CFUNR(V,R1)
        IR2 = CFUNR(V,R2)
        IR3 = CFUNR(V,R3)
        I = IR1 + IR2 + IR3
        R = REFUNC(V,I)
        POWER = PFUNC(V,I,THETA)
        CALL OUTSUB(IR1,IR2,IR3,I,R,POWER)
        STOP
        END


**********************************************************
*                                                        *
*   OUTPUT THE COMPUTED VALUES                           *
*                                                        *
**********************************************************
*                                                        *
*   ARGUMENTS:                                           *
*                                                        *
*     CR1,CR2,CR3 - COMPUTED CURRENTS (AMPS)             *
*     CR          - TOTAL CURRENT (AMPS)                 *
*     RES         - EFFECTIVE RESISTANCE (OHMS)          *
*     POWATT      - POWER LOSS ACROSS CIRCUIT (VOLTS)*
*                                                        *
*   OUTPUT VARIABLES:                                    *
*                                                        *
*     CR1,CR2,CR3 - COMPUTED CURRENTS (AMPS)             *
*     CR          - TOTAL CURRENT (AMPS)                 *
*     RES         - EFFECTIVE RESISTANCE (OHMS)          *
*     POWATT      - POWER LOSS ACROSS CIRCUIT (VOLTS)*
*                                                        *
**********************************************************

        SUBROUTINE OUTSUB (CR1,CR2,CR3,CR,RES,POWATT)
        REAL CR1,CR2,CR3,CR,RES,POWATT

        WRITE (*,1000) CR1,CR2,CR3
1000    FORMAT(/1X,'CURRENT ACROSS RESISTANCE R1 ='
       1        ,F8.2
       2        /1X,'CURRENT ACROSS RESISTANCE R2='
       3        ,F8.2
       4        /1X,'CURRENT ACROSS RESISTANCE R3 ='
       5        ,F8.2)
        WRITE(*,2000) CR,RES,POWATT
2000    FORMAT(1X,'TOTAL CURRENT =',F8.2
       1        /1X,'EFFECTIVE RESISTANCE =',F8.2
       2        /1X,'POWER DROP =',F8.2)
        RETURN
        END
```

Output

```
INPUT DATA
220. 75.  100. 50.  30.

          OUTPUT DATA

CURRENT ACROSS RESISTANCE R1 =    2.93
CURRENT ACROSS RESISTANCE R2 =    2.20
CURRENT ACROSS RESISTANCE R3 =    4.40
TOTAL CURRENT =    9.53
EFFECTIVE RESISTANCE =    23.08
POWER DROP = 1816.34
```

5.6.8 Current in Series Circuit

Problem

Write a program to compute the current in an AC circuit that has three resistances in series. Compute the voltage drops across the resistances.

Method

Input the voltage V and the resistances R1, R2, and R3. Use a function to compute the voltage drop across each resistance. Use a subroutine to output the current and the voltage drops. The circuit is as follows:

effective resistance $R = R1 + R2 + R3$ (ohms)

current $I = \dfrac{V}{R}$ (amps)

voltage drop across R1 $V1 = I\,R1$

voltage drop across R2 $V2 = I\,R2$

voltage drop across R3 $V3 = I\,R3$

total voltage $V = V1 + V2 + V3$

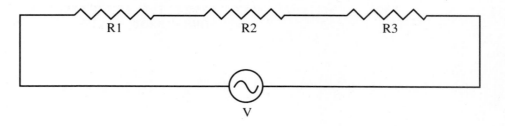

Program

```
***********************************************************
*                                                         *
*   COMPUTE THE CURRENT AND VOLTAGE DROP IN AN AC         *
*   SERIES CIRCUIT                                        *
*                                                         *
***********************************************************
*                                                         *
*   INPUT VARIABLES:                                      *
*                                                         *
*      VOLTAG   - VOLTAGE OF CIRCUIT (VOLTS)              *
*      R1,R2,R3 - RESISTANCES IN SERIES (OHMS)            *
*                                                         *
*   STATEMENT FUNCTIONS:                                  *
*                                                         *
*      VOLTDP   - VOLTAGE DROP ACROSS RESISTOR (VOLTS)*
*                                                         *
*   SUBPROGRAMS:                                          *
*                                                         *
*      SUBOUT   - OUTPUT SUBROUTINE                       *
*                                                         *
***********************************************************
        REAL VOLTAG,R1,R2,R3,R,I
        REAL VR1,VR2,VR3,V,CI,RES

        VOLTDP(CI,RES) = CI * RES

        WRITE (*,1000)
1000    FORMAT(1X,'INPUT DATA')
        READ (*,1500) VOLTAG,R1,R2,R3
1500    FORMAT(4F8.0)
        WRITE (*,1600)
1600    FORMAT(40X,'OUTPUT DATA')
        R = R1 + R2 + R3
        I = VOLTAG / R
        VR1 = VOLTAG(I,R1)
        VR2 = VOLTDP(I,R2)
        VR3 = VOLTDP(I,R3)
        V = VR1 + VR2 + VR3
        IF(ABS(V - VOLTAG) .LE. .001) THEN
           CALL SUBOUT(I,VR1,VR2,VR3)
        ELSE
           WRITE (*,2000)
2000       FORMAT(30X,'ERROR IN COMPUTATION')
        ENDIF
        STOP
        END
```

```
***********************************************************
*                                                         *
*   OUTPUT THE CIRCUIT VALUES                             *
*                                                         *
***********************************************************
*                                                         *
*   ARGUMENTS:                                            *
*                                                         *
*      IC          - CURRENT (AMPS)                       *
*      VDPR1,VDPR2,VDPR3 - VOLTAGE DROPS (VOLTS)          *
*                                                         *
*   OUTPUT VARIABLES:                                     *
*                                                         *
*      IC          - CURRENT (AMPS)                       *
*      VDPR1,VDPR2,VDPR3 - VOLTAGE DROPS (VOLTS)          *
*                                                         *
***********************************************************

       SUBROUTINE SUBOUT(IC,VDPR1,VDPR2,VDPR3)
       REAL IC,VDPR1,VDPR2,VDPR3

       WRITE (*,1000) IC,VDPR1,VDPR2,VDPR3
1000   FORMAT(/25X,'CURRENT IN THE CIRCUIT ='
     1        ,F8.2
     2        /25X,'VOLTAGE DROP ACROSS ',
     3        'RESISTANCE R1 =',F8.2
     4        /25X,'VOLTAGE DROP ACROSS ',
     5        'RESISTANCE R2 =',F8.2
     6        /25X,'VOLTAGE DROP ACROSS ',
     7        'RESISTANCE R3 =',F8.2)
       RETURN
       END
```

Output

```
INPUT DATA
220.bbbb|50.bbbbb|100.bbbb|150.bbbb|
                                   OUTPUT DATA

                CURRENT IN THE CIRCUIT =    0.73
                VOLTAGE DROP ACROSS RESISTANCE R1 =   36.67
                VOLTAGE DROP ACROSS RESISTANCE R2 =   73.33
                VOLTAGE DROP ACROSS RESISTANCE R3 =  110.00
```

Chapter Summary

FORTRAN provides several types of subprograms for implementing modules of a program. Three of them were presented in this chapter. The general form of the definition of a statement function is:

```
funcname(par1,par2,...,parn) = expr
```

A statement function is local to the routine in which it is defined. It may be used many times in that routine, but cannot be passed to other routines. Besides having parameters, a statement function may refer to other variables of the routine. If a parameter name duplicates the name of the other variable, the other variable is inaccessible for the duration of the execution of the statement function. Statement functions may not be explicitly typed.

The basic differences between function and subroutine subprograms are:

Functions	*Subroutines*
Invoked by using as a variable	Invoked by a CALL statement
Returns one value through function name	May return values through argument list
Can only return scalar values	Can return any type of value
Should not alter parameters unless returns error flag	May alter parameters
Used to calculate value	Used for input/output or to alter storage by assignment
Has a data type associated with the function name	Has no relationship to any specific data type
Must be written with parentheses even when there are no arguments	Are written without parenthesis if there are no arguments

The general form of a function call is:

```
funcname(arg1,arg2,...,argn)
```

The general form of a function subprogram is:

```
type FUNCTION funcname(arg1,arg2,...,argn)
 .
 .
 .
funcname = expr
 .
 .
 .
RETURN
END
```

A value must be assigned to the name of a function subprogram at least one place in the routine.

The general form of a subroutine call is:

```
CALL subname(arg1,arg2,...,argn)
```

The general form of a subroutine subprogram is:

```
SUBROUTINE subname(arg1,arg2,...,argn)
.
.
.
RETURN
END
```

The subroutine name is used only in calls to the subroutine. Values are returned to the calling program by assigning them to parameters.

Data can also be communicated between the main program and the subroutines and functions through the use of common areas with the COMMON statement. The COMMON statement has the form:

```
COMMON var1,var2,var3 ...,varn
```

When counters or other local variables must be retained from one invocation of a subprogram to another, the SAVE statement is used.

Exercises

1. Write and test a function subprogram COMB(N,K) to calculate the number of combinations of N objects taken K at a time. The formula is:

$$C_{n,k} = \frac{n!}{k! \, (n-k)!}$$

   where $n! = 1 \times 2 \times 3 \ldots \times n$

   Do not write a separate subprogram to calculate n! because for most values of n, it is too large to store in an integer variable.

2. Write a main program to calculate the stress and strain in a steel rod of diameter D (in.) and length L (in.) for compression loads P of 10,000 pounds to 1000,000 pounds in increments of 10,000. The modulus of elasticity E for steel is 30×10^6. Use a subroutine for the computations and a separate subroutine to print the load, stress, and strain. The formulas are:

$$\text{stress} \quad p = \frac{P}{A} \qquad\qquad \text{where} \quad A = \pi R^2$$

$$\text{elongated or shortened length} \quad \Delta L = \frac{p \, L}{E}$$

$$\text{strain} \quad e = \frac{\Delta L}{L}$$

3. Write a function subprogram to compute the tip speed of a propeller whose shaft speed S varies from 1000 to 10,000 revolutions per minute in increments of 1000. Pass the diameter D of the propeller to the function from a driver program, which also prints the tip speeds. The angular velocity in radians/sec. is computed from the formula

$$\omega = \frac{2\pi S}{60}$$

4. Write a subroutine to compute and print the mass M of air in a balloon inflated to V cu ft, at P pounds of pressure, at a temperature of T degrees. Call it from a driver program that reads values for the pressure P, volume V, and temperature T. The formula relating the variables is:

$$PV = .42\ M(T + 460)$$

5. Write a main program to input the inner radius Ri and the outer radius Ro of a hollow steel sphere and call a function subprogram to compute the volume of steel in the sphere. The formula for the volume of a sphere is:

$$V = \frac{4\pi R^3}{3}$$

6. Write a subroutine to compute and print the retarding force required to stop a train of weight m lbs. traveling at velocity V mi/sec within distances of 100, 200, 300, 400, and 500 ft. Use a driver program to input the weight M and velocity V. The formula for acceleration is:

$$a = \frac{V_f^2 - V_0^2}{2d} \qquad \text{where} \quad \text{a is acceleration}$$

$$V_f \text{ is final velocity}$$

$$V_0 \text{ is initial velocity}$$

$$d \text{ is distance}$$

retarding force $F = ma$

7. Write a function subroutine to compute the total mass of nitrogen in a storage tank. The capacity of the tank is V cu ft. The tank contains V_1 cu ft of liquid nitrogen at temperature T°R and V_g cu ft of nitrogen gas at T°R. Use a driver program to test the function.

The specific volume of liquid nitrogen is S_1 ft³/lb.m.
The specific volume of gaseous nitrogen is S_g ft³/lb.m.
The mass is computed as follows:

$$\text{for liquid nitrogen} \quad m_1 = \frac{V_1}{S_1}\ \text{lbm}$$

$$\text{for gaseous nitrogen} \quad m_g = \frac{V_g}{S_g}\ \text{lbm}$$

total mass $m = m_1 + m_g$

8. Write a subroutine to compute the amount of steel and concrete required to build a cooling tank having internal length l, width w, and height h. The wall thickness and the floor thickness are t_1 and t_2 respectively. Assume the ratio of steel to concrete is 1:5. Print the total steel and concrete required from the driver program.

6

One-Dimensional Arrays

Objective: To process collections of data stored as lists and vectors.

*A*n array is a simple, elegant, yet powerful data structure in FORTRAN 77. Arrays provide a convenient way of storing collections of data in list form: lists of measurements, names, real or integer numbers, items, prices, weights, and so on. The data items stored in the form of a list must all be of the same data type and represent the same thing. Engineering and scientific data in list form can be conveniently stored and manipulated by using arrays.

Certain operations performed on the data, such as sorting, require that the entire list be in memory. The arrays in FORTRAN make it possible to store the entire set of data in the form of a list before processing it.

An array is a named collection of memory locations. Each location, called an element of the array, is identified by a unique number called the index. The following example shows an array INUM that has five named elements, INUM(1), INUM(2), INUM(3), INUM(4), and INUM(5). The storage organization of this array is as follows:

INUM(1)
INUM(2)
INUM(3)
INUM(4)
INUM(5)

The number of memory locations allocated for INUM is five. They are named INUM(1), INUM(2), INUM(3), INUM(4), and INUM(5).

The arithmetic and logical operations that can be performed on single variables can also be performed on elements of an array. Numeric data as well as character data can be stored in arrays.

6.1 Concept of One-Dimensional Arrays

In mathematical formulas, a subscripted variable is used to indicate a particular one of a number of possible values. For example, the altitude of a rocket on takeoff is represented as h_0 where the subscript 0 represents time zero. At time t, its altitude is represented as h_t, where t is the subscript. In FORTRAN programming, the subscript must be an integer. In ordinary usage, ten different measurements of altitude could be written as:

h_t t$= 1,2,3,4,5,6,7,8,9,10$

representing the measurements h_1, h_2, h_3, . . ., h_{10}. The subscript values do not represent the elapsed time, but the order of the measurements. The rocket velocities corresponding to these altitudes would be:

v_t t$= 1,2,3,4,5,6,7,8,9,10$

representing the velocity values v_1, v_2, v_3, . . ., v_{10}. Velocity v_1 is at altitude h_1, velocity v_2 at altitude h_2, and so forth. Each value of the subscript is used to identify corresponding values of altitude and velocity. Under certain circumstances the subscripts might have meanings other than that of ordering and identifying array elements. If the altitudes and velocities were being calculated for 1 min, 2 min, 3 min, . . . after takeoff, then the subscripts would accurately represent time as well as order. Notice that each value of h_t must be measured in the same units and represent the same physical element—the altitude of the rocket. In a similar fashion, each value of v_t represents the same physical element and is measured in the same units, for example, miles per second.

If there is any natural order to the values, an order given by time or distance, or a desired output order such as that of cost, it should be the basis of storage. Many sorting and searching methods have been developed for changing the order of data.

6.1.1 Subscripts and Subscripted Variables

The name of a one-dimensional array can be used with a subscript as a subscripted variable. The name by itself, for example V, represents the whole array. Used in a subscripted variable, for example V_3, it represents a single element of the array.

x_5 names the fifth element of the array x
a_i names the ith element of the array a

These are abstract notations until values have been assigned to i and to the specific array elements referenced.

In programming languages, there are two ways to represent subscripted variables. The components of an abstract array x written mathematically as

x_i i = 1 to 10

can be represented as

```
X1, X2, X3, X4, X5, X6, X7, X8, X9, X10
```

which are ten different variables, related in the programmer's eye because of their similar names, but unrelated in the computer's understanding. This form is often convenient for small arrays. The coefficients of a quadratic equation could be called C1, C2, C3 rather than A, B, and C. But variables named this way are not truly subscripted. XI cannot represent them, but is itself just another variable. If

x_i i = 1 to 10

is represented as

```
X(1), X(2), X(3), X(4), X(5), X(6), X(7), X(8),
X(9), X(10)
```

then X is the collective name of the 10 elements, each one of which is identified by a unique subscript. Any one of them can be represented by X(I) provided I is given a value from 1 to 10. Using a variable or an expression as a subscript and changing its value provides a convenient and systematic way of accessing the array elements.

The short statement

```
WRITE (*,*) X
```

is equivalent to:

```
WRITE (*,*) X(1),X(2),X(3),X(4),X(5),X(6),X(7),
            X(8),X(9),X(10)
```

The DO-loop

```
      DO 50 I = 1,5
         X(I) = 0
50       CONTINUE
```

is equivalent to:

```
      X(1) = 0
      X(2) = 0
      X(3) = 0
      X(4) = 0
      X(5) = 0
```

An array subscript must be of the integer type, but it may be a constant, variable, or expression. The following are legitimate subscripted variables:

Algebraic form	FORTRAN form
X_5	X(5)
Y_i	Y(I)
Z_{x+1}	Z(X + 1) provided X is integer
W_{2i+j}	W(2*I + J)

6.1.2 Declaration of Arrays (INTEGER, REAL)

A declaration statement is essential when allocating storage to an array variable. Earlier versions of FORTRAN used a DIMENSION statement, which is still available in FORTRAN 77 for recompiling old programs. But it can be eliminated by using the type declaration statements to declare the array type and its size. In this book we use type statements to declare arrays and their size.

Programming Hint

> Reliability: Use type declaration statements to declare storage for arrays.

The general forms of the declaration statement are:

type variable (ub)
type variable (lb:ub)

where the type could be real, integer, double precision, complex, logical, or character. We present mainly real and integer variable types in this chapter.

The variable name is a symbolic name for the array as a whole. An array name follows the FORTRAN naming rules: it can be at most six characters long; the first character must be a letter and the other characters may be letters or digits. The upper bound is ub and the lower bound is lb; the upper bound must be greater than or equal to the lower bound. When the lower bound is not specified, it defaults to one; in which case the upper bound must be positive.

The declaration of the real array variable

```
REAL X(8)
```

is equivalent to:

```
REAL X(1:8)
```

The declaration of the integer array variable

```
INTEGER VELCTY(8)
```

is equivalent to:

```
INTEGER VELCTY(1:8)
```

Declarations of arrays may be combined into a single statement:

```
REAL VELCTY(100), PRESSR(10), TEMPR(100)
```

is equivalent to:

```
REAL PRESSR(10)
REAL TEMPR(100)
REAL VELCTY(100)
```

All these arrays have a subscript lower bound of one.

*Programming
Hint*

> It is often useful to give an array a larger size than necessary.

The following examples show lower bounds other than one:

```
INTEGER A(3:10),B(-5:5),C(-8:-3)
```

is equivalent to:

```
INTEGER A(3:10)
INTEGER B(-5:5)
INTEGER C(-8:-3)
```

Notice that the subscripts can be positive, negative, or zero, and that the lower bounds are less than the upper bounds in all these examples.

The declarations of arrays and single variables can be combined as follows:

```
REAL X(20), Y(20), TOTAL
INTEGER ICON, JMAX(10), VAL(20)
LOGICAL P(100), Q(50), R
```

Notice that arrays and single variables may be declared in the same statement. Storage for arrays is set up before program execution begins. Any type declarations are processed by the compiler while the program is being compiled. Therefore, if changes need to be made in the size of an array, the program must be recompiled.

6.1.3 Implied DO-loops

A special form of DO-loop can be used in DATA statements and in array input and output statements. This is known as the implied DO-loop because the DO and

CONTINUE statements are implicit rather than explicit. This form of DO-loop is used primarily to initialize, read, and write arrays.

The form of the implied DO-loop is:

(I/O sublist, var = v1,v2,v3)

where var is the loop index variable, v1 is the initial value, v2 is the final value, v3 is the step size.

Simple Implied DO-loops

The simple implied DO-loop is a loop with a single index variable and one or more values to be input or output. For example:

	Values of	
(I, I = 1, 10)	I	1, 2, . . . , 10
(SQRT(X), X = 1.0,25.0)	SQRT(X)	1.0, 1.414, . . . , 5.0
(K, K*K, K = 1, 5)	K,K*K	1 1, 2 4, . . . , 5 25
(N, N = 5, 0, -1)	N	5, 4, . . . , 0
(A, A = 1.0,10.0,2.0)	A	1.0, 3.0, . . . , 9.0
('*',J, J=0,5)	'*',J	* 0, * 1, . . . , * 5

When the implied DO-loop is used inside a list-directed output statement, all the values are printed on a single line, unless there is not enough space or the format indicates different spacing (in a formatted output statement). Given

```
WRITE (*,*) (I, I=1,10)
```

the output is:

```
1    2    3    4    5    6    7    8    9    10
```

If the printing is controlled by a regular DO-loop,

```
      DO 10 I = 1, 10
         WRITE (*,*) I
10       CONTINUE
```

the output is aligned vertically, one value on each line:

```
   1
   2
   3
   4
   5
   6
   7
   8
   9
  10
```

Given

```
    WRITE (*,*) (I,2*I,3*I, I=1,4)
```

the output is:

```
  1    2    3    2    4    6    3    6    9    4    8    12
```

Given

```
        WRITE (*,1000) (I,I=1,16)
  1000  FORMAT (1X,16I5)
```

the output is:

```
    1    2    3    4    5    6    7    8    9   10   11   12   13   14   15   16
```

printed on a single line in 16 fields of five columns each.
    Given

```
        WRITE (*,1000) (I,I=1,16)
  1000  FORMAT (2(1X,8I5))
```

or

```
  1000  FORMAT (1X,8I5)
```

the output is:

```
      1    2    3    4    5    6    7    8
      9   10   11   12   13   14   15   16
```

printed on two lines, each having eight fields of five columns each.
    An implied DO-loop can be used to number columns of output:

```
        WRITE (*,1000) (K,K=1,5)
  1000  FORMAT (5(5X,'COLUMN',I2))
```

or to number rows:

```
        WRITE (*,1000) (K,K=1,5)
  1000  FORMAT (/5X,'ROW',I2)
```

Nested Implied DO-loops

Nested implied DO-loops are similar to ordinary nested DO-loops:

```
      DO 20 I = 1,2
        DO 10 J = 1,3
```

```
            WRITE (*,*), I,J
10       CONTINUE
20     CONTINUE
```

and

```
    WRITE (*,*)((I,J,J=1,3),I=1,2)
```

produce the same values, but these values are spaced differently in the output. Every time a print statement executes, a new output line starts. Therefore the output from the ordinary nested DO-loops is:

```
    1       1
    1       2
    1       3
    2       1
    2       2
    2       3
```

while the output from the implied DO-loops is:

```
 1    1    1    2    1    3    2    1    2    2    2    3
```

In both examples the inner index J varies most rapidly and all the J values are printed for each value of the outer index I.

Given

```
        WRITE (*,1000) (I,(J, J=1,3),I=1,2)
1000    FORMAT (1X,I5,5X,3I5)
```

the output is:

```
    1       1    2    3
    2       1    2    3
```

The I value is being used to number the lines, each of which contains all the values.

6.1.4 Storage Allocation and Access

A type declaration statement is used to allocate storage for an array. Since this is done at compile time, the maximum amount of storage needed must be allocated. In the following example, five numbers at most can be stored under the name X:

REAL X(5)

```
X(1) ┌─────────┐
X(2) ├─────────┤
X(3) ├─────────┤
X(4) ├─────────┤
X(5) └─────────┘
```

Notice that five consecutive storage locations are allocated to the variable X. Since the declared type is real, each storage location can hold one real number. There are five array elements in all.

The following storage arrangements show storage for arrays having explicit lower bounds:

REAL A(−5:5)   REAL B(3:10)

```
A(−5) ┌─────────┐      B(3)  ┌─────────┐
A(−4) ├─────────┤      B(4)  ├─────────┤
A(−3) ├─────────┤      B(5)  ├─────────┤
A(−2) ├─────────┤      B(6)  ├─────────┤
A(−1) ├─────────┤      B(7)  ├─────────┤
A(0)  ├─────────┤      B(8)  ├─────────┤
A(1)  ├─────────┤      B(9)  ├─────────┤
A(2)  ├─────────┤      B(10) └─────────┘
A(3)  ├─────────┤
A(4)  ├─────────┤
A(5)  └─────────┘
```

REAL C(−6:−2)

```
C(−6) ┌─────────┐
C(−5) ├─────────┤
C(−4) ├─────────┤
C(−3) ├─────────┤
C(−2) └─────────┘
```

Notice that the array A has 11 elements; B has eight elements; C has five elements. The subscript indicates the relative position in terms of the order of the elements, not the absolute position in the array.

Array Access

Arrays may be accessed in three different ways: as a whole, by selecting one element, or by indicating a range of elements to be selected one by one in a particular order.

Given the declaration A(10),

the name	A	accesses	the entire array for input/output
	A(8)	"	the eighth element of the array
	(A(I),I=1,4)	"	the first four elements

(A(I),I = 1,10)	"	all elements of the array
(A(I),I = 1,10,2)	"	all elements with odd subscripts
(A(I),I = 2,10,2)	"	all elements with even subscripts
(A(I),I = 10,1, − 1)	"	all elements, backwards

Given the declaration X(− 2:7),

the name X	accesses	the entire array
X(5)	"	the eighth element of the array
(X(I),I = − 2,1)	"	the first four elements
(X(I),I = − 2,7)	"	all elements of the array

If the array has been declared larger than necessary, or if some of the array elements have not been given values, take care not to access any undefined elements. Also, be careful that array subscripts do not exceed the bounds declared for the array in the type statement.

Programming Warning

Out-of-bounds subscripts will cause serious errors.

When subscripts are being calculated or obtained from the input, they must be validated before being used to access an array.

The size of an array is the number of elements it contains. If an array has a default lower bound of one, its size is the same as its upper bound.

Declaration	Size
REAL X(10)	10
REAL X(20)	20
REAL X(150)	150

But if an array is declared with an explicit lower bound, its size is computed as follows:

$$\text{size} = \text{upper bound} - \text{lower bound} + 1$$

The following examples show this:

Declaration	Size
INTEGER X(3:10)	$10 - 3 + 1 = 8$
INTEGER X(− 6:8)	$8 - (-6) + 1 = 15$
INTEGER X(− 20: − 5)	$-20 - (-5) + 1 = 16$

6.1.5 Initialization of Arrays (DATA statement)

Arrays that have constant values—that contain tables needed for calculations—can be initialized by the DATA statement. Values to be changed, such as initial zeros, may also be initialized through the use of the DATA statement. This is efficient because the initialization takes place at compile time. The DATA statement should not be used to initialize constants. PARAMETER statement should be used for single-value constants, DATA for arrays. The general form of the DATA statement is:

DATA arrname/value1,value2,...,valuen/

The number of values must equal the number of elements in the array arrname. This is shown in the following examples:

```
INTEGER NUM(10)
DATA NUM/0,21,2,34,5,61,-6,1293,17,9/
```

initializes the integer array as:

NUM(1)	0
NUM(2)	21
NUM(3)	2
NUM(4)	34
NUM(5)	5
NUM(6)	61
NUM(7)	−6
NUM(8)	1293
NUM(9)	17
NUM(10)	9

and

```
REAL X(5)
DATA X/2.5,3.2,6.5,-7.9,12.7/
```

initializes the real array as:

X(1)	2.5
X(2)	3.2
X(3)	6.5
X(4)	−7.9
X(5)	12.7

A repetition factor can be used to condense a list of values where several are alike.

Given

```
INTEGER X(5), Y(8)
```

then

```
DATA X/5*0/        is equivalent to  DATA X/0,0,0,0,0/
DATA Y/3*1,5*-1/   is equivalent to  DATA Y/1,1,1,-1,-1,
                                          -1,-1,-1/
```

The first of these statements initializes all five elements of the array X to zero; the second initializes the first three elements of Y to one and the other five elements to minus one.

If only a few array elements are to be initialized, the individual elements may be named:

```
REAL A(5)
DATA A(1),A(3),A(4)/8.9,7.6,3.9/
```

initializes the real array as:

A(1)	8.9
A(2)	/ / / / /
A(3)	7.6
A(4)	3.9
A(5)	/ / / / /

The elements that are not assigned values by the DATA statement are undefined. In this example, A(2) and A(5) are undefined.

Implied DO-Loop in DATA Statement

An implied DO-loop may perform systematic initialization of parts of an array.

```
INTEGER M(10)
DATA (M(I), I=1,5)/5*0/
```

initializes the first five elements of the array M, giving them the value zero. The other five elements are undefined.

```
INTEGER M(10)
DATA (M(I), I=1,10,2)/5*0/
```

initializes the elements of the array with odd subscripts, giving them the value zero.

6.1.6 Review Questions

1. Write declaration statements for the following subscripted variables and give the size of each array:

   a. real X_i i = 1 through 15, real Y_j j = 1 through 25
   b. integer A_n n = 1 through 8, integer B_j j = 8 through 35
   c. logical P_k k = -20 through -5, logical Q_m m = 15 through 25
   d. real W_n n = -30 through -15, integer Y_m m = -3 through 45,
      real Z_k k = 20 through 30

2. Draw a picture of the storage allocation for each of the following variables:

   a. REAL A(5)
   b. INTEGER B($-15:-8$)
   c. REAL C(8:12)
   d. LOGICAL D($-1:6$)

3. Write DO statements for accessing all elements of each of the following arrays, in increasing order of subscripts:

   a. REAL X(20)
   b. INTEGER Y(10:30)
   c. INTEGER Z($-15:-4$)
   d. REAL W($-5:25$)

6.2 Input of One-Dimensional Arrays

Arrays may be input as a whole, referring to the array name, or element by element, using a subscript to identify each element. Either method may use list-directed or formatted input. If the array is input by array name, there must be enough data to fill the entire array. If an array is to be partly filled with data, or if a very large array is being filled so that the data may be counted incorrectly, subscripts should be used. Subscripts should also be used if the order of the data values is not the same as the order in which the values are to be stored.

Data for a one-dimensional array can be thought of as a list of values or a vector. These values should be entered in an easy-to-use form, either all on a single line or arranged in columns.

6.2.1 List-Directed Input

If data values are entered separated by commas or blanks, with no regard to spacing, no input format is used. The computer will locate as many values as needed, continuing to as many records of input as necessary.

Given the code segment

```
REAL X(5)
READ (*,*) X
```

or

```
READ (*,*) X(1),X(2),X(3),X(4),X(5)
```

or

```
READ (*,*) (X(K), K = 1,5)
```

and the input

```
8.5,   10.6,   128.05,   31.2,   6.4
```

or

```
8.5
```

```
10.6
```

```
128.05
```

```
31.2
```

```
6.4
```

or

```
8.5    10.6    128.05
```

```
31.2,    6.4
```

the values stored are:

X(1)	8.5
X(2)	10.6
X(3)	128.05
X(4)	31.2
X(5)	6.4

The five values needed for the array X may be entered as a single record, several records, or as many records as desired. The first five values found are used. They are stored starting at the beginning of the array, in the order of increasing subscript values.

If only the array name is used, the first value is placed in the first position of the array, the second value in the second position, and so forth, regardless of the values of the subscripts. If subscripts are used, they control the placement of the values.

Given the input data

```
8.5    10.6    128.05    31.2    6.4
```

and the code segment

```
REAL Y(6:10)
READ (*,*) Y
```

the values stored are:

Y(6)	8.5
Y(7)	10.6
Y(8)	128.05
Y(9)	31.2
Y(10)	6.4

With the code segment

```
REAL Y(6:10)
READ (*,*) Y(8),Y(9),Y(10),Y(6),Y(7)
```

the values stored are:

Y(6)	31.2
Y(7)	6.4
Y(8)	8.5
Y(9)	10.6
Y(10)	128.05

With the code segment

```
REAL Y(6:10)
READ*, (Y(K), K=10,6,-1)
```

the values stored are:

Y(6)	6.4
Y(7)	31.2
Y(8)	128.05
Y(9)	10.6
Y(10)	8.5

Programming Warning

When the array name is used in the input list without subscripts, if there is not enough input data to fill the entire array, an error will occur.

When an explicit DO-loop is used to input the values of an array, the input list of the READ statement controls the number of data values to be taken from each input record.

Given the code segment

```
      INTEGER ARAY(5)
      DO 10 I = 1,5
         READ (*,*) ARAY(I)
10    CONTINUE
```

and the input data

```
132
```

```
9      31
```

```
-125
```

```
16
```

```
8
```

the values stored are:

ARAY(1)	132
ARAY(2)	9
ARAY(3)	− 125
ARAY(4)	16
ARAY(5)	8

Since the READ statement is executed five times, it uses five separate records of input. Since the input list in the READ statement only contains one variable, only one value is read from each record. Any extra input values are ignored. This means that the value 31 in the second line of input is ignored.

When there is not enough input data to fill the array, subscripting must be used.

Given the code segment

```
      REAL X(10)
      DO 10 I=1,6
        READ (*,*) X(I)
10      CONTINUE
```

only six input values are needed. Unless array elements $X(7)$, $X(8)$, $X(9)$, and $X(10)$ have already been given values, they are undefined. If they already have values, those values are not changed. If the exact number of data values is uncertain, the following form should be used:

```
      INTEGER NUM(10)
      I = 1

*     DO WHILE(I .LE. 10)

5     IF (I .LE. 10) THEN
        READ (*,1000,END= 20) NUM(I)
1000    FORMAT(I5)
        I = I + 1
        GO TO 5
      ENDIF

*     ENDDO

20    CONTINUE
      I = I - 1
```

Notice that when this code completes executing, the variable I is equal to the number of values in the array.

When more than one measurement is being taken at a time, the input may consist of several sets of data. For example:

Length	Weight
14	2.5
23	3.7
41	9.9
62	0.0
70	6.8
80	7.4

The data is more conveniently input as matching pairs of length and weight. There must be two arrays; the input data alternates between them.

```
14   2.5
```

```
23   3.7
```

```
41   9.9
```

```
62   0.0
```

```
70   6.8
```

```
80   7.4
```

These values can be read using the following code:

```
      INTEGER LNG(6)
      REAL WT(6)
      DO 10 I = 1,6
         READ (*,*) LNG(I),WT(I)
10    CONTINUE
```

or

```
14   2.5   23   3.7   41   9.9   62   0.0   70   6.8   80   7.4
```

which can be read using

```
INTEGER LNG(6)
REAL  WT(6)
READ (*,*)(LNG(I),WT(I), I=1,6)
```

For each value of I in the implied DO statement, a value of LNG and a value of WT is read.

6.2.2 Formatted Input

Array input is formatted when the programmer needs to control the spacing of the input data.

Programming Warning

> Array input formats must match the type, number, and arrangement of array elements being read.

Given the program segment

```
      REAL X(5)
      READ (*,1000) X
1000  FORMAT(F4.0)
```

there must be five values, one on each record. For example:

```
-.75
```

```
9.65
```

```
 .07
```

```
6.54
```

```
7.82
```

Given the program segment

```
      REAL X(5)
      READ (*,1000) X
1000  FORMAT(5F4.0)
```

there must be five values on a single record. For example:

```
-.759.65 .076.547.82
```

Given the program segment

```
      REAL X(5)
      READ (*,1000) X
1000  FORMAT(3F4.0)
```

there must be five values, at most three on the first record and two on the second.

|-|.|7|5|9|.|6|5|ь|.|0|7|

|ь|.|5|4|7|.|8|2|

In these examples, only one READ statement is executed. When the format contains fewer than five field specifications, the format repeats until five values have been read. When the format contains more field specifications than needed, the extra field specifications are ignored.

Programming Warning

> Every time a format is repeated, a new input record is used.

Using explicit indexing, only one data value is read from each record.

```
      REAL TEMP(5)
      DO 10 I = 1,5
         READ (*,1000) TEMP(I)
1000     FORMAT(F5.1)
10    CONTINUE
```

is equivalent to

```
      REAL TEMP(5)
      READ (*,1000) TEMP
1000  FORMAT(F5.1)
```

Using an implied DO loop, the format controls the number of data values read from each record.

```
      REAL TEMP(5)
      READ (*,1000) (TEMP(I),I=1,5)
1000  FORMAT(5F5.1)
```

is equivalent to

```
      REAL TEMP(5)
      READ (*,1000) TEMP
1000  FORMAT(5F5.1)
```

In this case, five data values are read from one input record.

```
      REAL TEMP(5)
      READ (*,1000) (TEMP(I),I=1,5)
1000  FORMAT(2F5.1)
```

is equivalent to

```
          REAL TEMP(5)
          READ (*,1000) TEMP
1000   FORMAT(2F5.1)
```

In this case, two data values are read from each input record, therefore three input records are needed.

6.2.3 Review Questions

1. Write the list-directed input statements to read a list of data values into an array CONS(7). The data values are 10.5, 8.6, 5.2, 9.7, 20.7, 2.5, −6.9. Show the input statements as well as the input records.

   a. input using the array name only
   b. input using an explicit DO-loop
   c. input using an implied DO-loop

2. Write the formatted input statements to read a list of data values into an array VAL(5). The data values are 12.395, 16.728, 125.625, 17.9, −28.63. Show the input statements as well as the input records. Use as few input records as possible.

   a. input using the array name only
   b. input using an explicit DO-loop
   c. input using an implied DO-loop

3. Given an array dimensioned as X(20)
   a. and the input statement

```
          READ (*,1000) X
```

   how many input records are needed with each of the following formats?

   i.   FORMAT (F8.2)
   ii. FORMAT (5F8.2)
   iii. FORMAT (10F8.2)
   iv. FORMAT (7F8.2)

   b. and the input code

```
          DO 20 I=1,20
             READ (*,*) X(I)
20        CONTINUE
```

   how many input records are needed?
   c. and the input code

```
          DO 20 J=1,20
             READ (*,1000) X(J)
1000         FORMAT(2F8.2)
20        CONTINUE
```

   how many input records are needed?
   d. and the input statement

```
          READ (*,1000) (X(K), K=1,20)
```

   how many input records are needed with each of the following formats?
   i. FORMAT (F8.2)
   ii. FORMAT (5F8.2)

      iii. FORMAT (10F8.2)
      iv. FORMAT (7F8.2)

4. Write an input statement to read the following arrays X(20), Y(20), and Z(20) using implied DO-loops for the following cases:

  a. The X values are read first, the Y values are read next, and the Z values are read last.
  b. The values are in the order X(1), Y(1), Z(1), X(2), Y(2), Z(2), ...

5. For each of the following segments of code, what is the final value of K if the array is filled? If it is not filled?

a.
```
        INTEGER ARR(10)
        K = 0

*       DO WHILE (K .LT. 10)

10      IF(K.LT. 10) THEN
          K = K + 1
          READ (*,1000,END=20) ARR(K)
1000      FORMAT(I5)
          GO TO 10
        ENDIF

*       ENDDO

20      CONTINUE
```

b.
```
        INTEGER ARR(10)
        K = 1

*       DO WHILE (K .LE. 10)

10      IF(K.LE. 10) THEN
          READ (*,1000,END=20) ARR(K)
1000      FORMAT(I5)
          K = K + 1
          GO TO 10
        ENDIF

*       ENDDO

20      CONTINUE
```

c.
```
        INTEGER ARR(10)
        DO 10 K=1,10
          READ (*,1000,END=20) ARR(K)
1000      FORMAT(I5)
10      CONTINUE
20      CONTINUE
```

6.3 Output of One-Dimensional Arrays

The purpose of output is to produce some readable results, either printed on paper or displayed on a screen. One-dimensional arrays will usually be output either horizontally on a single line or vertically in a column. List-directed output provides a simple way of aligning data values in a column. Usually formatted output is needed for horizontal alignment because of the limited amount of space available. An array may be output either by using the name of the array or by indexing through the array one element at a time, as in input.

6.3.1 List-Directed Output

List-directed output of arrays assumes the use of the default field specifications. An array of just a few elements will fit on a single line, while a larger array will continue from one line to the next.

Given the program segments

```
REAL X(5)
WRITE (*,*) X
```

or

```
WRITE (*,*) (X(I), I=1,5)
```

and the values

X(1)	138.25
X(2)	326.78
X(3)	39.15
X(4)	−86.76
X(5)	158.62

the output is:

```
 138.25      326.78      39.15      -86.76      158.62
```

The entire array is printed in the order in which it is stored. Using the name of the array is equivalent to using an implied DO-loop when the entire array is to be printed.

Using an explicit DO-loop has the effect of printing each element of the array on a separate line. Given the program segment

```
      REAL X(5)
      DO 10 I=1,5
         WRITE (*,*) X(I)
10    CONTINUE
```

and the values

X(1)	138.25
X(2)	326.78
X(3)	39.15
X(4)	− 86.76
X(5)	158.62

the output is:

```
 138.25
 326.78
  39.15
 -86.76
 158.62
```

If there are several arrays they can be printed together and the lines numbered. Given the program segment

```
      INTEGER N(5)
      REAL X(5)
      DO 10 I=1,5
         WRITE (*,*) I,N(I),X(I)
10       CONTINUE
```

and the values

N(1)	14	X(1)	138.25
N(2)	26	X(2)	326.78
N(3)	−6	X(3)	39.15
N(4)	0	X(4)	− 86.76
N(5)	81	X(5)	158.62

the output is:

```
1       14      138.25
2       26      326.78
3       -6       39.15
4        0      -86.76
5       81      158.62
```

Or the order of the output can be changed by changing the order of the indexing.

Given the program segment

```
      INTEGER N(5)
      REAL X(5)
      DO 10 I=5,1,-1
         WRITE (*,*) I,N(I),X(I)
10       CONTINUE
```

and the values

N(1)	14		X(1)	138.25
N(2)	26		X(2)	326.78
N(3)	−6		X(3)	39.15
N(4)	0		X(4)	−86.76
N(5)	81		X(5)	158.62

the output is:

```
5        81      158.62
4         0      -86.76
3        -6       39.15
2        26      326.78
1        14      138.25
```

6.3.2 Formatted Output

If an array is to be printed in several columns or in a particular column of the output, a format is needed. The name of the array can be used without indexing, or a regular or implied DO-loop can be used.

Given the program segment

```
      REAL PRESR(10)
      WRITE (*,5000) PRESR
5000  FORMAT(1X,F6.2)
```

and the values

PRESR(1)	16.32
PRESR(2)	12.75
PRESR(3)	18.16
PRESR(4)	11.25
PRESR(5)	9.86
PRESR(6)	−3.75
PRESR(7)	11.88
PRESR(8)	39.75
PRESR(9)	18.32
PRESR(10)	16.98

the output will have one value on each line.

Given the format

```
5000  FORMAT(1X,2F6.2)
```

two values will be printed on each of five lines.

Given the format

```
5000  FORMAT(1X,5F8.2)
```

the output is:

```
ƀƀƀ16.32ƀƀƀ12.75ƀƀƀ18.16ƀƀƀ11.25ƀƀƀƀ9.86
ƀƀƀ-3.75ƀƀƀ11.88ƀƀƀ39.75ƀƀƀ18.32ƀƀƀ16.98
```

Notice that the number of values printed on each line is controlled by the repeat factor in the format. The spacing of the values is controlled by the field widths.

One-dimensional arrays may be printed using regular or implied DO-loops. The following examples show the output:

```
REAL X(6)
DATA X/1.5,6.5,8.5,9.6,3.5,12.8/
```

X(1)	1.5
X(2)	6.5
X(3)	8.5
X(4)	9.6
X(5)	3.5
X(6)	12.8

The output using regular DO-loops is:

```
      DO 10 I=1,6
         WRITE (*,1000) X(I)
1000     FORMAT(1X,F8.2)
10    CONTINUE
```

The WRITE statement is executed six times; therefore six lines of output are printed:

```
    1.50
    6.50
    8.50
    9.60
    3.50
   12.80
```

If a format such as (1X,3F8.2) were used, the output would be the same. The repeat factor of 3 would have no effect on the number of values printed on each line. The maximum number of values that can be printed on each line is controlled by the output statement; but the actual number of values printed on each line is provided by the FORMAT statement, as long as it is not greater than the maximum. With the regular DO-loop of the example above, only one value is printed, so the format repeat factor has no effect.

The elements of the array X can be numbered by printing the index as well as the values of the array:

```
      DO 10 I=1,6
         WRITE (*,1000) I,X(I)
1000     FORMAT(1X,I5,F8.1)
10    CONTINUE
```

The output is:

```
1       1.5
2       6.5
3       8.5
4       9.6
5       3.5
6      12.8
```

Notice that the output is printed in columns by using regular DO-loops, because every time the print statement executes, it causes the printer to print an entire line. Regular DO-loops will not print the output across the page. Instead, implied DO-loops must be used to print the output across the page. The following examples show the use of implied DO-loops:

```
      WRITE (*,1000) (X(I),I=1,6)
1000  FORMAT(1X,6F8.1)
```

```
    1.5      6.5      8.5      9.6      3.5     12.8
```

The WRITE statement is executed only once; therefore all the values can be printed on a single line, depending on the repeat factor. But the repeat factor indicates that six values should be printed on each line and there are exactly six values.

The following example shows the effect of the repeat factor in the format:

```
      WRITE (*,1000) (X(I),I=1,6)
1000  FORMAT(1X,3F8.1))
```

The output is:

```
    1.5      6.5      8.5
    9.6      3.5     12.8
```

Notice that the WRITE statement is executed only once as before, causing six values to be printed, but the format only permits three values to be printed on each line. After printing the first three values, the format repeats. This causes the next set of three values to be printed starting at the beginning of the next line. The repeat factor controls the number of values printed per line.

The values can be numbered in two ways when they are printed across the page:

```
      WRITE (*,1000) (I,X(I),I=1,6)
1000  FORMAT(1X,6(I4,F5.1))
```

The output is:

```
   1  1.5   2  6.5   3  8.5   4  9.6   5  3.5   6 12.8
```

Notice that the repeat factor 6 in the format prints all the six pairs of values in the WRITE statement across the page. In the following example, the indices are printed on the top line and the values on the next line:

```
        WRITE (*,1000) (I,I=1,6)
1000    FORMAT(1X,8I5)
        WRITE (*,2000) (X(I),I=1,6)
2000    FORMAT(1X,6F8.1)
```

The output is:

```
      1         2         3         4         5         6
    1.5       6.5       8.5       9.6       3.5      12.8
```

6.3.3 Review Questions

1. Show the output for each of the following implied DO-loops:

   a. WRITE (*,*) (I, I=1,20,2)
   b. WRITE (*,*) (JSUM+J, J=1,5)   assume JSUM=0 at beginning
   c. WRITE (*,*) (K, K=10,1,−1)
   d. WRITE (*,*) (2*M, M=5,10,2)
   e. WRITE (*,*) (N+4, N=1,5)

2. Show the output for each of the following nested implied DO-loops:
   a. WRITE (*,*) ((I,J,J=5,10),I=1,2)
   b. WRITE (*,*) ((I+J,J=1,4),I=1,3)
   c. WRITE (*,*) ((I+5,J*3,J=1,3),I=1,3)
   d. WRITE (*,*) ((I,J=1,4),I,I=1,3)

3. Show the output for each of the following formatted implied DO-loops:

   a.   WRITE (*,100) (M, M=1,15)
       100   FORMAT(1X,10I5)
   b.   WRITE (*,100) ((I,J,J=1,5),I=1,2)
       100   FORMAT(1X,5(I4,I2))
   c.   WRITE (*,100) ((K,L, L=1,10,2),K=1,3)
       100   FORMAT(1X,10I5)
   d.   WRITE (*,*) (I,I=1,5),(J,J=1,5)
       100   FORMAT(1X,10I5)
   e.   WRITE (*,100) (K, (L, L=1,5) ,K=1,3)
       100   FORMAT(1X,6I5)

4. Write the list-directed output statements to print the array declared as Y(20) using

   a. the array name only
   b. an explicit DO-loop
   c. an implied DO-loop

5. Describe the arrangement of the output produced by each of the following code segments:

   a. REAL Y(20)
      WRITE (*,*) (Y(I), I=1,10),(Y(I), I=11,20)

```
   b. REAL Y(20)
      WRITE (*,*) (Y(I), I=1,10)
      WRITE (*,*) (Y(I), I=11,20)

   c.        REAL Y(20)
             DO 10 I=1,10
               WRITE (*,*)Y(I)
      10      CONTINUE
             DO 20 I=11,20
               WRITE (*,*) Y(I)
      20      CONTINUE

   d.        REAL Y(20)
             DO 10 I=1,4
               WRITE (*,*)(Y(J), J=1,20,4)
      10      CONTINUE
```

6. Write the formatted output statements to print the array declared as VALUE(100) using field specification F6.2 and

   a. printing four values per line, using the array name only
   b. printing four values per line, using an explicit DO-loop
   c. printing four values per line, using an implied DO-loop

7. Write the formatted output statements to print the arrays declared as

   ```
   REAL XVAL(100),YVAL(100),ZVAL(100)
   ```

   in three columns, one for each array, using field specification F6.3 for each,

   a. using an explicit DO-loop
   b. using an implied DO-loop

8. Write the formatted output statements to print the arrays declared as

   ```
   INTEGER ACON(10), BCON(10)
   ```

   one below the other, on a line having length 80, with the following labeling and layout:

	1	2	3	4	5	6	7	8	9	10
ACON	xxxx	xxxx	xxxx	xxxx	xxxx	xxxx	xxxx	xxxx	xxxx	xxxx
BCON	xxxx	xxxx	xxxx	xxxx	xxxx	xxxx	xxxx	xxxx	xxxx	xxxx

9. Write the output statements to print an array declared as SALE(400) using field specification F7.2, arranged 10 values per line evenly spaced on paper that holds 120 characters per line. Print 10 lines per page.

6.4 Manipulation of Arrays

Any operation can be performed on individual elements of an array that can be performed on individual variables of the same type as the array. Numeric array elements may be used in arithmetic calculations and logical array elements may be used in logical operations. When an operation is to be performed on all elements of an array, an explicit DO-loop is usually used.

6.4.1 Array Assignments

The values of the elements of an array may be copied to another array using an explicit DO-loop. If the source and destination arrays do not have compatible data types, type conversion occurs. The elements are copied one by one in the order in which they are stored, as shown in the following code. The program segment

```
REAL X(5),Y(5)
 .  .  .
DO 10 I=1,5
   X(I) = Y(I)
10    CONTINUE
```

will have the following effect on X:

Before

X(1)	16.2	Y(1)	19.5
X(2)	12.2	Y(2)	17.2
X(3)	13.5	Y(3)	16.1
X(4)	26.3	Y(4)	13.5
X(5)	−7.1	Y(5)	37.6

After

X(1)	19.5	Y(1)	19.5
X(2)	17.2	Y(2)	17.2
X(3)	16.1	Y(3)	16.1
X(4)	13.5	Y(4)	13.5
X(5)	37.6	Y(5)	37.6

The values of the X array are replaced by the corresponding values of the Y array, which are not themselves altered.

Given the program segment

```
REAL X(7),Y(5)
 .  .  .
J = 0
DO 10 I=5,1,-1
   J = J + 1
   X(J) = Y(I)
10    CONTINUE
```

with the following effect:

Before

X(1)	16.2	Y(1)	19.5
X(2)	12.2	Y(2)	17.2
X(3)	13.5	Y(3)	16.1
X(4)	26.3	Y(4)	13.5
X(5)	−7.1	Y(5)	37.6
X(6)	7.9		
X(7)	−11.4		

After

X(1)	37.6	Y(1)	19.5
X(2)	13.5	Y(2)	17.2
X(3)	16.1	Y(3)	16.1
X(4)	17.2	Y(4)	13.5
X(5)	19.5	Y(5)	37.6
X(6)	7.9		
X(7)	−11.4		

The five elements of array Y, using index J, are copied into the first five positions of array X in reverse order. The last two elements of X are unchanged, as are the elements of Y.

The assignment statement can be used to initialize arrays to a single scalar value. If the entire array is to be initialized, an explicit DO-loop may be used.

The program segment

```
      INTEGER X(10)
      DO 10 I=1,10
         X(I) = 0
10    CONTINUE
```

has the following effect:

Before   *After*

X(1)	16	X(1)	0
X(2)	12	X(2)	0
X(3)	13	X(3)	0
X(4)	26	X(4)	0
X(5)	−7	X(5)	0
X(6)	7	X(6)	0
X(7)	−11	X(7)	0
X(8)	81	X(8)	0
X(9)	43	X(9)	0
X(10)	1	X(10)	0

One common programming situation, exchanging the values of two arrays, is accomplished by using an explicit DO-loop, as follows:

```
      REAL X(10),Y(10),TEMP
      . . .
      DO 50 I=1,10
         TEMP = X(I)
         X(I) = Y(I)
         Y(I) = TEMP
50    CONTINUE
```

Another common programming situation is moving some of the elements of a list down one position in order to insert a new element. In the following example, assume that the Kth element is to be placed at position J, J < K, by moving the elements X(J), X(J + 1), . . . , X(K − 1) down one position.

```
          REAL X(10),TEMP
          . . .
          TEMP = X(K)
          DO 50 I=K-1,J,-1
            X(I+1) = X(I)
50        CONTINUE
          X(J) = TEMP
```

This operation is the basis of a simple but not very efficient method of sorting an array that rearranges the values in ascending order. The smallest element is located at position K and placed in the first position by moving elements 1 through K-1 down one position. Then the second smallest element is located at position K (a new K) and placed in the second position by moving elements 2 through K-1 down one position. Each time through the array, the smallest remaining element is placed in position, until the whole array has been sorted. This is shown in the following example:

```
*   SIMPLE SORTING ROUTINE

          REAL X(10),TEMP
          . . .
          DO 70 J = 1,9
            TEMP = X(J)
            DO 30 I = J+1,10
              IF (X(I) .LT. TEMP) THEN
                TEMP = X(I)
                K = I
              ENDIF
30          CONTINUE
            DO 50 I=K-1,J,-1
              X(I+1) = X(I)
50          CONTINUE
            X(J) = TEMP
70        CONTINUE
```

Lists of numbers are sorted when it is necessary to find particular values quickly. They are also sorted for some statistical operations such as finding the median value. Section 6.6 gives complete programs showing sorting and searching.

6.4.2 Arithmetic Operations

Addition, subtraction, multiplication, division, and exponentiation can be performed on the elements of arrays using an explicit DO-loop to vary the subscript. Subscripted array elements may be used in expressions wherever a simple variable can be used. If more than one array is used in an expression, the arrays must be the same size. A variety of uses are shown below in several program segments and their respective effects. Given the integer array IARR(5):

```
          DO 10 I=1,5
            IARR(I) = IARR(I) + 8
10        CONTINUE
```

	Before	*After*
IARR(1)	12	20
IARR(2)	−6	2
IARR(3)	18	26
IARR(4)	20	28
IARR(5)	5	13

```
      DO 10 I=1,5
        IARR(I) = IARR(I) - 3
10      CONTINUE
```

	Before	*After*
IARR(1)	12	9
IARR(2)	−6	−9
IARR(3)	18	15
IARR(4)	20	17
IARR(5)	5	2

```
      DO 10 I=1,5
        IARR(I) = IARR(I) * 3
10      CONTINUE
```

	Before	*After*
IARR(1)	12	36
IARR(2)	−6	−18
IARR(3)	18	54
IARR(4)	20	60
IARR(5)	5	15

```
      DO 10 I=1,5
        IARR(I) = IARR(I) / 2
10      CONTINUE
```

	Before	*After*
IARR(1)	12	6
IARR(2)	−6	−3
IARR(3)	18	9
IARR(4)	20	10
IARR(5)	5	2

```
      DO 10 I=1,5
        IARR(I) = IARR(I) ** 2
10      CONTINUE
```

	Before	*After*
IARR(1)	12	144
IARR(2)	−6	36
IARR(3)	18	324
IARR(4)	20	400
IARR(5)	5	25

In these examples, each element of the array is treated in the same way.

Arithmetic is performed on corresponding elements according to the order in which they are stored. This is shown in the following program segments and their respective effects. Given the integer arrays A(5), B(5), C(5):

```
      DO 10 I=1,5
        C(I) = A(I) + B(I)
10      CONTINUE
```

A	B	C
8	6	14
12	3	15
9	10	19
5	-8	-3
3	6	9

```
      DO 10 I=1,5
        C(I) = A(I) - B(I)
10      CONTINUE
```

A	B	C
8	6	2
12	3	9
9	10	-1
5	-8	13
3	6	-3

```
      DO 10 I=1,5
        C(I) = A(I) * B(I)
10      CONTINUE
```

A	B	C
8	6	48
12	3	36
9	10	90
5	-8	-40
3	6	18

```
      DO 10 I=1,5
        C(I) = A(I) / B(I)
10      CONTINUE
```

A	B	C
8	6	1
12	3	4
9	10	0
5	-8	0
3	6	0

6.4.3 Review Questions

1. Given the real arrays X(3) and Y(3), show the results of the following program segments:

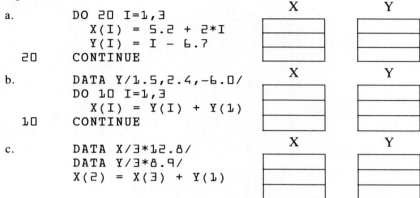

   a.
```
        DO 20 I=1,3
          X(I) = 5.2 + 2*I
          Y(I) = I - 6.7
20        CONTINUE
```

   b.
```
        DATA Y/1.5,2.4,-6.0/
        DO 10 I=1,3
          X(I) = Y(I) + Y(1)
10        CONTINUE
```

   c.
```
        DATA X/3*12.8/
        DATA Y/3*8.9/
        X(2) = X(3) + Y(1)
```

2. Given the integer arrays IA(6) and IB(6) with the following values, what is the result of each of the following segments of code?

IA	IB
25	
7	
14	
−6	
−21	
1	

   a.
```
        DO 10 I=1,6
          IB(I) = IA(I) + 6
10        CONTINUE
```

   b.
```
        DO 10 I=1,6
          IB(I) = IA(I) * 2
10        CONTINUE
```

   c.
```
        DO 10 I=1,6
          IB(I) = IA(I) / 4
10        CONTINUE
```

   d.
```
        DO 10 I=1,6
          IB(I) = IA(I) - 8
10        CONTINUE
```

   e.
```
        DO 10 I=1,6
          IB(I) = IA(I) ** 2
10        CONTINUE
```

6.5 Arrays in Subroutines and Functions

Most scientific and engineering application programs using arrays are complex, requiring many lines of code for each array manipulation. These array manipulations should be written using subroutines and functions.

6.5.1 Argument and Parameter Passing

Subroutines and functions are compiled separately as program units and invoked in the main program or other subprograms. Communicating information among them can be accomplished through argument passing. Arrays are passed to subroutines and functions by passing a reference to the location of the array. The subprogram can locate the argument array and can access values, if it is an input array, or store values, if it is an output array. The array must be declared in both the subprogram and the calling program. Each argument array must match its corresponding parameter array in data type, number of arrays passed, and their order in the argument list. The argument list of the calling program may contain arrays and simple variables. The parameter list of the subprogram must match the argument list of the calling program. The arrays and the variables must match as to type, number, order and size. The following example shows argument passing that includes arrays:

```
REAL X(10),Y(15)
INTEGER N,K(20)
  .
  .
  .
CALL SUMXYZ(X,N,Y,K)
  .
  .
  .
STOP
END

SUBROUTINE SUMXYZ(A,M,B,L)
REAL A(10),B(15)
INTEGER M,L(20)
  .
  .
  .
RETURN
END
```

The arguments X, N, Y, and K match the corresponding parameters A, M, B, and L exactly in type, number, size, and order.

The following example shows a subroutine that sums the numbers in an array, computes the average, and returns the sum and average to the main program. The values are passed as shown in Fig. 6.1.

```
********************************************************
*                                                      *
*    MAIN PROGRAM - DRIVER                             *
*                                                      *
********************************************************

      REAL X(20),XSUM,XAVRG
      INTEGER I

      READ (*,1000)(X(I),I=1,20)
1000  FORMAT(10F8.0)
      CALL XSMAVG(X,XSUM,XAVRG)
      WRITE (*,1100) (X(I),I=1,20)
1100  FORMAT(1X,10F10.2)
      WRITE (*,1200) XSUM,XAVRG
```

```
1200   FORMAT(//1X,'SUM =',F12.2,10X,'MEAN =',F12.2)
       STOP
       END

**********************************************************
*                                                        *
*   COMPUTE THE SUM AND AVERAGE OF THE ELEMENTS OF       *
*   AN ARRAY                                             *
*                                                        *
**********************************************************
*                                                        *
*   INPUT PARAMETERS:                                    *
*                                                        *
*     Y(20)     - A REAL ARRAY                           *
*                                                        *
*   OUTPUT PARAMETERS:                                   *
*                                                        *
*     YSUM      - SUM OF ELEMENTS OF THE ARRAY Y         *
*     YAVRG     - AVERAGE OF THE ELEMENTS OF THE         *
*                 ARRAY Y                                *
*                                                        *
**********************************************************

       SUBROUTINE XSMAVG(Y,YSUM,YAVRG)
       REAL Y(20),YSUM,YAVRG
       INTEGER I

       YSUM = 0.0
       DO 10 I=1,20
         YSUM = YSUM + Y(I)
10     CONTINUE
       YAVRG = YSUM / 20.0
       RETURN
       END
```

Figure 6.1

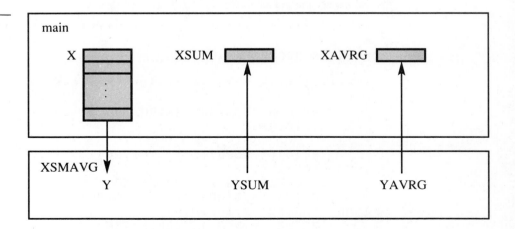

Figure 6.2

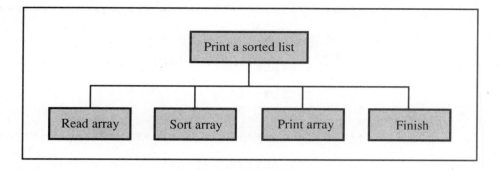

Arguments are passed to subroutines the same way they are passed to functions. Arrays are passed by reference. Changes to arrays are carried out immediately. In working with array parameters that are being changed, only the values of the elements can be changed. Since the array actually exists in the calling program, it is impossible for a subprogram to change the amount of storage space allocated. The documentation should state the assumed size of an array parameter.

Programming Warning

When processing an array passed to a subprogram, make sure the subscript is within the array bounds.

The following example uses subroutines to read, sort, and print an array. Each subroutine corresponds to a module on the hierarchy chart as shown in Fig. 6.2.

```
**********************************************************
*                                                        *
*   PRINT A SORTED LIST                                  *
*                                                        *
**********************************************************

        INTEGER L,N
        PARAMETER (L=100)
        REAL X(L)

        CALL GET(X,L,N)
        IF (N .EQ. 0) STOP
        CALL SORT(X,N)
        CALL PRINT(X,N)
        STOP
        END
```

```
      *****************************************************
      *                                                   *
      *    GET A LIST OF AT MOST L VALUES                 *
      *                                                   *
      *    PARAMETERS:                                    *
      *                                                   *
      *       OUTPUT: LIST                                *
      *               N                 0 < N < L+1       *
      *                                                   *
      *****************************************************

            SUBROUTINE GET(LIST,L,N)
            REAL LIST(L)
            INTEGER L,N

            N = 1

      *     DO WHILE (N .LE. L)

      5     IF(N .LE. L) THEN
               READ (*,1000,END=10) LIST(N)
      1000     FORMAT(F10.0)
               N = N + 1
               GO TO 5
            ENDIF

      *     ENDDO

      10    N = N - 1
            RETURN
            END
```

(The SORT and PRINT subroutines were not shown. Appropriate subroutines are found elsewhere in this chapter.)

The following example shows the use of an array as an argument to a function. The function computes the sum of the elements of the array X(40) and returns the sum to the main program.

```
      *****************************************************
      *                                                   *
      *    MAIN PROGRAM - DRIVER                          *
      *                                                   *
      *****************************************************

            REAL X(40),XSUM
            REAL XFNSUM
            INTEGER I

            READ (*,1000) (X(I),I=1,40)
      1000  FORMAT(20F4.0)
            XSUM = XFNSUM(X)
            WRITE (*,1200) XSUM
      1200  FORMAT(//1X,'SUM =',F12.2)
            STOP
            END
```

```
*******************************************************
*                                                     *
*    COMPUTE THE SUM OF THE ELEMENTS OF AN ARRAY      *
*                                                     *
*******************************************************
*                                                     *
*    INPUT PARAMETERS:                                *
*                                                     *
*      Y(40)      - A REAL ARRAY                      *
*                                                     *
*******************************************************

        REAL FUNCTION XFNSUM(Y)
        REAL Y(40),SUM
        INTEGER I

        SUM = 0.0
        DO 10 I=1,40
          SUM = SUM + Y(I)
10      CONTINUE
        XFNSUM = SUM
        RETURN
        END
```

Notice that the sum of the elements of the array is computed using a variable local to the function XFNSUM. The resulting sum is assigned to the function name and returned to the place in the main program where the function is invoked. There the value is assigned to the variable XSUM.

Programming Warning

> Do not change the values of the parameters of a function subprogram. This may cause unexpected side effects.

6.5.2 Adjustable Array Dimensioning

When arrays are passed to subroutine or function subprograms, to avoid errors in dimensioning the arrays, the array size or the number of valid data items in the array may also be passed. This size variable is then used to dimension the array in the subprogram. Passing the array size writes a general subprogram that can be used with an array of any size, the size being determined by the calling program. Then the size of the array in the main program can be changed without having to make changes to the code of the subprogram.

Programming Hint

> Pass the size of an array argument to the subprogram and use it to dimension the dummy argument array.

This is shown in the following example:

```
REAL X(10),Y(10)
INTEGER N
PARAMETER (N=10)

CALL XYSUM(X,Y,N)
    .
    .
    .
STOP
END

SUBROUTINE XYSUM(Z,W,M)
REAL Z(M),W(M)
INTEGER M
    .
    .
    .
RETURN
END
```

The argument value N is accessed as the dummy argument M at execution time, and this value is used in the declarations of the arrays Z and W. If the type and parameter statements of the calling program are changed, the same subroutine can be used without any changes. The value of N passed to the subroutine can be less than or equal to the declared size of the array in the main program.

```
******************************************************
*                                                    *
*    MAIN PROGRAM - DRIVER                            *
*                                                    *
******************************************************

      REAL X(40),Y(15),XSUM,YSUM
      REAL ARRSUM
      INTEGER NX,NY,I
      PARAMETER (NX=40,NY=15)

      READ (*,1000) (X(I),I=1,NX)
1000  FORMAT(20F4.0)
      XSUM = ARRSUM(X,NX)
      WRITE (*,1200)XSUM
1200  FORMAT(//1X,'SUM =',F12.2)

      READ (*,2000) (Y(I),I=1,NY)
2000  FORMAT(20F4.0)
      YSUM = ARRSUM(Y,NY)
      WRITE (*,2200) YSUM
2200  FORMAT(//1X,'SUM =',F12.2)
      STOP
      END
```

```
***************************************************************
*                                                             *
*    COMPUTE THE SUM OF THE ELEMENTS OF AN ARRAY              *
*                                                             *
***************************************************************
*                                                             *
*    INPUT PARAMETERS:                                        *
*                                                             *
*      Z(K)       - A REAL ARRAY                              *
*      K          - THE SIZE OF THE ARRAY                     *
*                                                             *
***************************************************************

        REAL FUNCTION ARRSUM(Z,K)
        REAL Z(K),SUM
        INTEGER K,I

        SUM = 0.0
        DO 10 I=1,K
          SUM = SUM + Z(I)
10      CONTINUE
        ARRSUM = SUM
        RETURN
        END
```

Notice that the first time the function is invoked, the array size NX = 40 is passed to the parameter K of the function and the 40 elements of the array X are summed. The second time the function is invoked, the array size NY = 15 is passed to the parameter K of the function and the 15 elements of the array Y are summed.

Since the size of the array is passed separately from the array itself, be careful that the size passed is correct–a runtime error will occur if the size is greater than the declared size in the calling program. However, if the size is too small, elements from only part of the array would be summed. If an array is not full, it can be processed by passing a count of the number of elements in the array. This is shown in the following example.

Programming Warning

> The size of an array in a called subprogram must not exceed the size of the corresponding array in the calling program module.

```
***************************************************************
*                                                             *
*    MAIN PROGRAM - DRIVER                                    *
*                                                             *
***************************************************************

        REAL X(40)
        REAL XSUM,FSUM
        INTEGER N,I

        N = 1
```

```
*         DO WHILE (N .LE. 40)

10        IF (N .LE. 40) THEN
            READ (*,1000,END=20) X(N)
1000        FORMAT(F4.0)
            N = N + 1
            GO TO 10
          ENDIF

*         ENDDO

20        N = N - 1
          XSUM = FSUM(X,N)
          WRITE (*,1200) XSUM
1200      FORMAT(//1X,'SUM =',F12.2)
          STOP
          END


*****************************************************
*                                                   *
*   COMPUTE THE SUM OF THE ELEMENTS OF AN ARRAY     *
*                                                   *
*****************************************************
*                                                   *
*   INPUT PARAMETERS:                               *
*                                                   *
*     Y(N)        - A REAL ARRAY                    *
*     N           - THE SIZE OF THE ARRAY           *
*                                                   *
*****************************************************

          REAL FUNCTION FSUM(Y,N)
          REAL Y(N),SUM
          INTEGER N,I

          SUM = 0.0
          DO 10 I=1,N
            SUM = SUM + Y(I)
10        CONTINUE
          FSUM = SUM
          RETURN
          END
```

Notice that there is no conflict in using the same line numbers and the same variable name N in both routines because they are compiled separately. The value of N is the exact number of values in the array. The array elements can be accessed in the function without looking at the empty array positions; the two routines understand the array storage areas to be different sizes, but starting in the same location. The calling program contains an array of 40 elements, some of which may not contain values, while the function subprogram accesses an array of N elements, all of them containing values.

6.5.3 Shared Arrays

Arrays may be shared between routines without passing them as arguments by placing them in COMMON. This is shown in the following example, which calls a subroutine to calculate the sum and the average of the numbers in an array. The results of the calculation are also placed in COMMON.

```
         COMMON N,X(10),XSUM,XAVR
         REAL X,XSUM,XAVR
         INTEGER N,I

         READ (*,1000) N
1000     FORMAT(I5)
         READ (*,2000) (X(I),I=1,N)
2000     FORMAT(10F5.0)
         CALL SUMAVR
         WRITE (*,3000) (X(I),I=1,N)
3000     FORMAT (1X,10F12.2)
         WRITE (*,4000) XSUM,XAVR
4000     FORMAT(1X,'SUM =',F12.2,20X,'AVERAGE =',F12.2)
         STOP
         END

*********************************************************
*                                                       *
*    CALCULATE SUM AND AVERAGE OF ELEMENTS OF A LIST    *
*                                                       *
*********************************************************

         SUBROUTINE SUMAVR
         COMMON M,Y(10),YSUM,YAVR
         REAL Y,YSUM,YAVR
         INTEGER M,I

         YSUM = 0.0
         DO 10 I=1,M
            YSUM = YSUM + Y(I)
10       CONTINUE
         YAVR = YSUM / M
         RETURN
         END
```

Fig. 6.3 shows the movement of data into and out of the routines through both the input/output data files and the COMMON area. Since the names of the elements of COMMON are not the same in the two routines, additional documentation would be needed to show that the N and X initialized by the main program are the M and Y used by the subroutine SUMAVR.

The following example uses both argument passing and shared data. The space allocated for COMMON must be greater than the amount of space actually needed.

Figure 6.3

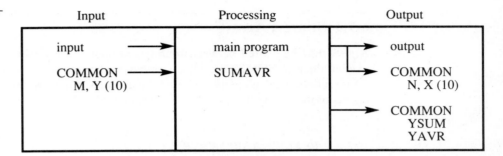

```
      COMMON Z(100)
      REAL X(100),Y(100),Z
      INTEGER N,I

      READ (*,*) N
      IF (N .GE. 1 .AND. N .LE. 100) THEN
         READ (*,*) (X(I),I=1,N)
         READ (*,*) (Y(I),I=1,N)
         CALL PRODZ(X,Y,N)
         WRITE (*,1000) (Z(I),I=1,N)
1000     FORMAT(1X,10E12.5)
      ENDIF
      STOP
      END

***************************************************************
*                                                             *
*   CALCULATE VECTOR PRODUCT                                  *
*                                                             *
*   PARAMETERS:                                               *
*                                                             *
*      INPUT:    W(M), U(M)                                   *
*                M             0 < M < 101                    *
*                                                             *
***************************************************************

      SUBROUTINE PRODZ(W,U,M)
      COMMON V(100)
      REAL W(M),U(M),V
      INTEGER M,I

      DO 10 I=1,M
         V(I) = W(I) * U(I)
10    CONTINUE
      RETURN
      END
```

Notice that all three arrays are described in the subroutine as having length M.
COMMON statements do not have to match as to length and type of storage
described. However, be careful not to exceed the bounds of the stored values. It is
best to use identical descriptions of COMMON in each routine that references it.

6.5.4 Review Questions

1. Write a header and declaration statement for the subroutine called by each of the following code segments:

   a. ```
   REAL X(10),XSUM
   INTEGER N,M
   CALL SUB1(N,M,X,XSUM)
   ```

   b. ```
   REAL A(10),B(10)
   CALL SUBSUM(A,B)
   ```

   c. ```
   INTEGER P(10),Q(20)
   INTEGER PLIM,QLIM
   PARAMETER (PLIM=10,QLIM=20)
   CALL CALC(P,PLIM)
   CALL CALC(Q,QLIM)
   ```

2. Write a function subprogram SUM(ARR1,N1,ARR2,N2) where ARR1 and ARR2 are one-dimensional real arrays of length N1 and N2, respectively. The function should check that the arrays are the same size, return zero if they are not, and return the value

$$\sum_{k=1}^{n} ARR1(k) * ARR2(k)$$

   if they are the same size.
3. Write a logical function subprogram VALID(ARR,N,LB,UB) that returns the value true if all elements in ARR are between LB and UB inclusively, and false otherwise. ARR, LB, and UB are real. ARR has N elements.
4. Write a function POS to compute the sum of all the positive elements and a function NEG to compute the sum of all the negative elements of a real array declared as COMMON ARR(100).
5. Write a subroutine to print the elements of any one-dimensional real array A in a column.
6. Write a subroutine to read values into a one-dimensional integer array M of size K and return the count N of the actual number of elements in the array.

# 6.6  Sample Programs

In these examples we show the use of arrays in sorting, searching, finding standard deviations, and in other problems where data is stored in one-dimensional arrays. These programs have been executed interactively on the Digital Equipment Corporation (DEC) computer model VAX 11/780. When both the input and output are shown, they are identified.

## 6.6.1 Maximum and Minimum Values

### Problem

Write a program that prints the maximum and minimum values in an array.
   ```

Pseudocode

```
Main program
   Input the array X with N elements
   Call MAXMIN(N,X,XMAX,XMIN)
   Print XMAX and XMIN
   Stop
Subroutine MAXMIN
   XMAX ← ARR(1)
   XMIN ← ARR(1)
   For each array element i
      if ARR(i) > XMAX then
         XMAX ← ARR(i)
      else if ARR(i) < XMIN then
         XMIN ← ARR(i)
   end for
Return
```

Program

```
*************************************************************
*                                                           *
*    MAIN PROGRAM - DRIVER                                   *
*                                                           *
*    SUBROUTINE:                                            *
*                                                           *
*       MAXMIN - COMPUTES MAXIMUM AND MINIMUM                *
*                                                           *
*************************************************************

      REAL X(20),XMAX,XMIN
      INTEGER N,I

      WRITE (*,*) 'INPUT THE SIZE, AND ELEMENTS OF ',
     1       'THE ARRAY'
      READ (*,1000) N
1000  FORMAT(I5)
      READ (*,1100) (X(I),I=1,N)
1100  FORMAT(10F8.0)
      CALL MAXMIN(N,X,XMAX,XMIN)
      WRITE (*,1150)
1150  FORMAT(//1X,'OUTPUT')
      WRITE (*,1200) XMAX,XMIN
1200  FORMAT(/1X,'MAX VALUE =',F10.2/1X,'MIN VALUE ='
     1        ,F10.2)
      STOP
      END
```

```
****************************************************************
*                                                              *
*    LOCATE THE MAXIMUM AND MINIMUM ELEMENTS OF                *
*    AN ARRAY                                                  *
*                                                              *
****************************************************************
*                                                              *
*    INPUT PARAMETERS:                                         *
*                                                              *
*      ARR(M)    - A REAL ARRAY                                *
*      M         - THE SIZE OF THE ARRAY                       *
*                                                              *
*    OUTPUT PARAMETERS:                                        *
*                                                              *
*      ARRMAX    - THE LARGEST ARRAY VALUE                     *
*      ARRMIN    - THE SMALLEST ARRAY VALUE                    *
*                                                              *
****************************************************************

        SUBROUTINE MAXMIN(M,ARR,ARRMAX,ARRMIN)
        REAL ARR(M),ARRMAX,ARRMIN
        INTEGER M,I

        ARRMAX = ARR(1)
        ARRMIN = ARR(1)
        DO 10 I=1,M
          IF (ARR(I) .GT. ARRMAX) THEN
            ARRMAX = ARR(I)
          ELSEIF (ARR(I) .LT. ARRMIN) THEN
            ARRMIN = ARR(I)
          ENDIF
10      CONTINUE
        RETURN
        END
```

Output

```
 INPUT THE SIZE, AND ELEMENTS OF THE ARRAY
     5
 2.      11.      17.      22.      39.


 OUTPUT

 MAX VALUE =      39.00
 MIN VALUE =       2.00
```

6.6.2 Sorting Arrays

In scientific and engineering applications, sorting the data is often necessary to find critical values. Sorting is simply arranging the data in ascending or descending order. Two types of sorts are the simple selection sort and the bubble sort.

Selection sort

Problem

To sort a one-dimensional array in ascending order using the selection sort.

Method

This sort proceeds by repeatedly comparing all the elements, first to find the smallest element and place it in the first position, then to find the next smallest element and place it in the second position, and so forth.

Pseudocode

```
Main program
    Call INPUT to input the array X
    Call SLSORT to sort the array X
    Call OUTPUT to output the sorted array X
    Stop
Subroutine INPUT
    Read N, X
Return
Subroutine SLSORT
    For each element I from 1 to N − 1
        For each element J from I + 1 to N
            if X(I) > X(J) then
                XTEMP ← X(I)
                X(I) ← X(J)
                X(J) ← XTEMP
            end if
        end for
    end for
Return

Subroutine OUTPUT
    For each element I from 1 to N
        print I and X(I)
    end for
Return
```

Flowchart

The main program and sort subroutine are shown in Fig. 6.4. Notice the special symbol in the flowchart for the main program that indicates a subprogram.

Figure 6.4

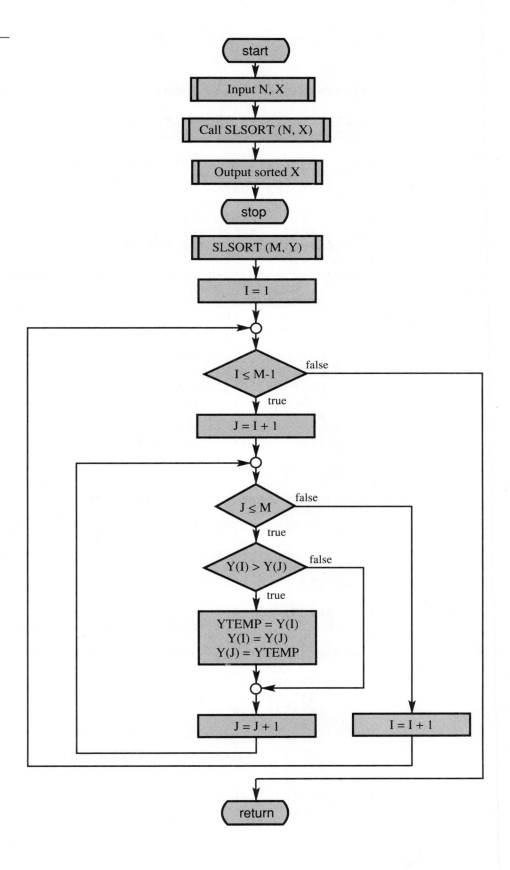

Program

```
*************************************************************
*                                                           *
*    SORT AN ARRAY OF NUMBERS INTO ASCENDING ORDER          *
*    USING A SELECTION SORT                                 *
*                                                           *
*************************************************************
*                                                           *
*    SUBROUTINES USED:                                      *
*                                                           *
*      INPUT:    INPUT VALUES INTO THE ARRAY                *
*      SLSORT:   SELECTION SORT, ASCENDING ORDER            *
*      OUTPUT:   PRINT THE SORTED ARRAY                     *
*                                                           *
*************************************************************

        INTEGER N,K
        PARAMETER (N=20)
        REAL X(N)

        CALL INPUT(X,N,K)
        CALL SLSORT(X,K)
        CALL OUTPUT(X,K)
        STOP
        END


*************************************************************
*                                                           *
*    INPUT AN ARRAY                                         *
*                                                           *
*************************************************************
*                                                           *
*    INPUT PARAMETERS:                                      *
*                                                           *
*      N          - THE SIZE OF THE ARRAY                   *
*                                                           *
*    OUTPUT PARAMETERS:                                     *
*                                                           *
*      ARR(N)    - A REAL ARRAY                             *
*      K          - THE NUMBER OF VALUES IN THE ARRAY       *
*                                                           *
*************************************************************

        SUBROUTINE INPUT(ARR,N,K)
        REAL ARR(N)
        INTEGER N,K

        WRITE (*,1000)
1000    FORMAT(1X,'INPUT: UNSORTED ARRAY')
        K = 1

*       DO WHILE (K .LE. N)
```

```
10      IF (K .LE. N) THEN
          READ (*,1100,END=20) ARR(K)
1100      FORMAT(F8.0)
          K = K + 1
          GO TO 10
        ENDIF

*       ENDDO

20      K = K - 1
        RETURN
        END


****************************************************************
*                                                              *
*   SELECTION SORT OF ARRAY IN ASCENDING ORDER                 *
*                                                              *
****************************************************************
*                                                              *
*   INPUT PARAMETERS:                                          *
*                                                              *
*     ARR(M)    - A REAL ARRAY                                 *
*     M         - THE SIZE OF THE ARRAY                        *
*                                                              *
*   OUTPUT PARAMETERS:                                         *
*                                                              *
*     ARR(M)    - THE SORTED ARRAY                             *
*                                                              *
*   SUBROUTINES CALLED:                                        *
*                                                              *
*     SWAP:   EXCHANGES TWO ARRAY ELEMENTS                     *
*                                                              *
****************************************************************

        SUBROUTINE SLSORT(ARR,M)
        REAL ARR(M)
        INTEGER M,I,J

        DO 20 I=1,M-1
          DO 10 J=I+1,M
            IF(ARR(I) .GT. ARR(J)) THEN
              CALL SWAP(ARR,I,J,M)
            ENDIF
10        CONTINUE
20      CONTINUE
        RETURN
        END
```

```
      *********************************************************
      *                                                       *
      *    EXCHANGES ELEMENTS I AND J OF ARRAY                *
      *                                                       *
      *********************************************************
      *                                                       *
      *    INPUT PARAMETERS:                                  *
      *                                                       *
      *      ARR(L)    - A REAL ARRAY                         *
      *      J         - INDEX OF ELEMENT TO BE SWAPPED       *
      *      I         - INDEX OF ELEMENT TO BE SWAPPED       *
      *      L         - SIZE OF ARRAY                        *
      *                                                       *
      *    OUTPUT PARAMETERS:                                 *
      *                                                       *
      *      ARR(L)    - THE ARRAY WITH ELEMENTS I AND J      *
      *                  SWAPPED                               *
      *                                                       *
      *********************************************************

            SUBROUTINE SWAP(ARR,I,J,L)
            REAL ARR(L),ATEMP
            INTEGER I,J,L

            ATEMP = ARR(I)
            ARR(I) = ARR(J)
            ARR(J) = ATEMP
            RETURN
            END


      *********************************************************
      *                                                       *
      *    OUTPUT AN ARRAY, 10 VALUES PER LINE                *
      *                                                       *
      *********************************************************
      *                                                       *
      *    INPUT PARAMETERS:                                  *
      *                                                       *
      *      ARR(M)    - A REAL ARRAY                         *
      *      M         - SIZE OF ARRAY                        *
      *                                                       *
      *********************************************************

            SUBROUTINE OUTPUT(ARR,M)
            REAL ARR(M)
            INTEGER M,I

            WRITE (*,1000)
      1000  FORMAT(/1X,'OUTPUT: SORTED ARRAY')
            WRITE (*,1100) (ARR(I),I=1,M)
      1100  FORMAT(1X,10F8.2)
```

```
RETURN
```

```
INPUT: UNSORTED ARRAY
33.
12.
78.
8.
2.
29.

OUTPUT: SORTED ARRAY
    2.00      8.00     12.00     29.00     33.00     78.00
```

Bubble Sort

In the bubble sort, the elements of the array are scanned from the bottom up. When any two adjacent elements are out of order, they are exchanged. This results in the smallest element floating to the top when the array is to be sorted in ascending order, or the largest element moving to the top when the array is to be sorted in descending order. The following example shows the results of the three passes needed to sort a short list in descending order.

Original list	Pass 1	Pass 2	Pass 3
8	12	12	12
10	8	10	10
6	10	8	9
9	6	9	8
12	9	6	6

We give pseudocode for the basic bubble sort and also for an optimized bubble sort. The basic bubble sort is not very efficient; therefore small improvements are usually included in a program. The following subroutine exchanges elements when they are out of order, the larger element rising toward the top of the list. A flag is used in the optimized sort to indicate whether the elements of the list are in the final order at the completion of a pass. This eliminates the need for any further passes. Since the kth pass places the correct element in the kth position, on the k + 1st pass, the first k elements do not need to be scanned.

Figure 6.5

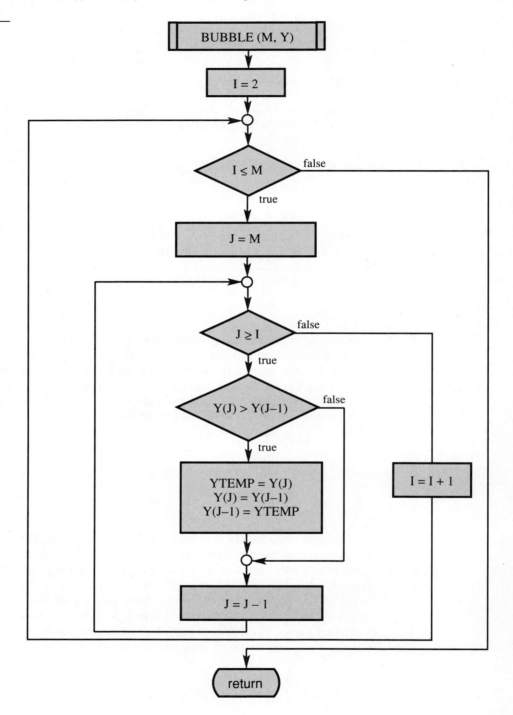

Pseudocode

```
Subroutine BUBBLE (bubble sort - descending order)
    For each position I from 2 to M
        For each element J from M to I
            If Y(J) > Y(J − 1) then
                YTEMP ← Y(J)
                Y(J) ← Y(J − 1)
                Y(J − 1) ← YTEMP
            end if
        end for
    end for
Return
```

This subroutine could be run with the same driver, input, and output routines as the selection sort above.

Flowchart

The flowchart is given in Fig. 6.5.

Program

```
*****************************************************
*                                                   *
*   MAIN PROGRAM — DRIVER                           *
*                                                   *
*****************************************************

      REAL X(20)
      INTEGER N,I

      WRITE (*,*) 'INPUT: THE SIZE AND ELEMENTS OF ',
     1        'THE ARRAY:'
      READ (*,1000) N
1000  FORMAT(I5)
      READ (*,1100) (X(I),I=1,N)
1100  FORMAT(10F8.0)
      CALL BUBBLE(X,N)
      WRITE (*,1150)
1150  FORMAT(//1X,'OUTPUT: SORTED ARRAY')
      WRITE (*,1200) (X(I),I=1,N)
1200  FORMAT(/1X,10F8.2)
      STOP
      END
```

```
******************************************************
*                                                    *
*   BASIC BUBBLE SORT OF ARRAY IN DESCENDING ORDER   *
*                                                    *
******************************************************
*                                                    *
*   INPUT PARAMETERS:                                *
*                                                    *
*     Y(M)      - A REAL ARRAY                       *
*     M         - THE SIZE OF THE ARRAY              *
*                                                    *
*   OUTPUT PARAMETERS:                               *
*                                                    *
*     Y(M)       - THE SORTED ARRAY                  *
*                                                    *
******************************************************

      SUBROUTINE BUBBLE(Y,M)
      REAL Y(M),YTEMP
      INTEGER M,I,J

      DO 20 I = 2,M
        DO 10 J=M,I,-1
          IF(Y(J) .GT. Y(J-1)) THEN
            YTEMP = Y(J)
            Y(J) = Y(J-1)
            Y(J-1) = YTEMP
          ENDIF
10      CONTINUE
20      CONTINUE
      RETURN
      END
```

Output

```
INPUT: THE SIZE AND ELEMENTS OF THE ARRAY:
     5
99.     11.     44.     33.     40.


OUTPUT: SORTED ARRAY

   99.00   44.00   40.00   33.00   11.00
```

Pseudocode

Subroutine BUBBLE (optimized bubble sort—descending order)
  I ← 2
  Set FLAG to false
  Do while I ≤ M and .NOT. FLAG
    set FLAG to true
    for each element J from M to I
      if Y(J) > Y(J − 1) then
        YTEMP ← Y(J)
        Y(J) ← Y(J − 1)
        Y(J − 1) ← YTEMP
        set FLAG TO false
      end if
    end for
    I = I + 1
  end do
Return

Flowchart

The flowchart for the optimized bubble sort is shown in Fig. 6.6.

Program

```
**********************************************************
*                                                        *
*   MAIN PROGRAM - DRIVER                                *
*                                                        *
**********************************************************

      REAL X(20)
      INTEGER N,I

      WRITE (*,*) 'INPUT: THE SIZE AND ELEMENTS OF ',
     1      'THE ARRAY:'
      READ (*,1000) N
1000  FORMAT(I5)
      READ (*,1100) (X(I),I=1,N)
1100  FORMAT(10F8.0)
      CALL BUBBLE(X,N)
      WRITE (*,1150)
1150  FORMAT(//1X,'OUTPUT: SORTED ARRAY')
      WRITE (*,1200) (X(I),I=1,N)
1200  FORMAT(/1X,10F8.2)
      STOP
      END
```

Figure 6.6

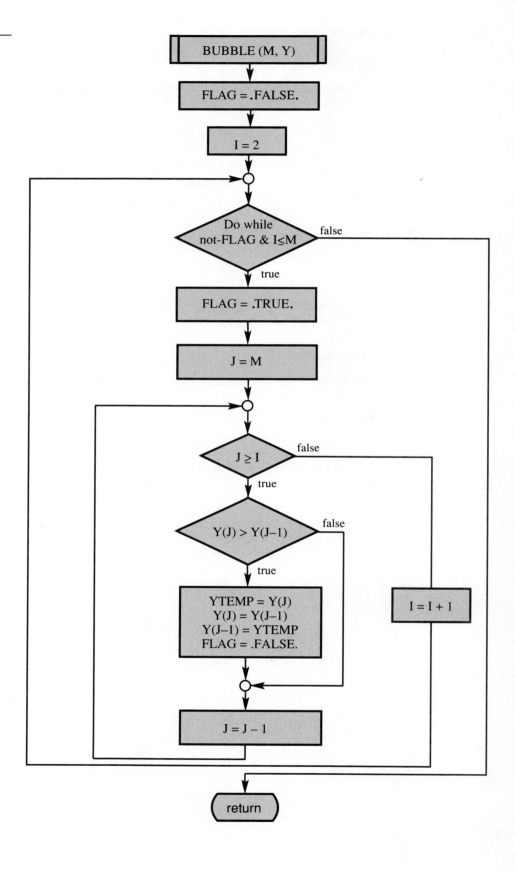

```
************************************************************
*                                                        *
*    PARTLY OPTIMIZED BUBBLE SORT OF ARRAY               *
*    IN DESCENDING ORDER                                 *
*                                                        *
************************************************************
*                                                        *
*    INPUT PARAMETERS:                                   *
*                                                        *
*      Y(M)      - A REAL ARRAY                          *
*      M         - THE SIZE OF THE ARRAY                 *
*                                                        *
*    OUTPUT PARAMETERS:                                  *
*                                                        *
*      Y(M)      - THE SORTED ARRAY                      *
*                                                        *
************************************************************

        SUBROUTINE BUBBLE(Y,M)
        REAL Y(M),YTEMP
        INTEGER M,I,J
        LOGICAL FLAG

        FLAG = .FALSE.
        I = 2

*       DO WHILE (.NOT. FLAG .AND. I .LE. M)

10      IF(.NOT. FLAG .AND. I .LE. M) THEN
          FLAG = .TRUE.
          DO 20 J=M,I,-1
            IF(Y(J) .GT. Y(J-1)) THEN
              YTEMP = Y(J)
              Y(J) = Y(J-1)
              Y(J-1) = YTEMP
              FLAG = .FALSE.
            ENDIF
20        CONTINUE
          I = I + 1
          GO TO 10

*       ENDDO

        ENDIF
        RETURN
        END
```

Output

```
INPUT: THE SIZE AND ELEMENTS OF THE ARRAY:
   6
72.      22.       39.       19.       26.       41.


OUTPUT: SORTED ARRAY

   72.00    41.00    39.00    26.00    22.00    19.00
```

Notice that the flag is true when no changes have been made during a pass through the array, and false when elements have been rearranged.

6.6.3 Searching Arrays

The method used to search for a particular value in an array depends on whether or not the array has been sorted. In these search algorithms, we assume that there are no duplicate values in the arrays. When a list of numbers has not been sorted, a linear search must be used. A binary search is much more efficient to use on sorted lists.

Linear Search

The linear search is an element-by-element scan of the array, looking for the desired value. If it is not there, the entire array must be searched. When it is there, the search stops as soon as the value is located. This routine returns a logical flag indicating the success of the search. The position of the value in the array is returned through an argument.

Pseudocode

```
Subroutine LNSRCH
   I ← 1
   Set FOUND to false
   Do while I ≤ M and not FOUND
     If Y(I) = ITEM then
        set FOUND to true
     else
        I ← I + 1
     end if
   end do
Return success flag FOUND
```

Program

```
*****************************************************
*                                                   *
*   MAIN PROGRAM - DRIVER                            *
*                                                   *
*****************************************************

      REAL X(20),ITEM
      INTEGER N,I,LOC
      LOGICAL ITMFND,LNSRCH

      WRITE (*,*) 'INPUT: THE SIZE AND ELEMENTS OF ',
     1      'THE ARRAY:'
      READ (*,1000) N
1000  FORMAT(I5)
      READ (*,1100) (X(I),I=1,N)
1100  FORMAT(10F8.0)
      WRITE (*,*) 'INPUT NUMBER TO BE FOUND'
      READ (*,1200) ITEM
1200  FORMAT(F8.0)
      WRITE (*,1250)
1250  FORMAT(//1X,'OUTPUT')
      ITMFND = LNSRCH(X,N,ITEM,LOC)
      IF (.NOT. ITMFND) THEN
         WRITE (*,1300)
1300     FORMAT(/1X,'ELEMENT NOT FOUND')
      ELSE
         WRITE (*,1400) X(LOC),LOC
1400     FORMAT(/1X,'ELEMENT ',F8.2,' FOUND AT ',
     1          'POSITION',I5)
      ENDIF
      STOP
      END


*****************************************************
*                                                   *
*   LINEAR SEARCH OF UNSORTED ARRAY                  *
*                                                   *
*****************************************************
*                                                   *
*   INPUT PARAMETERS:                                *
*                                                   *
*     ARR(M)    - A REAL ARRAY                       *
*     M         - THE SIZE OF THE ARRAY              *
*     ITEM      - THE ITEM WANTED                    *
*                                                   *
*   OUTPUT PARAMETERS:                               *
*                                                   *
*     I         - POSITION OF ITEM IN ARRAY          *
*   RETURNS     - SUCCESS FLAG                       *
*                                                   *
*****************************************************
```

```
          LOGICAL FUNCTION LNSRCH(ARR,M,ITEM,I)
          REAL ARR(M),ITEM
          INTEGER M,I,K
          LOGICAL FOUND

          I = 1
          FOUND = .FALSE.

*         DO WHILE (I .LE. M .AND. .NOT. FOUND)

10        IF(I .LE. M .AND. .NOT. FOUND) THEN
            IF(ARR(I) .EQ. ITEM) THEN
              FOUND = .TRUE.
            ELSE
              I = I + 1
            ENDIF
            GO TO 10
          ENDIF

*         ENDDO

          LNSRCH = FOUND
          RETURN
          END
```

Output

```
INPUT: THE SIZE AND ELEMENTS OF THE ARRAY:
    5
9.       4.       8.       5.       2.
INPUT NUMBER TO BE FOUND
5.


OUTPUT

ELEMENT      5.00 FOUND AT POSITION    4


INPUT: THE SIZE AND ELEMENTS OF THE ARRAY:
    6
22.      34.      13.      45.      29.      61.
INPUT NUMBER TO BE FOUND
27.


OUTPUT

ELEMENT NOT FOUND
```

Binary Search

The linear search is inefficient for sorted data. Instead, a binary search should be used. A binary search uses a probing process to look at the middle element of the list and detemine which half the desired item is in. Then it looks at the middle element of that half to determine which quarter of the list contains the desired element. By repeatedly halving the search space, the item can be located very quickly. If the item is not in the list, this search locates the position where it belongs.

Suppose we want the number 24 in the following list:

Sorted list	Probe 1	Probe 2	Probe 3
2			
7			
8			
11			
13			
17			
20	--20--	------	
24			--24--
31			
39		--39--	
45			
57			
62	------		

Pseudocode

```
Function BNSRCH (using data in ascending order)
    POS ← 0
    FIRST ← 1
    LAST ← M
    Do while FIRST ≤ LAST and POS = 0
        MID ← (FIRST + LAST) / 2
        If Y(MID) > ITEM then
            LAST ← MID − 1
        else if Y(MID) < ITEM then
            FIRST ← MID + 1
        else
            POS ← MID
        end if
    end do
Return
```

Flowchart

The flowchart is given in Fig. 6.7.

Figure 6.7

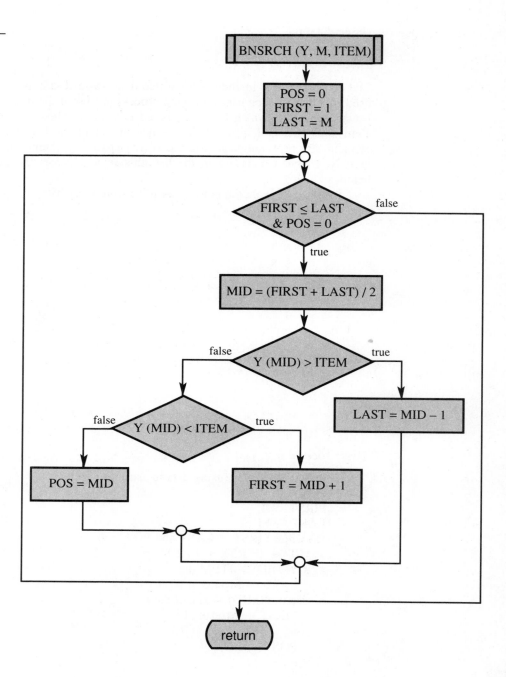

Program

```
****************************************************
*                                                  *
*   MAIN PROGRAM - DRIVER                           *
*                                                  *
****************************************************
```

```
          REAL X(20),ITEM
          INTEGER N,I,LOC,BNSRCH

          WRITE (*,*) 'INPUT: THE SIZE AND ELEMENTS OF ',
         1      'THE SORTED ARRAY:'
          READ (*,1000) N
1000      FORMAT(I5)
          READ (*,1100) (X(I),I=1,N)
1100      FORMAT(10F8.0)
          WRITE (*,*) 'INPUT NUMBER TO BE FOUND'
          READ (*,1200) ITEM
1200      FORMAT(F8.0)
          WRITE (*,1250)
1250      FORMAT(//1X,'OUTPUT')
          LOC = BNSRCH(X,N,ITEM)
          IF (LOC .EQ. 0) THEN
             WRITE (*,1300)
1300         FORMAT(/1X,'ELEMENT NOT FOUND')
          ELSE
             WRITE (*,1400) X(LOC),LOC
1400         FORMAT(/1X,'ELEMENT ',F8.2,' FOUND AT ',
         1            'POSITION',I5)
          ENDIF
          STOP
          END

*****************************************************
*                                                   *
*   BINARY SEARCH OF ARRAY SORTED IN ASCENDING ORDER *
*                                                   *
*****************************************************
*                                                   *
*   INPUT PARAMETERS:                               *
*                                                   *
*     ARR(M)     - A REAL ARRAY                     *
*     M          - THE SIZE OF THE ARRAY            *
*     ITEM       - THE ITEM WANTED                  *
*                                                   *
*   RETURNS      - LOCATION OF ITEM IN THE ARRAY    *
*                                                   *
*****************************************************

          INTEGER FUNCTION BNSRCH(ARR,M,ITEM)
          REAL ARR(M),ITEM
          INTEGER M,FIRST,LAST,MID,POS

          POS = 0
          FIRST = 1
          LAST = M

*         DO WHILE (FIRST .LE. LAST .AND. POS .EQ. 0)
```

```
10      IF(FIRST .LE. LAST .AND. POS .EQ. 0) THEN
          MID = (FIRST + LAST) / 2
          IF(ARR(MID) .GT. ITEM) THEN
            LAST = MID - 1
          ELSEIF(ARR(MID) .LT. ITEM) THEN
            FIRST = MID + 1
          ELSE
            POS = MID
          ENDIF
          GO TO 10
        ENDIF

*       ENDDO

        BNSRCH = POS
        RETURN
        END
```

Output

```
INPUT: THE SIZE AND ELEMENTS OF THE SORTED ARRAY:
     6
2.       4.       13.      25.      47.      63.
INPUT NUMBER TO BE FOUND
25.


OUTPUT

ELEMENT    25.00 FOUND AT POSITION    4


INPUT: THE SIZE AND ELEMENTS OF THE SORTED ARRAY:
     6
2.       4.       13.      25.      47.      63.
INPUT NUMBER TO BE FOUND
22.


OUTPUT

ELEMENT NOT FOUND
```

6.6.4 Standard Deviation

Problem

Compute the standard deviation of a set of values, then print the values that are outside one standard deviation of the mean.

Pseudocode

Input the values into an array
Calculate the mean and the standard deviation
Print the values outside the standard deviation
Stop

The formula for the standard deviation is:

$$
S.D. = \sqrt{\frac{\sum_{i=1}^{n} P_i^2 - \frac{1}{n}\left(\sum_{i=1}^{n} P_i\right)^2}{n-1}}
$$

Program

```
*************************************************************
*                                                           *
*    STANDARD DEVIATION AND EXTREME VALUES                  *
*                                                           *
*************************************************************
*                                                           *
*    INPUT VARIABLES:                                       *
*                                                           *
*      P(N)  - A REAL ARRAY                                 *
*                                                           *
*    OUTPUT VARIABLES:                                      *
*                                                           *
*      STDEV - STANDARD DEVIATION                           *
*                                                           *
*************************************************************

        REAL P(40), SUMSQR, SQRSUM, SUM, MEAN, STDEV
        REAL SDPLUS, SDMINS
        INTEGER I, N
        PARAMETER (N=10)

        WRITE (*,*) 'INPUT 10 ELEMENTS'
        READ (*,1000) (P(I),I=1,N)
1000    FORMAT(10F5.0)
        SUMSQR = 0.0
        SUM = 0.0
        DO 10 I=1,N
           SUMSQR = SUMSQR + P(I) * P(I)
           SUM = SUM + P(I)
10      CONTINUE
        SQRSUM = SUM * SUM
        MEAN = SUM / N
        STDEV = SQRT((SUMSQR - SQRSUM/N)/(N-1))
        WRITE (*,1100) STDEV
1100    FORMAT(/1X,'STANDARD DEVIATION =',F12.2/1X)
        SDPLUS = MEAN + STDEV
        SDMINS = MEAN - STDEV
        WRITE (*,*) 'EXTREME VALUES'
```

```
              DO 20 I=1,N
                IF(P(I) .LT. SDMINS .OR. P(I) .GT. SDPLUS)THEN
                   WRITE (*,*) P(I)
                ENDIF
     20       CONTINUE
              STOP
              END
```

Output

```
INPUT 10 ELEMENTS
13.   5.    2.   19.   7.    11.   6.    15.   10.   12.

STANDARD DEVIATION =        5.10

EXTREME VALUES
   2.000000
   19.00000
```

6.6.5 Table Lookup

Problem

Look up in a table the critical temperatures at which a gas liquifies and solidifies.

Method

GAS(20) contains the identifications for 20 gases. LIQTMP(20) contains the temperatures at which those gases liquify, and SOLTMP(20) contains the temperatures at which those gases solidify.

Pseudocode

```
Input the tables, in order by chemical formula
Input the formula of the gas to be looked up
Scan the array GAS looking for the formula
If it is found then
    print the temperatures
else
    print an error message
end if
Stop
```

Program

```
**************************************************************
*                                                            *
*  LOOK UP CRITICAL TEMPERATURES OF GASES                    *
*                                                            *
**************************************************************
*                                                            *
*  INPUT VARIABLES:                                          *
*                                                            *
*    GAS(N)    - I.D. NUMBERS OF GASSES                      *
*    LIQTMP(N)- TEMPERATURES OF LIQUIFICATION                *
*    SOLTMP(N)- TEMPERATURES OF SOLIDIFICATION               *
*    WANTED   - I.D. OF GAS WANTED                           *
*                                                            *
*  OUTPUT VARIABLES:                                         *
*                                                            *
*    LIQTMP    - LIQUIFICATION TEMPERATURE OF GAS            *
*                WANTED                                       *
*    SOLTMP    - SOLIDIFICATION TEMPERATURE OF GAS           *
*                WANTED                                       *
*                                                            *
**************************************************************

      INTEGER LIQTMP(20), SOLTMP(20)
      INTEGER GAS(20), WANTED
      INTEGER I, N
      PARAMETER (N=5)

      WRITE (*,*) 'INPUT 5 SETS OF DATA'
      READ (*,1000) (GAS(I),LIQTMP(I),SOLTMP(I),
     1     I=1,N)
1000  FORMAT(I10,I5,I5)
      WRITE (*,*) 'ENTER I.D. OF GAS WANTED'
      READ (*,1100) WANTED
1100  FORMAT(I10)
      I = 1

*     DO WHILE (I .LT. N .AND. GAS(I) .LT. WANTED)

10    IF (I .LT. N .AND. GAS(I) .LT. WANTED) THEN
        I = I + 1
        GO TO 10
      ENDIF

*     ENDDO

      IF( GAS(I) .EQ. WANTED) THEN
        WRITE (*,*) WANTED,'  LIQUIFIES AT',LIQTMP(I)
        WRITE (*,*) '  SOLIDIFIES AT  ',SOLTMP(I)
      ELSE
        WRITE (*,*) WANTED,'  NOT IN TABLE'
      ENDIF
      STOP
      END
```

Output

```
INPUT 5 SETS OF DATA
         1     5   100
         2    10   110
         3    15   120
         4    20   130
         5    25   140
 ENTER I.D. OF GAS WANTED
         3
         3   LIQUIFIES AT              15
    SOLIDIFIES AT              120

INPUT 5 SETS OF DATA
         1     5   100
         2    10   110
         3    15   120
         4    20   130
         5    25   140
 ENTER I.D. OF GAS WANTED
         8
         8   NOT IN TABLE
```

6.6.6 Evaluation of a Polynomial

Problem

Evaluate a polynomial in X having at most six coefficients.

Method

Use Horner's method. For a polynomial of degree 5 having six coefficients, the formula is:

$$y = ((((c_0 * x + c_1) * x + c_2) * x + c_3) * x + c_4) * x + c_5$$

Pseudocode

Read the coefficients
Read the value of X
Use a loop to calculate the value of Y
Output the value of Y
Stop

Program

```
*****************************************************************
*                                                               *
*   EVALUATE A POLYNOMIAL OF DEGREE NOT GREATER                 *
*   THAN 5                                                       *
*                                                               *
*****************************************************************
*                                                               *
*   INPUT VARIABLES:                                            *
*                                                               *
*     C(N)        - COEFFICIENTS OF THE POLYNOMIAL              *
*     X           - VALUE OF VARIABLE                           *
*                                                               *
*   OUTPUT VARIABLES:                                           *
*                                                               *
*     Y           - THE VALUE OF THE POLYNOMIAL                 *
*                                                               *
*****************************************************************

        REAL C(0:5),X,Y
        INTEGER I, N

        WRITE (*,*) 'INPUT 6 COEFFICIENTS'
        READ (*,*) (C(I), I=0,5)
        I = 6
        N = I - 1
        WRITE (*,*) 'INPUT THE VARIABLE X OF THE ',
     1        'FUNCTION'
        READ (*,*) X
        Y = C(0)
        DO 30 I=1,N
           Y = Y * X + C(I)
30      CONTINUE
        WRITE (*,*) 'X =',X,'    Y =',Y
        STOP
        END
```

Output

```
 INPUT 6 COEFFICIENTS
 6.,3.,5.,2.,1.,6.
 INPUT THE VARIABLE X OF THE FUNCTION
 2.5
 X =    2.500000         Y =    802.2500
```

In this example, the array of coefficients may not be full. The variable N is the subscript of the last coefficient.

6.6.7 Inventory of an Engineering Parts Supply Firm

Problem

Calculate the total value of the parts belonging to a supply firm.

Method

Use three arrays, the first for the number of items of each part type in the inventory, and the second for the cost of each item. Calculate the value of the inventory of each part type, the total number of items in the inventory, and the total value of the inventory. Also calculate the percent of the inventory value that is invested in each part type. In the third array, store the total value of each part type.

Pseudocode

```
Input the number of types of parts in the inventory
For each part type
    Input the number of items, and the value per item
end for
Initialize the totals
    INVTOT ← 0
    INVCST ← 0
For each part type
    Add number of items to INVTOT
    Calculate total cost
    Add total cost to INVCST
end for
For each part type
    Calculate percent of INVCST
    Output number of items, value per item, total cost,
        percent of INVCST
end for
Output INVTOT, INVCST
Stop
END
```

Program

```
*****************************************************
*                                                   *
*   INVENTORY OF A PARTS SUPPLIER                   *
*                                                   *
*****************************************************
*                                                   *
*   INPUT VARIABLES:                                *
*                                                   *
*     M       - NUMBER OF PART TYPES IN INVENTORY   *
*                                                   *
*   SUBPROGRAMS:                                    *
*                                                   *
*     INPUT  - SUBROUTINE TO INPUT PARTS INFORMATION*
*     COMPUT - SUBROUTINE TO COMPUTE THE COSTS      *
*     OUTPUT - SUBROUTINE TO PRINT THE INVENTORY    *
*              REPORT                               *
*                                                   *
*****************************************************

      COMMON ITEM(100), ITMCST(100), TOTCST(100)
      INTEGER ITEM,INVTOT,M
      REAL ITMCST,TOTCST,INVCST

      WRITE (*,*) 'INPUT THE NUMBER OF ITEMS:'
      READ (*,1000) M
1000  FORMAT(I5)
      CALL INPUT(M)
      CALL COMPUT(M,INVCST,INVTOT)
      CALL OUTPUT(M,INVCST,INVTOT)
      STOP
      END


*****************************************************
*                                                   *
*   INPUT THE INFORMATION FOR EACH PART TYPE        *
*                                                   *
*****************************************************
*                                                   *
*   INPUT VARIABLES:                                *
*                                                   *
*     M         - NUMBER OF PART TYPES IN INVENTORY *
*     ITEM(M)   - NUMBER OF ITEMS OF EACH PART TYPE *
*     ITMCST(M) - COST PER ITEM OF EACH PART TYPE   *
*                                                   *
*****************************************************

      SUBROUTINE INPUT(N)
      COMMON ITEM(100),ITMCST(100),TOTCST(100)
      INTEGER ITEM,N,I
      REAL ITMCST,TOTCST
```

```
          WRITE (*,500)
500       FORMAT(/1X,'INPUT ITEM QUANTITY AND COST ',
     1        'PER ITEM')
          DO 10 I=1,N
            READ (*,1000),ITEM(I),ITMCST(I)
1000        FORMAT(I5,F10.2)
10        CONTINUE
          RETURN
          END


     ********************************************************
     *                                                      *
     *   CALCULATE THE INVENTORY TOTALS AND COSTS           *
     *                                                      *
     ********************************************************
     *                                                      *
     *   INPUT VARIABLES:                                   *
     *                                                      *
     *     M           - NUMBER OF PART TYPES IN INVENTORY  *
     *     ITEM(M)     - NUMBER OF ITEMS OF EACH PART TYPE  *
     *     ITMCST(M)   - COST PER ITEM OF EACH PART TYPE    *
     *                                                      *
     *   OUTPUT VARIABLES:                                  *
     *                                                      *
     *     ITMTOT(M)   - TOTAL VALUE OF EACH PART TYPE      *
     *     INVTOT      - TOTAL NUMBER OF ITEMS IN INVENTORY *
     *     INVCST      - TOTAL VALUE OF INVENTORY           *
     *                                                      *
     ********************************************************


          SUBROUTINE COMPUT(N,INVTOT,INVCST)
          COMMON ITEM(100),ITMCST(100),TOTCST(100)
          INTEGER ITEM,N,I,IVNTOT
          REAL ITMCST,TOTCST,INVCST

          INVTOT = 0
          INVCST = 0.0
          DO 10 I=1,N
            TOTCST(I) = ITEM(I) * ITMCST(I)
            INVTOT = INVTOT + ITEM(I)
            INVCST = INVCST + TOTCST(I)
10        CONTINUE
          RETURN
          END
```

```
      ************************************************************
      *                                                          *
      *   OUTPUT THE INFORMATION FOR EACH PART TYPE              *
      *                                                          *
      ************************************************************
      *                                                          *
      *   INPUT VARIABLES:                                       *
      *                                                          *
      *     M            - NUMBER OF PART TYPES IN INVENTORY     *
      *                                                          *
      *   OUTPUT VARIABLES:                                      *
      *                                                          *
      *     ITEM(M)      - NUMBER OF ITEMS OF EACH PART TYPE     *
      *     ITMCST(M)    - COST PER ITEM OF EACH PART TYPE       *
      *     TOTCST(M)    - TOTAL VALUE OF INVENTORY OF EACH      *
      *                    PART                                  *
      *     PCTCST       - PERCENT OF INVENTORY OF EACH PART     *
      *                    TYPE                                  *
      *     INVTOT       - NUMBER OF ITEMS IN INVENTORY          *
      *     INVCST       - TOTAL VALUE OF INVENTORY              *
      *                                                          *
      ************************************************************

            SUBROUTINE OUTPUT(N,INVTOT,INVCST)
            COMMON ITEM(100),ITMCST(100),TOTCST(100)
            INTEGER ITEM,INVTOT,N,I
            REAL ITMCST,TOTCST,INVCST,PCTCST

            WRITE (*,1000)
      1000  FORMAT(43X,'PERCENT'/4X,'PART',3X,'NO. ON',4X
           1         'PART',8X,'TOTAL',7X,'OF'/5X,'NO.',
           2         4X,'HAND',5X,'COST',8X,'COST',5X,'INVENTORY')
            DO 10 I=1,N
              PCTCST = TOTCST(I) / INVCST
              WRITE(*,1100) I,ITEM(I),ITMCST(I),TOTCST(I),PCTCST
      1100    FORMAT(/4X,I3,6X,I2,5X,F6.2,5X,F8.2,5X,F4.2)
      10      CONTINUE
            WRITE(*,1200) INVTOT,INVCST
      1200  FORMAT(//1X'TOTALS',T11,I5,T30,F10.2)
            RETURN
            END
```

Output

```
INPUT THE NUMBER OF ITEMS:
    5

INPUT ITEM QUANTITY AND COST PER ITEM
   10   50.
   14   75.
    5   20.
   20   15.
   25   40.

        PART    NO. ON    PART        TOTAL       PERCENT
        NO.     HAND      COST        COST          OF
                                                  INVENTORY

          1      10      50.00       500.00        0.17

          2      14      75.00      1050.00        0.36

          3       5      20.00       100.00        0.03

          4      20      15.00       300.00        0.10

          5      25      40.00      1000.00        0.34


     TOTALS      74                 2950.00
```

Chapter Summary

One-dimensional arrays are used for storing a list or vector of like items. Storage for an array should be explicitly allocated by a type statement:

INTEGER arr(lb:ub),...

lb and ub are the lower and upper bounds of the array, respectively.

REAL arr(lb:ub),...
LOGICAL arr(lb:ub),...

The lower and upper bounds of an array must be integers. The upper bound must be specified, but the lower bound may default to one. When only the upper bound is specified, it must be greater than zero.

An explicit DO-loop is used when an array is used in calculations. Input/ output may be controlled by an explicit DO-loop, by an implied DO-loop, or by using the name of the array.

DO K I=N,M	reads ARR(N), . . . , ARR(M)
READ (*,*) ARR(I)	
k CONTINUE	each from a separate record
READ (*,*) (ARR(I), I=N,M)	reads ARR(N), . . . , ARR(M)
READ (*,*) ARR	reads an entire array

As with simple variables, array input/output may be list-directed or formatted.

Array elements may be used in arithmetic operations like any other variables. Two arrays are compatible if they are both numeric, both logical, or both character and have the same size.

A one-dimensional array is used when a set of data is being processed more than once, a set of data is being sorted, or values are being looked up in a set of data.

Exercises

1. Write a program to input data into an array X(100). Compute the sum and average. Then count the number of values of X greater than the average and the number less than the average. Print the values, the average, and the two counts.

2. Write a program to read a set of 100 integers between 1 and 10 and count the number of times each integer appears in the set. Print the integers in order of frequency, placing the number occurring the highest number of times first.

3. Build a table of the velocity of flow of a liquid through a frictionless pipe for various levels of pressure heads.

   Let h be the pressure head in feet
   g 32 ft/sec^2
   v be the velocity of flow
   then v = $\sqrt{2\,g\,h}$ h = 100, 200, 300, . . . , 10000

4. Write a program that plots a graph of an equation in polar coordinates on a 24 × 80 screen.

$$X = R \cos\theta$$
$$Y = R \sin\theta$$

   where θ = 0.0°, 10.0°, 20.0°, . . . 360°

5. Write a program that builds tables of the tip speed of a propeller having diameter D (an input value) for various shank speeds s, measured in revolutions per minute. Let s = 1000, 2000, 3000, . . . , 80,000. Store the tip speeds and shank speeds in tables; then print the tables. The formula for computing the angular velocity in radians per second is:

$$w = \frac{2\,\pi\,s}{60} \qquad v = \frac{w\,d}{2}$$

6. When surveying for road construction, 1000 survey data values were recorded in a one-dimensional array. The locations were numbered and the data was stored in the input file in order by location numbers. Write a program that reads the data and stores each value in the position corresponding to the location number in one of two arrays. Array A contains measurements that are above a common datum; Array B contains measurements

that are below the common datum. Write a subroutine CREATE to create the two arrays and call another subroutine OUTPUT to print the two arrays, 20 values per line.

7. Write a program that stores the IDs, ages, and weights of laboratory animals in arrays. Call a subroutine to sort the information into ascending order according to the age of the animals. Print the sorted information.

8. A farmer keeps a list of his beef cattle on a computer. Every month he sells the heaviest animals. Write a program that reads the IDs and weights of the animals into an array, calls a subroutine to sort the array into descending order by weight, and prints the information on the K heaviest animals.

7 *Multidimensional Arrays*

Objective: To process data stored by rows and columns in tables.

*D*ata that would be written by hand in the form of a table, data positioned in terms of space/time coordinates, values of functions of two or more independent variables—all must be represented using two or more subscripts and stored in arrays having two or more dimensions. Examples of a two-dimensional array include theater seats arranged by row and postion within the row, rate of water flow over dams on a river at noon each day, or value of f(x,y) for integer values of x and y. Mathematical matrices of two or more dimensions are implemented as arrays. These often represent sets of vectors, for example, the coefficients of simultaneous equations. Thus a two-dimensional array can store a table of values of a single type, or a set of vectors of a single type. A three-dimensional array can store a three-dimensional matrix or a set of two-dimensional tables. In FORTRAN 77, arrays may have up to seven dimensions.

7.1 Concept of Two-Dimensional Arrays

A two-dimensional arrangement of data is normally considered to consist of rows and columns. For example, minimum water levels at three stations on a river for the past four years might be given as:

	station 1	station 2	station 3
year 1	14.7	−6.3	9.2
year 2	29.6	8.9	17.4
year 3	−0.1	7.9	6.0
year 4	5.5	14.2	−3.7

Each value in this arrangement can be uniquely identified by indicating its row and its column. If this arrangement of data is collectively named X, then the mathematical notation for any single element of the arrangement is given by

$X_{i,j}$ i = 1,2,3,4 and j = 1,2,3
where   i is the row subscript (year)
          j is the column subscript (station)

The values in the table are assigned names as follows:

	column 1	column 2	column 3
row 1	$X_{1,1}$	$X_{1,2}$	$X_{1,3}$
row 2	$X_{2,1}$	$X_{2,2}$	$X_{2,3}$
row 3	$X_{3,1}$	$X_{3,2}$	$X_{3,3}$
row 4	$X_{4,1}$	$X_{4,2}$	$X_{4,3}$

The first subscript is called the row subscript because it is the same for each element in a row, and the second subscript is called the column subscript because it is the same for each element in a column. You can see that the position of each element in a row is indicated by the second or column subscript and the position of each element in a column is indicated by the first or row subscript.

A two dimensional array can be accessed at three levels: as a whole, as a single row or a single column, or as a single element.

Algebra	*FORTRAN*	
X	X	refers to the whole array
$X_{2,j}$	(X(2,J), J = 1,3)	refers to row 2
$X_{i,1}$	(X(I,1), I = 1,4)	refers to column 1
$X_{2,1}$	X(2,1)	refers to row 2, column 1

Programming Hint

> Vary column subscripts to access elements by rows, and row subscripts to access elements by columns.

In FORTRAN notation, the elements of the two-dimensional array X are identified as follows:

	column 1	column 2	column 3
row 1	X(1,1)	X(1,2)	X(1,3)
row 2	X(2,1)	X(2,2)	X(2,3)
row 3	X(3,1)	X(3,2)	X(3,3)
row 4	X(4,1)	X(4,2)	X(4,3)

7.1.1 Declaration Statement

A type declaration statement must be used to specify the data type, give a name, and allocate the storage space for a two-dimensional array. In has the general form

type arr($l_r : u_r$, $l_c : u_c$)

where $u_r \geq l_r$, $u_c \geq l_c$

For example:

```
REAL X(1:4,1:3)
```

where l and u refer to the lower and upper bounds, respectively. Subscripts r and c refer to rows and columns, or

type arr(u_r , u_c)

where $u_r \geq 1$, $u_c \geq 1$

For example:

```
REAL X(4,3)
```

The size of these arrays X is 12, four rows by three columns. The upper bound must be specified. When only the upper bound is specified for a dimension, the lower bound defaults to 1. The type may be integer, real, logical, double precision, complex, or character.

The formula for calculating the size of a two-dimensional array is:

$$size = (u_r - l_r + 1) \times (u_c - l_c + 1)$$

For the array $X(4,3)$, size = $(4 - 1 + 1) \times (3 - 1 + 1) = 12$. When a program contains many large arrays, the size of the arrays may affect the efficiency of the program. The following type declarations allocate storage for arrays of various sizes:

Declaration	Rows	Columns	Size
REAL A(5,5)	5	5	25
INTEGER B(3:8,5)	6	5	30
LOGICAL C(5:16,6:18)	12	13	156
INTEGER D(-5:0,5:10)	6	6	36
REAL E(0:7,-3:5)	8	9	72
REAL D(-8:-2,-5:-1)	7	5	35

7.1.2 Storage Allocation

The computer uses the array declaration to set up the allocation of memory space for the array when the program is compiled. The amount of space assigned cannot be changed without recompiling the program. Unlike most computer languages, FORTRAN stores two-dimensional arrays by columns, even though this is not the natural order for writing values by hand or entering them on a terminal. The storage order is shown below:

```
        REAL  X(4,3)

X(1,1)    X(1,2)    X(1,3)
X(2,1)    X(2,2)    X(2,3)
X(3,1)    X(3,2)    X(3,3)
X(4,1)    X(4,2)    X(4,3)
```

	X(1,1)
col 1	X(2,1)
	X(3,1)
	X(4,1)
	X(1,2)
col 2	X(2,2)
	X(3,2)
	X(4,2)
	X(1,3)
col 3	X(2,3)
	X(3,3)
	X(4,3)

Notice that the four elements of the first column are stored ahead of the elements of the second column, and that the third column is last. The elements of each column are stored in order of increasing row number, and the columns are stored in order of increasing column number. In this order, the first subscript, which is the row subscript, changes more rapidly than the column subscript. This is known as column-major order.

As the following example shows, the elements are ordered by columns regardless of the values of the subscripts.

```
      INTEGER N(3:4,-1:1)
```

```
N(3,-1)   N(3,0)   N(3,1)
N(4,-1)   N(4,0)   N(4,1)
```

col 1	$N(3,-1)$	
	$N(4,-1)$	----
col 2	$N(3,0)$	
	$N(4,0)$	----
col 3	$N(3,1)$	
	$N(4,1)$	

Programming Warning

> Two-dimensional arrays are stored by columns rather than by rows.

Initialization of Two-Dimensional Arrays

Two-dimensional arrays may be initialized through the use of data statements, either by array name or by an implied DO-loop, as shown:

```
REAL X(4,3)
DATA X/12*0.0/
```

is equivalent to

```
REAL X(4,3)
DATA ((X(I,J), I=1,4), J=1,3)/12*0.0/
```

They may also be initialized by using the index values of DO-loops to vary the subscripts in an assignment statement.

```
      REAL X(4,3)
      DO 20 J=1,3
        DO 10 I=1,4
          X(I,J) = 0.0
10      CONTINUE
20    CONTINUE
```

These examples assign the value of zero to all twelve elements of the array X. Notice that the size of the array is used in the DATA statement. With the nested DO-loops, the assignment statement in the inner loop is executed four times for each of the three times through the outer loop, a total of 12. Using the second subscript for the outer DO-loop and the first subscript for the inner loop is natural for the implied DO-loops since the first is written ahead of the second. For each column J, a value is stored for each element of the column. The row subscript changes more rapidly than the column subscript.

```
INTEGER N(2,3)
DATA N/1,2,3,4,5,6/
```

N(1,1)	1
N(2,1)	2
N(1,2)	3
N(2,2)	4
N(1,3)	5
N(2,3)	6

is equivalent to

```
INTEGER N(2,3)
DATA ((N(I,J),I=1,2),J=1,3)/1,2,3,4,5,6/
```

If these array elements are arranged two-dimensionally, they have the following form:

$$\begin{array}{lll} & \text{array N} & \\ N(1,1)=1 & N(1,2)=3 & N(1,3)=5 \\ N(2,1)=2 & N(2,2)=4 & N(2,3)=6 \end{array}$$

The following example shows the initialization of an array with explicit lower bounds:

```
REAL X(-3:0,2:6)
DATA X/20*0.0/
```

is equivalent to

```
REAL X(-3:0,2:6)
DATA ((X(I,J), I=-3,0), J=2,6)/20*0.0/
```

The DATA statement can be used when arrays such as those used for counters or accumulating totals must be initialized to values that will change during program execution. The PARAMETER statement should be used for constant values, that is, values that will not change during program execution.

Programming
Hint

> Maintainability: Use the DATA statement to initialize variables and the PARAMETER statement to intialize constants.

The following example shows the use of a DATA statement to initialize a vector to hold the row totals of a two-dimensional array:

```
REAL X(4,3),XROW(4)
DATA XROW/0.0,0.0,0.0,0.0/

DO 20 I=1,4
   DO 10 J=1,3
      XROW(I) = XROW(I) + X(I,J)
10    CONTINUE
20 CONTINUE
```

When arrays are to be processed by row rather than by column, the index of the inner DO-loop corresponds to the column subscript. In this case the array elements are not processed in the order in which they are stored. This is shown in the following example:

```
INTEGER N(2,3)
DATA ((N(I,J), J=1,3), I=1,2)/1,2,3,4,5,6/
```

is equivalent to

```
INTEGER N(2,3)
K = 1
DO 20 I=1,2
   DO 10 J=1,3
      N(I,J) = K
      K = K + 1
10    CONTINUE
20 CONTINUE
```

N(1,1)	1
N(2,1)	4
N(1,2)	2
N(2,2)	5
N(1,3)	3
N(2,3)	6

If these array elements are arranged two-dimensionally, they have the following form:

array N

$$N(1,1) = 1 \quad N(1,2) = 2 \quad N(1,3) = 3$$
$$N(2,1) = 4 \quad N(2,2) = 5 \quad N(2,3) = 6$$

The following examples show arrays accessed by rows and by columns:

Array
REAL X(3,4)

Row access	*Column access*
((X(I,J), J = 1,4), I = 1,3)	((X(I,J), I = 1,3), J = 1,4)
or	or

```
      DO 20 I = 1,3              DO 20 J = 1,4
         DO 10 J = 1,4              DO 10 I = 1,3
            X(I,J) ...                X(I,J) ...
   10    CONTINUE           10    CONTINUE
   20 CONTINUE              20 CONTINUE
```

Array
REAL X(−8:4,12:40)

Row access	*Column access*
((X(I,J), J = 12,40), I = −8,4)	((X(I,J), I = −8,4), J = 12,40)
or	or

```
      DO 20 I = −8,4            DO 20 J = 12,40
         DO 10 J = 12,40           DO 10 I = −8,4
            X(I,J) ...                X(I,J) ...
   10    CONTINUE           10    CONTINUE
   20 CONTINUE              20 CONTINUE
```

7.1.3 Review Questions

1. Write declarations for the following arrays:

   a. real $X_{i,j}$ i = 1,5   j = 1,8
   b. integer $y_{i,j}$ i = −2,7   j = 1,12
   c. logical $p_{i,j}$ and $q_{i,j}$ i = 3,8   j = 0,6

2. For each of the following arrays, show the storage allocation:
   a. REAL A(2,4)
   b. REAL B(3:6,4:6)
   c. INTEGER C(−2:0,−5:−3)
   d. INTEGER D(2:4,−3:−1)

3. For each of the following arrays, give the upper and lower bound of the row subscript, the upper and lower bound of the column subscript:

   a. INTEGER X(8,6)
   b. LOGICAL Y(3:7,8:16)
   c. REAL Z(−5:3,−7:−2)

4. For each of the following arrays, show the nesting of DO-loops that would process the array by columns:

   a. REAL X(6,7)
   b. REAL Y(5:8,6:12)

   c. REAL Z$(-5:2, -6:-2)$
   d. REAL W$(-8:-2, 9:11)$

5. For each of the following arrays, show the nesting of DO-loops that would process the array by rows:

   a. REAL X(6,7)
   b. REAL Y(5:8,6:12)
   c. REAL Z$(-5:2, -6:-2)$
   d. REAL W$(-8:-2, 9:11)$

7.2 Input of Two-Dimensional Arrays

Data can be input into two-dimensional arrays by using the array name, by using implied DO-loops, or by using nested DO-loops. When the unsubscripted array name is used, there must be enough data to fill the array, and it must be provided by the input device and ordered by columns. If the array may not be filled, or if the data is presented in row order, either DO-loops or implied DO-loops must be used.

7.2.1 Input by Array Name

When data is input by array name, it is stored sequentially in the space allocated for the array. Since the array is stored in column-major order, the data must be presented in column-major order, as shown in the following example:

array X			
12.8	6.7	13.9	139.5
3.6	18.3	6.7	19.3
7.5	9.4	8.5	240.0

Given the program segment

```
REAL X(3,4)
READ*,X
```

and the data

```
12.8    3.6    7.5
```

```
6.7    18.3    9.4
```

```
13.9    6.7    8.5
```

```
139.4    19.3    240.0
```

the values are stored as shown:

X(1,1)	12.8
X(2,1)	3.6
X(3,1)	7.5
X(1,2)	6.7
X(2,2)	18.3
X(3,2)	9.4
X(1,3)	13.9
X(2,3)	6.7
X(3,3)	8.5
X(1,4)	139.5
X(2,4)	19.3
X(3,4)	240.0

7.2.2 Input Using DO-Loops

By controlling the order of the indexing, two-dimensional arrays can be input in row order.

array X

12.8	6.7	13.9	139.5
3.6	18.3	6.7	19.3
7.5	9.4	8.5	240.0

Given the program segment

```
REAL X(3,4)
READ (*,*) ((X(I,J), J=1,4), I=1,3)
```

and the data

```
12.8    6.7    13.9    139.5
```

```
3.6    18.3    6.7    19.3
```

```
7.5    9.4    8.5    240.0
```

the values are stored as shown:

X(1,1)	12.8
X(2,1)	3.6
X(3,1) ----	7.5
X(1,2)	6.7
X(2,2)	18.3
X(3,2) ----	9.4
X(1,3)	13.9
X(2,3)	6.7
X(3,3) ----	8.5
X(1,4)	139.5
X(2,4)	19.3
X(3,4)	240.0

Since the array is the same as in the previous example, the same values are stored in the same locations. The input data, however, resembles the array rather than its transpose. Since the data is not in column-major order, subscripting is used to control the storing of the values.

If the data is being entered by rows, an entire row at once, either of the following segments of code can be used:

```
      REAL X(3,4)
      READ (*,1000) ((X(I,J), J=1,4), I=1,3)
1000  FORMAT(4F5.0)
```

is equivalent to

```
      REAL X(3,4)
      DO 20 I=1,3
        READ (*,1000) (X(I,J), J=1,4)
1000    FORMAT(4F5.0)
20    CONTINUE
```

With the implied DO, the repeat factor in the format controls the number of values to be read from each input record. If there are four values per record, then three records are read, one for each row. When the implied DO is nested inside the regular DO-loop, the READ statement is executed three times, once for each record.

If the data is being entered by rows, one value at a time, either of the following segments of code can be used:

```
      REAL X(3,4)
      READ (*,1000) ((X(I,J), J=1,4), I=1,3)
1000  FORMAT(F5.0)
```

is equivalent to

```
      REAL X(3,4)
      DO 20 I=1,3
        DO 10 J=1,4
          READ (*,1000) X(I,J)
1000      FORMAT(F5.0)
10      CONTINUE
20    CONTINUE
```

Both of these two looping constructs require 12 records of input data.

Programming Hint

> Efficiency: Use a nested implied DO-loop to input data into two-dimensional arrays, provided there is enough data to fill the array.

7.2.3 Review Questions

1. Write an input statement to read the following data by name, formatted, four values per record. Show how the data is arranged in the input records and in storage.

   array N

1	2	3	4
5	6	7	8
9	10	11	12
13	14	15	16

   a. Read the values in row-major order.
   b. Read the values in column-major order.

2. Write an input statement to read the following data if all the values are in a single record. Show how the data is arranged in the record and in storage.

   array A

8.5	6.2	7.5
9.8	7.6	3.9
6.8	9.4	8.3

   a. Read the values in row-major order.
   b. Read the values in column-major order.

3. Write an input statement to read data into the first 10 rows of the array declared as REAL X(100,5), assuming each row is in a separate record.

4. Write an input statement to read data into the array declared as REAL Y(20,10), assuming each row is in a separate record. Also assume that there may be fewer than 20 records.

5. For each of the following program segments, how many input records are needed?

   a.
   ```
        DO 50 I=1,10
          DO 20 J=1,5
            READ (*,*) A(I,J)
   20       CONTINUE
   50     CONTINUE
   ```

   b.
   ```
        DO 50 J=1,5
          DO 20 I=1,10
            READ (*,*) A(I,J)
   20       CONTINUE
   50     CONTINUE
   ```

   c.
   ```
        DO 50 I=1,10
          READ (*,2000) (A(I,J), J=1,5)
   ```

```
              2000      FORMAT(5F12.5)
              50        CONTINUE

        d.              DO 10 J=1,5
                          READ (*,3000) (A(I,J), I=1,10)
              3000      FORMAT(10F8.5)
              10        CONTINUE

        e.              READ (*,5000) ((A(I,J), J=1,5),I=1,10)
              5000    FORMAT(5F10.2)
```

7.3 Output of Two-Dimensional Arrays

Two-dimensional arrays should be output in readable form. They should be printed
or displayed by rows, with the columns aligned. To output two-dimensional arrays,
use either a combination of regular implied DO-loops or nested implied DO-loops.
The number of values printed on each line can be controlled by the format repeat
factor. The examples in this section show such looping and format-controlled
structures.

*Programming
Warning*

> If a two-dimensional array is output by name, the data will be printed in column-
> major order.

7.3.1 Output Using DO-Loops

In the following example, the WRITE statement executes once for each row. This
causes each of the rows of the array to be printed on a separate line. The actual
number of values printed on each line is limited by the default fields in the list-
directed output. But each time the WRITE statement executes, the output will start
on a new line.

```
        REAL X(8,10)
        . . .
        DO 30 I=1,8
          WRITE (*,*) (X(I,J), J=1,10)
30      CONTINUE
```

In the following example, the WRITE statement executes once. The repeat
factor in the format statement controls the number of values printed on each line.
Each row of the array is printed on a separate line.

```
        REAL X(8,10)
        . . .
        WRITE (*,1000) ((X(I,J), J=1,10), I=1,8)
1000    FORMAT(1X,10F12.4)
```

The following example shows an array printed with the rows and columns numbered. Given the program segment

```
      INTEGER M(3,3)
      WRITE (*,1000)(J, J=1,3)
1000  FORMAT(4X,3I10//)
      DO 10 I=1,3
         WRITE (*,2000) I,(M(I,J), J=1,3)
2000     FORMAT(1X,I3,3I10)
10    CONTINUE
```

and the data

M(1,1)	380
M(2,1)	960
M(3,1) - - -	125
M(1,2)	875
M(2,2)	962
M(3,2) - - -	735
M(1,3)	935
M(2,3)	176
M(3,3)	82

the output is as follows:

```
                 1           2           3

      1         380         875         935
      2         960         962         176
      3         125         735          82
```

When an array has too many elements in each row to print each row on a single line, several lines should be used for each row. The array will be readable if the first line of each row is labeled and the rows are separated by blank lines, as in the following example:

```
      REAL VAL(100,100)
       . . .
      DO 10 I=1,100
         WRITE (*,1000) I,(VAL(I,J), J=1,20)
1000     FORMAT(///1X,I4,20F5.2)
         WRITE (*,2000) (VAL(I,J), J=21,100)
2000     FORMAT(5X,20F5.2)
10    CONTINUE
```

The 100 values in each row of the array are printed 20 to a line in five lines. Two blank output lines are left between rows of the array. The first line of each row of the array is numbered. The entire array will use 700 lines of output, approximately 13 pages.

Efficiency: Very large arrays should be processed in column-major order to avoid excessive disk access.

7.3.2 Review Questions

1. Given an array stored as shown, write the output statements to print the array N:

   a. by rows, one row per line
   b. by columns, one column per line
   c. by rows, with the rows numbered
   d. by rows, with the columns numbered

N(1,1)	25
N(2,1)	− 8
N(3,1)	286
N(4,1)	23
N(1,2)	7
N(2,2)	62
N(3,2)	0
N(4,2)	116
N(1,3)	− 27
N(2,3)	780
N(3,3)	5
N(4,3)	176

2. Given the array REAL X(10,10), how many lines of output are produced by each of the following program segments?

   a.
   ```
           DO 10 I=1,10
             WRITE (*,5000) (X(I,J), J=1,10)
   5000      FORMAT(1X,5F10.2)
   10      CONTINUE
   ```

   b.
   ```
           DO 10 I=1,10
             WRITE (*,5000) (X(I,J), J=1,10)
   5000      FORMAT(1X,10F10.2)
   10      CONTINUE
   ```

   c.
   ```
           DO 10 I=1,10
             WRITE (*,*) (X(I,J), J=1,10)
   10      CONTINUE
   ```

3. Show the output of each of the following program segments, using the array of problem 1.

   a.
   ```
           WRITE (*,5000) ((N(I,J), J=1,3), I=1,4)
   5000    FORMAT(1X,3I5)
   ```

   b.
   ```
           WRITE (*,5000) (I,(N(I,J), J=1,3), I=1,4)
   5000    FORMAT(1X,4I5)
   ```

```
   c.          WRITE (*,5000) ((J,N(I,J), J=1,3), I=1,4)
        5000  FORMAT(1X,6I5)
```

4. Write a code segment to print each of the following arrays, one row per line:
   a. REAL X(−5: −3,7)
   b. INTEGER IVAL(0:4,0:6)
   c. REAL ARR(−3:3, −2:5)

7.4 Manipulation of Arrays

When arrays are used in arithmetic, it is always the individual elements that are used. The whole array is processed by indexing through all the subscripts.

7.4.1 Array Assignment

For efficient initialization of a two-dimensional array, use nested DO-loops. The outer loop indexes the column subscript and the inner loop indexes the row subscript, as in the following example:

```
        INTEGER A(3,4),ROW,COL
        DO 20 COL=1,4
          DO 10 ROW=1,3
            A(ROW,COL) = 0
  10        CONTINUE
  20      CONTINUE
```

A value of zero is assigned to each element of the array.

If one array is being copied into another, the same set of indexes can be used as subscripts for both, as in the following example:

```
*  COPY AN ARRAY

        INTEGER X(3,4),Y(3,4)
        . . .
        DO 20 J=1,4
          DO 10 I=1,3
            Y(I,J) = X(I,J)
  10        CONTINUE
  20      CONTINUE
```

Each element of the array X is copied into the corresponding position in array Y. Again, column-major order is used for efficiency.

To form the transpose of a matrix, use the indexes as subscripts for both arrays. Process one in column-major order and one in row-major order, as in the following example:

```
*  FORM THE TRANSPOSE OF AN ARRAY

        INTEGER ARR(3,4),TRANSP(4,3)
        . . .
```

```
        DO 20 J=1,4
          DO 10 I=1,3
            TRANSP(J,I) = ARR(I,J)
10        CONTINUE
20      CONTINUE
```

```
        ARR                 TRANSP
     1   2   3           1   2   3   4
1    .   .   .      1    .   .   .   .
2    .   .   .      2    .   .   .   .
3    .   .   .      3    .   .   .   .
4    .   .   .
```

In this example, the first column of array ARR is copied to the first row of array TRANSP, the second column to the second row, and so forth.

By varying only one subscript, a single row or column may be accessed, as in the following examples:

```
*   STORE 5 IN COLUMN 3          *   STORE 5 IN ROW 3

        REAL W(5,7)                      REAL W(5,7)
        . . .                            . . .
        DO 10 I = 1,5                    DO 10 J = 1,7
          W(I,3) = 5.0                     W(3,J) = 5.0
10      CONTINUE                 10      CONTINUE
```

By using a single index for the subscripts, the diagonals of an array may be accessed, as in the following examples:

```
*   STORE 5 ON MAJOR DIAGONAL

        INTEGER Q(10,10),N
        N = 10
        DO 10 I = 1,N
          Q(I,I) = 5
10      CONTINUE
```

```
*   STORE 5 ON MINOR DIAGONAL

        INTEGER Q(10,10),N
        N = 10
        DO 50 I = 1,N
          Q(I,N+1-I) = 5
50      CONTINUE
```

7.4.2 Matrix Operations on Arrays

When arrays represent mathematical matrices, implement the matrix arithmetic operations by using DO-loops to index through the arrays. Below are the calculations of the mathematical sum and difference of two matrices:

```
*   MATRIX ADDITION: C = A + B

        REAL A(N,M),B(N,M),C(N,M)
        INTEGER I,J,N,M
        . . .
        DO 20 J = 1,M
          DO 10 I = 1,N
            C(I,J) = A(I,J) + B(I,J)
10        CONTINUE
20      CONTINUE

*   MATRIX SUBTRACTION: C = A - B

        REAL A(N,M),B(N,M),C(N,M)
        INTEGER I,J,N,M
        . . .
        DO 20 J = 1,M
          DO 10 I = 1,N
            C(I,J) = A(I,J) - B(I,J)
10        CONTINUE
20      CONTINUE
```

Notice that the arrays are being processed in column-major order. Corresponding elements of array A and array B are added or subtracted with the result stored in array C. All three arrays are the same size, with the same size rows and the same size columns.

Matrix addition and subtraction are element by element addition and subtraction, but matrix multiplication is not element by element multiplication. Instead, it is an inner product. In mathematical terms,

$$c_{i,j} = \sum_{k=1}^{l} a_{i,k} \, b_{k,j}$$

```
*   MATRIX MULTIPLICATION: C = A * B

        SUBROUTINE MATMLT(A,B,C,N,L,M)
        REAL A(N,L),B(L,M),C(N,M),SUM
        INTEGER I,J,K,L,M,N
        . . .
        DO 30 J = 1,M
          DO 20 I = 1,N
            SUM = 0.0
            DO 10 K=1,L
              SUM = SUM + A(I,K) * B(K,J)
10          CONTINUE
            C(I,J) = SUM
20        CONTINUE
30      CONTINUE
```

This product is shown in the following matrices:

$$A = \begin{bmatrix} a_{11} & a_{12} \\ a_{21} & a_{22} \end{bmatrix} \qquad B = \begin{bmatrix} b_{11} & b_{12} & b_{13} \\ b_{21} & b_{22} & b_{23} \end{bmatrix}$$

$$C = \begin{bmatrix} a_{11}b_{11} + a_{12}b_{21} & a_{11}b_{12} + a_{12}b_{22} & a_{11}b_{13} + a_{12}b_{23} \\ a_{21}b_{11} + a_{22}b_{21} & a_{21}b_{12} + a_{22}b_{22} & a_{21}b_{13} + a_{22}b_{23} \end{bmatrix}$$

Row I of matrix A is multipied by column J of matrix B and the sum of the individual products is stored in C(I,J), for all I and J. Multiplication of matrices A and B is possible if and only if the number of columns of matrix A is the same as the number of rows of matrix B.

Calculating a power of a matrix is a special case of matrix multiplication. Matrix powers can only be calculated for square matrices.

```
*   POWER OF A MATRIX: C = A²

        SUBROUTINE POWER(A,C,N)
        REAL A(N,N),C(N,N),SUM
        INTEGER I,J,K,N
        . . .
        DO 30 J = 1,N
          DO 20 I = 1,N
            SUM = 0.0
            DO 10 K=1,N
              SUM = SUM + A(I,K) * A(K,J)
10          CONTINUE
            C(I,J) = SUM
20        CONTINUE
30      CONTINUE
```

Notice that multiplication of large matrices is time consuming for the computer. This algorithm for calculating the square of an n x n matrix executes the assignment statement inside the innermost loop n^3 times. For a 100×100 matrix, this is 1,000,000 times.

7.4.3 Review Questions

1. Using the following two-dimensional arrays A and B, show the result of each of the segments of code.

	array A			array B	
3.5	6.8	9.2	2.0	3.0	4.0
8.5	7.6	12.7	1.0	2.0	6.0
5.2	4.6	7.2	7.0	5.0	3.0

a.
```
        DO 10 I=1,3
          A(I,2) = A(I,3) + A(I,3)
10      CONTINUE
```

b.
```
        DO 10 J=1,3
          B(2,J) = B(2,J) + B(3,J)
10      CONTINUE
```

c.
```
        DO 60 I=1,3
          DO 50 J=2,3
            A(I,J) = B(I,J) * 2
```

```
      50        CONTINUE
      60      CONTINUE

  d.          DO 30 I=1,2
                DO 20 J=1,3
                  B(I,J) = A(I,J) + B(I,J)
      20        CONTINUE
      30      CONTINUE
```

2. Given the two-dimensional array A(6,8), write a code segment to do each of the following:

   a. Compute the sum of each row and store the row sums in a one-dimensional array.
   b. Compute the sum of each column and store the column sums in a one-dimensional array.
   c. Compute the sum of all the elements in the array.

3. Given the square matrix X(10,10), write a code segment to do each of the following:

   a. Compute the sum of the elements of the major and minor diagonals.
   b. Compute the sum of the elements in the upper triangular matrix.
   c. Compute the sum of the elements in the lower triangular matrix.

4. Given the square matrix A(N,N), write a code segment to calculate A^3, the third power of the matrix.

7.5 Concept of Higher Dimension Arrays

In engineering and the physical sciences, problems expressed in terms of three dimensions or even four (three of space and one of time) are common. Much of modern physics postulates even more dimensions. Arrays of up to seven dimensions can be used in FORTRAN 77.

Applications in engineering and science that involve three-dimensional objects often require the use of three-dimensional arrays. Some common examples are heat conduction through three-dimensional bodies, fluid flow over airfoils, wave propagation through three-dimensional bodies, vibrations of three-dimensional objects, stress analysis in human bones, and so on.

One way of imagining arrays of more than two dimensions is in terms of tables that are printed on more than one sheet of paper. A large table might require more than one volume of a book. Then the book itself might have several printings, the printings might be for several editions, and the editions might be translated into several languages. Thus a multidimensional array of numbers could be interpreted as:

two dimensions
    array(row,column)
three dimensions
    array(row,column,sheet)
four dimensions
    array(row,column,sheet,volume)
five dimensions
    array(row,column,sheet,volume,printing)

six dimensions
  array(row,column,sheet,volume,printing,edition)
seven dimensions
  array(row,column,sheet,volume,printing,edition,language)

The value X(6,5,2,1,4,3,7) would then be the number in row 6, column 5 (or the sixth number in column 5) on the second sheet of the first volume of the fourth printing of edition three in language seven. Notice that the last subscript represents the largest category.

In mathematical terms, a multidimensional array represents values of a function of more than one variable, where the independent variables can only assume integer values.

two dimensions
  f(x,y) x and y integers
three dimensions
  f(x,y,z) x, y, and z integers
four dimensions
  f(x,y,z,w) x, y, z, and w integers
and so forth

7.5.1 Declarations and Storage Allocation

The general form of an array declaration for a multidimensional array is

$$\text{type arr}(l_r:u_r,l_c:u_c,l_s:u_s,\ldots)$$

or

$$\text{type arr}(u_r,u_c,u_s,\ldots)$$

where u and l are the upper and lower bounds and r, c, and s are the row, column, and sheet subscripts. The lower bound default value is one. In the example

```
REAL X(3,4,2)
```

space is allocated for a three-dimensional array having three rows and four columns on each of two sheets. Geometrically, the three-dimensional array can be shown as in Fig. 7.1.

The arrangement of the elements is as follows:

sheet 1	$X_{1,1,1}$	$X_{1,2,1}$	$X_{1,3,1}$	$X_{1,4,1}$
	$X_{2,1,1}$	$X_{2,2,1}$	$X_{2,3,1}$	$X_{2,4,1}$
	$X_{3,1,1}$	$X_{3,2,1}$	$X_{3,3,1}$	$X_{3,4,1}$

sheet 2	$X_{1,1,2}$	$X_{1,2,2}$	$X_{1,3,2}$	$X_{1,4,2}$
	$X_{2,1,2}$	$X_{2,2,2}$	$X_{2,3,2}$	$X_{2,4,2}$
	$X_{3,1,2}$	$X_{3,2,2}$	$X_{3,3,2}$	$X_{3,4,2}$

Notice that the third subscript is constant for a given sheet. The first two subscripts give the row and column position of the element on the sheet.

The elements of the array are stored by sheets and within these by columns, as follows:

Figure 7.1

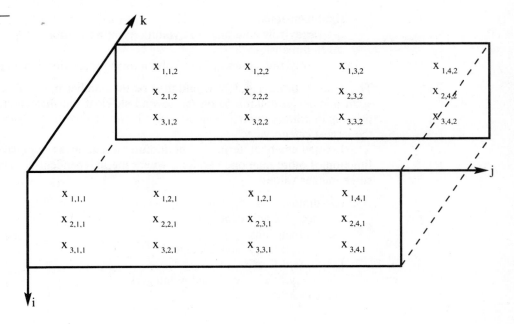

A(1,1,1)		
A(2,1,1)		column 1
A(3,1,1)		- - - - - - - -
A(1,2,1)		
A(2,2,1)		column 2
A(3,2,1)		- - - - - - - - sheet 1
A(1,3,1)		
A(2,3,1)		column 3
A(3,3,1)		- - - - - - - -
A(1,4,1)		
A(2,4,1)		column 4
A(3,4,1)		- - - - - - - - - - - - - - - - -
A(1,1,2)		
A(2,1,2)		column 1
A(3,1,2)		- - - - - - - -
A(1,2,2)		
A(2,2,2)		column 2
A(3,2,2)		- - - - - - - - sheet 2
A(1,3,2)		
A(2,3,2)		column 3
A(3,3,2)		- - - - - - - -
A(1,4,2)		
A(2,4,2)		column 4
A(3,4,2)		

Notice that the row subscript changes the most rapidly, then the column subscript. The sheet subscript changes the least rapidly. To access this array efficiently in the order in which it is stored, the DO-loops should be nested as an implied DO-loop:

```
*    SCAN A 3-DIMENSIONAL ARRAY IN STORAGE ORDER

     ... (((A(I,J,K), I=1,3), J=1,4), K=1,2)
```

or as an explicit DO-loop:

```
     DO 30 K=1,2
        DO 20 J=1,4
           DO 10 I=1,3
              A(I,J,K) ...
10            CONTINUE
20         CONTINUE
30      CONTINUE
```

For an array having more dimensions, the first subscript varies the most rapidly and the last subscript varies the least rapidly, as in the following example:

```
*    SCAN A 6-DIMENSIONAL ARRAY IN STORAGE ORDER

(((((((X(I,J,K,L,M,N), I=...), J=...), K=...), L=...),
        M=...), N=...)
```

or

```
     DO 60 N = ...
        DO 50 M = ...
           DO 40 L = ...
              DO 30 K=1,2
                 DO 20 J=1,4
                    DO 10 I=1,3
                       A(I,J,K,L,M,N) ...
10                     CONTINUE
20                  CONTINUE
30               CONTINUE
40            CONTINUE
50         CONTINUE
60      CONTINUE
```

This order of elements is used whenever the array is referenced by array name.

Three-dimensional arrays can be initialized using DATA statements, as in the following examples:

```
     REAL A(3,4,2)
     DATA A/24*0.0/
```

is equivalent to

```
     REAL A(3,4,2)
     DATA (((A(I,J,K), I=1,3), J=1,4), K=1,2)/24*0.0/
```

Given the program segment

```
REAL X(2,2,3)
DATA X/1.5,2.5,3.7,8.6,12.5,0.5,7.2,8.3,9.2,10.2,
       2.8,6.5/
```

the values are stored as:

X(1,1,1)	1.5	
X(2,1,1)	2.5	sheet 1
X(1,2,1)	3.7	
X(2,2,1)	8.6	------
X(1,1,2)	12.5	
X(2,1,2)	0.5	sheet 2
X(1,2,2)	7.2	
X(2,2,2)	8.3	------
X(1,1,3)	9.2	
X(2,1,3)	10.2	sheet 3
X(1,2,3)	2.8	
X(2,2,3)	6.5	

7.5.2 Input/Output Operations

Input/output of multidimensional arrays may be done by name or by using DO-loops. When the name is used, the data is input or output in storage order. For example:

```
REAL X(3,4,2)
READ (*,*) X
```

requires input data arranged by columns, one sheet at a time. Array input should be done in the most readable order, by rows, one sheet at a time, as in the following example:

```
*   READ A 3-DIMENSIONAL ARRAY BY ROWS

      REAL X(3,4,2)
      READ (*,*) (((X(I,J,K), J=1,4), I=1,3), K=1,2)
```

DO-loops should be used to control the output of mutidimensional arrays so that the data can be printed in the correct order. Take care to separate the sheets by several blank lines. When possible, sheets should not be broken between pages of output. In the following example, part of the third sheet could be placed on the first page, but the output is more readable if the third sheet is placed entirely on the second page.

```
*   PRINT A 3-DIMENSIONAL ARRAY BY ROWS

      SUBROUTINE OUTPUT(A,L,M,N)
      REAL A(L,M,N)
      INTEGER I,J,K,LINE

      LINE = 1
      DO 50 K=1,N
        IF (LINE .GT. 36) THEN
          WRITE (*,1000)
1000      FORMAT('1')
          LINE = 2
```

```
                ENDIF
                WRITE (*,2000)
2000            FORMAT(//)
                LINE = LINE + 2
                DO 30 I=1,20
                  WRITE (*,3000) (A(I,J,K), J=1,10)
3000            FORMAT(1X,10F12.5)
                  LINE = LINE + 1
30              CONTINUE
50          CONTINUE
```

The implied DO inside the regular DO prints the data by rows. The variable LINE counts the lines on the page and shows which line will be printed next. In this example, we assume that at most 55 lines can be printed on each page. Therefore, when 36 lines have been printed, there is no room on the page for another sheet of the array. Inside the loop, the line counter is initialized with the value 2 because the first line of the page has been printed in the process of starting the page. This example shows a general method that can be used for all arrays.

When an array of more than three dimensions is printed, each volume of sheets must start on a new page. This is shown in the following example:

```
*   PRINT A 4-DIMENSIONAL ARRAY BY ROWS

        SUBROUTINE OUTPUT(A,N1,N2,N3,N4)
        INTEGER N1,N2,N3,N4,I,J,K,L
        REAL A(N1,N2,N3,N4)
        . . .
        DO 70 L = 1,N4
          WRITE (*,1000)
1000      FORMAT('1')
          LINE = 2
          DO 50 K=1,N3
            IF (LINE .GT. 36) THEN
              WRITE (*,2000)
2000          FORMAT('1')
              LINE = 2
            ENDIF
            WRITE (*,3000)
3000        FORMAT(//)
            LINE = LINE + 2
            DO 30 I=1,N2
              WRITE (*,4000) (A(I,J,K,L), J=1,N1)
4000          FORMAT(1X,10F12.5)
              LINE = LINE + 1
30          CONTINUE
50        CONTINUE
70      CONTINUE
```

In this example, the line counter is initialized for every volume and each volume starts on a new page. Then as many sheets are printed on each page as will fit. The data is printed by rows with two blank rows between sheets. The line counter is initialized with the value 2 because the first line of the page has been printed in the process of starting the page.

7.5.3 Manipulation of Arrays

As with other arrays, elements of multidimensional arrays can be used in arithmetic expressions and assignment statements. For efficiency, whenever possible the elements should be processed in the order in which they are stored. The following example forms a three-dimensional "image" of a solid sphere, storing a one at all points inside or on the surface of the sphere and a zero at all points outside. Both the initialization of the array and the calculation of the points proceed in storage order.

```
*    REPRESENTATION OF SOLID SPHERE X² + Y² + Z² = 100

         INTEGER SPHERE(-12:12,-12:12,-12:12)
         PARAMETER (RSQ=100,LB=-12,UB=12)
         INTEGER RSQ,LB,UB
         INTEGER I,J,K,IBEG,IEND,JBEG,JEND,KBEG,KEND

         DO 30 K = LB,UB
            DO 20 J = LB,UB
               DO 10 I= LB,UB
                  SPHERE(I,J,K) = 0
10             CONTINUE
20          CONTINUE
30       CONTINUE

         KEND = SQRT(RSQ)
         KBEG = - KEND
         DO 60 K = KBEG,KEND
            JEND = SQRT(RSQ - K*K)
            JBEG = - JEND
            DO 50 J = JBEG,JEND
               IEND = SQRT(RSQ - J*J - K*K)
               IBEG = - IEND
               DO 40 I = IBEG,IEND
                  SPHERE(I,J,K) = 1
40             CONTINUE
50          CONTINUE
60       CONTINUE
```

Each sheet of this array represents a cross-section of the sphere. By printing the sheets with a different symbol for each sheet, a three-dimensional image could be produced.

7.5.4 Review Questions

1. Write the array declaration for each of the following variables and give the size of each array:

   a. real $x_{i,j,k}$ where i = 1,5   j = -1,0   k = 1,4
   b. real $y_{i,j,k}$ where i = -5,5   j = -3,2   k = 4,8
   c. integer $a_{i,j,k}$ where i = 0,5   j = 0,2   k = 0,10

2. Write the input code to read the integer array K(3,4,5) given the following data arrangements:

   a. by sheets, with each row on a separate record
   b. by sheets, with each column on a separate record
   c. all the elements on a single record, in storage order
   d. each element on a separate record, in storage order

3. Write the output code to print the integer array N(40,20,10), each sheet on a separate page, using the format 2016 for each line.

7.6 Arrays and Subprograms

Complex problems in science and engineering use multidimensional arrays, for example, to solve systems of equations. When such problems are divided logically into functional modules, the input, output and computational manipulation of the arrays is complex enough to require the use of subprograms.

7.6.1 Argument and Parameter Passing

It is important to note that arrays are not passed to subprograms by copying the array, but by informing the subprogram of the location of the array, "passing by address." When an array is specified as an argument, its address is passed to the parameter. The computer does not check the specifications to make sure that the array is specified the same way in both the calling routine and the called routine. This provides the programmer with a certain amount of freedom, but also can easily lead to errors. Through the parameter name, the subprogram can access the argument array to obtain values or to store values. A two-dimensional array must have the same size in each routine that references the array elements. However, it may be declared with a larger size in the main program, provided that the elements are not accessed there.

The following example shows the use of a subroutine to input an array and a function to sum the values in the array. The array has the same dimensions in all three routines.

```
***********************************************************
*                                                         *
*    MAIN DRIVER PROGRAM                                  *
*                                                         *
***********************************************************
       INTEGER N
       PARAMETER (N=10)
       REAL X(N,N),XSUM,XFUN

       CALL SUBINP(X)
       XSUM = XFUN(X)
       WRITE (*,1000) XSUM
1000   FORMAT(1X,'X-ARRAY SUM =',F10.2)
```

```
      STOP
      END

*********************************************************
*                                                       *
*   INPUT SUBROUTINE                                    *
*                                                       *
*********************************************************
*                                                       *
*   OUTPUT PARAMETERS:                                  *
*                                                       *
*     Y(10,10)          - REAL ARRAY                    *
*                                                       *
*********************************************************

      SUBROUTINE SUBINP(Y)
      REAL Y(10,10)
      INTEGER I

      DO 10 I=1,10
        READ (*,1000) (Y(I,J), J=1,10)
1000    FORMAT(10F8.0)
10    CONTINUE
      RETURN
      END

*********************************************************
*                                                       *
*   FUNCTION TO COMPUTE SUM OF ARRAY ELEMENTS           *
*                                                       *
*********************************************************
*                                                       *
*   INPUT PARAMETERS:                                   *
*                                                       *
*     Z(M,N)            - REAL ARRAY                    *
*                                                       *
*********************************************************

      REAL FUNCTION XFUN(Z)
      REAL Z(10,10),SUM
      INTEGER I,J

      SUM = 0.0
      DO 20 J=1,10
        DO 10 I=1,10
          SUM = SUM + Z(I,J)
10      CONTINUE
20    CONTINUE
      XFUN = SUM
      RETURN
      END
```

The array X(10,10) is actually allocated storage in the data area of the main program. When it is passed to the subroutine SUBINP, inputting values into the array Y actually stores them in the space allocated for X. The function then uses these values under the name Z. Note that when there is not enough data in the input file, the subroutine prints an error message and execution stops.

The following example shows the use of a single subroutine to print two different arrays, which are generated in the main program by the use of parametric equations. The two arrays have the same dimensions.

```
**********************************************************
*                                                        *
*    PRINT TABLES OF VALUES OF X AND Y                   *
*    FOR                                                 *
*            X = A SIN(.23T)                             *
*            Y = 1 - .5A COS(.68T)                       *
*                                                        *
*                              A = 1 ... 10,             *
*                              T = .01,.02,...1.0        *
*                                                        *
**********************************************************

         REAL X(10,10),Y(10,10),T
         INTEGER A,K

         T = 0.0
         DO 20 K = 1,10
           T = T + .01
           DO 10 A=1,10
             X(A,K) = A * SIN(0.23 * T)
             Y(A,K) = 1 - .5 * A * COS(0.68 * T)
10        CONTINUE
20       CONTINUE
         WRITE (*,*) 'X VALUES'
         CALL OUTSUB(X)
         WRITE (*,*) 'Y VALUES'
         CALL OUTSUB(Y)
         STOP
         END


**********************************************************
*                                                        *
*    OUTPUT SUBROUTINE                                   *
*                                                        *
**********************************************************
*                                                        *
*    INPUT PARAMETERS:                                   *
*                                                        *
*    Z(10,10)                 - REAL ARRAY               *
*                                                        *
**********************************************************

         SUBROUTINE OUTSUB(Z)
         REAL Z(10,10),T
         INTEGER A,K

         WRITE (*,1000) (T, T=0.1,1.0,0.1)
```

```
1000    FORMAT (10X,'A',35X,'T'/11X,10F8.1)
        DO 10 A = 1,10
           WRITE (*,1100) (A,(Z(A,K), K=1,10))
1100       FORMAT(1X,I10,10F8.1)
10      CONTINUE
        RETURN
        END
```

The routine OUTSUB is called twice. First, the array X is passed to the dummy argument Z and printed. Second, the array Y is passed and printed. Notice that the arrays X, Y, and Z match in type and size.

Programming Warning

> The size of dummy argument arrays must not be greater than the size of the actual argument arrays.

In the examples above, if an array size is changed in the main program, it must also be changed in the subroutines. The upper bounds of the DO-loops must be changed too, to correspond to the array size. This maintenance problem can be avoided by using adjustable dimensions in the subprograms, which we discuss in the following section.

7.6.2 Adjustable Array Dimensioning

It is good programming practice to pass both the array and its bounds as arguments. The same array bounds must be passed to all subprograms that access the elements of a single array. This defines the effective array dimensions. The array declaration in the main program may allocate more space than is needed by the effective array. When a general program is written, the array bounds in the main program should be the maximum possible size corresponding to the largest potential amount of data to be stored. Both the actual array bounds and the effective array bounds should be passed to the subprograms. Then, when the declared size of the array is changed in the calling routine, no code changes are needed in the called routines. In addition, the same subprogram can be used with arrays of different sizes as arguments. The following examples show the use of adjustable arrays in the subroutines.

In the following program, the subroutine INSUB reads a set of not more than R input records, each containing C values. The function XMAXFN locates and returns the maximum element of the array.

```
**********************************************
*                                            *
*    MAIN DRIVER PROGRAM                      *
*                                            *
**********************************************

      INTEGER N,M,R,C
      PARAMETER (N=10,M=20)
      REAL X(N,M),XMAXFN
```

```
         READ (*,*) R,C
         IF (R .EQ. N .AND. C .LE. M) THEN
            CALL INSUB(X,R,C)
            XMAX = XMAXFN(X,R,C)
            WRITE (*,1000) XMAX
1000        FORMAT(1X,'X-MAXIMUM =',F10.2)
         ELSE
            WRITE (*,*) 'ARRAY SIZE ERROR'
         ENDIF
         STOP
         END

*****************************************************
*                                                   *
*   INPUT SUBROUTINE                                *
*                                                   *
*****************************************************
*                                                   *
*   INPUT PARAMETERS:                               *
*                                                   *
*      R,C              - EFFECTIVE ARRAY BOUNDS    *
*                                                   *
*   OUTPUT PARAMETERS:                              *
*                                                   *
*      Y(R,C)           - REAL ARRAY                *
*                                                   *
*****************************************************

         SUBROUTINE INSUB(Y,R,C)
         REAL Y(R,C)
         INTEGER I,J,R,C

         DO 10 I=1,R
            READ (*,1000) (Y(I,J), J=1,C)
1000        FORMAT(10F8.0)
10       CONTINUE
         RETURN
         END

*****************************************************
*                                                   *
*   FUNCTION TO FIND MAXIMUM ARRAY ELEMENT          *
*                                                   *
*****************************************************
*                                                   *
*   INPUT PARAMETERS:                               *
*                                                   *
*      Z(R,C)           - REAL ARRAY                *
*                                                   *
*   OUTPUT:                                         *
*                                                   *
*      RETURNS          - MAXIMUM VALUE IN ARRAY    *
*                                                   *
*****************************************************
```

```
      REAL FUNCTION XMAXFN(Z,R,C)
      INTEGER I,J,R,C
      REAL Z(R,C),ZMAX

      ZMAX = Z(1,1)
      DO 20 J=1,C
        DO 10 I=1,R
          IF (Z(I,J) .GT. ZMAX) THEN
            ZMAX = Z(I,J)
          ENDIF
10      CONTINUE
20      CONTINUE
      XMAXFN = ZMAX
      RETURN
      END
```

Notice that the effective array size was read in the main program. Then the array storage area and the effective size were passed to each subprogram. By using the PARAMETER statement in the main program and passing the effective array size, any change in the maximum array declaration will require only a change in the PARAMETER statement of the main program. The array is processed in row-major order in the input program, because that is the most convenient order for the user. It is processed in column-major or storage order in the function, because that is the most efficient order for the computer.

Progamming Hint

> Generality: Use adjustable arrays in subprograms.

When a programmer team is working on a large project, using adjustable dimensions in subprograms makes it possible for different programmers to use the same subprograms with arrays of different sizes.

7.6.3 Review Questions

1. Indicate whether each of the following statements is true or false:

   a. A two-dimensional array is passed to a subprogram by using the array name.
   b. When two-dimensional arrays are passed to subprograms, their values are copied to the subprograms.
   c. Corresponding argument and parameter arrays must match in type.
   d. Corresponding argument and parameter arrays do not need to match in the number of dimensions.
   e. A parameter array in a subprogram may be smaller than the corresponding argument array.
   f. A function subprogram can return an array through the function name.
   g. A function subprogram can return an element of an array through the function name.
   h. A subroutine should be used rather than a function to input or output an array.
   i. If a subprogram has an adjustable dimension array, the size of the array must be passed from the calling program.

2. Write a function subprogram to compute the sum of the elements on the main diagonal of a real array X(N,N).

3. Write a subroutine subprogram to generate the transpose XTRANS(M,N) of a real array X(N,M).

4. Write a subroutine subprogram to initialize a three-dimensional array ARR(8,9,10) to all zeros.

5. Write a subroutine to output the two-dimensional integer array MAT(9,9), labeling each element as follows:

> (1,1) nnn (1,2) nnn . . . (1,9) nnn
> .
> .
> .
> (9,1) nnn (9,2) nnn . . . (9,9) nnn

7.7 Sample Programs

Most of the programs in this section involve two-dimensional arrays. Arrays of higher dimensions are rarely used. These programs have been executed interactively on the Digital Equipment Corporation (DEC) computer model VAX 11/780. The output is shown. Where the input is also shown, both are identified.

7.7.1 Rotation of a Line

Problem

An array P(2,2) contains the coordinates of the endpoints of a line.

> P(1,1) is x_1 P(1,2) is y_1 of point (x_1,y_1)
> P(2,1) is x_2 P(2,2) is y_2 of point (x_2,y_2)

Calculate the coordinates of the endpoints of the line when it has been rotated through an angle A about the origin. The angle A is measured in radians.

Method

Multiply the array P by the array

$$TA = \begin{matrix} \cos(\theta) & \sin(\theta) \\ -\sin(\theta) & \cos(\theta) \end{matrix}$$

This converts the original array

> x_1 y_1
> x_2 y_2

to the array

> $x_1\cos(\theta) - y_1\sin(\theta)$ $x_1\sin(\theta) + y_1\cos(\theta)$
> $x_2\cos(\theta) - y_2\sin(\theta)$ $x_2\sin(\theta) + y_2\cos(\theta)$

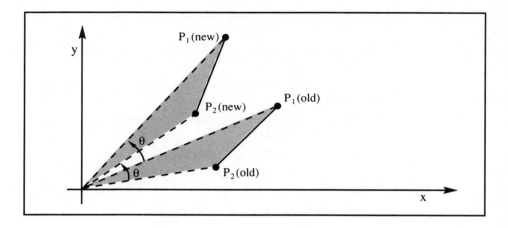

Program

```
*************************************************************
*                                                         *
*   ROTATION OF A LINE ABOUT THE ORIGIN                   *
*                                                         *
*************************************************************

      REAL P(2,2),TA(2,2),NEWP(2,2)
      REAL THETA,ANGLE,PI
      INTEGER I,J
      PARAMETER (PI=3.14159)

*   INITIALIZE ARRAYS

      WRITE (*,1000)
1000  FORMAT(1X,'INPUT DATA: ENTER ANGLE IN ',
     1     'DEGREES AND '/1X,'COORDINATES OF ENDPOINTS ',
     2     'OF TWO LINES')
      READ (*,*) THETA
      ANGLE = PI / 180.0 * THETA
      READ (*,*) ((P(I,J), J=1,2), I=1,2)
      TA(1,1) = COS(ANGLE)
      TA(1,2) = SIN(ANGLE)
      TA(2,1) = - TA(1,2)
      TA(2,2) = TA(1,1)

*   MULTIPLY ARRAYS (MATRIX MULTIPLICATION)

      WRITE (*,1100)
1100  FORMAT(//1X,'COORDINATES OF OLD LINE',3X,
     1            'COORDINATES OF NEW LINE')
      NEWP(1,1) = P(1,1) * TA(1,1) + P(1,2) * TA(2,1)
      NEWP(1,2) = P(1,1) * TA(1,2) + P(1,2) * TA(2,2)
      NEWP(2,1) = P(2,1) * TA(1,1) + P(2,2) * TA(2,1)
```

```
                 NEWP(2,2) = P(2,1) * TA(1,2) + P(2,2) * TA(2,2)
                 WRITE (*,1200) P(1,1),P(1,2),NEWP(1,1),NEWP(1,2)
                 WRITE (*,1200) P(2,1),P(2,2),NEWP(2,1),NEWP(2,2)
      1200       FORMAT(/1X,2F8.2,11X,2F8.2)
                 STOP
                 END
```

Output

Two sets of data are output:

```
INPUT DATA: ENTER ANGLE IN DEGREES AND
COORDINATES OF ENDPOINTS OF TWO LINES
180
-3.5,4.0,6.0,4.0


COORDINATES OF OLD LINE     COORDINATES OF NEW LINE

   -3.50     4.00                  3.50    -4.00

    6.00     4.00                 -6.00    -4.00


INPUT DATA: ENTER ANGLE IN DEGREES AND
COORDINATES OF ENDPOINTS OF TWO LINES
45
2.0,2.0,4.0,4.0


COORDINATES OF OLD LINE     COORDINATES OF NEW LINE

    2.00     2.00                  0.00     2.83

    4.00     4.00                  0.00     5.66
```

7.7.2 Rotation of a Set of Lines

Problem

An array P(2,2,10) contains the coordinates for the endpoints of 10 lines. Each sheet of the array represents one line.

P(1,1,L)   is the x coordinate of one end of line L
P(1,2,L)   is the y coordinate of one end of line L
P(2,1,L)   is the x coordinate of the other end of L
P(2,2,L)   is the y coordinate of the other end of L

Rotate all the lines around the origin by an angle θ.

Method

Multiply the coordinates of each point by the rotation matrix given in problem 7.7.1.

Program

```
***********************************************************
*                                                         *
*   ROTATION OF A SET OF LINES ABOUT THE ORIGIN           *
*                                                         *
***********************************************************

      REAL THETA,PI,ANGLE
      INTEGER I,J,N,K
      PARAMETER (N=2,PI=3.14159)
      REAL P(2,2,N)),TA(2,2),NEWP(2,2,N)

*   INITIALIZE ARRAYS

      WRITE (*,1000)
1000  FORMAT(1X,'INPUT DATA: ENTER ANGLE IN ',
     1      'DEGREES AND COORDINATES'/1X'OF ENDPOINTS ',
     2      'OF TWO LINES')
      READ (*,*) THETA
      ANGLE = PI / 180.0 * THETA
      READ (*,*) (((P(I,J,K), J=1,2), I=1,2), K=1,N)
      TA(1,1) = COS(ANGLE)
      TA(1,2) = SIN(ANGLE)
      TA(2,1) = - TA(1,2)
      TA(2,2) = TA(1,1)

*   MULTIPLY ARRAYS (MATRIX MULTIPLICATION)

      WRITE (*,1100)
1100  FORMAT(//1X,'COORDINATES OF OLD ',
     1            'LINES',3X,'COORDINATES OF NEW ',
     2            'LINES')
      DO 50 K=1,N
         NEWP(1,1,K) = P(1,1,K) * TA(1,1) + P(1,2,K) *
     1                 TA(2,1)
         NEWP(1,2,K) = P(1,1,K) * TA(1,2) + P(1,2,K) *
     1                 TA(2,2)
         NEWP(2,1,K) = P(2,1,K) * TA(1,1) + P(2,2,K) *
     1                 TA(2,1)
         NEWP(2,2,K) = P(2,1,K) * TA(1,2) + P(2,2,K) *
     1                 TA(2,2)
        WRITE(*,1200) P(1,1,K),P(1,2,K),NEWP(1,1,K),
     1       NEWP(1,2,K)
        WRITE(*,1200) P(2,1,K),P(2,2,K),NEWP(2,1,K),
     1       NEWP(2,2,K)
1200  FORMAT(/1X,2F8.2,11X,2F8.2)
50    CONTINUE
```

```
```

```
INPUT DATA: ENTER ANGLE IN DEGREES AND COORDINATES
OF ENDPOINTS OF TWO LINES
180
2.0,5.5,4.0,9.5
0.0,-5.0,4.0,-8.0


COORDINATES OF OLD LINES    COORDINATES OF NEW LINES

     2.00     5.50              -2.00    -5.50

     4.00     9.50              -4.00    -9.50


     0.00    -5.00               0.00     5.00

     4.00    -8.00              -4.00     8.00
```

7.7.3 Value of a Determinant

Problem

Calculate the value of a 3 × 3 determinant.

Pseudocode

Read the determinant into the first three columns of a 3 × 5 array.
Copy the first two columns into the last two columns so that the array
has the form

$$M = \begin{matrix} a_1 & b_1 & c_1 & a_1 & b_1 \\ a_2 & b_2 & c_2 & a_2 & b_2 \\ a_3 & b_3 & c_3 & a_3 & b_3 \end{matrix}$$

Calculate the value of the determinant as

$$\det = \sum_{j=1}^{3} m_{1,j} \ (m_{2,j+1} \ m_{3,j+2} - m_{2,j+2} \ m_{3,j+1})$$

Program

```
**************************************************************
*                                                            *
*    CALCULATE THE VALUE OF THE DETERMINANT OF A             *
*    3 X 3 MATRIX                                            *
*                                                            *
**************************************************************
```

```
          REAL M(3,5),DET
          INTEGER I,J,K

          WRITE (*,1000)
1000      FORMAT(1X,'INPUT A 3 X 3 MATRIX:'/)
          READ (*,*) ((M(I,J), J=1,3), I=1,3)
          DO 10 I = 1,3
             M(I,4) = M(I,1)
             M(I,5) = M(I,2)
10        CONTINUE

*   CALCULATE THE DETERMINANT

          DET = 0.0
          DO 20 J = 1,3
             DET = DET + M(1,J) * (M(2,J+1)*M(3,J+2)
     1                        -    M(2,J+2)*M(3,J+1))
20        CONTINUE
          WRITE (*,2000)
2000      FORMAT(/1X,T25,'OUTPUT OF 3 X 3 MATRIX')
          DO 30 I = 1,3
             WRITE (*,3000) (M(I,J),J=1,3)
3000         FORMAT(/1X,T22,3F8.2)
30        CONTINUE
          WRITE (*,4000) DET
4000      FORMAT(/1X,'DETERMINANT OF MATRIX =',F8.2)
          STOP
          END
```

Output

```
INPUT A 3 X 3 MATRIX:

1.5,9.0,3.5
2.0,6.5,8.5
5.5,7.0,1.0

                   OUTPUT OF 3 X 3 MATRIX

                   1.50      9.00      3.50

                   2.00      6.50      8.50

                   5.50      7.00      1.00

DETERMINANT OF MATRIX =   247.13
```

7.7.4 Locate a Saddle Point

Problem

Write a program to locate all the mountain passes in an array of elevations.

Method

A mountain pass takes the form of a saddle point in the array. A saddle point is a point that is the maximum in its row and the minimum in its column, or the minimum in its row and the maximum in its column.

Pseudocode

> For each row and each column, find the maximum and minimum in the row and the maximum and minimum in the column (assume there are no duplicates).
> Check each row maximum to see whether it is also a column minimum.
> If so, print its position.
> Check each row minimum to see whether it is also a column maximum.
> If so, print its position.

Program

```
************************************************************
*                                                        *
*    LOCATE SADDLE POINTS IN AN ARRAY.                   *
*                                                        *
************************************************************

      INTEGER I,J,K,N
      PARAMETER(N=5)
      REAL ELEV(N,N)
      REAL ROWMAX(N),ROWMIN(N),COLMAX(N),COLMIN(N)
      INTEGER JRMAX(N),JRMIN(N),ICMAX(N),ICMIN(N)

      WRITE (*,1000)
1000  FORMAT(1X,'INPUT A 5 X 5 ARRAY'/)
      DO 10 I=1,N
         READ (*,*) (ELEV(I,J), J=1,N)
10    CONTINUE

*   INITIALIZE MAX AND MIN VECTORS

      DO 20 K=1,N
         ROWMAX(K) = ELEV(K,1)
         ROWMIN(K) = ELEV(K,1)
         COLMAX(K) = ELEV(1,K)
         COLMIN(K) = ELEV(1,K)
         JRMAX(K)  = 1
         JRMIN(K)  = 1
```

```
                ICMAX(K) = 1
                ICMIN(K) = 1
 20         CONTINUE

 *    FIND ROW AND COLUMN MAXIMUMS AND MINIMUMS

            DO 40 J=1,N
              DO  30 I = 1,N
                IF (ROWMAX(I) .LT. ELEV(I,J)) THEN
                   ROWMAX(I) = ELEV(I,J)
                   JRMAX(I) = J
                ENDIF
                IF (ROWMIN(I) .GT. ELEV(I,J)) THEN
                   ROWMIN(I) = ELEV(I,J)
                   JRMIN(I) = J
                ENDIF
                IF (COLMAX(J) .LT. ELEV(I,J)) THEN
                   COLMAX(J) = ELEV(I,J)
                   ICMAX(J) = I
                ENDIF
                IF (COLMIN(J) .GT. ELEV(I,J)) THEN
                   COLMIN(J) = ELEV(I,J)
                   ICMIN(J) = I
                ENDIF
 30           CONTINUE
 40         CONTINUE

 *    COMPARE MAXIMUMS AND MINIMUMS TO FIND SADDLE
      POINTS

            WRITE (*,2000)
 2000       FORMAT(///26X,'OUTPUT OF SADDLE POINTS',//
     1              25X,'I',9X,'J',6X,'ELEVATION'/)
            DO 50 I = 1,N
              J = JRMAX(I)
              IF (ICMIN(J) .EQ. I) THEN
                 WRITE (*,3000) I,J,ELEV(I,J)
 3000            FORMAT(16X,2I10,4X,F8.1)
              ENDIF
              J = JRMIN(I)
              IF (ICMAX(J) .EQ. I) THEN
                 WRITE (*,4000) I,J,ELEV(I,J)
 4000            FORMAT(16X,2I10,4X,F8.1)
              ENDIF
 50         CONTINUE
            STOP
            END
```

Output

```
INPUT A 5 X 5 ARRAY

1.0,2.0,3.0,4.0,5.0
2.0,3.0,4.0,5.0,6.0
3.0,4.0,5.0,6.0,7.0
4.0,5.0,6.0,7.0,8.0
5.0,6.0,7.0,8.0,9.0




                OUTPUT OF SADDLE POINTS

        I           J           ELEVATION

        1           5           5.0
        5           1           5.0
```

7.7.5 Sort the Rows of a Two-Dimensional Array

Problem

Write a program to sort the rows of a two-dimensional array.

Pseudocode

```
Call INPUT to input the array
Call SLSORT to sort the array
    (use the selection sort of Section 6.6.2)
Call OUTPUT to output the sorted array
```

Program

```
*******************************************************
*                                                     *
*   MAIN PROGRAM - DRIVER                              *
*                                                     *
*******************************************************

      INTEGER N,M,K,L
      PARAMETER (K=10,L=10)
      REAL X(K,L)

      WRITE (*,1000)
1000  FORMAT(/1X,'INPUT THE SIZE OF THE ARRAY:')
      READ (*,*) N,M
      CALL INPUT(X,N,M)
      CALL SLSORT(X,N,M)
```

```
          CALL OUTPUT(X,N,M)
          STOP
          END

**********************************************************
*                                                        *
*    INPUT AN ARRAY                                      *
*                                                        *
**********************************************************
*                                                        *
*    INPUT PARAMETERS:                                   *
*                                                        *
*      N,M        - THE EFFECTIVE SIZE OF THE ARRAY      *
*                                                        *
*    OUTPUT PARAMETERS:                                  *
*                                                        *
*      ARR(N,M) - A REAL ARRAY                           *
*                                                        *
**********************************************************

          SUBROUTINE INPUT(ARR,N,M)
          REAL ARR(N,M)
          INTEGER I,J,N,M

          WRITE (*,1000)
1000      FORMAT(/1X,'INPUT THE ARRAY TO BE SORTED:'/)
          DO 10 I = 1,N
            READ (*,*) (ARR(I,J), J=1,M)
10        CONTINUE
          RETURN
          END

**********************************************************
*                                                        *
*    SELECTION SORT OF ARRAY ROWS IN ASCENDING ORDER     *
*                                                        *
**********************************************************
*                                                        *
*    INPUT PARAMETERS:                                   *
*                                                        *
*      ARR(N,M) - A REAL ARRAY                           *
*                                                        *
*    OUTPUT PARAMETERS:                                  *
*                                                        *
*      ARR(N,M) - THE SORTED ARRAY                       *
*                                                        *
**********************************************************

          SUBROUTINE SLSORT(ARR,N,M)
          REAL ARR(N,M),TEMP
          INTEGER N,M,I,J,K
```

```
              DO 40 I=1,N
                DO 30 J=1,M-1
                  DO 20 K = J+1,M
                    IF (ARR(I,J) .LT. ARR(I,K)) THEN
                      TEMP = ARR(I,J)
                      ARR(I,J) = ARR(I,K)
                      ARR(I,K) = TEMP
                    ENDIF
20                CONTINUE
30              CONTINUE
40            CONTINUE
              RETURN
              END


**************************************************
*                                                *
*   OUTPUT AN ARRAY, M VALUES PER LINE           *
*                                                *
**************************************************
*                                                *
*   INPUT PARAMETERS:                            *
*                                                *
*     ARR(N,M) - A REAL ARRAY                    *
*                                                *
*   OUTPUT VARIABLES:                            *
*                                                *
*     ARR(N,M) - THE SORTED ARRAY                *
*                                                *
**************************************************

              SUBROUTINE OUTPUT(ARR,N,M)
              REAL ARR(N,M)
              INTEGER N,M,I,J

              WRITE (*,1000)
1000          FORMAT(///1X,'OUTPUT OF SORTED ARRAY'/)
              DO 10 I = 1,N
                WRITE (*,1100) (ARR(I,J), J=1,M)
1100            FORMAT(1X,10F8.2)
10            CONTINUE
              RETURN
              END
```

Output

```
INPUT THE SIZE OF THE ARRAY:
5,5

INPUT THE ARRAY TO BE SORTED:

2.0,3.1,5.5,9.9,4.1
6.4,2.0,7.7,8.8,3.3
7.9,2.3,6.6,4.0.1.9
8.3,6.9,0.5,3.7,2.9
4.5,1.8,5.9,9.8,2.5


OUTPUT OF SORTED ARRAY
        2.00      3.10      4.10      5.50      9.90
        2.00      3.30      6.40      7.70      8.80
        1.90      2.30      4.00      6.60      7.90
        0.50      2.90      3.70      6.90      8.30
        1.80      2.50      4.50      5.90      9.80
```

Notice that as each element in a row is compared, the rows are scanned for the first corresponding elements that differ. Then if these elements are out of order, they and the remaining elements of the rows are exchanged.

7.7.6 Inventory of ABC Tyre Company

Problem

ABC Tyre Company retails tyres for foreign cars. Write a program that prints the item and cost inventory for the five stores owned by the company.

Method

The main program should call an input subroutine, a computational subroutine, and an output subroutine. The input subroutine reads a table of the tyre inventory of the company and a table of the tyre costs of the company. Each row of the tables represents a single tyre size and each column of the tables represents a single outlet store. The computational subroutine calculates the total number of tyres of each size, the total value of tyres of each size, the total number of tyres stocked by each store, the total value of the tyres stocked by each store, and the overall total number of tyres and total value. The output subroutine prints the inventory report.

Program

```
*****************************************************************
*                                                               *
*    INVENTORY OF ABC TYRE COMPANY                              *
*                                                               *
*****************************************************************
*                                                               *
*    PARAMETERS:                                                *
*                                                               *
*       20    TYRE SIZES MAXIMUM                                *
*       10    STORES MAXIMUM                                    *
*                                                               *
*    SUBPROGRAMS CALLED:                                        *
*                                                               *
*       DATAIN      - READS ITEM AND COST TABLES               *
*       COMSUB      - COMPUTES ITEM AND COST TOTALS PER        *
*                     STORE                                     *
*       TYRFNC      - COMPUTES TOTAL ITEM INVENTORY           *
*       CSTFNC      - COMPUTES TOTAL INVENTORY COST           *
*       DATOUT      - PRINTS THE INVENTORY REPORT             *
*                                                               *
*****************************************************************

      INTEGER M,N, STORE, SIZE
      PARAMETER (M=20,N=10)
      INTEGER ITMTYR(M,N),SIZTYR(M),STRTYR(N)
      REAL UNTCST(M,N),TYRCST(M,N),SIZCST(M),
     1            CTRCST(N)
      REAL TOTCST,CSTFNC
      INTEGER TOTTYR,TYRFNC

      WRITE (*,*) 'INPUT THE NUMBER OF TYRE SIZES ',
     1        '(MAXIMUM OF 20) AND THE NUMBER OF ',
     2        'STORES (MAXIMUM OF 10)'
      READ (*,*) SIZE,STORE
      CALL DATAIN(ITMTYR,UNTCST,SIZE,STORE)
      CALL COMSUB(ITMTYR,UNTCST,TYRCST,SIZTYR,STRTYR,
     1            SIZCST,STRCST,SIZE,STORE)
      TOTTYR = TYRFNC(SIZTYR,SIZE)
      TOTCST = CSTFNC(SIZCST,SIZE)
      CALL DATOUT(ITMTYR,UNTCST,TYRCST,SIZTYR,STRTYR,
     1            TOTTYR,STRCST,SIZCST,TOTCST,SIZE,
     2            STORE)
      STOP
      END
```

```
      ************************************************************
      *                                                          *
      *    SUBROUTINE TO INPUT DATA                              *
      *                                                          *
      ************************************************************
      *                                                          *
      *    INPUT PARAMETERS:                                     *
      *                                                          *
      *      SIZE          - ACTUAL NUMBER OF TYRE SIZES         *
      *      STORE         - ACTUAL NUMBER OF STORES             *
      *                                                          *
      *    OUTPUT PARAMETERS:                                    *
      *                                                          *
      *      TYRITM(SIZE,STORE) - ARRAY OF TYRE INVENTORY        *
      *      CSTUNT(SIZE,STORE) - ARRAY OF TYRE COSTS            *
      *                                                          *
      ************************************************************

            SUBROUTINE DATAIN(TYRITM,CSTUNT,SIZE,STORE)
            INTEGER STORE,SIZE
            INTEGER ITMTYR(SIZE,STORE)
            REAL UNTCST(SIZE,STORE)
            INTEGER I,J

      *    INPUT THE INVENTORY TABLES

            WRITE (*,1000)
      1000  FORMAT(//1X,'INPUT THE NUMBER OF TYRES BY ',
           1        'SIZE AND STORE')
            DO 10 I=1,SIZE
              READ (*,*) (TYRITM(I,J),J=1,STORE)
      10    CONTINUE
            WRITE (*,2000)
      2000  FORMAT(//1X,'INPUT THE COST PER TYRE BY ',
           1        'SIZE AND STORE')
            DO 20 I=1,SIZE
              READ (*,*) (CSTUNT(I,J),J=1,STORE)
      20    CONTINUE
            RETURN
            END
```

```
*******************************************************
*                                                     *
*   SUBROUTINE TO COMPUTE THE ITEM TOTALS AND COST    *
*   TOTALS                                            *
*                                                     *
*******************************************************
*                                                     *
*   INPUT PARAMETERS:                                 *
*                                                     *
*     TYRITM(SIZE,STORE)    - ARRAY OF ITEMS IN       *
*                              INVENTORY              *
*     CSTUNT(SIZE,STORE)    - ARRAY OF COSTS OF TYRE  *
*                              TYPES                  *
*     SIZE           - ACTUAL NUMBER OF TYRE SIZES    *
*     STORE          - ACTUAL NUMBER OF STORES        *
*                                                     *
*   OUTPUT PARAMETERS:                                *
*                                                     *
*     CSTTYR(SIZE,STORE) - ARRAY OF INVENTORY VALUE   *
*     TYRSIZ(SIZE)    - ARRAY IF INVENTORY ITEMS BY   *
*                          TYRE SIZE                  *
*     TYRSTR(STORE)   - ARRAY OF INVENTORY ITEMS BY   *
*                          STORE                      *
*     CSTSIZ(SIZE)    - ARRAY OF INVENTORY VALUE BY   *
*                          TYRE SIZE                  *
*     CSTSTR(STORE)   - ARRAY OF INVENTORY VALUE BY   *
*                          STORE                      *
*                                                     *
*******************************************************

      SUBROUTINE COMSUB(TYRITM,CSTUNT,CSTTYR,TYRSIZ,
     1    TYRSTR,CSTSIZ,CSTSTR,SIZE,STORE)
      INTEGER STORE,SIZE
      INTEGER TYRITM(SIZE,STORE),TYRSIZ(SIZE),
     1    TYRSTR(STORE)
      REAL CSTUNT(SIZE,STORE),CSTTYR(SIZE,STORE)
      REAL CSTSIZ(SIZE),CSTSTR(STORE)
      INTEGER I,J

      DO 20 J = 1,STORE
        DO 10 I = 1,SIZE
          CSTTYR(I,J) = TYRITM(I,J) * CSTUNT(I,J)
10      CONTINUE
20    CONTINUE
      DO 40 I = 1,SIZE
        TYRSIZ(I) = 0
        CSTSIZ(I) = 0.0
        DO 30 J = 1,STORE
          TYRSIZ(I) = TYRSIZ(I) + TYRITM(I,J)
          CSTSIZ(I) = CSTSIZ(I) + CSTTYR(I,J)
30      CONTINUE
40    CONTINUE
```

```
          DO 60 J = 1,STORE
            TYRSTR(J) = 0
            CSTSTR(J) = 0.0
            DO 50 I = 1,SIZE
              TYRSTR(J) = TYRSTR(J) + TYRITM(I,J)
              CSTSTR(J) = CSTSTR(J) + CSTTYR(I,J)
50          CONTINUE
60        CONTINUE
          RETURN
          END


*********************************************************
*                                                       *
*   FUNCTION TO COMPUTE OVERALL TOTAL NUMBER OF TYRES*
*                                                       *
*********************************************************
*                                                       *
*   INPUT PARAMETERS:                                   *
*                                                       *
*     TYRES(SIZE)    - TOTAL NUMBER OF TYRES            *
*                                                       *
*   RETURNS          - TOTAL NUMBER OF TYRES IN COMPANY*
*                      INVENTORY                        *
*                                                       *
*********************************************************

          INTEGER FUNCTION TYRFNC(TYRES,SIZE)
          INTEGER SUMTYR,I,SIZE
          INTEGER TYRES(SIZE)

          SUMTYR = 0
          DO 10 I = 1,SIZE
            SUMTYR = SUMTYR + TYRES(I)
10        CONTINUE
          TYRFNC = SUMTYR
          RETURN
          END


*********************************************************
*                                                       *
*   FUNCTION TO COMPUTE THE TOTAL VALUE OF INVENTORY  *
*                                                       *
*********************************************************
*                                                       *
*   INPUT PARAMETERS:                                   *
*                                                       *
*     COST(SIZE) - TOTAL COST OF TYRES                 *
*                                                       *
*   RETURNS        - TOTAL VALUE OF TYRES IN COMPANY   *
*                    INVENTORY                          *
*                                                       *
*********************************************************
```

```
      REAL FUNCTION CSTFNC(COST,SIZE)
      INTEGER I,SIZE
      REAL COST(SIZE),SUMCST

      SUMCST = 0.0
      DO 10 I = 1,SIZE
        SUMCST = SUMCST + COST(I)
10    CONTINUE
      CSTFNC = SUMCST
      RETURN
      END


***********************************************************
*                                                         *
*   SUBROUTINE TO PRINT THE INVENTORY REPORT              *
*                                                         *
***********************************************************
*                                                         *
*   INPUT PARAMETERS:                                      *
*                                                         *
*     TYRITM(SIZE,STORE)   - ARRAY OF TYPES OF TYRES       *
*                             PER STORE                    *
*     CSTUNT(SIZE,STORE)   - ARRAY OF COSTS PER TYRE       *
*                             PER STORE                    *
*     CSTTYR(SIZE,STORE)   - ARRAY OF TYRE VALUES PER      *
*                             STORE                        *
*     TYRSIZ(SIZE)   - COMPANY INVENTORY OF TYRES OF       *
*                       EACH SIZE                          *
*     TYRSTR(STORE)  - COMPANY INVENTORY OF TYRES PER      *
*                       STORE                              *
*     TYRTOT         - TOTAL TYRE INVENTORY OF COMPANY     *
*     CSTSTR(STORE)  - VALUE OF INVENTORY OF EACH          *
*                       STORE                              *
*     CSTSIZ(SIZE)   - VALUE OF INVENTORY OF EACH TYRE     *
*                       SIZE                               *
*     CSTTOT         - TOTAL VALUE OF COMPANY              *
*                       INVENTORY                          *
*                                                         *
***********************************************************
      SUBROUTINE DATOUT(TYRITM,CSTUNT,CSTTYR,TYRSIZ,
     1        TYRSTR,TYRTOT,CSTSTR,CSTSIZ,CSTTOT,
     2        SIZE,STORE)
      INTEGER I,J,STORE,SIZE,TYRTOT
      INTEGER TYRITM(SIZE,STORE),TYRSIZ(SIZE),
     1        TYRSTR(STORE)
      REAL CSTUNT(SIZE,STORE),CSTTYR(SIZE,STORE),
     1      CSTSTR(STORE)
      REAL CSTSIZ(SIZE),CSTTOT

      WRITE (*,1000)
1000  FORMAT('1',12X,'INVENTORY OF TYRES BY SIZE ',
     1        'AND STORE')
```

```
      WRITE (*,1050)
1050  FORMAT('+',12X,'_____ __ _____ __ ____ ',
     1       '___ _____')
      WRITE (*,1100) (I, I=1,STORE)
1100  FORMAT(//1X,'STORE NUMBER:',5I5,1X,'TOTALS')
      WRITE (*,1200)
1200  FORMAT(/1X,'TYRE TYPE')
      DO 10 I=1,SIZE
         WRITE (*,2000) I,(TYRITM(I,J), J=1,STORE),
     1           TYRSIZ(I)
2000     FORMAT(1X,I5,8X,6I5)
10    CONTINUE
      WRITE (*,3000) (TYRSTR(I), I=1,STORE),TYRTOT
3000  FORMAT(/1X,'TOTALS:',6X,6I5)

      WRITE (*,4000)
4000  FORMAT('1',12X,VALUE OF INVENTORY BY SIZE ',
     1       ' AND STORE')
      WRITE (*,4050)
4050  FORMAT('+',12X,'_____ __ _____ __ ____ ',
     1       '___ _____')
      WRITE (*,5000) (I,I=1,STORE)
5000  FORMAT(//1X,'STORE NUMBER:',5I8,4X,'TOTALS')
      WRITE (*,6000)
6000  FORMAT(/1X,'TYRE TYPE')
      DO 20 I=1,SIZE
         WRITE(*,7000) I,(CSTTYR(I,J), J=1,STORE),
     1           CSTSIZ(I)
7000     FORMAT(1X,I5,8X,6F8.2)
20    CONTINUE
      WRITE (*,8000) (CSTSTR(I), I=1,STORE),CSTTOT
8000  FORMAT(/1X,'TOTALS:',6X,6F8.2)
      RETURN
      END
```

Output

```
INPUT THE NUMBER OF TYRE SIZES (MAXIMUM OF 20)
AND THE NUMBER OF STORES (MAXIMUM OF 10)
4,5


INPUT THE NUMBER OF TYRES BY SIZE AND STORE
10,20,30,40,50
20,30,40,50,60
30,40,50,60,70
40,50,60,70,80


INPUT THE COST PER TYRE BY SIZE AND STORE
15.0,15.5,16.0,16.5,17.0
12.0,12.5,13.0,13.5,14.5
9.0,9.5,10.0,10.5,11.0
6.0,6.5,7.0,7.5,8.0
```

INVENTORY OF TYRES BY SIZE AND STORE

STORE NUMBER:	1	2	3	4	5	TOTALS
TYRE TYPE						
1	10	20	30	40	50	150
2	20	30	40	50	60	200
3	30	40	50	60	70	250
4	40	50	60	70	80	300
TOTALS:	100	140	180	220	260	900

VALUE OF INVENTORY BY SIZE AND STORE

STORE NUMBER:	1	2	3	4	5	TOTALS
TYRE TYPE						
1	150.00	310.00	480.00	660.00	850.00	2450.00
2	240.00	375.00	520.00	675.00	870.00	2680.00
3	270.00	380.00	500.00	630.00	770.00	2550.00
4	240.00	325.00	420.00	525.00	640.00	2150.00
TOTALS:	900.00	1390.00	1920.00	2490.00	3130.00	9830.00

Chapter Summary

Two-dimensional arrays are used for storing the rows and columns of tables and matrices. The storage must be allocated explicitly:

LOGICAL array($l_r : u_r$, $l_c : u_c$)

where l_r and u_r, l_c and u_c are the lower and upper bounds of the rows and columns, respectively. The lower and upper bounds must be integers such that $l_r \leq u_r$ and $l_c \leq u_c$. When the lower bound is not specified, the default value is one and the upper bound must be positive.

All processing of two-dimensional arrays should be done by indexing through the subscripts, since the arrays are stored in column-major order. The processing is most efficient when the elements are processed in order by columns. Array elements can be used anywhere simple variables of the same type can be used.

Arrays of more than two dimensions are rarely used. However, FORTRAN 77 supports arrays of as many as seven dimensions. The declaration of a multidimensional array has the form

$$\text{REAL array}(l_1 : u_1, \, l_2 : u_2, \, l_3 : u_3, \, \ldots \, l_n : u_n)$$
$$\text{INTEGER array}(l_1 : u_1, \, l_2 : u_2, \, l_3 : u_3, \, \ldots \, l_n : u_n)$$

where for all i, $l_i \leq U_i$. Elements of multidimensional arrays are used in the same way as elements of one- or two-dimensional arrays.

Input/output of two-dimensional arrays may be done by referencing the name of the array, using regular or implied DO-loops, or using combinations of these. Arrays can be used in subroutines and functions. Array are passed by reference to the array location. Adjustable dimensioning of arrays makes a program more flexible.

Exercises

1. Alter the program of Section 7.7.4 so that the row and column maximum and minimum values are not stored in vectors. That is, as each row maximum or minimum is found, search the column containing it to determine whether it is a column minimum or maximum.

2. Write a program to sort a two-dimensional real array A(20,20). The elements in a row should not be rearranged, but the rows should be moved so that

    $A(1,1) \geq A(i,1)$ $i > 1$
    $A(2,1) \geq A(i,1)$ $i > 2$
    $. . .$

    If any two rows have the same first element, they should be arranged in order according to their second element, and so forth.

3. A magic square is an n $\times$ n array of integers having the same value for all the row sums, column sums, and sums of the two main diagonals. For example:

    $$\begin{array}{ccc} 4 & 9 & 2 \\ 3 & 5 & 7 \\ 8 & 1 & 6 \end{array}$$

    is a 3 $\times$ 3 magic square with the sum of the rows, columns, and diagonals equal to 15. The algorithm for forming an n $\times$ n magic square when n is odd is as follows:

    a. Generate the integers from 1 through n^2.
    b. As this is done, place the first number in the middle of the bottom row of the array in position A(i,j).

   c. Place the next number in position A(mod(i,n) + 1,mod(j,n) + 1), unless a number is already there. In that case place it in position A(i − 1,j).

   d. Repeat step 3 until all the integers have been placed in the array.

   Write a program that generates and prints magic squares of sizes n = 3,5,7,9,11,13,15.

4. A point P(x,y,z) in three-dimensional space is rotated an angle xrad around the x-axis by multiplying the vector P by the array XROT, an angle yrad around the y-axis by multiplying it by YROT, and an angle zrad around the z-axis multiplying it by ZROT, where

$$XROT = \begin{matrix} 1 & 0 & 0 \\ 0 & \cos(xrad) & -\sin(xrad) \\ 0 & \sin(xrad) & \cos(xrad) \end{matrix}$$

$$YROT = \begin{matrix} \cos(yrad) & 0 & \sin(yrad) \\ 0 & 1 & 0 \\ -\sin(yrad) & 0 & \cos(yrad) \end{matrix}$$

$$ZROT = \begin{matrix} \cos(zrad) & -\sin(zrad) & 0 \\ \sin(zrad) & \cos(zrad) & 0 \\ 0 & 0 & 1 \end{matrix}$$

   Write a program that takes as input three angles: xrad, yrad, and zrad, and calculates a single rotational matrix ROT, which has the effect of performing the x rotation, then the y rotation, then the z rotation. Input coordinates of points. For each point print out its original location and its location after the combined rotation.

5. An n × n array contains the costs of flying nonstop between n different cities. Generate an n × n array that contains the minimum cost of flying with one stop between each pair of cities for which such a flight is possible. Print both arrays.

6. A population study is being done on the spread of disease. A logical n × n array A of zeros and ones shows which of n people have had direct contact with which others in the last two weeks (1 for contact, 0 for no contact). Calculate the kth power of the array such that $A^k = A^{k-1}$. This array shows which people have had any contact at all, direct or indirect, within the two weeks. Print the original array and the final array.

7. Write a set of subroutines that
   a. input a two-dimensional matrix
   b. multiply two matrices using matrix multiplication
   c. print a two-dimensional matrix
   Test these routines with a matrix A(3,5) and B(5,8).

8. Write a function subprogram SUM(ARR,N,M,DIM,K) that calculates the sum of the elements in row K of ARR if DIM = 1, and the sum of the elements in column K if DIM = 2. Test this function by filling a vector R(20) wih the row sums of A(20,20) and a vector C(20) with the column sums of A. Then compute the sum of R and the sum of C. Hint—pass R and C as having dimension N = 20, M = 1.

9. Write a program that calculates the line of least strain and the line of greatest strain on a two-dimensional flat plate under uniform loading, given the measurements of strain. The measurements are taken at grid points and stored in an array ST(100,100). Use a subroutine to locate the lines of maximum and minimum strain. Use another subroutine to output the array and the lines of maximum and minimum strain. Store the array in common.

8 *Character Data Manipulation*

*C*haracter data manipulation was introduced in 1977 in FORTRAN V and later became part of standard FORTRAN 77. Originally it was felt that a scientific and engineering language only had to handle numeric computations, provided there were ways of labeling output. However, experience showed that sometimes it is necessary to label input for proper identification, and that a character code or ID is more appropriate than a numeric one. In many applications, character strings

385

are an essential part of the data. FORTRAN 77 has the essential operators and built-in functions for convenient manipulation of character data.

The characters permitted are the 49 recognized by FORTRAN 77. They are coded in a standard character code such as ASCII, EBCDIC, or BCD. This data is stored as a string of individual characters assigned to a character constant or a character variable. Since character data is stored differently from numeric data, the character string '123' is different from the number 123 and cannot be used in arithmetic expressions. The numeric value can be used in numeric operations, assignments, and comparisons. The character string value can be used in character operations, assignments, and comparisons.

Input/output of character values can be carried out with or without formats. If formats are used, they differ from numeric formats. Assignment and comparison of character data use the same operators as numeric data. But arithmetic operators cannot be used with character values, and the special character operators and functions cannot be used with numeric data.

The basic operations used in character data manipulation are concatenation, which constructs longer strings from short strings, and substring, which extracts a short string from a longer string. The following are typical examples of character data:

Character string	Use
JOHN THOMPSON	name
1453 S. PARK AVE.	address
(012)345-6789	telephone number
555 32412 00	account ID
15R6T	location ID
NE	directional code
$ (IN 1000S)	column heading

Character strings may contain blank spaces, digits, letters, and special symbols that FORTRAN recognizes. Strings of digits should be stored as character strings if they are used for identification rather than computation; for example, social security numbers and telephone numbers. The basic operations on character strings are insertion, deletion, extraction, assignment, and comparison. In addition, very often data of character type must be stored in some type of sorted order. Most scientific and engineering data requiring the use of IDs, such as inventory identification numbers or codes for test locations, is more readable if alphabetic IDs are used rather than numeric codes. Numeric IDs should be used only when a large number of items are to be identified and special security measures are necessary to avoid transcription errors.

8.1 Character Constants and Variables

A FORTRAN 77 character literal is a character string enclosed within single quotation marks. We have seen character literals in input/output statements and in formats. They are also used to initialize character constants and variables. The following examples show all these different uses:

```
PRINT*,'THE END'
FORMAT('0')
PARAMETER (CODE = 'XYZ')
STR = 'REPORT OF 5/10/88'
```

As with numeric identifiers, character identifiers name constants when they are initialized by a PARAMETER statement and are never given a new value. They name variables when they are initialized by an assignment statement or a READ statement.

The length of a character string is significant. The following examples show character literals of different lengths:

Character string	*Length*
'UNIVERSITY'	10
'AMERICANƀNATIONALS'	18
'THEƀBIGƀBIRDƀBLUE'	17
'+*A−*CD/*KM'	11
'IƀSHOULDN''TƀTALKƀSOƀMUCH'	24
'HEƀSAID,ƀ''HELLO'''	16

To determine the length of a string, count the characters inside the enclosing quotation marks, including the blank spaces. If a single quotation mark or apostrophe is to be included as part of the literal, it is represented by two adjacent single quotation marks, but they are only counted as one.

The length of a character constant or variable must be included in the declaration. The length provides a maximum size for the values that can be stored in the character variable.

8.1.1 Declaration (CHARACTER statement)

There are no default character types in FORTRAN. A character variable must be declared by using a CHARACTER statement. The general form of the declaration is:

CHARACTER charvarname1*length1,charvarname2*length2,...

This form is used when the different character variables have different lengths, as in the following examples:

```
CHARACTER STR*8
CHARACTER NAME*10,LOC*20,DATE*6,CODE
```

When a length is not given, a default length of one is used; thus CODE takes as its value a single character. If the variables have the same length, the general form is:

CHARACTER*length charvarname1,charvarname2,...

For example,

```
CHARACTER*20 NAME,ADDR,JOB
```

The declaration causes contiguous storage to be set aside for the individual characters of each character variable. The storage assigned by these declarations is as follows:

STR   [ ][ ][ ][ ][ ][ ][ ][ ]

NAME   [ ][ ][ ][ ][ ][ ][ ][ ][ ][ ]

LOC   [ ]

DATE   [ ][ ][ ][ ][ ][ ]

CODE   [ ]

Note that when no length is specified, the default length of a character string is one. Eight bytes of storage have been assigned to STR, 10 to NAME, 20 to LOC, six to DATE, and a default length of one to CODE.

When several variables are to have the same length, the declarations may be combined, as follows:

```
CHARACTER*8 NAME1,NAME2,NAME3
```

Eight bytes are allocated for each variable name. The general and specific declarations of length may be used in the same declaration, as follows:

```
CHARACTER*10 STR1,STR2*8,STR3,STR4*5
```

which allocates 10 bytes for STR1 and STR3, eight bytes for STR2, and five bytes for STR4.

Both a type delaration and a PARAMETER statement are needed to initialize a character constant to a value that will not be changed during program execution. The declaration and DATA statement are used to initialize character variables. The following examples show the use of both the PARAMETER and DATA statements:

```
CHARACTER DIGIT*10
PARAMETER (DIGIT='0123456789')
```

In the case of a character constant, the length may be obtained from the literal in the parameter statement, as in the following example:

```
CHARACTER DIGIT*(*)
PARAMETER (DIGIT='0123456789')
```

In both of these examples, the storage is initialized to the same value.

DIGIT   [0][1][2][3][4][5][6][7][8][9]

One character is stored in each byte of storage.

Character variables may be initialized using either a DATA statement or an assignment statement, for example:

```
CHARACTER PLACE*14
DATA PLACE/'CONSTANTINOPLE'/
```

or

```
PLACE = 'CONSTANTINOPLE'
```

The string in the variable PLACE is stored as shown:

PLACE `C O N S T A N T I N O P L E`

If the character string does not fit the storage space exactly, it is stored left-justified with the right end truncated or padded with blanks, as in the following examples:

```
CHARACTER*10 METAL,EARTH
DATA METAL,EARTH/'ALUMINUM','DIATOMACEOUS'/
```

The strings are stored as shown below:

METAL `A L U M I N U M ␢ ␢`

EARTH `D I A T O M A C E O`

The DATA statement is also used to initialize arrays, even when they hold constants:

```
CHARACTER GRADE(5)
DATA (GRADE(I),I=1,5)/'A','B','C','D','F'/
```

The strings are stored as shown below:

```
GRADE(1)  A
GRADE(2)  B
GRADE(3)  C
GRADE(4)  D
GRADE(5)  E
```

8.1.2 Assignment of Character Data

Using assignment statements, character data may be assigned only to character variables. The data assigned may be in the form of a literal or may already be stored in a character constant or variable. In the following example,

```
CHARACTER*5 STR, STRCON, TEMP
PARAMETER (STRCON='ABCDE')

TEMP = STRCON
STR = 'W␢X␢Y'
```

the storage locations before the execution of the assignment statements hold

STR `/ / / / /`   STRCON `A B C D E`   TEMP `/ / / / /`

and after the assignments they hold

STR `W ␢ X ␢ Y`   STRCON `A B C D E`   TEMP `A B C D E`

The original data in STR and TEMP is lost, the value in STRCON is copied into TEMP, and the literal 'W␢X␢Y' is placed in STR.

Character variables do not always match in length the value being assigned to them. Behind the scenes, the assignment is made one character at a time, starting at the left end of storage. As many characters as possible are stored. If there is extra space, it is filled with blanks. There are three possibilities:

Exact Length Character Value

```
CHARACTER STR*10
STR = 'UNIVERSITY'
```

STR ⟦U⟧N⟧I⟧V⟧E⟧R⟧S⟧I⟧T⟧Y⟧

All the characters are stored, because the character string has the same length as the storage.

Long Character Value

```
CHARACTER STR*10
STR = 'SOUTHERNᵇTECH'
```

STR ⟦S⟧O⟧U⟧T⟧H⟧E⟧R⟧N⟧ᵇ⟧T⟧

The character literal is stored left-justified, and the three rightmost characters in the string are truncated.

Short Character Value

```
CHARACTER STR*10
STR = 'Aᵇ&ᵇM'
```

STR ⟦A⟧ᵇ⟧&⟧ᵇ⟧M⟧ᵇ⟧ᵇ⟧ᵇ⟧ᵇ⟧ᵇ⟧

The character literal is stored left-justified, and the five extra bytes are filled with blanks.

8.1.3 Comparison of Character Data

Character constants and character variables can be compared for equality. Any of the relational operators presented in section 4.1.2 can be used with character strings. If the character values include special characters other than letters and blank spaces, the ordering depends on the underlying order of the processor's collating sequence. A collating sequence is the numerical order of character representations in an internal code such as ASCII or EBCDIC. ANSI FORTRAN 77 uses the ASCII collating sequence. Other implementations use EBCDIC or other collating sequences, which are usually machine dependent. The ASCII and EBCDIC collating sequences are given in Appendix A. In ASCII, the 'ᵇ' precedes all other special characters and all the special characters precede the digits, which in turn precede the alphabetical characters.

The computer compares character strings, character by character, from left to right until it finds unequal characters. If the character strings are not the same length, if necessary the computer considers the shorter one to be extended to the length of the longer one with blank spaces. For example,

```
CHARACTER STR1*10,STR2*7
STR1 = 'UNIVERSITY'
STR2 = 'UNIVERSITY'
```

are stored as

STR1 `U N I V E R S I T Y`   STR2 `U N I V E R S`

When these are compared for equality,

```
IF (STR1 .EQ. STR2)
```

they are compared as

STR1 `U N I V E R S I T Y`   STR2 `U N I V E R S ƀ ƀ ƀ`

and the result is false because the 'ƀ' in position eight of STR2 is not equal to the 'I' in position eight of STR1.

The following examples show the results of comparisons:

Relational expression			*Truth value*	*Comment*
'WXYZ'	.LT.	'WXPR'	false	'P' precedes 'Y'
'WXYZ'	.GT.	'ABCD'	true	'A' precedes 'W'
'WXYZ'	.LE.	'WXY'	false	'ƀ' precedes 'Z'
'WXYZ'	.NE.	'WXYZƀ'	false	'ƀ' equals 'ƀ'
'2+3'	.LT.	'5'	true	'2' precedes '5'
'TƀP'	.LT.	'TP'	true	'ƀ' precedes 'P'

An important part of a sorting routine consists of comparing two character strings and swapping them if they are not already in order. This is shown in the following code segment:

```
CHARACTER*10 STR1, STR2, TEMP
. . .
IF (STR1 .GT. STR2) THEN
   TEMP = STR1
   STR1 = STR2
   STR2 = TEMP
ENDIF
```

When data is searched for a particular piece of information identifiable by the ID, the character string comparison controls the search. This is shown in the following code segment:

```
       SUBROUTINE FIND(ID)
       CHARACTER*4  ID,INFOID
       CHARACTER*76 INFO

       READ (*,*,END=100) INFOID,INFO

*      DO WHILE (INFOID .NE. ID)

10     IF (INFOID .NE. ID) THEN
          READ (*,*,END=100) INFOID,INFO
          GO TO 10
       ENDIF

*      ENDDO

*  RECORD WANTED HAS BEEN FOUND
          . . .
```

```
*   RECORD WANTED IS MISSING

100    CONTINUE
```

LGE, LGT, LLE, and LLT Functions

When FORTRAN 77 programs are transported from one machine to another, because of a difference in character codes, the collating sequences may not be the same. This may cause problems in execution and the production of different answers on different machines. FORTRAN 77 has special library functions that may be used in the comparison of character strings, which produce the same results on all machines. Essentially they compare character strings according to the order of the ASCII collating sequence. These functions are:

LGE(str1,str2)	str1 lexicographically greater than or equal to str2
LGT(str1,str2)	str1 lexicographically greater than str2
LLE(str1,str2)	str1 lexicographically less than or equal to str2
LLT(str1,str2)	str1 lexicographically less than str2

The following examples show the use of these functions:

```
CHARACTER*N STR1,STR2
IF (LGE(STR1,STR2)) THEN
```

> true if STR1 = STR2 or STR1 follows STR2 in the ASCII collating sequence, otherwise false

```
IF (LGT(STR1,STR2)) THEN
```

> true if STR1 follows STR2 in the ASCII collating sequence, otherwise false

```
IF (LLE(STR1,STR2)) THEN
```

> true if STR1 = STR2 or STR1 precedes STR2 in the ASCII collating sequence, otherwise false

```
IF (LLT(STR1,STR2)) THEN
```

> true if STR1 precedes STR2 in the ASCII collating sequence, otherwise false

ICHAR and CHAR Functions

The functions ICHAR and CHAR are used to convert characters to integers and integers to characters. The ICHAR function converts a single character in the FORTRAN character set to the integer that identifies its place in the collating sequence. The general form of the function is

ICHAR(char)

where char is a single character. The value returned is the position of the character in the collating system, numbered from 0 through $n-1$ for a set of n characters. If the character ' + ' is the eleventh character, then it is in position 10 and ICHAR(' + ') is 10. Since 'B' precedes 'X' in the collating sequence, the value of ICHAR('B') is less than ICHAR('X').

The function CHAR takes as its argument an integer specifying a position in the collating sequence and returns the character in that position. The general form of the function is

CHAR(integer)

where the integer must be in the range 0 through $n-1$ for a set of n characters. For example, CHAR(71) is 'G' if 'G' is in position 71 of the collating sequence.

The CHAR and ICHAR functions are inverses of each other. For example,

```
CHAR(ICHAR('B'))
```

is 'B' and

```
ICHAR(CHAR(42))
```

is 42. The following example shows how to assign the collating sequence positions to the letters of the alphabet:

```
      CHARACTER LETTER(26)
      INTEGER NUM(26),I
      DATA(LETTER(I),I=1,26)/'A','B','C','D','E','F',
     1     'G','H','I','J','K','L','M','N','O','P',
     2     'Q','R','S','T','U','V','W','X','Y','Z'/

      DO 10 I=1,26
         NUM(I) = ICHAR(LETTER(I))
10    CONTINUE
```

8.1.4 Input/Output of Character Data (A format)

Input/output of character data can be handled in two ways. If the data has been free-formatted, the computer automatically determines the spacing. The formatted form uses spacing supplied by the programmer.

List-Directed Input

When character data is free-formatted, the character values are already in the form of character literals, separated by commas or blanks in the input stream. The input list of the READ statement directs the computer where to store the values.

Programming Warning

> Character data used as list-directed input must be enclosed in single quotation marks.

Given the code segment

```
CHARACTER NAME*20, ADDR*30
READ (*,*) NAME,ADDR
```

and the input stream

```
'TERRY␢K.␢DRINKWATER','8␢VALLEY␢DR.,␢LR,␢AR␢11251'
```

the values stored are

NAME ┌─┬─┬─┬─┬─┬─┬─┬─┬─┬─┬─┬─┬─┬─┬─┬─┬─┬─┐
     │T│E│R│R│Y│␢│K│.│␢│D│R│I│N│K│W│A│T│E│R│␢│

ADDR │8│␢│V│A│L│L│E│Y│␢│D│R│.│,│␢│L│R│,│␢│A│R│

     │␢│1│1│2│5│1│␢│␢│␢│␢│

Note that the data must be separated by commas or blanks because two adjacent quotation marks would be interpreted as a quoted apostrophe. When, as in this example, the data does not have the same length as the variable, the value is stored left-justified, truncated or padded as necessary.

List-Directed Output

Free-formatted output of character strings does not use default spacing. Character values are printed without any intervening blanks. If values are to be aligned in columns they must have the same explicit size.

Given the code segment

```
CHARACTER A*10,B*12

A = 'ABCDEFGHIJ'
B = 'WXYƎ87ZPQRST'
WRITE (*,*) A, B
```

the output will be

```
ABCDEFGHIJWXYƎ87ZPQRST
```

Note that the output does not contain any quotation marks and the values are juxtaposed in the output line.

Given the code segment

```
CHARACTER A*10,B*12

A = 'ABCDEFGHIJ'
B = 'WXYƎ87ZPQRST'
WRITE (*,*) A, B
WRITE (*,*) B, A
```

the output will be

```
ABCDEFGHIJWXYƎ87ZPQRST
WXYƎ87ZPQRSTABCDEFGHIJ
```

Note that the second variables are not aligned.

The columns of data can be spaced apart by including blanks in the output list. The is shown in the following example. Given the code segment

```
CHARACTER A*10,B*12

A = 'ABCDEFGHIJ'
B = 'WXY387ZPQRST'
WRITE (*,*) A, '    ', B
WRITE (*,*) B, '    ', A
```

the output will be

```
ABCDEFGHIJ    WXY387ZPQRST
WXY387ZPQRST    ABCDEFGHIJ
```

Note that the quoted blank spaces in the output list form an actual character string, therefore they are printed as part of the output. If character data output is to be aligned in columns, it is best to use formatted output.

Formatted Input

Using formatted input, the programmer can control the spacing of character data in the input record. Since specific fields are identified, the input character strings are not enclosed in quotation marks.

*Programming
Warning*

> Do not enclose character input data in quotation marks when formatted input is used.

Input data is read using the A format for the field specifications. This is shown in the following example. Given the code segment

```
        CHARACTER STR1*8, STR2*10

        READ 1000, STR1,STR2
1000    FORMAT(A8,A10)
```

and the input record

```
|A|B|C|D|E|F|G|H|K|L|M|N|O|P|Q|R|S|T|
     A8              A10
```

the input values are stored as

STR1 `A|B|C|D|E|F|G|H`   STR2 `K|L|M|N|O|P|Q|R|S|T`

The A8 field specification identifies the characters in the first eight columns of the record with the variable name STR1. The A10 specification identifies the characters in the next 10 positions with the variable name STR2. When character data does not exactly fit the specified fields, it should be left-justified in the fields, as shown in the following example. Given the code segment

```
CHARACTER NAME*10, ADDR*20

READ 1100, NAME,ADDR
1100   FORMAT(A10,A20)
```

and the input record

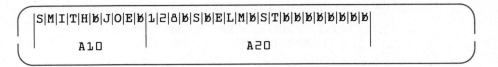

the input values are stored as

```
NAME   S M I T H b J O E b
```

```
ADDR   1 2 8 b S b E L M b S T b b b b b b b b
```

Blank spaces in the input data are read and stored the same way as other characters.

If the field lengths of the character input specifications do not match the lengths of the input variables, the values are stored left-justified in the input variables with the right ends truncated or padded with blanks to fit the space. This is shown in the following example. Given the code segment

```
CHARACTER FIRST*10, LAST*10

READ 1100, FIRST,LAST
1100   FORMAT(A6,A12)
```

and the input record

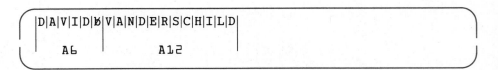

the input values are stored as

```
FIRST   D A V I D b b b b b
```

```
LAST    V A N D E R S C H I
```

The following example shows input containing both character strings and numbers. The format specifications describe the data fields in order from left to right. Given the code segment

```
CHARACTER STUID*9, NAME*11
INTEGER GR1, GR2, GR3, GR4
```

```
            READ 2000, STUID,NAME,GR1,GR2,GR3,GR4
2000   FORMAT(A9,A11,4I3)
```

the input record has the form

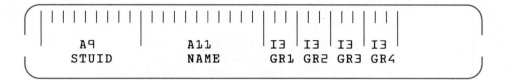

Formatted Output

When the programmer wishes to control the spacing of output data, formatted output should be used. Character strings are printed right-justified in the fields specified. Since the character values are left-justified in the storage locations, this results in the output data being aligned left-justified in columns, provided the variables printed in the same position have the same declared length. Extra space can be left between columns of output by overspecifying the field width or by explicit use of spacing specifications. The following example shows this. Given the code segment

```
    CHARACTER PARTNO*4, DESCRP*10, SOURCE*12

    PRINT 1000, PARTNO, DESCRP, SOURCE
     . . .
    PRINT 1000, PARTNO, DESCRP, SOURCE
1000 FORMAT(1X,A8,' ',A10,A12)
```

then the output might be

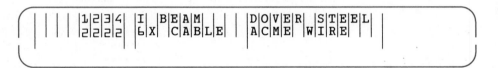

Note that numbers are printed right-justified in an over-specified field. The specifications for DESCRP and SOURCE exactly match the character string declarations, therefore they are printed exactly as the values are stored. The 1X specification produces a blank space for the carriage control character.

8.1.5 Review Questions

1. Write the declaration statements for the following character strings:

    a. STR1 = 'FORTRAN 77'
    b. STR2 = 'IBM VERSION (1984)'
    c. STR3 = 'ƀƀƀ'
    d. STR4 = '"HI"'
    e. STR5 = ''

2. Write declaration statements for the following character strings:

   a. STRA having length 20, STRB having length 16, STRC having length 12
   b. STRX, STRY, STRZ, STRW all having length 25
   c. STR1, STR3, STR5 which have lengths 4, 5, and 6 respectively

3. Write declaration and parameter statements to initialize the following character constants:

   a. TITLE = 'ANNUALⱫREPORT'
   b. DEPT = 'ENGINEERING'
   c. SECT = 'PRODUCTⱫREVIEW'
   d. YEAR = '1989'

4. Indicate whether each of the following comparisons is true or false:

   a. 'CONSTANT' .GT. 'CONSTANTINOPLE'
   b. 'MAGNESIUM' .LT. 'MANGANESE'
   c. 'MCKENZIE' .LE. 'MCKNIGHT'
   d. 'BACON' .GE. 'EGGS'
   e. 'EGGS' .GE. 'EGGSⱫ'
   f. LGE('0123','123')
   g. LLT('ⱫⱫ','ⱫB')

5. Write input statements to read the following character data into appropriately named variables:

   a. 'CASTⱫIRON', 'STEEL','ALUMINUM','COPPERⱫALLOY'
   b. 'FRAMES','HANDLES', 'WHEELS', 'PEDALS'
   c. 'DEPTH','WIDTH','HEIGHT'

6. Write output statements to print the following:

   a. 'METALⱫPROCESSINGⱫINDUSTRY' centered at the top of the page
   b. 'PRECIOUSⱫMETALSⱫSALVAGEDⱫ-' at the beginning of the fifth row
   c. 'GOLD','SILVER','PLATINUM' as column headings in positions 20, 40, and 60

7. Write the output statements to print the following logo:

```
        *
       ***
      *****
     *******
    *********
     *******
      *****
       ***
        *
```

8.2 Operations on Character Data

Character data manipulation consists of building strings, taking strings apart, locating characters and substrings in strings, and replacing substrings. The only basic operation for string manipulation in FORTRAN is concatenation, attaching strings together to form a larger string. All other character string manipulations are accomplished through the use of built-in character functions.

8.2.1 Concatenation

The double slash symbol (//) used for concatenation builds a longer string out of shorter strings.

```
'MAN' // 'Ƅ' // 'MACHINE' // 'Ƅ' // 'INTERFACE'
```

is equivalent to

```
'MANƄMACHINEƄINTERFACE'
```

Several concatenation operations may be included in the same expression and any string literals may be used, including blanks. Character literals and variables may be combined, but concatenation of variables preserves any leading or trailing blanks in the variables, as shown in the following example. Given the code segment

```
CHARACTER*4  STR1,STR2,STR3,STR4
CHARACTER    RESULT*17
   . . .
STR1 = 'THE'
STR2 = 'SKY'
STR3 = 'IS'
STR4 = 'BLUE'
RESULT = STR1 // STR2 // STR3 // STR4 // '.'
```

```
RESULT is 'THEƄSKYƄISƄƄBLUE.'
```

The length of the RESULT variable was carefully selected so that the value would fit exactly. If it had not been an exact match, the right end of the value would have been truncated if it was longer or padded with blanks if it was shorter. Spacing the words equally, as in this example, is possible using built-in functions to locate the end of each word.

8.2.2 Built-in Character Functions

There are two built-in FORTRAN functions that can be used to obtain information about strings:

LEN(string)   returns the number of characters in the string
INDEX(string,substr) returns the location of the substring substr in the string

In both cases, the value returned is an integer.

Length Function

The function LEN can take as its argument any character variable, constant, or expression. The number returned can be thought of as being either the number of characters in the argument string, including blanks, or as the number of bytes of storage used by the argument string. This is shown in the following examples:

```
CHARACTER VERSE*45, RHYME*45
VERSE = 'THE FLOWERS THAT BLOOM IN THE SPRING, TRA LA'
```

```
RHYME = 'HI HO, HI HO, IT''S OFF TO WORK WE GO'
N = LEN(VERSE)               result is            N = 45
N = LEN(RHYME)                   ''               N = 45
N = LEN('APPLES ARE RED')        ''               N = 14
N = LEN('THE'//' ')              ''               N = 4
N = LEN(' '//VERSE)              ''               N = 46
```

In the case of variables, the declared length is used regardless of the number of nonblank characters stored. In the case of literals, the number of characters in the literal is used. In the case of an expression, the function returns the number of characters in the value of the expression.

At this point you may not think this function is very useful. You will see its value when you write subprograms that have character arguments of adjustable length.

Index Function

The INDEX function searches a string for a specific substring and returns the starting position of the first occurrence of that substring. This is shown in the following examples:

```
CHARACTER AXIOM*51
AXIOM = 'COMPUTER PROGRAMMING IS MORE OF AN ART THAN
        A SCIENCE'
 .  .  .
L = INDEX(AXIOM,'M')        result is    L = 3   First 'M'
L = INDEX(AXIOM,'AMM')          ''       L = 15  'A' of 'AMM'
L = INDEX(AXIOM,'IS')           ''       L = 22  'I' of 'IS'
L = INDEX(AXIOM,'ꞵISꞵ')         ''       L = 21
L = INDEX(AXIOM,'CAN')          ''       L = 0   not found
```

The arguments of this function may be variables, literals, or character expressions, as in the following examples:

```
CHARACTER   WORD*5
WORD = 'BREAD'
K = INDEX('BREADFRUIT',WORD)         result is      K = 1
K = INDEX('CONSTANTINOPLE','N')          ''         K = 3
K = INDEX(WORD//'S','ADS')               ''         K = 4
K = INDEX('ALUMINUM','UM')               ''         K = 3
```

One special use of the INDEX function is for data validation. A single character used as a code can be validated by

```
IF (INDEX('valid chars',char) .NE. 0) THEN valid
```

as in the following examples:

```
(INDEX('0123456789',CH) .NE. 0)    CH is a digit
(INDEX('+-*/',CH) .NE. 0)      CH is an arithmetic operator
```

Another special use is the conversion of a character to a numeric code, as in the following examples. If CH is a digit, then given

```
CODE = INDEX('0123456789',CH) - 1
```

CODE is the value of the digit. If CH is one of the letters 'A', 'B', 'C', or, 'D',

```
VALUE = INDEX('DCBA',CH)
```

VALUE is 1 if CH is 'D', 2 if 'C', 3 if 'B', 4 if 'A'.

8.2.3 Substring Manipulation

Characters may be extracted from a character string or inserted into a character string by referring to their positions in the string. The general form

> string(i:j)

refers to character positions i through j in the string. If i is missing, the substring is assumed to start in the first position; If j is missing, the substring is assumed to end in the last position. When this notation is used in an expression, the substring in the indicated postions is used. If the notation is used as a receiving field for an assignment, the substring in those positions is changed.

Substring Extraction

The following examples show the use of substring access to copy part of a character string. Given the code segment

```
CHARACTER STRING*20, STR1*6, STR2*6

STRING = 'COMMONFACTOR'
STR1 = STRING(1:6)            or      STRING(:6)
STR2 = STRING(7:12)
```

STRING `C O M M O N F A C T O R ƀ ƀ ƀ ƀ ƀ ƀ ƀ ƀ`

STR1 `C O M M O N`   STR2 `F A C T O R`

the value of STR1 is 'COMMON' and of STR2 is 'FACTOR'. The value of STRING has not been changed. STRING(:6) is the same as STRING(1:6), but STRING(7:) is not the same as STRING(7:12). As the former is longer, it has more trailing blanks. STRING(0:6) or STRING(7:22) would be in error because it attempts to access characters beyond the bounds of the string.

Programming Warning

> String access must not attempt to go outside the limits of the character string.

Given a character string STR of length N,

STR(1:N) refers to the entire string.
STR(I:J) refers to a substring where $1 \leqslant I \leqslant J \leqslant N$

A particular position in the string may be referenced by a numeric constant, variable, or expression. The following example shows several ways of extracting the same substring:

```
CHARACTER   NAME*20, WORD*10
NAME = 'PULASKI COUNTY'

WORD = NAME(1:7)              is 'PULASKI'

K = INDEX(NAME,' ')-1
WORD = NAME(1:K)              is 'PULASKI'

WORD = NAME(:INDEX(NAME,' ')-1)    is 'PULASKI'
```

When a character string consists of several parts, the parts may be located and separated, as shown in the following example:

```
        CHARACTER*20 NAME, WORD1, WORD2
        READ (*,*) NAME

*   REMOVE LEADING BLANKS

*       DO WHILE (NAME(1:1) .EQ. ' ')

10      IF(NAME(1:1) .EQ. ' ') THEN
           NAME = NAME(2:)
           GO TO 10
        ENDIF

*       ENDDO

        K = INDEX(NAME,' ')
        WORD1 = NAME(:K-1)
        WORD2 = NAME(K+1:)
```

Note that this program segment is not robust and will not work if the input string is entirely blank or does not contain any blanks.

Substring Insertion

Substrings are inserted into strings either by separating the string into pieces and rebuilding it by concatenation, or by replacing one substring by another of the same length. In the following example, the middle initial is to be used instead of the middle name. Since this involves a change of length, the first and last names are extracted and the full name is rebuilt.

```
        CHARACTER NAME*20, FIRST*4, INITL*1, LAST*5

        NAME = 'RAMA NARAYANA REDDY'
        FIRST = NAME(:4)
        INITL = NAME(6:6)
        LAST = NAME(15:)
        NAME = FIRST // ' ' // INITL // '. ' // LAST
```

This example assumes that the lengths of the parts of the name are known. If they are not known, the INDEX function can be used to locate the blanks between names and the example becomes

```
CHARACTER NAME*20, FIRST*4, INITL*1, LAST*5
. . .
NAME = 'RAMA NARAYANA REDDY'
I = INDEX(NAME,' ')
J = INDEX(NAME(I+1:),' ') + I
FIRST = NAME(:I-1)
INITL = NAME(I+1:I+1)
LAST = NAME(15:)
NAME = FIRST // 'ƀ' // INITL // '.ƀ' // LAST
```

FIRST ⟦R⟧⟦A⟧⟦M⟧⟦A⟧   INITIAL ⟦N⟧   LAST ⟦R⟧⟦E⟧⟦D⟧⟦D⟧⟦Y⟧

The result of the concatenation is:

NAME ⟦R⟧⟦A⟧⟦M⟧⟦A⟧⟦ƀ⟧⟦N⟧⟦.⟧⟦ƀ⟧⟦R⟧⟦E⟧⟦D⟧⟦D⟧⟦Y⟧⟦ƀ⟧⟦ƀ⟧⟦ƀ⟧⟦ƀ⟧⟦ƀ⟧⟦ƀ⟧⟦ƀ⟧

NAME is 'RAMAƀN.ƀREDDYƀƀƀƀƀƀƀ' in either case.

If names are to be rearranged so that the substrings no longer divide the string in the same way, the same method of extraction and concatenation is used.

```
CHARACTER NAME*20, FIRST*4, MIDDLE*8, LAST*5

NAME = 'RAMA NARAYANA REDDY'
FIRST = NAME(:4)
MIDDLE = NAME(6:13)
LAST = NAME(15:)
NAME = LAST // 'ƀ' // MIDDLE // 'ƀ' // FIRST
```

As a result, NAME is 'REDDYƀNARAYANAƀRAMAƀ'.

The following example shows the insertion of a substring using the same method:

```
CHARACTER DATE*12, MONTH*4, YEAR*4

DATE = 'MAY 1989'
MONTH = DATE(:4)
YEAR = DATE(5:)
DATE = MONTH // '23,ƀ' // YEAR
```

as a result, DATE is 'MAY 23, 1989'.

When one string is replaced by another of the same length, it may be inserted without taking apart the context string. This is shown in the following example:

```
CHARACTER DATE*12

DATE = 'MAY 23,ƀ1989'
DATE(5:6) = '30'
```

As a result, DATE is 'MAY 30, 1989'.

Substrings may be extracted and inserted in the same statement. This does not rearrange the substrings; it copies one of them, as in the following example:

```
CHARACTER WORD*12
```

```
WORD = 'COMMANDMENTS'
WORD(:3) = WORD(11:)
```

As a result, WORD is 'TSƀMANDMENTS'. The last two letters were extracted, expanded with a trailing blank, and placed in the first three positions. When extracting and replacing in the same statement, be careful not to overlap the accessed substrings.

8.2.4 Review Questions

1. Given

   ```
   CHARACTER STR1*5,STR2*3,STR3*6
   ```

   ```
   PARAMETER (STR1='WATER', STR2='IS', STR3='LIQUID')
   ```

   show the result of each of the following expressions:

   a. STR1 // 'ƀ' // STR2 // 'Aƀ' // STR3
   b. STR3 // STR1
   c. STR1 // 'ƀ' // STR2 // STR1 // '.'

2. Given

   ```
   CHARACTER TEXT*50
   ```

   ```
   TEXT = 'UNIVERSITIES ARE INSTITUTIONS OF LEARNING.'
   ```

   show the value of each of the following expressions:

   a. TEXT(:12)
   b. TEXT(14:16)
   c. TEXT(20:)
   d. TEXT(7:7)

3. Given

   ```
   CHARACTER DEPT*25
   ```

   ```
   DEPT = 'ELECTRICAL ENGINEERING'
   ```

   give the value of each of the following expressions:

   a. LEN(DEPT)
   b. LEN(DEPT(:5))
   c. LEN(DEPT(2:17))
   d. LEN(DEPT // 'RMƀ103')

4. Given

   ```
   CHARACTER*30 SENT
   ```

   ```
   SENT = 'ALLOY METALS ARE STRONG.'
   ```

   give the value of each of the following expressions:

   a. INDEX(SENT,'ALLOY')
   b. INDEX(SENT,'SƀARE')

    c. INDEX(SENT,'b')

    d. INDEX(SENT,'S')

5. Given

```
CHARACTER*3 STR1*5,STR2, STR3

DATA STR1,STR2,STR3/'ROSES','ARE','RED'/
```

show the result of each of the following expressions:

    a. STR1(:4) // STR3

    b. INDEX(STR1,'S')

    c. INDEX(STR1,STR3(2:2))

    d. INDEX(STR1//STR2,'SA')

    e. STR1(INDEX(STR1,'O'):INDEX(STR1,'E'))

6. Write an expression that

    a. is true if CH is a letter of the alphabet

    b. converts 'M' to 1, 'F' to 2

    c. is false if a string STR is not completely blank

    d. gives the length of the substring of LINE that precedes the first blank

8.3 Character Data and Arrays

Whenever an application requires a list of character data, an array may be used to store the data. This would include such things as a list of student names, a list of parts to build a machine, a list of metals in an alloy, or a list of locations of test data. Each element of a character array is a character string.

8.3.1 Declaration of Character Arrays

An array used for storing character data must be declared as to the array size, the data type, and the length of the character strings. All character string elements have the same length. The following example,

```
CHARACTER XARY(20)*5
```

allocates array storage under the name XARY for 20 elements, each of which is a character string having five characters. Several arrays may be declared in the same statement:

```
CHARACTER*10 XARY(15),YARY(20),ZARY(10)
```

or

```
CHARACTER XARY(15)*10,YARY(20)*10,ZARY(10)*10
```

The array XARY has 15 elements of 10 characters each. YARY has 20 elements of 10 characters each and ZARY has 10 elements of 10 characters each.

8.3.2 Input/Output of Character Arrays

The input/output of character arrays is similar to that of numeric arrays except for the data type. Either list-directed or formatted instructions and either explicit or implied DO-loops may be used.

List-Directed Input/Output

Character string data for list-directed input must be enclosed in single quotation marks. The following examples show list-directed input of character strings:

```
CHARACTER ARAY(10)*8

DO 50 I=1,10
   READ (*,*) ARAY(I)
50    CONTINUE
```

The input consists of 10 records, each having a character string in quotation marks. For example,

```
'XXXXXXX'
      .
      .
      .
```

Given the program segment

```
CHARACTER YARY(10)*6,ZARY(10)*10

DO 50 I=1,10
   READ (*,*) YARY(I),ZARY(I)
50    CONTINUE
```

the data has the form

```
'XXXXX',   'YYYYYYYYYY'
      .
      .
      .
```

List-directed output of arrays of character data is shown in the following examples:

```
CHARACTER ARAY(10)*5

DO 50 I=1,10
   WRITE (*,*) I,'        ',ARAY(I)
50    CONTINUE
```

The output is printed on 10 lines:

```
  1         XXXXX
  2         XXXXX
  .
  .
  .
 10         XXXXX
```

Given the program segment

```
      CHARACTER STRRAY(10)*6,CHARY(10)*8

      DO 50 I=1,10
         WRITE (*,*) I,'      ',STRRAY(I),'      ',CHARY(I)
50    CONTINUE
```

the two arrays are printed side by side on 10 lines:

```
  1         SSSSSS      CCCCCCCC
  2         SSSSSS      CCCCCCCC
  .
  .
  .
 10         SSSSSS      CCCCCCCC
```

Note that the columns must be explicitly spaced apart. With list-directed output, character strings are printed in consecutive fields.

Formatted Input/Output of Character Arrays

The following examples show the use of formats in the input of data into character arrays:

```
      CHARACTER XRAY(10)*15

      DO 50 I=1,10
         READ (*,1000) ARAY(I)
1000  FORMAT(A15)
50    CONTINUE
```

The input consists of 10 records, each having the first 15 columns treated as a character string. No quotation marks are used. The input data has the following form:

```
|X|X|X|X|X|X|X|X|X|X|X|X|X|X|X|
```

Given the program segment

```
CHARACTER YARY(20)*10,ZARY(20)*15

DO 50 I=1,20
   READ (*,1000) YARY(I), ZARY(I)
1000   FORMAT(A10,A15)
50     CONTINUE
```

the input consists of 20 records, each containing two character strings, in the first 10 and the next 15 columns. The input data has the following form:

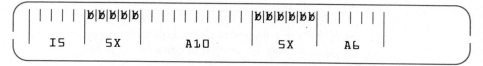

Formatted output of character arrays is shown in the following example:

```
CHARACTER ARAY(10)*10,BARY(10)*6

DO 50 I=1,10
   WRITE (*,1000) I,ARAY(I),BARY(I)
1000   FORMAT(1X,I5,5X,A10,5X,A6)
50     CONTINUE
```

There will be 10 numbered lines of output, each line containing one value for each array. The output has the following form:

```
|  |  |  |  |  | ƀ|ƀ|ƀ|ƀ|ƀ|  |  |  |  |  |  |  |  |  |  | ƀ|ƀ|ƀ|ƀ|ƀ|ƀ|  |  |  |  |  |
|    I5    |    5X    |       A10      |    5X    |      A6     |
```

While the column of numbers is right-justified, the character strings in each of the arrays are left-justified in their respective fields because the character field specifications match the array declarations.

8.3.3 Manipulation of Character Arrays

Character arrays can be manipulated element by element in the same way as simple character variables. Array elements can be concatenated, substrings can be extracted and replaced, and built-in functions can be used to manipulate the elements. Character array elements can be assigned to single variables. Logical operations can be performed using relational operators to compare array elements or using the lexicographical built-in function. The following examples show how character arrays may be processed:

```
CHARACTER XARY(10)*8,YARY(10)*6,RARY(10)*14

DO 10 I=1,10
  L = INDEX(XARY(I),' ')
  RARY(I) = XARY(I)(1:L) // YARY(I)
10     CONTINUE
```

This example shows the formation of the elements of array RARY from the leading substrings of the array XARY and the array YARY. Each element of XARY must have at least one blank. For example, given

XARY(I) `⟨R⟩⟨O⟩⟨S⟩⟨E⟩⟨S⟩⟨b⟩⟨b⟩⟨b⟩`   YARY(I) `⟨R⟩⟨E⟩⟨D⟩⟨b⟩⟨b⟩⟨b⟩`

the result is:

RARY(I) `⟨R⟩⟨O⟩⟨S⟩⟨E⟩⟨S⟩⟨b⟩⟨R⟩⟨E⟩⟨D⟩⟨b⟩⟨b⟩⟨b⟩⟨b⟩⟨b⟩`

Note that only one blank from XARY(I) is included in the concatenated result.

The following example has an array containing names: first name, middle name, and last name, separated by blanks. The names are printed in the order last name, middle name, and first name.

```
      CHARACTER NAME(20)*30,TEMP*30
      CHARACTER FIRST*30, MIDD*30, LAST*30

      DO 10 I=1,20
        L =INDEX(NAME(I),' ')
        FIRST = NAME(I)(1:L-1)
        TEMP = NAME(I)(L+1:)
        L = INDEX(TEMP,' ')
        MIDD = TEMP(1:L-1)
        LAST = TEMP(L+1:)
        TEMP = LAST(1:INDEX(LAST,' ')) //
     1    MIDD(1:INDEX(MIDD,' ')) //
     2    FIRST(1:INDEX(FIRST,' '))
        WRITE (*,1000) TEMP
1000    FORMAT(1X,A30)
10    CONTINUE
```

The use of the INDEX function and concatenation to form the character string TEMP for output adjusts the spacing, so that there is exactly one blank between each of the parts of the name being printed.

In the following example, a character string is separated into words and the words are stored in an array:

```
      CHARACTER SENT*44
      CHARACTER WORDS(7)*10
      DATA WORDS/7*' '/

      I = 1
      L = INDEX(SENT,' ')

*      DO WHILE (L .GT. 1 .AND. I .LE. 7)

10    IF (L .GT. 1 .AND. I .LE. 7) THEN
        WORDS(I) = SENT(1:L-1)
        SENT = SENT(L+1:)
        I = I + 1
        L = INDEX(SENT,' ')
        GO TO 10
      ENDIF

*      ENDDO
```

Given the data

```
SENT = 'COMPUTERS MUST BE INSTRUCTED TO DO SOMETHING'
```

the words are stored as

```
WORDS(1)   COMPUTERSƀ
WORDS(2)   MUSTƀƀƀƀƀ
WORDS(3)   BEƀƀƀƀƀƀƀ
WORDS(4)   INSTRUCTED
WORDS(5)   TOƀƀƀƀƀƀƀ
WORDS(6)   DOƀƀƀƀƀƀƀ
WORDS(7)   SOMETHINGƀ
```

Note that the words are stored left-justified with blank fill.

8.3.4 Review Questions

1. Write declaration statements to declare the following character arrays:

   a. XSTR having 15 elements of 20 characters each
   b. STRX, STRY, and STRZ having 10, 15, and 20 elements respectively of length 8, 12, and 15 characters
   c. ST1, ST2, ST3, and ST4 each having 40 elements, but having lengths of 10, 10, 15, and 20 characters respectively

2. Given the following array, write a program segment using a DO-loop to construct a sentence in a single character string:

```
WORD(1)   THEƀƀ
WORD(2)   TIGER
WORD(3)   ISƀƀƀ
WORD(4)   BLACK
WORD(5)   INƀƀƀ
WORD(6)   COLOR
```

   The words should be concatenated in such a way that there is exactly one blank between words.

3. Write a program segment to separate the following paragraph into sentences and store them in an array:

   THE FOREST HAS TREES. ALL THE TREES ARE GREEN IN SUMMER. BIRDS BUILD NESTS IN THE TREES. SQUIRRELS LIVE IN HOLES IN THE TRUNKS. OTHER ANIMALS BURROW UNDER THE ROOTS. ONE TREE CAN SHELTER MANY ANIMALS.

8.4 Character Data and Subprograms

Character data may be passed to subroutines or functions. It may be returned from subroutines through changed parameters, it may be returned from functions. Like other types of programs, programs using character data should have a modular design, with subprograms used for complicated input/output and for complex calculations.

8.4.1 Argument and Parameter Passing

The argument lists of subprograms may contain a variety of types of data. As with other types, when character variables are passed as arguments, the parameters must match as to type and length. Since it is the address of the variable that is actually passed, to obtain the location of the character value, the subprogram can only access the string correctly by having a local declaration that matches. Character arguments and parameters may be single character strings or arrays containing character data.

The following example shows the passing of character strings to a subroutine. The third character string is being used as a pattern for the concatenation of the first two, and the fourth character string holds the result. Since the pattern string has the form 'ABBA', the first two strings will be concatenated in the order ASTR // BSTR // BSTR // ASTR.

```
      CHARACTER*4 ASTR,BSTR,PAT*8,RESULT*40

      READ (*,*) ASTR,BSTR
      PAT = 'ABBA'
      CALL CONCAT(ASTR,BSTR,PAT,RESULT)
      WRITE (*,*) RESULT
      STOP
      END

      SUBROUTINE CONCAT(STR1,STR2,CODE,ANS)
      CHARACTER STR1*4,STR2*4,CODE*8,ANS*40
      CHARACTER CH
      INTEGER K,I
*
      ANS = ' '
      K = 1
      L = 1
      CH = CODE(K:K)

*     DO WHILE (K .LE. 8)

10    IF (K .LE. 8) THEN
         CH = CODE(K:K)
         IF (CH .EQ. 'A') THEN
            ANS(L:L+3) = STR1
         ELSE IF (CH .EQ. 'B') THEN
            ANS(L:L+3) = STR2
         ENDIF
         K = K + 1
         L = L + 4
         GO TO 10
      ENDIF

*     ENDDO
```

```
         RETURN
         END
```

Note that the dummy arguments STR1,STR2, CODE, and ANS are declared as having the same respective lengths as the actual arguments ASTR, BSTR, PAT, and RESULT.

The following example shows the use of subroutines to input and output an array containing character data, and a function to locate the longest character string in the array. The effective length is the number of characters preceding the trailing blanks.

```
         CHARACTER*12 CHARY(20)
         INTEGER N,LOC,LONG

         READ (*,1000) N
 1000    FORMAT(I5)
         IF (N .LE. 12) THEN
            CALL INARY (N,CHARY)
            LOC = LONG(N,CHARY)
            CALL OUTARY(N,CHARY)
            WRITE (*,2000) CHARY(LOC),LOC
 2000       FORMAT(1X,'THE STRING ',A12,' IN ',
        1          'POSITION',I2,' IS THE LONGEST')
         ELSE
            WRITE (*,*) 'ERROR IN INPUT VALUE'
         ENDIF
         STOP
         END


*****************************************************************
*                                                               *
*   SUBROUTINE TO INPUT AN ARRAY OF CHARACTER                   *
*   STRINGS                                                      *
*                                                               *
*****************************************************************

         SUBROUTINE INARY(M,STARY)
         CHARACTER*12 STARY(M)
         INTEGER I,M

         DO 10 I=1,M
            READ (*,1000,END=50) STARY(I)
 1000       FORMAT(A12)
 10      CONTINUE
         RETURN
 50      WRITE (*,*) 'DATA MISSING'
         STOP
         END
```

```
      ***********************************************************
      *                                                         *
      *   SUBROUTINE TO OUTPUT AN ARRAY OF CHARACTER            *
      *   STRINGS                                               *
      *                                                         *
      ***********************************************************

            SUBROUTINE OUTARY(K,STARX)
            CHARACTER*12 STARX(K)
            INTEGER K,I

            DO 10 I=1,K
               WRITE (*,1000) I,STARX(I)
      1000     FORMAT(1X,I5,5X,A12)
      10       CONTINUE
            RETURN
            END

      ***********************************************************
      *                                                         *
      *   FUNCTION TO FIND THE LONGEST VALUE IN A               *
      *   CHARACTER ARRAY                                       *
      *                                                         *
      ***********************************************************

            INTEGER FUNCTION LONG(Z,STARZ)
            CHARACTER*12 STARZ(Z)
            INTEGER Z,I,K,POS,L

            L = 0
            POS = 0
            DO 20 I=1,Z
               K = 12

      *         DO WHILE (K.GT.L.AND.STARZ(I)(K:K).EQ.' ')

      10        IF (K.GT.L .AND. STARZ(I)(K:K).EQ.' ') THEN
                  K = K - 1
                  GO TO 10
               ENDIF

      *         ENDDO

               IF (K .GT. L) THEN
                  L = K
                  POS = I
               ENDIF
      20       CONTINUE
            LONG = POS
            RETURN
            END
```

8.4.2 Adjustable-Length Character Variables

Subprograms using character variables may be generalized by passing the lengths of the character strings as well as their locations. This makes it possible to use the same subprogram with character strings of different sizes. The following example shows the adjustable description of character variables in a subroutine that prints character variables left-justified in a field of width 20.

```
      CHARACTER STR1*10,STR2*14

      READ (*,1000) STR1,STR2
1000  FORMAT(A10,A14)
      CALL SUBOUT(STR1)
      CALL SUBOUT(STR2)
      STOP
      END


      SUBROUTINE SUBOUT(STRNG)
      INTEGER M
      CHARACTER STRNG*(*),FIELD*20

      M = LEN(STRNG)
      FIELD = ' '
      FIELD(1:M) = STRNG

      WRITE (*,1000) FIELD
1000  FORMAT(1X,A20)
      RETURN
      END
```

For example, when STR1 = 'ELECTRONIC' and STR2 = 'MAGNETIC FIELD', the output is as shown below:

```
|ELECTRONIC          |
|MAGNETIC FIELD      |
```

The first time the subroutine is called, a character string of length 10 is passed. This length is then used to direct the placement of the character string in positions 1 through 10 of FIELD, as shown. The second time the subroutine is called, a character string of length 14 is passed. This string is placed in positions 1 through 14 of FIELD.

Programming Warning

> The declaration of a character string parameter in a subprogram must not exceed the length of the actual character string argument.

8.4.3 Review Questions

1. Indicate whether the following statements are true or false:

   a. Character data can be passed to subroutines just like numeric data.
   b. Character variables passed to subroutines do not have to be declared in the subroutines.
   c. Character strings passed as arguments automatically have the same length in the subprograms.
   d. Functions may return character strings.
   e. Character strings stored in an array must all have the same length.

2. Write a subroutine CONCAT that is passed the three character strings ST1 = 'ROSES', ST2 = 'ARE', and ST3 = 'RED' and that builds and returns the string ST = 'ROSESbAREbRED' to the calling program.

3. Write a subroutine REVERS that is passed a character string STR of length N and reverses the order of the characters in the string, returning the reversed string to the calling program.

4. Write a logical function VALID that is passed a character string NUM of length N, returning true if NUM contains only digits, otherwise returning false.

5. Write a subroutine INPUT that reads character strings into an array DATA(20)*10 and returns the array and a logical variable, which is true if the elements of the array are in alphabetical order, false otherwise.

8.5 Sample Programs Using Character Data

The most common uses of character routines are for editing and validating data, arranging data for storage, and setting up displays. The character data itself may be IDs, pictures, information, or simply numbers being stored in character form. These programs have been executed interactively on the Digital Equipment Corporation (DEC) computer model VAX 11/780.

8.5.1 Data Compression

Problem

Write a program to remove the blank spaces from a character string, separating the data values by commas and compressing the string. (Trailing blanks will remain.) For example,

```
'  24.903  -125 XYZ64 .036 1.8E-17    '
```

will become

```
'24.903,-125,XYZ64,.036,1.18E-17'
```

Pseudocode

Locate the last nonblank character.
For each set of blanks preceding the last nonblank character (remove it
    from the string)
        concatenate the preceding and succeeding character strings,
            separated by a comma
Replace the string by the result

Program

```
**********************************************************
*                                                        *
*       CHARACTER STRING COMPRESSION                     *
*                                                        *
**********************************************************
*                                                        *
*       OUTPUT VARIABLES:                                *
*                                                        *
*         LINE   - COMPRESSED CHARACTER STRING           *
*                                                        *
**********************************************************

        INTEGER K,N,M
        CHARACTER LINE*55

*       ASSIGN THE CHARACTER STRING TO VARIABLE LINE

        LINE = ' 24.903 -125 XYZ64 .036 1.8E-17  '

        IF (LINE .EQ. ' ') THEN
           WRITE (*,1000)
1000       FORMAT(/1X,'THE LINE IS BLANK')
           STOP
        ENDIF

*       REMOVE LEADING BLANKS

        M = 1

*       DO WHILE (LINE(M:M) .EQ. ' ')

10      IF (LINE(M:M) .EQ. ' ') THEN
           M = M + 1
           GO TO 10
        ENDIF

*       ENDDO

        LINE = LINE(M:)

*       FIND LAST NONBLANK CHARACTER

        K = LEN(LINE)
```

```
*         DO WHILE (LINE(K:K) .EQ. ' ')

20        IF (LINE(K:K) .EQ. ' ') THEN
             K = K - 1
             GO TO 20
          ENDIF

*         ENDDO

*         LOCATE SET OF BLANKS AND REMOVE THEM

          N = INDEX(LINE,' ')
          IF (N .NE. 0) THEN

*            DO WHILE (N .LT. K)

30           IF (N .LT. K) THEN
                M = N + 1

*               DO WHILE (LINE(M:M) .EQ. ' ')

40              IF (LINE(M:M) .EQ. ' ') THEN
                   M = M + 1
                   GO TO 40
                ENDIF

*               ENDDO

                LINE = LINE(:N-1) // ',' // LINE(M:)
                K = K - M + N + 1
                N = INDEX(LINE,' ')
                GO TO 30
             ENDIF

*            ENDDO

          ENDIF
          WRITE (*,2000)
2000      FORMAT(1X,'OUTPUT OF THE COMPRESSED STRING'/)
          WRITE (*,*) LINE
          STOP
          END
```

Output

```
OUTPUT OF THE COMPRESSED STRING
24.903,-125,XYZ64,.036,1.8E-17
```

This type of processing would be used when as much data as possible is being stored in as small a space as possible.

8.5.2 Data Conversion

Problem

A record contains an unknown number of integers separated by one or more blanks. Print the numbers in a column, right-justified. For example,

```
12645   3547        -1   46  -458762'
```

should be printed as

```
   12645
    3547
      -1
      46
 -458762
```

Pseudocode

> For each number
>   Remove leading blanks
>   Find the first trailing blank following the digits
>   Extract the number (maximum of 11 digits)
>   Convert the number to integer
>   Print the number
> End for
> Stop

Program

```
****************************************************************
*                                                              *
*   PRINT NUMBERS FROM A RECORD                                *
*                                                              *
****************************************************************
*                                                              *
*   INPUT VARIABLES:                                           *
*                                                              *
*     RECORD - CHARACTER STRING CONTAINING SIGNED              *
*              NUMBERS                                         *
*                                                              *
*   OUTPUT VARIABLES:                                          *
*                                                              *
*     NUMVAL - NUMERIC VALUE OF SIGNED STRING OF               *
*              DIGITS                                          *
*                                                              *
****************************************************************
```

```
        INTEGER N, NUMVAL
        CHARACTER RECORD*50, NUMSTR*11

        WRITE (*,*) 'INPUT THE CHARACTER STRING'
        READ (*,1000) RECORD
1000    FORMAT(A50)

        WRITE (*,2000)
2000    FORMAT(//X,'OUTPUT OF THE INTEGERS'/)

*       DO WHILE (RECORD .NE. ' ')

10      IF (RECORD .NE. ' ') THEN

*       REMOVE LEADING BLANKS

            N = 1

*           DO WHILE (RECORD(N:N) .EQ. ' ')

20          IF (RECORD(N:N) .EQ. ' ') THEN
              N = N + 1
              GO TO 20
            ENDIF

*           ENDDO

*       EXTRACT, CONVERT, AND PRINT THE INTEGERS

            N = N - 1
            RECORD = RECORD(N+1:)
            N = INDEX(RECORD,' ')
            NUMSTR = ' '
            NUMSTR(13-N:) = RECORD(:N-1)
            READ (UNIT=NUMSTR,FMT=3000) NUMVAL
3000        FORMAT(I11)
            WRITE (*,4000) NUMVAL
4000        FORMAT(5X,I11)
            RECORD = RECORD(N+1:)
            GO TO 10
        ENDIF

*       ENDDO

        STOP
        END
```

Output

```
 ┌─────────────────────────────────────────────────────────────
 │  INPUT THE CHARACTER STRING
 │    723419 -2810578    4172      6348192
 │
 │
 │  OUTPUT OF THE INTEGERS
 │
 │         723419
 │       -2810578
 │           4172
 │        6348192
 └─────────────────────────────────────────────────────────────
```

This type of input processing can be used when nothing is known about the spacing of the input data and the individual data values are wanted.

8.5.3 Number Verification

Problem

Read an integer from the first 10 positions of a record. Verify that the field actually contains a single integer number. For example,

'ƀƀ49751ƀƀƀ'	is correct
'ƀƀ-4681ƀƀƀ'	is correct
'ƀƀ874-1539'	is not correct
'23ƀƀƀ745ƀ'	is not correct
'25ƀƀABCƀƀƀ'	is not correct
'ƀƀƀƀƀƀƀƀƀƀ'	is not correct
'ƀƀ39X1ƀƀƀƀ'	is not correct

Method

Check for each of the following conditions:

Only leading blanks
Integer must start with $+$, $-$, 0–9
Integer must continue with 0–9
Only trailing blanks

Program

```
*****************************************************************
*                                                               *
*    VERIFY THAT FIELD CONTAINS AN INTEGER                      *
*                                                               *
*****************************************************************
*                                                               *
*    INPUT VARIABLES:                                           *
*                                                               *
*      RECORD - CHARACTER STRING TO BE VALIDATED                *
*                                                               *
*    OUTPUT VARIABLES:                                          *
*                                                               *
*      FIELD  - VALID OR INVALID FIELD                          *
*                                                               *
*****************************************************************

      LOGICAL INTG
      INTEGER K
      CHARACTER RECORD*50, FIELD*11

      WRITE (*,*) 'INPUT THE CHARACTER STRING'
      READ (*,1000) RECORD
1000  FORMAT(A50)
      FIELD = RECORD(:10)
      INTG = .FALSE.

*     FIND AND VALIDATE FIRST NONBLANK CHARACTER

      K = 1

*     DO WHILE (FIELD(K:K) .EQ. ' ')

10    IF (FIELD(K:K) .EQ. ' ') THEN
         K = K + 1
         GO TO 10
      ENDIF

*     ENDDO

      IF(INDEX('+-0123456789',FIELD(K:K)).NE.0) THEN
         INTG = .TRUE.
      ENDIF

*     VALIDATE CHARACTERS BEFORE NEXT BLANK

      K = K + 1

*     DO WHILE (FIELD(K:K) .NE. ' ')

20    IF (FIELD(K:K) .NE. ' ') THEN
         IF(INDEX('0123456789',FIELD(K:K)).EQ.0) THEN
            INTG = .FALSE.
```

```
          ENDIF
          K = K + 1
          GO TO 20
       ENDIF

*      ENDDO

*      VALIDATE CHARACTER AFTER INTEGER

       IF(FIELD(K:) .EQ. ' ' .AND. INTG) THEN
          WRITE (*,2000) FIELD
2000      FORMAT(/1X,'OUTPUT OF THE RESULTS'/1X,A11,
     1           'IS AN INTEGER')
        ELSE
          WRITE (*,3000) FIELD
3000      FORMAT(/1X,'OUTPUT OF THE RESULTS'/1X,A11,
     1           'IS NOT AN INTEGER')
        ENDIF
        STOP
        END
```

Output of Four Runs

```
INPUT THE CHARACTER STRING
   123

OUTPUT OF THE RESULTS
   123      IS AN INTEGER



INPUT THE CHARACTER STRING
123 123

OUTPUT OF THE RESULTS
123 123      IS NOT AN INTEGER



INPUT THE CHARACTER STRING
123A

OUTPUT OF THE RESULTS
123A         IS NOT AN INTEGER



INPUT THE CHARACTER STRING
123a

OUTPUT OF THE RESULTS
123a         IS NOT AN INTEGER
```

We used several "tricks of the trade" in this program. The variable FIELD is longer than necessary so that its value contains trailing blanks. A flag, INTG, is used to keep track of the results of the tests performed on the field. Initially INTG is .FALSE. until it is known that FIELD has at least one nonblank substring. Then it is assumed that FIELD contains an integer. Therefore INTG is .TRUE. unless one of the tests fails. The test for valid characters is performed by checking each character against a string of valid characters. Once the end of the string is found, a simple comparison with 'b' will determine whether the rest of the field is blank.

8.5.4 Graph of Sine and Cosine Functions

Problem

Plot longitudinally along the paper the graphs of $\sin(\theta)$ and $\cos(\theta)$ for $0 \leq \theta \leq 360°$.

Method

Use a character string for the line to be printed. Place an asterisk at each point on the sine and cosine curves. Space the points 10° apart.

Program

```
******************************************************
*                                                    *
*    PRINT THE SINE AND COSINE WAVES                 *
*                                                    *
******************************************************
*                                                    *
*    OUTPUT VARIABLES:                               *
*                                                    *
*    LINE    - PRINT LINE OF POINTS ON THE CURVES    *
*                                                    *
******************************************************

        INTEGER I,S,C
        REAL THETA,CONST
        CHARACTER LINE*80,STAR
        PARAMETER (PI=3.14159,STAR='*')

        WRITE (*,1000)
1000    FORMAT(/27X,'SINE WAVE',15X,'COSINE WAVE'/)
        CONST = 10.0 * PI / 180.0
        THETA = 0.0
        DO 10 I = 0,360,10
           S = 25 * SIN(THETA)
           C = 25 * COS(THETA)
           LINE = ' '
           LINE(30+S:30+S) = STAR
           LINE(30+C:30+C) = STAR
           WRITE (*,2000) LINE
```

```
2000      FORMAT(A80)
          THETA = THETA + CONST
10        CONTINUE
          STOP
          END
```

Output

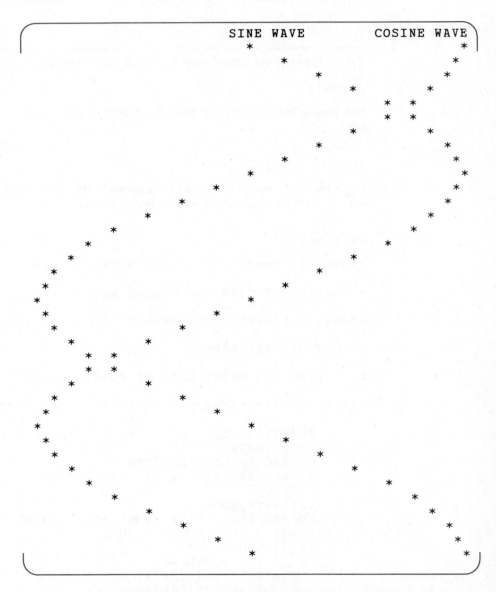

The graph could be drawn without using a character string for the output by calculating the positions of the asterisks in the output and overprinting the two graphs. Use the following output statements:

```
        WRITE (*,2000) (' ',K = 1,30+S),STAR
2000    FORMAT(1X,80(A))
        WRITE (*,2500) (' ',K = 1,30+C),STAR
2500    FORMAT('+',80(A))
```

8.5.5 Class Grade Report

Problem

Print an end-of-semester report of the grades of students in a computer class, sorted according to average grade.

Method

Use (1) a subroutine to input the test scores, (2) a subroutine to compute student averages and a class average, (3) a subroutine to assign letter grades to the students, (4) a sort subroutine, and (5) an output subroutine.

Program

```
****************************************************************
*                                                              *
*   PRINT A REPORT OF STUDENT GRADES                           *
*                                                              *
****************************************************************
*                                                              *
*   SUBROUTINES USED:                                          *
*                                                              *
*     INPUT    - READS THE STUDENT RECORDS                     *
*     COMPUT   - COMPUTES THE STUDENT SEMESTER                  *
*                AVERAGE                                        *
*     LTRGRD   - ASSIGNS THE STUDENT LETTER GRADES             *
*     SORT     - SORTS THE RECORDS IN DESCENDING               *
*                ORDER BY SEMESTER AVERAGE, USING A            *
*                TAG SORT                                       *
*     OUTPUT   - PRINTS THE GRADE REPORT                        *
*                                                              *
****************************************************************

        CHARACTER NAME (75)*24,COURSE*80,ID(75)*6,
     1      GRD(75)
        REAL AVG(75),WT(17),CLSAVG
        INTEGER GRADE(75,17),ORDER(75),J,K,N

        DO 10 J=1,75
          ORDER(J) = J
          AVG(J) = 0
10      CONTINUE

        CALL INPUT(NAME,ID,GRADE,WT,COURSE,K,N)
```

```
           IF (N .GT. 0) THEN
              CALL COMPUTE(GRADE,WT,AVG,CLSAVG,K,N)
              CALL LTRGRD(AVG,GRD,N)
              CALL SORT(AVG,ORDER,N)
              CALL OUTPUT(COURSE,NAME,ID,GRADE,GRD,AVG,
     1           ORDER,CLSAVG,WT,K,N)
            ELSE
              WRITE (*,1000)
 1000       FORMAT('1',T10,'NO DATA FOUND')
           ENDIF
           STOP
           END

     *********************************************************
     *                                                       *
     *   INPUT SUBROUTINE                                    *
     *                                                       *
     *********************************************************
     *                                                       *
     *   INPUT VARIABLES:                                    *
     *                                                       *
     *     NAME      - STUDENT NAME                          *
     *     ID        - STUDENT ID NUMBER                     *
     *     GR        - STUDENT TEST SCORE                    *
     *     WT        - WEIGHT OF TEST SCORE                  *
     *     COURSE    - HEADING FOR COURSE GRADE REPORT       *
     *     NGR       - NUMBER OF TEST SCORES (FEWER THAN 18)*
     *     NSTU      - NUMBER OF STUDENTS (NOT MORE THAN 75)*
     *                                                       *
     *   OUTPUT PARAMETERS:                                  *
     *                                                       *
     *     NAME(NSTU)     - ARRAY OF STUDENT NAMES           *
     *     ID(NSTU)       - ARRAY OF STUDENT ID NUMBERS      *
     *     GR(NSTU,NGR)   - ARRAY OF STUDENT TEST SCORES     *
     *     WT(NGR)        - ARRAY OF WEIGHTS OF TEST SCORES  *
     *     NGR            - NUMBER OF TEST SCORES            *
     *     NSTU           - NUMBER OF STUDENTS               *
     *                                                       *
     *********************************************************

           SUBROUTINE INPUT(NAME,ID,GR,WT,COURSE,NGR,NSTU)
           CHARACTER NAME(75)*24,COURSE*80,ID(75)*6
           REAL WT(17)
           INTEGER GR(75,17),J,NGR,NSTU

           NSTU = 1
           WRITE (*,*) 'INPUT HEADINGS'
           READ (*,1000,END=999) COURSE
 1000      FORMAT(A80)
           WRITE (*,*) 'INPUT WEIGHTS OF GRADES'
           READ (*,2000,END=999) NGR,(WT(J),J=1,NGR)
 2000      FORMAT(I2,17F4.2)
           WRITE (*,*) 'INPUT ID, NAME, GRADES'
```

```
            DO 20 NSTU=1,75
               READ (*,3000,END=999) ID(NSTU),NAME(NSTU),
     1              (GR(NSTU,J),J=1,NGR)
3000        FORMAT(A6,T8,A24,17I4)
20          CONTINUE
            NSTU = 75
            RETURN

999         NSTU = NSTU - 1
            RETURN
            END


***********************************************************
*                                                         *
*    SUBROUTINE TO COMPUTE AVERAGE GRADES                 *
*                                                         *
***********************************************************
*                                                         *
*    INPUT PARAMETERS:                                    *
*                                                         *
*      GRADE(NSTU,NGR) - ARRAY OF STUDENT TEST SCORES     *
*      WT(NGR)         - WEIGHT OF TEST SCORES            *
*      NGR      - NUMBER OF TEST SCORES (FEWER THAN 18)*
*      NSTU     - NUMBER OF STUDENTS (NOT MORE THAN 75)*
*                                                         *
*    OUTPUT PARAMETERS:                                   *
*                                                         *
*      AVG(NSTU)  - ARRAY OF AVERAGE STUDENT SCORES       *
*      CAVG       - AVERAGE SCORE IN CLASS                *
*                                                         *
***********************************************************

            SUBROUTINE COMPUTE(GRADE,WT,AVG,CAVG,NGR,NSTU)
            REAL WT(17),AVG(75),CAVG,SUM
            INTEGER GRADE(75,17),NGR,NSTU,C,R

            SUM = 0.0
            DO 20 R=1,NSTU
              DO 10 C=1,NGR
                AVG(R) = AVG(R) + GRADE(R,C) * WT(C)
10            CONTINUE
              SUM = SUM + AVG(R)
20          CONTINUE
            CAVG = SUM / NSTU
            RETURN
            END
```

```
*****************************************************
*                                                   *
*    SUBROUTINE TO ASSIGN LETTER GRADES             *
*                                                   *
*****************************************************
*                                                   *
*    INPUT PARAMETERS:                              *
*                                                   *
*      NSTU    - NUMBER OF STUDENTS (NOT MORE THAN 75)*
*      AVG(NSTU) - ARRAY OF AVERAGE STUDENT SCORES  *
*                                                   *
*    OUTPUT PARAMETERS:                             *
*                                                   *
*      GRD(NSTU) - ARRAY OF STUDENT LETTER GRADES   *
*                                                   *
*****************************************************

        SUBROUTINE LTRGRD(AVG,GRD,NSTU)
        REAL AVG(75)
        INTEGER NSTU,I
        CHARACTER GRD(75)

        DO 10 I=1,NSTU
          IF(AVG(I) .GE. 90.0) THEN
            GRD(I) = 'A'
          ELSEIF(AVG(I) .GE. 80.0) THEN
            GRD(I) = 'B'
          ELSEIF(AVG(I) .GE. 65.0) THEN
            GRD(I) = 'C'
          ELSEIF(AVG(I) .GE. 50.0) THEN
            GRD(I) = 'D'
          ELSE
            GRD(I) = 'F'
          ENDIF
10      CONTINUE
        RETURN
        END


*****************************************************
*                                                   *
*   SORT SUBROUTINE: SORTS IN DESCENDING ORDER OF AVG*
*                                                   *
*****************************************************
*                                                   *
*    INPUT PARAMETERS:                              *
*                                                   *
*      AVG(NSTU) - ARRAY OF AVERAGE STUDENT SCORES  *
*      O(NTSU)   - INDEX OF STUDENT RECORDS         *
*      NSTU    - NUMBER OF STUDENTS (NOT MORE THAN 75) *
*                                                   *
*    OUTPUT PARAMETERS:                             *
*                                                   *
*      O(NSTU)   - SORTED INDEX OF STUDENT RECORDS  *
*                                                   *
*****************************************************
```

```
      SUBROUTINE SORT(AVG,O,NSTU)
      REAL AVG(75)
      INTEGER O(75),NSTU,I,J,TEMP

      DO 20 J=1,NSTU-1
        DO 10 I=1,NSTU-J
          IF(AVG(O(I)) .LT. AVG(O(I+1))) THEN
            TEMP = O(I)
            O(I) = O(I+1)
            O(I+1) = TEMP
          ENDIF
10      CONTINUE
20    CONTINUE
      RETURN
      END


*******************************************************
*                                                     *
*   OUTPUT SUBROUTINE TO PRINT GRADE REPORT           *
*                                                     *
*******************************************************
*                                                     *
*   INPUT PARAMETERS & OUTPUT VARIABLES:              *
*                                                     *
*     HEADS            - COURSE HEADING               *
*     NAME(NSTU)       - ARRAY OF STUDENT NAMES       *
*     ID(NSTU)         - ARRAY OF STUDENT ID NUMBERS  *
*     GRADE(NSTU,NGR)  - ARRAY OF STUDENT TEST SCORES *
*     GRD(NSTU)        - ARRAY OF STUDENT LETTER      *
*                        GRADES                       *
*     AVG(NSTU)        - ARRAY OF AVERAGE STUDENT     *
*                        SCORES                       *
*     O(NSTU)          - INDEX ARRAY TO STUDENT       *
*                        RECORDS                      *
*     CAVG             - CLASS AVERAGE                *
*     WT(NGR)          - ARRAY OF WEIGHTS OF TEST     *
*                        SCORES                       *
*     NGR              - NUMBER OF TEST SCORES (UNDER *
*                        18)                          *
*     NSTU             - NUMBER OF STUDENTS (NOT MORE *
*                        THAN 75)                     *
*                                                     *
*   SUBROUTINE USED:                                  *
*                                                     *
*     HEAD     - PRINTS THE HEADINGS FOR THE REPORT   *
*                                                     *
*******************************************************

      SUBROUTINE OUTPUT(HEADS,NAME,ID,GRADE,GRD,
     1                  AVG,O,CAVG,WT,NGR,NSTU)
      CHARACTER HEADS*80,NAME(75)*24,ID(75)*6,GRD(75)
      REAL AVG(75),CAVG,WT(17)
      INTEGER GRADE(75,17),O(75),NGR,NSTU,R,
     1                  CNT,PG,I,J
```

```
          CNT = 100
          PG = 0
          DO 20 I=1,NSTU
            R = O(I)
            IF(CNT .GT. 50) THEN
              CALL HEAD(HEADS,WT,CNT,PG,NGR)
            ENDIF
            WRITE (*,1000) ID(R),NAME(R),AVG(R),GRD(R),
     1            (GRADE(R,J),J=1,NGR)
1000      FORMAT(T2,A6,T10,A24,F7.1,2X,A1,17I5)
            CNT = CNT + 1
20        CONTINUE
          WRITE (*,2000) CAVG
2000      FORMAT(//,T20,'CLASS AVERAGE = ',F6.2)
          RETURN
          END


*****************************************************
*                                                   *
*   SUBROUTINE TO PRINT THE PAGE HEADINGS            *
*                                                   *
*****************************************************
*                                                   *
*   INPUT PARAMETERS:                                *
*                                                   *
*     HEADS       - COURSE HEADING                   *
*     WT(NGR)     - ARRAY OF WEIGHTS OF TEST SCORES  *
*     PG          - PAGE NUMBER                      *
*     CNT         - RECORD COUNT                     *
*     NGR         - NUMBER OF TEST SCORES (UNDER 18) *
*                                                   *
*   OUTPUT VARIABLES:                                *
*                                                   *
*     HEADS       - COURSE HEADING                   *
*     WT(NGR)     - ARRAY OF WEIGHTS OF TEST SCORES  *
*     PG          - PAGE NUMBER                      *
*                                                   *
*****************************************************

          SUBROUTINE HEAD(HEADS,WT,CNT,PG,NGR)
          INTEGER CNT,PG,NGR,I
          CHARACTER HEADS*80
          REAL WT(17)

          CNT = 0
          PG = PG + 1
          WRITE (*,1000) HEADS,PG
1000      FORMAT('1',T3,A80,4X,'PAGE',I3,//)
          WRITE (*,2000) (WT(I),I=1,NGR)
2000      FORMAT(T34,'WEIGHTS',T44,1X,17(F4.2,1X))
          WRITE (*,3000)
3000      FORMAT(/)
          RETURN
          END
```

Output

```
INPUT HEADINGS
COMPUTER SCIENCE
INPUT WEIGHTS OF GRADES
3,.25,.25,.5
INPUT ID, NAME, GRADES
11111   JOHN BENSON              88   84   90
22222   ANN SMITH                85   87   93
33333   BILL JOHNSON             70   78   75
44444   JOE WALTON               78   81   70
55555   DAVID CALHOUN            91   89   93
66666   DONNA DENTON             93   90   97
77777   MARY HILTON              82   86   85
88888   MARK STEVENS             65   80   69
99999   REBECCA ALLEN            78   74   83


COMPUTER SCIENCE
     PAGE  1


                            WEIGHTS     0.25 0.25 0.50


66666   DONNA DENTON        94.3  A     93   90   97
55555   DAVID CALHOUN       91.5  A     91   89   93
22222   ANN SMITH           89.5  B     85   87   93
11111   JOHN BENSON         88.0  B     88   84   90
77777   MARY HILTON         84.5  B     82   86   85
99999   REBECCA ALLEN       79.5  C     78   74   83
44444   JOE WALTON          74.8  C     78   81   70
33333   BILL JOHNSON        74.5  C     70   78   75
88888   MARK STEVENS        70.8  C     65   80   69


           CLASS AVERAGE = 83.03
```

In the main program, the arrays are declared to be the maximum size that might be needed. The same constant size declarations are used in all the routines, but only parts of the arrays actually contain data. In the INPUT subroutine, the number of student records are counted. The number of tests is the first input value of the list of test weights. Rather than calling a subroutine many times to calculate the average score of a single student, the subroutine is called once to calculate all the average scores. This is more efficient. Likewise, all the letter grades are assigned with a single subroutine call. The SORT subroutine rearranges a list of the record positions until it shows what order the sorted records should have. This type of tag sort is more efficient than actually rearranging all the arrays every time a exchange is made. The OUTPUT routine then uses the index array to determ the correct order for printing the records. The OUTPUT routine can be u print more than one page of output with a maximum of 50 records on each page. It calls a separate routine to print the page headings. Notice that the line count is checked immediately before each student record is printed.

Chapter Summary

Character strings are a specific nonnumeric type in FORTRAN 77. They are declared using the CHARACTER statement and may be initialized using the PARAMETER or DATA statement. Unlike numeric data types, the declaration for character strings must normally include the amount of storage to be set aside for the string. This is the same as the number of characters in the stored string. In all operations, blanks are considered to be part of the character string.

Character data can be

compared for equality, inequality, or lexicographical ordering
assigned to character variables
assigned to specific subfields of character variables
input or output using the A format
treated as an internal source for formatted input
treated as an internal destination for formatted output

Special notation is used to reference character substrings. The special operator for character data is concatenation. There are two built-in library functions, LEN and INDEX. By using them various operations can be performed on a character string:

creating a string	str = part 1 // part 2//....//partn
referencing specific positions	str(i:j)
extracting a substring	substr = str(i:j)
replacing a substring	str(i:j) = newsubstr
inserting a substring	str = str(:k)//substr//str(k + 1:)
deleting a substring	str = str(:k)//str(n:)
	or str(k + 1:) = str(n:)
locating a specific substring	INDEX(str,substr)
validating a character	INDEX(validchars,ch) .NE. 0
converting characters to numeric codes	INDEX(digits,ch) + 1
determining the length of a string	LEN(str)
determining the length of a substring	LEN(str(i:j))

Various small program segments are useful building blocks for character manipulation programs.

Locating the first character that belongs to a character set:

```
      K = 1

*     DO WHILE(INDEX(charset,str(K:K)) .EQ. 0)

10    IF(INDEX(charset,str(K:K)) .EQ. 0) THEN
         K = K + 1
```

```
                    GO TO 10
               ENDIF

*     ENDDO
```

str(K:K) is the desired character.

Locating the first character that does not belong to a character set:

```
          K = 1

*         DO WHILE(INDEX(charset,str(K:K)) .NE. 0)

10        IF(INDEX(charset,str,(K:K)) .NE. 0) THEN
             K = K + 1
             GO TO 10
          ENDIF

*         ENDDO
```

str(K:K) is the desired character.

Locating the last character that belongs to a character set:

```
          K = LEN(str)

*         DO WHILE(INDEX(charset,str(K:K)) .EQ. 0)

10        IF(INDEX(charset,str(K:K)) .EQ. 0) THEN
             K = K - 1
             GO TO 10
          ENDIF
*         ENDDO
```

str(K:K) is the desired character.

Locating the last character that does not belong to a character set:

```
          K = LEN(str)

*         DO WHILE(INDEX(charset,str(K:K)) .NE. 0)

10        IF(INDEX(charset,str(K:K)) .NE. 0) THEN
             K = K - 1
             GO TO 10
          ENDIF

*         ENDDO
```

str(K:K) is the desired character.

Removing all embedded blanks:

```
          N = LEN(str)
          K = INDEX(str,' ')
```

```
*       DO WHILE (K .LT. N)

10      IF(K .LT. N) THEN
          str(K:) = str(K+1:)
          K = INDEX(str,' ')
          N = N - 1
          GO TO 10
        ENDIF

*       ENDDO
```

Exercises

1. Write a program to read a set of data in which each 80-character record contains a character string of at most 10 nonblank characters. Find the longest and the shortest string. Print each string and its length. Also identify and print the longest and shortest strings.

2. Write a program to input character strings, using free-formatted input, determining for each character string whether it represents a real number or not. Print the real numbers in columns 1–10, the other character strings starting in column 20.

3. Write a program that reads text (80 column records) and replaces every English name of a digit by the digit itself, for example, 'ONE' by '1', and so on.

4. Write a program that reads data from 80 column records, replaces all substrings of more than one blank by a single blank, and builds 80 column output records, filling each record as full as possible. (The input records may not be full.)

5. Write a program to print an inventory report for an automobile parts store. Each input record contains a part inventory number, a part name, and the cost of the part. Print the main heading, "AUTO PARTS INVENTORY," on the first page and page numbers and column headings on every page. The information from the records should be listed, with not more than 51 lines including headings printed on each page. The output should look like this:

AUTO PARTS INVENTORY   PAGE 1

PART ID   PART NAME   COST

18375   BRAKE PADS   15.85
....

PAGE 2

PART ID   PART NAME   COST

18375   BRAKE PADS   15.85
...   .

9 *File and Data Manipulation*

Objective: To be able to store and maintain data for future use and to output data for immediate use or for long-term storage.

Scientific and engineering problems often deal with large volumes of data. Computers are used to analyze data collected by other instruments such as telescopes and telemonitoring devices. Data such as this is input data in machine-readable form. Other types of problems such as the structural analysis of buildings, wide-body aircraft, or steel bridges generate large volumes of data from basic engineering equations. This data might be output data designed for use on simulation or graphics equipment. In other applications, the output data may have to be in a form that people can read. Data also may be produced by one computer or computer program and used as input to another. Large amounts of this kind of data are stored on the computer in files known as data files. Both program files and data files are stored on the secondary storage devices.

This chapter is concerned with the creation, maintenance, and use of data files. From the vantage point of the computer, *input files* are collections of data to be read by the computer; *output files* are collections of data generated by the computer. Input and output are access specifications. At different times, a single physical file may serve as an output file or an input file. In addition, data files that already exist and are being modified may be accessed as update files.

Actual physical files are divided into physical records that are used to hold the data. The organization of the physical files into physical records depends on the device and operating system. From the point of view of the programmer, the file contains logical records. A *logical record* is the amount of data read or written at one time without the use of carriage control format characters.

Files must be opened before the records can be accessed and closed when the access is completed. An input file may only be read while it is open; an output file may only be written while it is open. An output data file can be used as an input data file in the same program if it is closed and then opened or it can be used a second time in a different program.

Files are normally stored on secondary storage devices such as magnetic tape, disks, or drums. This frees the main memory for use in computations. The choice of device affects the use of the file. Files are stored on magnetic tapes if they are to be used infrequently, because the tapes generally must be mounted manually. Larger installations have automatic tape loading and unloading systems. Tapes are also used for particularly large files. The choice of tape mandates the order of accessing of the records because tapes are generally processed from start to finish. Files that are needed only temporarily, that are needed frequently, or that must be updated regularly are generally stored on a magnetic disk or drum.

9.1 Concept of Files and File Access

To the programmer, a file is a logical entity containing a collection of records stored on a logical device. The system software hides the physical location, structure, and manipulation of the file. A data file can be created and data can be entered in the form of records by using an editor, or it can be created by a program through the use of an OPEN statement and a WRITE statement. The actual creation of the file may be separate from the entry of data. Once a file exists, the data in it can be accessed by using READ statements in a program.

Magnetic tapes that are used to store files are typically one-half-inch wide, coated with a magnetic material organized in tracks for digital recording. Most tapes have seven or nine tracks running longitudinally along the tape. One of the tracks is used for error checking; the other six or eight tracks contain the bits that make up one byte of data. The number of bytes that can be recorded per inch is the density of the tape, for example, 400, 600, 800, 1600 or more bpi (bytes per inch). When data is recorded on a tape, the tape accelerates from rest to its recording speed, leaving a gap ahead of the record. After the data has been recorded, the tape returns to a state of rest, again leaving a gap in the recording. These gaps between records, called interrecord gaps (IRGs), are approximately half an inch in length. Writing many small records to tape is inefficient because of the percentage of tape filled by the IRGs. Therefore, tape devices usually buffer the input and output, storing many records together in a buffer and reading or writing them all at once.

Unlike files on other storage media, tape files may contain records of various lengths. Special symbols are recorded to mark the beginning and end of records, and special records mark the beginning and end of files. More than one file may be recorded on a single tape, and a large file may require more than one tape. Tape files are used primarily as backup storage for large amounts of data. They provide a convenient way to ship or store data.

A magnetic disk contains platters coated with a magnetic material on which the tracks are laid out in concentric circles. The disk unit may consist of several platters that rotate on a central spindle. The disk is organized into cylinders, each cylinder consisting of the tracks that are in the same position on each of the different platters. There is a read/write head for each side of each platter. Tracks in a cylinder can be read or written without moving the read/write heads, but head motion is needed to access tracks on different cylinders. Each track is divided into sectors, and one sector is read or written at a time.

Data on a disk is organized according to the number of bits in a sector. Physically, data is located on a disk by its cylinder, track, and sector. This means that records in disk files may be accessed either sequentially or directly. Disk files are used for volatile data that changes rapidly, such as airline seat reservations, and for data that must be online at all times.

A magnetic drum has a cylindrical surface with parallel tracks around the circumference. There is a read/write head for each track, making file access on drums faster than disk access. Details about the physical arrangement of the data can be found in the system manuals. Magnetic drum files are used for storing system programs such as compilers and function libraries.

Small computers store programs and data on floppy disks or hard disks, both of which are organized similarly to magnetic disk files.

Generally, most large computer systems support three file organizations: sequential files, indexed or indexed sequential files, and direct files. Most FORTRAN 77 compilers only provide access to sequential and direct files. This is sufficient for all types of applications, but many manufacturers also provide varieties of indexed files to support database organizations. The type of file used depends on the device available and the application. Files stored on tapes can only be organized sequentially. A file stored on a disk can be either sequential or direct. Sequential files are used when the data is to be processed in the same order as it is stored. Direct files are used when the processing order is not known at the time the files are created.

Files can be created with either formatted or unformatted output. Files entered from a terminal or output to a printer are in a *formatted* form, that is, each record is a string of characters in a form that people can read. Input and output statements use formats or default formatting. With formatted input, the characters that form the input string are converted to internal coded binary representations, depending on the types of the variables in the input list. On output, the internal values are converted from binary to coded characters. The programmer sees the characters entered as input and the characters produced as output, but does not see the internal binary representations of the values. A formatted file is sometimes called a *character* file.

In an *unformatted* file, sometimes called a *binary* file, no conversion takes place on input or output. The values have the same binary representation on th file as in the computer memory. This means that they can be read by the machine, but not by people.

The actual form of the data on the file is machine dependent. Therefore, tape files that are being transferred between machines are usually formatted. Files that are being reused on the same machine are usually unformatted since unformatted input/output is more efficient than formatted input/output.

Data written to a file on an external storage device in unformatted form can be read only in that form. Data written to a file in formatted form can be read only by using formats. For this reason, the two types of data may not be mixed on a file.

9.1.1 OPEN and CLOSE Statements

The OPEN statement makes a file available to a program by establishing a logical connection between a physical file on a device and the program. If the file is to be used for input, it must already exist. If the file is to be used for output and does not already exist, it will be created upon opening.

The CLOSE statement breaks the logical connection between the physical file on the device and the program. A file that is open for output can be closed and opened again for input. FORTRAN has the fail-safe feature of automatically closing all files at the end of execution, if the programmer has not explicitly closed them.

OPEN Statement

The general form of the OPEN statement is:

OPEN (list of control parameters)

The possible control parameters are:

UNIT = integer expression   specifies the logical unit number to be assigned to the file being opened

FILE = character expression   specifies the external name of the file being opened, the name by which the file is known to the system

STATUS = character expression

The status may be 'OLD', 'NEW', or 'SCRATCH'. When the file already exists, it is designated as 'OLD'. If the file does not exist, 'NEW' is used for a file to be retained beyond the end of execution; 'SCRATCH' is used for a temporary file. A scratch file cannot be accessed after the file is closed.

ACCESS = character expression   specifies whether the file is 'SEQUENTIAL' or 'DIRECT'; the default value is 'SEQUENTIAL'

FORM = character expression   specifies whether the file is
                               'FORMATTED' or
                               'UNFORMATTED'; the default
                               value is 'FORMATTED'

IOSTAT = integer variable   specifies which variable is to be
                               used as a status indicator: a zero
                               value indicates successful opening
                               of the file; a positive value
                               indicates an opening error

ERR = line label   specifies the statement to be
                               executed if an error occurs on
                               opening the file

RECL = integer expression   specifies the record length for
                               a direct file

BLANK = character expression

If the character expression is 'ZERO', blanks within numeric fields in a formatted input file are interpreted as zeros. If the expression is 'NULL', the blanks are ignored, unless the entire field is blanks, in which case it is given the value zero.

The following example shows a minimal OPEN statement:

```
OPEN (UNIT=9, FILE ='INVENT', STATUS='OLD')
```

The logical unit number 9 is associated with the file having the external name 'INVENT'. The file already exists and is a sequential formatted file. Since the file is sequential, the record length is not required. Every OPEN statement must provide a logical unit number, a file name, and a file status.

The following example shows a more complex OPEN statement:

```
OPEN (UNIT=12,FILE='FILEZ',STATUS='OLD',
      IOSTAT=ICON,ERR=50,BLANK='ZERO')
```

In this example, the file is formatted and sequential. Throughout the program, the file will be referred to by the logical unit number 12. The file already exists. The value of the variable ICON and whether or not execution jumps to line 50 both indicate whether or not the opening of the file was error free. If ICON is not zero, its value indicates the type of error (refer to a FORTRAN manual). BLANK = 'ZERO' indicates that blanks embedded in numeric fields should be treated as zeros.

The following example shows a minimal OPEN statement for a direct file:

```
OPEN (UNIT=8,FILE='ABC',STATUS='OLD',
      ACCESS='DIRECT',RECL=30)
```

Since this is a direct access file, a record length is specified: the number of words in each record.

CLOSE Statement

Once processing of the file is completed, the CLOSE statement should be used to break the connection between the program and the actual file. The general form of the CLOSE statement is:

CLOSE (list of control parameters)

The possible control parameters are:

UNIT = integer expression   specifies the logical unit number of the file being closed

STATUS = character expression

The status may be 'DELETE' or 'KEEP'. When the file is not needed any longer, it is designated as 'DELETE'. 'KEEP' is used if the file is to be retained after being closed. The default value is 'KEEP' for all but scratch files, which cannot be kept.

IOSTAT = integer variable   specifies which variable is to be used as a status indicator: a zero value indicates successful closing of the file; a positive value indicates a closing error

ERR = line label   specifies the statement to be executed if an error occurs on closing the file

The following example shows a minimal CLOSE statement:

```
CLOSE (UNIT=12)
```

The file associated with the logical unit number 12 is disconnected from the program and preserved. If it should be needed again, it can be reconnected with the same or different logical unit by being opened again. In the following example,

```
CLOSE (UNIT=12,IOSTAT=ICON,ERR=80,STATUS='DELETE')
```

processing will continue with the next statement if there is no error. The file will be removed from the system because of the 'DELETE' option. If there is an error, an error code will be stored in ICON, processing will continue at line 80, and the file will not be deleted.

9.1.2 Input and Output Statements

Input and output statements were discussed at length in chapter 3. Standard system files were used for input and output. Using these files does not require OPEN and CLOSE statements. Although we already discussed the input and output statements READ, PRINT, and WRITE, we include them in this chapter for the sake of completeness. In the examples we assume that user files are being accessed rather than system files.

The general form of the READ statement is:

READ (list of control parameters) list of input variables

The possible control parameters are:

integer expression	specifies the logical unit number of the file being read
format specifier	format number or character format constant; the default is list-directed input
END = line label	specifies the statement where control is to transfer if there are no more data records in the input file
ERR = line label	specifies the statement to be executed if an error occurs on reading the file
IOSTAT = integer variable	specifies which variable is to be used as a status indicator: a zero value indicates successful reading of the input file; a positive value indicates an input error
REC = integer expression	specifies the record position in a direct file from which the record is to be read

The following examples show various uses of the READ statement:

```
      CHARACTER SSNO(50)*11
      CHARACTER NAME(50)*24,ADDR(50)*30
      INTEGER K

      OPEN (UNIT=12,FILE='CUSTMR',STATUS='OLD')
      DO 10 K=1,50
        READ (12,1000,END=80,ERR=90)SSNO(K),
     1        NAME(K),ADDR(K)
1000    FORMAT(A11,9X,A24,6X,A30)
10      CONTINUE
      STOP

90    WRITE (*,*) 'READ ERROR'
      STOP
      END
```

In this example the file 'CUSTMR' is read and the data is stored in arrays SSNO(50), NAME(50), and ADDR(50). Note that the input statement could also be written as

```
READ (12,'(A11,9X,A24,6X,A30)',
      END=80,ERR=90)SSNO,NAME,ADDR
```

If an error occurs in reading the file, such as a record of the wrong size or an invalid character, execution will continue at line 90. When the last record has been processed and the read attempt fails to find any data, the execution will continue at line 80.

```
      INTEGER STID,T1,T2,T3,STAT,ICN
      CHARACTER*24 NAME
      . . .
      OPEN (UNIT=15,FILE='STDFIL',STATUS='OLD',
     1      ACCESS='DIRECT',IOSTAT=ICN,
     2      BLANK='NULL',RECL=55)
      . . .
      READ (15,1200,IOSTAT=STAT,REC=3)
     1      STID,NAME,T1,T2,T3
1200  FORMAT(I6,4X,A24,6X,3I5)
      IF (ICN .GT. 0) THEN
         WRITE (*,*) 'ERROR',STAT
         STOP
      ENDIF
      . . .
```

This program segment opens an already existing direct file and reads record number 3. If there is an error, such as an invalid numeric field, the program will print an error code and stop.

WRITE Statement

The WRITE statement is used to store information in a file as logical records. The general form of the WRITE statement is:

WRITE (list of control parameters) list of output variables

The possible control parameters are:

integer expression	specifies the logical unit number of the file being written
format specifier	format number or character format constant; the default is list-directed output
ERR = line label	specifies the statement to be executed if an error occurs on writing to the file
IOSTAT = integer variable	specifies which variable is to be used as a status indicator: a zero value indicates successful writing of the file; a positive value indicates a writing error.

REC = integer expression   specifies the position in a direct
                                         file where the record is to be
                                         written

The following examples show various uses of the WRITE statement:

```
      CHARACTER*5 TSTSTA, TSTDAY
      REAL DPT,EVEL,ECDTY
      .  .  .
      OPEN (UNIT=12,FILE='TSTVAL',STATUS='NEW')
      .  .  .
      WRITE (12,2500,ERR=50) TSTSTA,TSTDAY,
     1      DPT,EVEL,ECDTY
2500  FORMAT(A5,A5,3F8.5)
      .  .  .
50    WRITE (*,*) 'OUTPUT ERROR'
      STOP
      .  .  .
```

This program segment creates the file TSTVAL. Values of the variables are input
or generated, then written to the file. If an error occurs, such as an incorrect format
size, not enough file space, or a transmission error, execution will jump to statement 50 and then terminate with a printed error message.

```
      INTEGER RECNO
      CHARACTER INFO*80
      .  ..
      OPEN (UNIT=15,FILE='INFOF',STATUS='NEW',
     1      ACCESS='DIRECT',RECL=80)
      DO 50 RECNO=1,100
      .  .  .
        WRITE (15,'(A80)',REC=RECNO) INFO
      .  .  .
50    CONTINUE
      CLOSE (UNIT=15,STATUS='KEEP')
      .  .  .
```

In this example, a direct file is being created by placing records in positions 1
through 100. The file is opened immediately before the loop that contains the
WRITE statements and closed immediately after the loop terminates. Every time
a file is opened, it is positioned at the beginning. Opening and closing a file for
every WRITE activity would be inefficient because the computer would have to
reconnect the program with the file each time and search for the correct position.

9.1.3 Sequential Files

A sequential file organization is one in which the records are always accessed in
the same order in which they were originally entered. It is not possible to access
the nth record without first accessing all the preceding $n - 1$ records.

   If only a few records are to be processed, efficiency may be increased by
sorting the records before the file is built and placing the most frequently used
records at the beginning. More commonly, the records are in ascending or descend

ing order according to some key field such as ID number or last name. If the file is to be printed in readable form, the records should be sorted in the file the same way they are to appear in the printed report. The last record of a sequential file is an endfile record. The first record is sometimes used for special information concerning the file.

A sequential file is updated by copying the file, making changes to the records. In the following example, the DATE field of each record is being changed to NEWDAT:

```
*   UPDATE A DATA FILE BY COPYING

        CHARACTER*8 DATE,NEWDAT
        REAL X(100)
        INTEGER OLDF,NEWF
        PARAMETER (OLDF=12,NEWF=15)

        READ (*,*) NEWDAT
        OPEN (UNIT=OLDF,FILE='AFILE1',STATUS='OLD')
        OPEN (UNIT=NEWF,FILE='AFILE2',STATUS='NEW')

*       DO WHILE (.NOT. END)

10      READ (OLDF,1000,END=40) DATE,X
          WRITE (NEWF,1000) NEWDAT,X
1000      FORMAT(A8,100F5.0)
        GO TO 10

*       ENDDO

40      CLOSE (UNIT=OLDF,STATUS='DELETE')
        CLOSE (UNIT=NEWF,STATUS='KEEP')
        STOP
        END
```

For ease in keeping track of the files, the logical units have been assigned names. The entire file would be copied even if only a few of the records were being altered. When a file is closed, the endfile record is automatically written in the next record position after the last previously written record. In this example, the old file is deleted from the system after the job terminates, but the new file is retained. Both files are opened immediately ahead of the read-write loop, and are closed immediately after it.

If changes to a master file are to be found on a transaction file, then both files must be sorted in the same order, on the same key field. In the following example, assume that ID is the key field, that the updating consists of replacing INFO with NEWINF, that the files are sorted in ascending order of ID, and that there is at most one transaction for each master record. As the master and transaction files are processed and matched, a new file is built as the updated master file. The basic algorithm for matching files is:

Case
    When master ID = transaction ID then
        modify master record

```
                write modified record to the new master file
                read another master record, another transaction record
            When master ID < transaction ID then
                write master record to the new master file
                read another master record
            When master ID > transaction ID then
                write an error message
                read another transaction record
        end case
```

```
*    UPDATE A MASTER DATA FILE FROM A TRANSACTION FILE

        CHARACTER*72 MINFO,TINFO
        INTEGER MFID,TFID
        INTEGER MASTF,TRANSF,NEWF
        PARAMETER (MASTF=12,TRANSF=15,NEWF=18)

        OPEN (UNIT=MASTF,FILE='AFILE1',STATUS='OLD')
        OPEN (UNIT=NEWF,FILE='AFILE2',STATUS='NEW')
        OPEN (UNIT=TRANSF,FILE='BFILE1',STATUS='OLD')
        READ (MASTF,1000,END=40) MFID,MINFO
        READ (TRANSF,1000,END=40) TFID,TINFO

*       DO WHILE (MFID .EQ. TFID)

10      IF (MFID .EQ. TFID) THEN
            WRITE (NEWF,1000) MFID,TINFO
            READ (MASTF,1000,END=40) MFID,MINFO
            READ (TRANSF,1000,END=50) TFID,TINFO

          ELSEIF (MFID .LT. TFID) THEN
            WRITE (NEWF,1000) MFID,MINFO
            READ (MASTF,1000,END=40) MFID,MINFO
          ELSEIF (MFID .GT. TFID) THEN
            WRITE (*,*) 'ERROR IN TRANSACTION ID'
            READ (TRANSF,1000,END=50) TFID,TINFO
          ENDIF
1000    FORMAT(A8,100F5.0)
        GO TO 10

*       ENDDO

*    PROCESS REST OF TRANSACTION FILE

40      WRITE (*,*) 'ERROR IN TRANSACTION ID'
        READ (TRANSF,1000,END=60) TFID,TINFO
        GO TO 40

*    PROCESS REST OF MASTER FILE

50      WRITE (NEWF,1000) MFID,MINFO
        READ (MASTF,1000,END=60) MFID,MINFO
        GO TO 50
```

```
60      CLOSE (UNIT=MASTF,STATUS='DELETE')
        CLOSE (UNIT=TRANSF,STATUS='DELETE')
        CLOSE (UNIT=NEWF,STATUS='KEEP')
        STOP
        END
```

9.1.4 Direct Access Files

Direct access files differ from sequential files in that the records are identified by their position in the file. They may be processed in any order by supplying the record position with each input and output statement. Unlike sequential files, all records of a direct access file must have the same length. When a large number of records are being accessed and access is in the order in which they are stored, processing them in sequential order is more efficient than processing them in random order. Direct access is more efficient when only a few records are being processed and they do not have to be in storage order. Some of the record positions of a direct access file may not be used. For example, records might be placed just in the odd-numbered positions. For this reason, files that have been created as direct access files may not be processed as sequential files.

As the following example shows, records in a direct access file may be updated in place provided that the record length is not changed:

```
*    UPDATE A DIRECT DATA FILE IN PLACE

        CHARACTER*8 DATE,NEWDAT
        REAL X(100)
        INTEGER RECNO

        READ (*,*) NEWDAT
        RECNO = 1
        OPEN (UNIT=12,FILE='DATFIL',STATUS='OLD',
     1          ACCESS='DIRECT',RECL=127)

*       DO WHILE (.NOT. END)

20      READ (12,1100,ERR=50,REC=RECNO) DATE,X
        WRITE (12,1100,REC=RECNO) NEWDAT,X
1100     FORMAT(A8,100F5.0)
        RECNO = RECNO + 1
        GO TO 20

*       ENDDO

50      CLOSE (UNIT=12,STATUS='KEEP')
        STOP
        END
```

In this example, each record is changed and rewritten as it is read. The value that was read into DATE is replaced by the value of NEWDAT. The rest of the record is rewritten, unchanged. This is done by using the same record number for the input and output statements. RECNO is used as a counter to access all the records in order. Execution will jump to statement 50 when RECNO is too large and the computer seeks a record that is not there. Execution also jumps to statement 50 when there is no data stored at the record position identified by RECNO. The value of IOSTAT could be used to distinguish between a record number that is out of bounds and a dummy record.

The following three-part example uses input data to create a direct access file, to update the file, and to query the file. Note that in all three parts, the record numbers are found in the input data. The file is created, modified, and queried in the order given by the input data, rather than in the order of the record numbers.

```
*    CREATE A DIRECT DATA FILE

        INTEGER NAVAIL,SIZE,WT,LGTH,PRODID

        OPEN (UNIT=12,FILE='PRODAT',STATUS='NEW',
     1          ACCESS='DIRECT',RECL=10)

*       DO WHILE (.NOT. END)

20      READ (5,1000,END=50) PRODID,NAVAIL,SIZE,WT,LGTH
1000      FORMAT(5I10)
          WRITE (12,1100,REC=PRODID)NAVAIL,SIZE,WT,LGTH
1100      FORMAT(4I10)
        GO TO 20

        ENDDO

50      CLOSE (UNIT=12,STATUS='KEEP')
        STOP
        END


*    UPDATE A DIRECT DATA FILE

        INTEGER NAVAIL,SIZE,WT,LGTH,PRODID,NUSED

        OPEN (UNIT=12,FILE='PRODAT',STATUS='OLD',
     1          ACCESS='DIRECT',RECL=10)

*       DO WHILE (.NOT. END)

20      READ (5,1000,END=50) PRODID,NUSED
1000      FORMAT(2I10)
          READ (12,1100,REC=PRODID) NAVAIL,SIZE,WT,LGTH
          NAVAIL = NAVAIL - NUSED
          WRITE (12,1100,REC=PRODID)NAVAIL,SIZE,WT,LGTH
1100      FORMAT(4I10)
        GO TO 20

        ENDDO

50      CLOSE (UNIT=12,STATUS='KEEP')
        STOP
        END
```

```
*    QUERY A DIRECT DATA FILE

     INTEGER NAVAIL,SIZE,WT,LGTH,PRODID,NUSED

     OPEN (UNIT=12,FILE='PRODAT',STATUS='OLD',
    1        ACCESS='DIRECT',RECL=40)

*    DO WHILE (.NOT. END)

20   READ (5,1000,END=50) PRODID
1000   FORMAT(I10)
       READ (12,1100,REC=PRODID) NAVAIL,SIZE,WT,LGTH
1100   FORMAT(4I10)
       WRITE (*,1200) PRODID,NAVAIL,SIZE,WT,LGTH
1200   FORMAT(1X,5I10)
     GO TO 20

*    ENDDO

50   CLOSE (UNIT=12,STATUS='KEEP')
     STOP
     END
```

Note that all three program segments are controlled by the list of PRODID values on the standard system input file. These values are part of the data, but they are not stored in the record. Instead, they are used to identify the position of the record in the file. Sometimes it is convenient to store the record numbers in the record and also use them as a storage key. The direct data file is opened and closed in each program that uses it. While it is open, both input and output may be done.

Programming Warning

All records on a direct access file must have the same length. Formats must be used with a formatted file.

9.1.5 Review Questions

1. Indicate whether each of the following statements is true or false:

   a. A file is a collection of related records.
   b. There are three file organizations in FORTRAN 77.
   c. Direct access may be used with either magnetic tape or magnetic disk files.
   d. Direct access may be used with either sequential or direct files.
   e. Record numbers must be used for input/output of records in direct files.
   f. Direct files must be formatted.
   g. An OPEN statement is used to make a file on a device available to a program.
   h. A CLOSE statement is used to disconnect a file from a program.
   i. The default access type is DIRECT because direct access is more efficient than SEQUENTIAL access.
   j. If the FORM option is not used in an OPEN statement, the file is unformatted.
   k. A formatted file may not contain numbers.
   l. An unformatted file may contain characters.

2. Write OPEN statements for the following files:

   a. The file 'ENERGY', a formatted sequential input file, is to be associated with logical unit 10. Use the status and error control options.
   b. The file 'CHEMT3', a formatted sequential output file, is to be associated with logical unit 12. Use the status and error control options.
   c. The file 'W5LAND', a formatted direct input file having records of length 70, is to be associated with logical unit 14. Use the status and error control options.
   d. The file 'FDAT3N', a formatted direct update file, is to be associated with logical unit 12. Use the status and error control options.

3. Write CLOSE statements for the following situations:

   a. Delete the sequential file connected to logical unit 15.
   b. Retain the direct file connected to logical unit 12.

4. Write an input/output statement and format to do each of the following:

   a. Input one record from the formatted sequential file connected to logical unit 17. The record layout is:

1   8   11   30 31   35 36   40
IDNO		DESCRP		PROJID	DATE	

   b. Input 10 records from a formated sequential file connected to logical unit INFILE into tables STEEL, COPPER, ALUM, and ZINC. The records contain the weight in tons of the metals supplied by 10 different companies. They have the following form:

1   10 11   20 21   30 31   40
steel	copper	aluminum	zinc	

   c. Input record 108 from a formatted direct file connected to logical unit DACC. The records are:

1   25 26 30 31   40 41   45 46   55 56   60
NAME		ADDR	AMTDUE	BAL	

5. Write an output statement and format for each of the following situations:

   a. A record with the following format is to be written to a sequential formatted file on logical unit 13. Use all forms of error detection.

Field	Cols
STUDID (character)	1−8
STNAME (character)	10−25
T1,T2,T3,T4 (integer)	31−42
AVGT (real)	45−50
GRADE (character)	55

b. A record with the following format is to be written to position 3127 of a direct formatted file on logical unit 18. Use all forms of error detection.

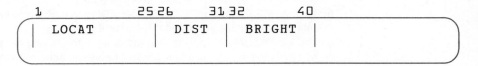

6. Write a program segment that stores INFO*80 in record position 291 of a direct formatted file on logical unit 12, provided there is no record already in that position. If there is a record, print an error message, 'DUPLICATE RECORD NUMBER'.

7. WRITE a program segment that replaces INFO*80 in record position 32 of a direct formatted file on logical unit 23 with DATA*80, provided there is a record in that position. If no record is found, print an error message, 'RECORD NOT FOUND'.

8. Write a program segment that reads INFO*80 from record position 8 of a direct formatted file on logical unit 15, provided there is a record in that position. If no record is found, print an error message, 'RECORD NOT FOUND'.

9.2 File Organization

Formatted and unformatted files are treated differently by the system. Formatted files are organized as *stream files;* that is, it appears that a stream of characters is transmitted between the file and the program on input or output. This stream of characters may represent all or part of an input/output list, depending on the format. Unformatted files are organized as *record files;* exactly the amount of data specified in the input/output list is transmitted at once.

9.2.1 Stream Files

The data in a stream file is stored in character form using an internal character coding scheme such as EBCDIC or ASCII. If the file is created by a program, either list-directed or formatted output is used. Any numeric values that are not stored in the computer in character form are converted to characters using either implicit or explicit formatting before being output. Data stored in a stream can be displayed on devices having different line lengths by automatic wrapping around from one line to the next. Line breaks can be forced by the use of a slash (/) in the format. Each output statement also forces a line break.

A stream input statement searches for the amount of data needed, ignoring line boundaries that may have been present when the input file was created. An advance to the next input line can be forced by the use of a slash in the format statement. Each time an input statement is executed, there is an advance to the next line of input.

When an input statement is executed, the data is not only transmitted from the input file to internal memory, but also separated into variables. Each value is converted to a machine-dependent internal representation. When an output statement is executed, the data is transmitted from the internal memory to the output file and also converted from the internal representation to the coded character form. Usually data stored in formatted stream files requires more space than unformatted data because of the character form and the spacing and special editing characters. A signed 11-digit integer requires 12 bytes of storage in character form compared to four bytes in binary form.

All the examples of files in the earlier chapters of this book were stream files.

9.2.2 Record Files

Record files are unformatted. The data is stored in the file in the same form in which it is stored internally in memory. When this type of file is used, the input/output statement does not refer to a format and the file is declared to be UNFOR-MATTED in the OPEN statement. Such a file cannot be printed or displayed because the data is not in readable form. It cannot be created except by using a program.

The following example shows the creation of a record file from a stream input file:

```
*       CREATING A RECORD FILE

        INTEGER LENGTH,WIDTH,HEIGHT,INT,VOLUME
*
        OPEN (UNIT=10,FILE='VOLFIL',STATUS='NEW',
     1           FORM='UNFORMATTED')

*       DO WHILE (.NOT. END .AND. .NOT. ERR)

10      READ (*,*,END=100) LENGTH,WIDTH,HEIGHT
           VOLUME = LENGTH * WIDTH * HEIGHT
           WRITE (10,IOSTAT=INT,ERR=50)
     1           LENGTH,WIDTH,HEIGHT,VOLUME
        GO TO 10

*       ENDDO

50      CONTINUE
        WRITE (*,*) 'FILE OUTPUT ERROR',INT
        STOP
100     CONTINUE
        CLOSE (UNIT=10,STATUS='KEEP')
        STOP
        END
```

Note that the new output file VOLFIL is being created. Each record has 16 bytes, four for each output variable, but the record length is not declared because the file is sequential.

9.2.3 Internal Files

Any character string can be treated as though it were an input or output device. Internal input/output provides another way of combining and separating character strings. It also provides an easy way to convert numbers to character strings and character strings to numbers.

Internal Input

The general forms of an internal input statement are:

READ (UNIT = string,FMT = formatno) input list
READ (UNIT = string,'(format)') input list

The format may be either a standard FORMAT statement or it may be quoted in the READ statement. This is shown in the following examples. Given the code segment

```
      CHARACTER NAME*20, FIRST*4, MIDDLE*8, LAST*5
      NAME = 'RAMA NARAYANA REDDY'
         . . .
      READ (UNIT=NAME,FMT=1000) FIRST, MIDDLE, LAST
1000  FORMAT(A4,1X,A8,1X,A5)
```

or

```
      READ (UNIT=NAME,'(A4,1X,A8,1X,A5)') FIRST,
     1        MIDDLE, LAST
```

the character string is treated as though it were a record:

```
1     5 6
| RAMA |  | NARAYANA |  | REDDY |
```

The result is:

```
FIRST is 'RAMA'
MIDDLE is 'NARAYANA'
LAST   is 'REDDY'
```

The following example shows the reuse of a string. The ID number is first read from it in character form, the preferred form for such numbers, then in integer form, which would be useful if calculations were to be performed on the number to check for transcription errors. Given the code segment

```
CHARACTER RECORD*40, IDSTR*5
INTEGER IDNUM
 . ..
READ (UNIT=RECORD,'(A5)') IDSTR
READ (UNIT=RECORD,'(I5)') IDNUM
```

and the value RECORD = '27369STEEL BALL BEARINGS', then the value of IDSTR is '27369' and the value of IDNUM is 27369. The values of IDSTR and IDNUM are not the same, because they are not variables of the same type. IDSTR can be compared with and assigned to other character variables, but not numeric variables. IDNUM can be compared with and assigned to other numeric variables, but not character variables. Concatenation can be used with IDSTR, but not with IDNUM. Arithmetic can be performed with IDNUM, but not with IDSTR.

Internal Output

The general forms for the internal output statement are:

> WRITE (UNIT = string,FMT = formatno) output list
> WRITE (UNIT = string,'(format)') output list

These are shown in the following example. Given the code segment

```
     CHARACTER LINE*40, TYPE*4
     TYPE = 'XYZ'
     CODE = 256
     LENGTH = 14.78
     WRITE (UNIT=LINE,FMT=1000)TYPE,CODE,LENGTH,'ƁCM.'
1000 FORMAT(10X,A5,I5,F10.2,A10)
```

or

```
     WRITE (UNIT=LINE,'(10X,A5,I5,F10.2,A10)')
          TYPE,CODE,LENGTH,'ƁCM.'
```

the value of LINE is:

> `'ƁƁƁƁƁƁƁƁƁƁXYZƁƁƁƁ256ƁƁƁƁƁ14.78ƁCM.ƁƁƁƁƁƁ'`

The internal output performs the type conversions from integer and real to character and concatenates the character strings, spacing them the same way as for ordinary output. The difference is that the character string LINE has not been printed, but it is still in memory. It can be used like any other character string.

9.2.4 Review Questions

1. Indicate whether each of the following statements is true or false:

   a. A stream file can be opened as an unformatted file.
   b. A record file is made up of characters.
   c. When using a stream file, the data is converted from external character form to an internal form or vice versa.
   d. A record file is written using formats.
   e. The records of a record file should be the length of the printer or display line.
   f. A record file is more efficient in terms of processing time.
   g. A record file is more efficient in terms of file space.
   h. When opening a record file, the access mode must be specified.
   i. When opening a stream file, the number of characters in the stream must be specified.

2. Given data REAL X, INTEGER N, DOUBLE PRECISION D, how many bytes of output is generated by each of the following?

   a.   `WRITE (10) X,N,D` where 10 is an unformatted file.

   b.   `WRITE (12,50) X,N,D`
        `50   FORMAT (I5,F6.2,D10.8)` where 12 is a formatted file.

   c.   `WRITE (15,50) X,N`
        `50   FORMAT (5X,I5,10X,F6.2)` where 15 is a formatted file.

3. Write a segment of FORTRAN code to copy an unformatted sequential file 'INFIL' into an unformatted sequential file 'OUTFIL'. The records contain 10 real variables.

4. Given

```
CHARACTER*20 LINE,STR1*5,STR2*5
LINE = '1234567890ABCDEFGHIJ'
```

show the result of each of the following operations:

```
a. READ (UNIT=LINE,'(I3,1X,F4.1)') I,X
b. READ (UNIT=LINE,'(8X,A4,1X,A5)') STR1,STR2
c. WRITE (UNIT=LINE,'(10X,A10)') 'PAGE 1'
d. WRITE (UNIT=LINE,'(F10.3,5X,I5)') LINE(2:4),LINE(:3)
```

9.3 File Status and Positioning

Being able to determine the status and positioning of a file is sometimes essential in file management. The status includes information on the access mode, format, and file type. Being able to control the positioning of a direct file affects the efficiency of file operations.

9.3.1 INQUIRE Statement

The INQUIRE statement is used to determine the status of a named file or a logical unit. A list of optional parameters is used to ask for particular information. The general forms of the INQUIRE statement are:

INQUIRE (file specifier, list of queries)

or

INQUIRE (unit specifier, list of queries)

The set of possible queries are as follows:

IOSTAT = integer variable	specifies the input/output status
ERR = label	specifies point of error processing
EXIST = logical variable or logical array element	true if file or unit exists, false if it does not exist
OPENED = logical variable	true if file or unit is open, false if it is not
NUMBER = integer variable	specifies the number of the unit connected to the file
NAMED = logical variable	true if the unit has been connected to a file, false otherwise

NAME = character variable	specifies the name of the file connected to the unit
ACCESS = character variable	either 'SEQUENTIAL' or 'DIRECT' in value
SEQUENTIAL = character variable	either 'YES', 'NO', or 'UNKNOWN' in value
DIRECT = character variable	either 'YES', 'NO', or 'UNKNOWN' in value
FORM = character variable	either 'FORMATTED' or 'UNFORMATTED' in value
FORMATTED = character variable	either 'YES', 'NO', or 'UNKNOWN' in value
UNFORMATTED = character variable	either 'YES', 'NO', or 'UNKNOWN' in value
RECL = integer variable	specifies the record length of the file
NEXTREC = integer variable	specifies the record number of the next record position
BLANK = character variable	either 'NULL' or 'ZERO'

If the query is inappropriate for the situation, for example, the form is requested when no file has been connected to the unit, the record length of a stream file is requested, or BLANK indicator of a record file, the status variable may become undefined, or may be given a value that is of no use to the programmer. For further details on these status queries, refer to a FORTRAN installation manual.

9.3.2 REWIND Statement

When a file is first opened by a program, it is always automatically positioned at the first record. If a tape file is to be reused, it must be explicitly positioned by the program. The REWIND statement is used for this. It must not be used when a sequential file is first created because the endfile marker will not be written unless the file is closed. The general forms of the REWIND statement are:

> REWIND logical unit number

or

> REWIND (list of control parameters)

The possible control parameters are:

UNIT = integer expression	specifies the logical unit number of the file being written
ERR = line label	specifies the statement to be executed if an error occurs on writing the file
IOSTAT = integer variable	specifies which variable is to be used as a status indicator: a zero value indicates successful rewinding of the file; a positive value indicates a rewinding error

The following examples show possible uses of this statement.

```
REWIND 12
```

This statement assumes that logical unit 12 has already been connected to a file. When the statement is executed, the file is repositioned at the beginning. If it is already in that position, nothing is done.

```
REWIND (UNIT=10,IOSTAT=INT,ERR=90)
```

This statement assumes that logical unit 10 has already been connected to a file. If this is not the case, execution continues at program line 90 with an error code stored in INT.

9.3.3 BACKSPACE Statement

The backspace statement is used to process a record for the second time. When a record is read or written, the record pointer is advanced to the next record. When the BACKSPACE statement is used, the record pointer is repositioned to the beginning of the preceding record. Through the use of the BACKSPACE statement, a record in either sequential or direct files can be read a second time, or can be read and then rewritten. The general forms of the BACKSPACE statement are:

BACKSPACE logical unit number

or

BACKSPACE (list of control parameters)

The possible control parameters are:

UNIT = integer expression	specifies the logical unit number of the file being backspaced
ERR = line label	specifies the statement to be executed if an error occurs on backspacing the file

IOSTAT = integer variable   specifies which variable is to be used as a status indicator: a zero value indicates successful backspacing of the file; a positive value indicates a backspacing error

The following examples show possible uses of this statement:

```
BACKSPACE 12
```

The file is positioned so that the most recently read or written record on the file connected to logical unit 12 can be reread or rewritten. If the file was already positioned at the beginning, nothing happens.

```
BACKSPACE (UNIT=13,IOSTAT=MINT,ERR=100)
```

This statement backspaces the file connected to logical unit 13 by one record. If an error occurs, execution continues at program line 100 with a status value in MINT.

9.3.4 ENDFILE Statement

The ENDFILE statement is used to explicitly write an endfile record. Then a sequential file need not be closed before being rewound. This statement is also used to write an endfile record in a direct file to set the upper bound of the area devoted to the file. The general forms of the ENDFILE statement are:

ENDFILE logical unit number

or

ENDFILE (list of control parameters)

The possible control parameters are:

UNIT = integer expression   specifies the logical unit number of the file being written

ERR = line label   specifies the statement to be executed if an error occurs on writing the file

IOSTAT = integer variable   specifies which variable is to be used as a status indicator; a zero value indicates successful writing of the endfile; a positive value indicates a writing error

The following examples show possible uses of this statement:

```
ENDFILE 12
```

This statement causes an endfile record to be written at the current position of the file connected to logical unit 12.

```
ENDFILE (UNIT=15,IOSTAT=KINT,ERR=150)
```

This statement writes an endfile record at the current position of the file connected to logical unit 15. If an error occurs, execution continues at program line 150 with a status value in KINT.

9.3.5 Review Questions

1. Write an INQUIRE statement to determine the following information for the file MYOUTF:

    a. the status of the file
    b. whether access has been declared SEQUENTIAL or DIRECT
    c. the number of the logical unit associated with the file
    d. whether the file has been declared FORMATTED or UNFORMATTED
    e. the length of a file record

2. Write a FORTRAN statement or statements to do each of the following tasks:

    a. Rewind the file connected to logical unit 20, using all the error detection options.
    b. Backspace the file connected to logical unit 13 by five records, using all the error detection options.
    c. Write an endfile record after the first 100 records of the sequential file connected to logical unit 16.

3. Write a FORTRAN program that creates an unformatted sequential file SEQTMP, filling it with 100 character strings of 80 characters each taken from the standard input unit 5, then rewinds the file without closing it, and prints the character strings.

4. Write a FORTRAN program that reads a formatted sequential file MYDATA, which contains character strings of 10 characters each and replaces every string of 10 blanks with a string of 10 zeros.

5. Write a FORTRAN program that creates an unformatted direct file ENGDAT, filling 100 records of length 40 with character strings of 40 blanks each.

9.4 Sample Programs Using Files

There are three basic file situations: creating a file, updating or maintaining a file, and querying a file. Since there are two types of files, sequential and direct, there are six basic kinds of file programs. The records for these files can be formatted or unformatted. The records have at least one key field by which they can be recognized. This key value may or may not be the same as the record's position in the file. Complications can be added by permitting duplicate keys, several key fields that are not ordered the same way, inactive records, variable length records, or records having different formats. The programs in this section show some of the simpler situations. The output was produced by interactive program execution on the Digital Equipment Corporation (DEC) computer model VAX 11/780.

9.4.1 Distance of Points from Origin

Problem

Write a program that reads the x and y coordinates of points from an input file, calculates the distance of each point from the point (0,0), and writes the coordinates and distance to a file, which should then be listed.

Method

Let 'CORIN' be the sequential input file and 'COROUT' be the unformatted sequential storage file.

$$dist = \sqrt{x^2 + y^2}$$

is the distance of a point from the origin.

Program

```
*****************************************************
*                                                   *
*   CREATING AND LISTING A FILE OF POINTS AND        *
*   DISTANCES                                        *
*                                                   *
*****************************************************
*                                                   *
*   INPUT FILE: 'CORIN'                              *
*                                                   *
*     VARIABLES:                                     *
*                                                   *
*       X, Y          - COORDINATES OF THE POINT     *
*                                                   *
*   INPUT/OUTPUT FILE: 'COROUT'                      *
*                                                   *
*     VARIABLES:                                     *
*                                                   *
*       X, Y          - COORDINATES OF THE POINT     *
*       DIST          - DISTANCE OF THE POINT FROM THE *
*                       ORIGIN                       *
*                                                   *
*****************************************************

        REAL X,Y,DIST
        INTEGER INFIL,NEWFIL
        PARAMETER (INFIL=12,NEWFIL=13)
```

```
*   CREATE THE NEW FILE

        OPEN (UNIT=INFIL,FILE='CORIN',STATUS='OLD',
     1           FORM='FORMATTED',ACCESS='SEQUENTIAL')
        OPEN (UNIT=NEWFIL,FILE='COROUT',STATUS='NEW',
     1           FORM='UNFORMATTED',ACCESS=
     2           'SEQUENTIAL')

*        DO WHILE (MORE DATA)

10      READ (INFIL,1000,END=40) X,Y
1000      FORMAT(2F10.0)
          DIST = SQRT(X*X + Y*Y)
          WRITE (NEWFIL) X,Y,DIST
        GO TO 10

*        ENDDO

40      CLOSE (UNIT=INFIL)
        CLOSE (UNIT=NEWFIL)

*   LIST THE NEW FILE

        OPEN (UNIT=NEWFIL,FILE='COROUT',STATUS='OLD',
     1           FORM='UNFORMATTED',ACCESS=
     2           'SEQUENTIAL')

        WRITE (*,1100) 'X','Y','DISTANCE'
1100    FORMAT(8X,A6,11X,A6,12X,A8)

*        DO WHILE (MORE DATA)

60      READ (NEWFIL,END=80) X,Y,DIST
          WRITE (*,1200) X,Y,DIST
1200      FORMAT(3(5X,F12.5))
        GO TO 10

*        ENDDO

80      CLOSE (UNIT=NEWFIL,STATUS='KEEP')
        STOP
        END
```

Output

```
                        type corin.dat
     2.0          4.0
     1.5          5.5
     6.0          7.5
    11.0          3.0
     2.0          9.0
     3.0          4.0
     4.0          6.0
     7.0          8.0




          X                   Y                DISTANCE
     2.00000             4.00000               4.47214
     1.50000             5.50000               5.70088
     6.00000             7.50000               9.60469
    11.00000             3.00000              11.40175
     2.00000             9.00000               9.21954
     3.00000             4.00000               5.00000
     4.00000             6.00000               7.21110
     7.00000             8.00000              10.63015
```

Notice that the format and the access are specified in the OPEN statements.
This is necessary only for the unformatted option because 'FORMATTED' and
'SEQUENTIAL' are default values. The file CORDOUT is open for output when
it is created, then closed and opened again for input. Closing the file causes an
end-of-file record to be written to the file. Opening the file a second time causes
the record pointer to be repositioned to the beginning of the file. The new file has
been given the same logical unit number both times, but this is not necessary.

9.4.2 Multiplication of Large Matrices

Problem

Write a program to multiply an $N \times M$ matrix A (each input record is a row of
matrix A), and an $M \times L$ matrix B (each input record is a column of matrix B).
Print the result.

Method

Each value of the output matrix is calculated as

$$c_{ij} = \sum_{k=1}^{M} a_{ik} b_{kj}$$

The matrices are stored in files 'MATF1' and 'MATF2'. The *i*th record of 'MATF1' contains the *i*th row of matrix A. The *j*th record of 'MATF2' contains the *j*th column of matrix B. For each row of A, it is necessary to read all the columns of B. If the B file were sequential, this could be done by closing and reopening the B file for each row of A. Since the B file is not sequential, it is done by reinitializing the record number.

Program

```
************************************************************
*                                                          *
*   MULTIPLICATION OF LARGE MATRICES STORED IN FILES  *
*                                                          *
************************************************************
*                                                          *
*   INPUT FILES:                                           *
*                                                          *
*      'MATF1'  - MATRIX A, STORED BY ROWS                 *
*                 (SEQUENTIAL FILE)                        *
*      'MATF2'  - MATRIX B, STORED BY COLUMNS (DIRECT *
*                 FILE)                                    *
*                                                          *
*   OUTPUT VARIABLES:                                      *
*                                                          *
*      CMAT      - ROW OF MATRIX C, PRODUCT OF             *
*                  MATRICES A AND B                        *
*                                                          *
************************************************************
        INTEGER I,J,K,AROW,ACOL,BROW,BCOL
        INTEGER INA,INB
        PARAMETER(AROW=4,ACOL=3,BROW=3,BCOL=3)
        PARAMETER(INA=12,INB=14)
        REAL AMAT(ACOL),BMAT(BROW),CMAT(BCOL)

        OPEN (UNIT=INA,FILE='MATF1',STATUS='OLD')

*       THE FILE 'MATF2' HAS BEEN CREATED ON THE VAX/
*       780 USING FDL.
*       DIRECT FILE HAS ALREADY BEEN CREATED AND THE
*       DATA FOR A 3 X 3 ARRAY HAS BEEN STORED IN
*       COLUMN ORDER AS RECORDS.
*       THE RECORD LENGTH FOR THIS ARRAY IS 12
*       CHARACTERS.

        OPEN (UNIT=INB,FILE='MATF2',STATUS='OLD',
     1        ACCESS='DIRECT',FORM='FORMATTED',
     2        RECL=12)

        WRITE (*,900)
900     FORMAT(/1X,'OUTPUT OF THE PRODUCT MATRIX'/)
        DO 80 I = 1,AROW
          READ (INA,1000) (AMAT(K),K=1,ACOL)
```

```
1000      FORMAT(4F4.1)
          DO 60 J = 1, BCOL
            CMAT(J) = 0.0
            READ (INB,1000,REC=J) (BMAT(K), K=1,BROW)
            DO 40 K = 1, BROW
              CMAT(J) = CMAT(J) + AMAT(K) * BMAT(K)
40          CONTINUE
60        CONTINUE
          WRITE (*,1200) (CMAT(J), J=1,BCOL)
1200      FORMAT (1X,5F10.2)
80     CONTINUE
       STOP
       END
```

Notice that the same counter is used to control the reading of the direct file and one of the DO-loops.

The problem can be solved by storing both files in sequential files, provided the file containing the B matrix is read completely through once for each record of the A matrix file. This could be done by closing and reopening INB, or by rewinding it as shown below:

```
       INTEGER I,J,K,AROW,ACOL,BROW,BCOL
       INTEGER INA,INB
       PARAMETER(AROW=4,ACOL=3,BROW=3,BCOL=3)
       PARAMETER(INA=12,INB=14)
       REAL AMAT(ACOL),BMAT(BROW),CMAT(BCOL)

       OPEN (UNIT=INA,FILE='MATF1',STATUS='OLD')
       OPEN (UNIT=INB,FILE='MATF2',STATUS='OLD')

       WRITE (*,900)
900    FORMAT(/1X,'OUTPUT OF THE PRODUCT MATRIX'/)
       DO 80 I = 1,AROW
         READ (INA,1000) (AMAT(K),K=1,ACOL)
1000     FORMAT(4F4.1)
         DO 60 J = 1 TO BCOL
           CMAT(J) = 0.0
           READ (INB,1000) (BMAT(K), K=1,BROW)
           DO 40 K = 1 TO BROW
             CMAT(J) = CMAT(J) + AMAT(K) * BMAT(K)
40         CONTINUE
60       CONTINUE
         WRITE (*,1200) (CMAT(J) J=1,BCOL)
1200     FORMAT (1X,5F10.2)
         REWIND (UNIT=INB)
80     CONTINUE
       STOP
       END
```

Output

```
 TYPE MATF1.DAT
1.0 1.0 1.0
2.0 2.0 2.0
3.0 3.0 3.0
4.0 4.0 4.0

 TYPE MATF2.DAT
5.0 5.0 5.0
6.0 6.0 6.0
7.0 7.0 7.0


OUTPUT OF THE PRODUCT MATRIX

    15.00        18.00        21.00
    30.00        36.00        42.00
    45.00        54.00        63.00
    60.00        72.00        84.00
```

9.4.3 Comparison of Air Samples

Problem

Air samples are collected from different parts of a city. As each sample is analyzed, the information is stored in a direct file under the number assigned to that location. If there was a previous sample from the same location, the two analyses are printed for visual comparison and the new information is stored.

Method

Since the data is not necessarily entered in order by location, the location number is used as a record key for a direct access file. Before storing the data, a check is made for previous information from that location. The input is found on the standard system input file.

Program

```
************************************************************
*                                                          *
*  UPDATE FILE OF CITY AIR SAMPLE ANALYSES                 *
*                                                          *
************************************************************
*                                                          *
*  MASTER FILE: 'SAMPLE' (DIRECT FILE)                     *
*                                                          *
*  INPUT VARIABLES:                                        *
*                                                          *
*      OLDINF  - OLD RECORD VALUE                          *
*      ANALYS  - NEW RECORD VALUE                          *
*                                                          *
*  OUTPUT VARIABLES:                                       *
*                                                          *
*      LOC     - LOCATION OF AIR SAMPLE ('SAMPLE'          *
*                KEY)                                      *
*      ANALYS  - ANALYSIS OF AIR SAMPLE                    *
*                                                          *
************************************************************

          CHARACTER*80 ANALYS,OLDINF
          INTEGER LOC,AIRFIL,RSTAT
          PARAMETER (AIRFIL=24)

          OPEN (UNIT=AIRFIL,FILE='SAMPLE',STATUS='OLD',
     1          ACCESS='DIRECT',FORM='UNFORMATTED',
     2          RECORDTYPE='FIXED')

*         DO WHILE MORE DATA

20        READ (5,1000,END=100) LOC,ANALYS
1000        FORMAT(I3,1X,A80)

*           CHECK FOR DUPLICATE RECORD

            READ (AIRFIL,REC=LOC,ERR=60,IOSTAT=RSTAT)
     1          OLDINF

*           WHEN DUPLICATE FOUND

            WRITE (*,1400) OLDINF,ANALYS
1400        FORMAT(//5X,A80/10X,A80)

*           STORE NEW ANALYSIS

60          WRITE (AIRFIL,REC=LOC) ANALYS
          GO TO 20

*         ENDDO
```

```
100      CLOSE (UNIT=AIRFIL,STATUS='KEEP')
         STOP
         END
```

No output is given for this program since the output was written to a direct access file rather than to the printer.

9.4.4 Inventory Report

Problem

Rewrite the program of Section 7.7.6 to read the inventory information from files TYRF and CSTF.

Method

Only the input subroutine DATAIN has to be changed. The new version is shown below.

Program

```
***********************************************************
*                                                         *
*    SUBROUTINE TO INPUT DATA                             *
*                                                         *
***********************************************************
*                                                         *.
*    INPUT PARAMETERS:                                    *
*                                                         *
*       SIZE          - ACTUAL NUMBER OF TYRE SIZES       *
*       STORE         - ACTUAL NUMBER OF STORES           *
*                                                         *
*    OUTPUT PARAMETERS:                                   *
*                                                         *
*       TYRITM(SIZE,STORE) - ARRAY OF TYRE INVENTORY      *
*       CSTUNT(SIZE,STORE) - ARRAY OF TYRE COSTS          *
*                                                         *
***********************************************************

         SUBROUTINE DATAIN(TYRITM,CSTUNT,SIZE,STORE)
         INTEGER STORE,SIZE
         INTEGER TYRITM(SIZE,STORE)
         REAL CSTUNT(SIZE,STORE)
         INTEGER I,J
         PARAMETER (TYRF=12,CSTF=13)

         OPEN (UNIT=TYRF,FILE='TYRES',STATUS='OLD')
         OPEN (UNIT=CSTF,FILE='COST',STATUS='OLD')

*    INPUT THE INVENTORY TABLES
```

```
         WRITE (*,1000)
1000     FORMAT(//1X,'INPUT THE NUMBER OF TYRES BY ',
     1           'SIZE AND STORE')
         DO 10 I=1,SIZE
           READ (TYRF,1500,END=30)
     1           (TYRITM(I,J),J=1,STORE)
1500       FORMAT(20I3)
10       CONTINUE
         WRITE (*,2000)
2000     FORMAT(//1X,'INPUT THE COST PER TYRE BY SIZE ',
     1           'AND STORE')
         DO 20 I=1,SIZE
           READ(CSTF,2500,END=30)
     1           (CSTUNT(I,J),J=1,STORE)
2500       FORMAT(20F4.1)
20       CONTINUE
         RETURN
30       WRITE (*,*) 'DATA MISSING'
         RETURN
         END
```

Summary

A data file is an organized collection of records. The file can be created outside a FORTRAN program through the use of an editor or within a FORTRAN program through output statements.

An OPEN statement is used to connect a file with a program. The OPEN statement assigns a logical unit number to the file and provides the computer with information about the organization of the file and the access mode being used. A CLOSE statement is used to disconnect a file from a program. The file can be retained for future use, or the file space can be released.

A program creates a file by opening it as 'NEW', then writing data to it. An 'OLD' file already exists. The data in it may be read or modified, and additional data may be added to it.

Either 'SEQUENTIAL' or 'DIRECT' access may be used. Sequential files are processed from beginning to end. Direct files may be processed in any order. Records in a direct file must all have the same length. A specific record is located by providing the record number of the record.

Files built using an editor and those that are to be printed or displayed must contain 'FORMATTED' records. These files are written and read using format statements. Files that are only processed through programs should be 'UNFORMATTED' because unformatted input/output is more efficient than formatted input/output.

The parameters of the OPEN statement for a file must be compatible with the file's actual physical characteristics. When the structure of a file is unknown, the INQUIRE statement can be used to discover it.

The various file control statements are:

OPEN	readies the designated file
CLOSE	disconnects the designated file
INQUIRE	determines the characteristics of a file
READ	retrieves data from a file
WRITE	stores data in a file
PRINT	stores data in a print file
REWIND	positions a file at the beginning
BACKSPACE	positions a file to the previous record
ENDFILE	writes an end marker on a file

Exercises

1. Write a program to read a 20 × 20 real matrix, which is stored one row per record in an unformatted file 'MATIN', and write the transpose of the matrix to the unformatted file 'MATOUT', also stored one row per record.

2. A file 'INFOF' contains mailing labels of the form

cols	1–20	name
	21–50	street address
	51–73	city
	74–75	state abbreviation
	76–80	zip code

   Write a program to sort the records in ascending order by zip codes.

3. The file 'DIFILE' contains tree IDs, dates, and diameter measurements for the trees in an experimental tree farm. Another file, 'HTFILE', contains tree IDs, dates, and height measurements. Both files are in order by the tree ID numbers. Write a program that creates a file 'TREFIL' containing, for each tree, the tree ID, date and diameter, date and height. Assume that each tree ID does not appear more than once in each file, but that some IDs may not be in both files.

4. Assume that the data files of Exercise 3 are not in order by tree IDs. Create 'TREFIL' as a direct file, using the tree IDs as keys.

5. The file 'INVF' is a direct file holding 3000 records of 80 bytes each. Some of the records contain data, some are dummy records. Write a program that copies the data from 'INVF' into a sequential file 'INVSEQ' using only the actual data records.

6. The sequential master file 'MFILE' has records of the form

cols	1–4	inventory number
	5–50	item description

   The sequential transaction file 'TFILE' has records of the form

cols	1–4	inventory number
	5–50	blanks for record to be deleted
	5–50	item description for record to be added

Both files are in order by inventory number. MFILE does not contain any duplicate inventory numbers. TFILE may contain duplicates. Create a new sequential file using the transaction file to update the master file. The new file should contain all records of MFILE that are not deleted and all records of TFILE that are added and not subsequently deleted.

10 *Additional FORTRAN Features*

*T*his chapter contains types of data declarations and control statements that are used infrequently in FORTRAN programming. The numeric data types REAL and INTEGER, introduced in the preceding chapters, are adequate for most scientific programming. On computers with a 32-bit word size, REAL numbers contain at most seven significant digits. Some applications require a higher degree of accuracy. In addition, some mathematical and electrical engineering applications require complex numbers. Normal REAL numbers require four bytes, or one word of storage in a computer. By allocating two words, complex numbers consisting of a real and an imaginary part or real numbers of higher precision can be stored. While FORTRAN 77 provides these data types, they may not be fully available on all machines.

The EQUIVALENCE statement is used mainly when it is necessary to look at and manipulate the actual storage representation of data, for example, in writing system programs.

The control statements discussed in this chapter are mostly of historical interest, having been retained from earlier versions of FORTRAN for reasons of compatibility.

10.1 Precision Specification of Numeric Variables

The precisions provided by FORTRAN are known as single precision and double precision. In a computer where a single-precision number contains a maximum of seven significant digits, a double-precision number will contain at most sixteen significant digits. On any machine, a double-precision number contains slightly more than twice as many significant digits as a single-precision number, with the same range of values. Both constants and variables can be specified in both precisions. To preserve numeric significance, related calculations in a program should involve only single-precision values, or only double-precision values. Mixing them causes a loss of significance and misleading answers.

10.1.1 Declaration of Precision

The DOUBLE PRECISION declaration allocates two words of storage for values having more than seven significant digits. The general form of the declaration is:

DOUBLE PRECISION var1,var2,var3,...,varn

The declaration of a variable as having double precision enables the computer to store more than seven digits, but it does not guarantee that all the digits are significant. The actual number of significant digits depends on the experimental or computational values stored in the variable. If a measurement has an accuracy of only four significant digits, using double precision will not increase the degree of significance. It is up to the user to ensure the significance of data and up to the programmer to preserve the significance of data.

The following example causes storage to be allocated as shown:

```
DOUBLE PRECISION A,B,C,D(5)
```

All the real variables in a program can be declared double precision by using implicit data names and the IMPLICIT statement, as follows:

```
IMPLICIT DOUBLE PRECISION (A-H,O-Z)
```

The effect of this statement is to make all undeclared variables with names starting with any of the letters A, B, . . . , H and O, P, . . . , Z into double-precision variables.

Programming Warning

> Maintainability: Avoid the use of IMPLICIT DOUBLE PRECISION in any program containing single-precision real numbers.

Double-precision numeric literals can only be written in exponential form. The letter D is used for the exponent, corresponding to the letter E for single-precision numeric literals.

Single precision	*Double precision*
0.8563E02	0.85632794D02
−0.039764E04	−0.039763978529D04
0.9665874E−05	0.9665874D−05
−95.672875E02	−95.672865493203D02

Just as with single-precision digits, the number that follows the letter D indicates a power of 10. The range of possible exponents is the same for double-precision real numbers as for single-precision numbers.

If the digits of the literal are all significant but the last digit represents a rounding of further digits or an estimate, then the number of significant digits in each of these values is as follows:

Value	Significant digits	Digits stored
0.8563E02	4	7
0.85632794D02	8	16
−0.039764E04	5	7
−0.039763978529D04	11	16
0.9665874E−05	7	7
0.9665874D−05	7	16
−95.672865E02	7	7
−95.672865493203D02	14	16

Notice that although a single-precision storage location always contains the same number of digits, not all of them are necessarily significant. In addition, if too many digits are specified in the literal, they will not all be stored. The same is true of double-precision values.

10.1.2 Input/Output of Double-Precision Values

The field specification Dw.d is available for the input and output of double-precision values that have more than seven significant digits. If they have fewer than seven significant digits, either the Ew.d or the Fw.d specification can be used.

Input of Double-Precision Values

As with single-precision values, the use of a decimal point in the input data over-rides the specification of fractional digits. The following examples show various types of input formats:

```
*        IMPLIED DECIMAL POINT, D FORMAT

         DOUBLE PRECISION A,B
         READ (*,1000) A,B
1000     FORMAT(D12.5,D15.3)
```

| 3 | 8 | 7 | 6 | 4 | 1 | 2 | 6 | 3 | D | 0 | 2 | | − | 1 | 8 | 9 | 5 | 3 | 4 | 8 | 8 | 2 | D | 0 | 1 |

as a result of the input

A = 3876.41263D02 = 0.387641263D06
B = −189534.882D01 = −0.189534882D07

```
*        EXPLICIT DECIMAL POINT, D FORMAT
```

```
       DOUBLE PRECISION X,Y
       READ (*,1000) X,Y
1000   FORMAT(D10.0,D13.0)
```

|2|1|.|5|7|2|9|D|0|2|−|6|3|.|5|9|1|1|0|2|D|−|3|

as a result of the input

X = 21.5729D02 = 0.215729D04
Y = −63.591102D−03 = −0.63591102D−01

```
*      EXPLICIT DECIMAL POINT, D FORMAT, NO EXPONENT
*      IN DATA

       DOUBLE PRECISION G,H
       READ (*,1000) G,H
1000   FORMAT(D15.0,D15.0)
```

| | | | |1|2|3|4|.|5|6|7|8|9|3| | |−|2|.|1|5|3|4|7|9|0|6|6|2|

as a result of the input

G = 1234.567893 = 0.1234567893D04
H = −2.1534790662 = −0.21534790662D01

Notice the use of the Dw.d format even when there are only seven significant digits. If the Ew.d or Fw.d format is used on input for numbers that have fractional parts, the storage representation will be less accurate than that obtained using the Dw.d format. If the input values are whole numbers of fewer than seven digits, as in the following example, these formats can be used to store them as double precision numbers:

```
*      EXPLICIT DECIMAL POINT, E or F FORMAT

       DOUBLE PRECISION P,Q
       READ (*,1000) P,Q
1000   FORMAT(E15.0,E10.0)  or  FORMAT(F15.0,F10.0)
```

| | | | |1|7|5|2|1|5|7|3|.|D|0| |−|.|0|2|6|1|D|0|4|

as a result of the input

P = 1752157.D0 = 0.1752157D07
Q = −.0261D04 = −0.261D03

Notice that at most seven digits are preserved.

Output of Double-Precision Values

If double-precision output values have more than seven significant digits, the Dw.d format specification should be used. The field width must be great enough to provide space for a sign, a decimal point, and a signed exponent:

Dw.d   with $w \geq d + 7$

The exact form of the output may vary from system to system. If the values have fewer than seven significant digits, the specification Ew.d can be used instead. In either case, the decimal part of the specification, d, should not be greater than the number of significant digits. The Fw.d specification can be used if the exponential form is not wanted. In this case, the d does not correspond to the number of significant digits. The following examples show the use of different output formats. Given

```
DOUBLE PRECISION A,B
A = 1896.7842D0
B = -0.000895D0
WRITE (*,1000) A,B
```

and the format

```
    1000    FORMAT(1X,D15.8,D13.6)
```

the output is printed as:

```
|b|0|.|1|8|9|6|7|8|4|2|D|b|0|4|-|0|.|8|9|5|0|0|0|D|-|0|3|
```

With the format

```
    1000    FORMAT(1X,E14.7,E13.6)
```

the output is printed as:

```
|b|0|.|1|8|9|6|7|8|4|E|b|0|4|-|0|.|8|9|5|0|0|0|E|-|0|3|
```

With the format

```
1000    FORMAT(1X,F11.4,F10.6)
```

the output is printed as:

```
|b|b|1|8|9|6|.|7|8|4|2|b|b|b|.|0|0|0|8|9|5|
```

Notice that when the E format is used, in addition to the leading zero, at most seven digits are printed.

10.1.3 Arithmetic and Library Functions

Arithmetic

All the arithmetic operators can be used with double-precision values. When a double-precision value is used in a mixed mode operation with an integer or single-precision value, the integer or single-precision value is converted to double precision before the operation is performed. The result is a double-precision value that has no more accuracy than the less accurate of the two operands. This is shown in the following examples:

```
DOUBLE PRECISION W,X,Y,Z
W = 123.456789D0
X = −.0000123456789D0
Y = 123456789.D0
Z = 12345.6789D0
```

		double-precision result is accurate to
W = W + 286.75		2 decimal places
X = X − 25318		11 decimal places (integers are exact)
Y = Y * 1.7		only 2 digits
Z = Z / 16.15		only 4 digits

Notice that all the arithmetic results are stored as double-precision values. However, the significance of the value stored depends on the significance of the operands. Since all the numeric literals are integer or single precision, they are converted to double precision before the arithmetic takes place. For these values, this conversion does not affect their accuracy.

Numeric type conversions take place only as needed. The following example shows the steps in the evaluation and assignment of a mixed mode expression:

```
DOUBLE PRECISION X,Y
REAL A,B,W
INTEGER I,K
```

expression	$W = A + I − B * K + 3.15 * X − Y / 5$
step 1	$W = A + I − \quad R1 \quad + \quad R2 \quad − R3$
	where R1 is a single-precision real result
	R2 is a double-precision real result
	R3 is a double-precision real result
step 2	$W = \quad R4 \quad − \quad R1 \quad + \quad R2 \quad − R3$
	where R4 is a single-precision real result
step 3	$W = \qquad R5 \qquad + \quad R2 \quad − R3$
	where R5 is a single-precision real result
step 4	$W = \qquad\qquad R6 \qquad − R3$
	where R6 is a double-precision real result
step 5	$W = \qquad\qquad\qquad R7$
	where R7 is the double-precision final result

The value R7 is stored in W. If W were a double-precision variable, the result R7 would be stored in the form it already had. But since W is single precision, the result R7 is rounded to seven digits and stored in a single word of memory.

Library Functions

The FORTRAN library includes versions of most of the scientific functions for double-precision computations. The ordinary version cannot be used, but the specific version designed to provide double-precision results. The name of this version is the same as the name of the single-precision function, except that it is preceded by a D. For example,

```
SQRT(X)          single-precision argument and result
DSQRT(X)         double-precision argument and result
```

These functions must have arguments of the correct type, as shown in the following example:

```
DOUBLE PRECISION X,Y
X = 3.0D0
Y = DSQRT(X)
```

Since 3.0 is a whole number, it would not seem to make any difference whether it is used as an integer, single-precision real, or double-precision real. However, the DSQRT function requires a double-precision argument. The result stored in Y is as accurate as the computer can make it. The language reference manual for your computer will have information on the error bounds of the library functions.

Table 10.1 shows the double-precision forms of the more common library functions. The complete list of functions is found in Appendix B.

Double-Precision Subprograms

The programmer may not write double-precision function subprograms since it would require returning values from two positions in memory. Instead, subroutine subprograms should be used. The arguments of the subroutine may be of any type, provided that the argument list matches the parameter list as to type, number, and order of the arguments. One of the arguments must be used to return the value of

Table 10.1

FUNCTION	ARGUMENT TYPE	RESULT TYPE
DABS(D)	double	double
DMOD(DX,DA)	"	"
DMAX1(DA,DB,...)	"	"
DMIN1(DA,DB,...)	"	"
DSQRT(D)	" $D \geqslant 0$	"
DEXP(D)	"	"
DLOG(D)	" $D > 0$	"
DLOG10(D)	" $D > 0$	"
DSIN(D)	"	"
DCOS(D)	"	"
DTAN(D)	" $D = 0$	"

the computation. This is shown in the following example of the computation of a double-precision cube root:

```
***********************************************************
*                                                         *
*    DOUBLE PRECISION CUBE ROOT                           *
*                                                         *
*    PARAMETER                                            *
*       INPUT:  X                                         *
*       OUTPUT: Y                                         *
*                                                         *
***********************************************************

      SUBROUTINE DCBRT(X,Y)
      DOUBLE PRECISION X,Y

      Y = EXP(DLOG(X)/3.0)
      RETURN
      END
```

10.1.4 Review Questions

1. Write the statements to declare the following as double-precision variables:

   a. AMAX, AVAL, CONST, CALC, VAL
   b. x_i, y_j i = 1 through 10, j = 1 through 25
   c. $a_{i,j}$, $b_{j,k}$ i = 1 through 20, j = 1 through 30, k = 1 through 40

2. Write input and FORMAT statements to read the following data into double-precision variables A, B, and C:

   a.

   ```
   189.8762|ᵇᵇ3976.0546D03|ᵇᵇ-0.00854D-02|
   ```

   b.

   ```
   -0.0672|ᵇᵇᵇ39547.621933|ᵇᵇ18954.678|
   ```

3. Write the output and FORMAT statements to print the following double-precision values in exponential form with decimal points aligned in columns 20, 40, and 60, using the D format:

   a. W = 389.625D0, X = 0.06784D0, Y = −3264.752D0
   b. P = 8764.13D0, Q = −0.000385D0, R = 164.756D0
   c. E = 39762.154D5, F = −076854.162D−7, G = 3176.8492D10

4. Write the output and FORMAT statements to print the following double-precision values in exponential form with decimal points aligned in columns 20, 40, and 60, using the F format:

a. W = 389.625D0, X = 0.06784D0, Y = −3264.752D0
b. P = 8764.13D0, Q = −0.000385D0, R = 164.756D0
c. E = 39762.154D5, F = −076854.162D−7, G = 3176.8492D1

5. Indicate the accuracy of the following double-precision values:

a. 5.0D0
b. DSIN(3.0D0)
c. .12345D − 5
d. .67890D8
e. 0.0D0
f. 2.79D0 + 1.3D0

10.2 Complex Variables

FORTRAN 77 supports the complex number data type needed for some applications in electrical engineering and mathematical physics. Mathematically, a complex number has a real and an imaginary part. It is written as

a + bi

      where a is the real part
          b is the imaginary part with $i^2 = -1$

Both a and b are represented as real numbers in the computer.

A numeric literal of the complex number type is written in FORTRAN as a pair of real numbers, as in the following examples:

Mathematics	*FORTRAN*
3.0 + 4.0i	(3.0,4.0)
6.0 − 7.5i	(6.0, −7.5)
−4.2 + 8.9i	(−4.2,8.9)
−.25 − 1.3i	(−.25, −1.3)

Storing the two parts of a complex value requires two words of memory. FORTRAN 77 supports input/output of complex numbers, arithmetic, and specific library functions for them. All of these operations automatically handle both the real and imaginary part of the values.

If x is a complex variable, then the real and imaginary parts of x can be referred to mathematically as:

$$x_{re} \text{ and } x_{imag}$$

and

$$x = x_{re} + x_{imag}$$

10.2.1 Declaration of Complex Variables

The general form of the declaration statement for complex variables is:

COMPLEX var1, var2, var3,...,varn

Two words of memory are allocated for each variable. The following example causes storage to be allocated as shown:

```
COMPLEX X,Y,Z,W(5)
```

In FORTRAN, the real and imaginary parts of a complex number X are referred to as

```
REAL(X) and AIMAG(X)
```

If X1 and X2 are both single- or both double-precision real numbers, then

```
X = COMPLX(X1,X2)
```

is a single- or double-precision complex number such that

```
X1 = REAL(X)
```

and

```
X2 = AIMAG(X)
```

10.2.2 Input/Output of Complex Values

There are no distinctive field specifications for complex values. Instead, a pair of real field specifications is used, one for the real part and one for the imaginary part of a complex number. Both parts are read or written as though they were real numbers. Thus either the F, E, or G specification is used.

Input

The following example shows the use of the F specification to input complex values:

```
      COMPLEX A,B,C
      READ (*,1200) A,B,C
1200  FORMAT(2F4.0,2F5.0,2F8.0)
```

A		3.50	re
		6.28	imag
B		7.56	re
		8.95	imag
C		9.876	re
		−12.625	imag

```
|3|.|5|0|6|.|2|8| |7|.|5|6| |8|.|9|5| | |9|.|8|7|6|−|1|2|.|6|2|5|
        A              B                      C
```

Notice that a pair of values is read for each variable as the variable has an undefined value unless both the real and imaginary components are stored. The letter i
is not part of the data. Mathematically, these values would be written as:

$$A = 3.50 + 6.28i$$
$$B = 7.56 + 8.95i$$
$$C = 9.876 - 12.625i$$

When values are input into a complex array, the order of the elements is as
shown in the following example:

```
      COMPLEX X(4)
      READ (*,1200) X
1200  FORMAT(2F5.0)
```

X(1)		8.2	re
		6.5	imag
X(2)		7.8	re
		0.3	imag
X(3)		3.7	re
		−7.9	imag
X(4)		12.8	re
		36.2	imag

```
|b|b|8|.|2|b|b|6|.|5|
```

```
|b|b|7|.|8|b|b|b|.|3|
```

```
|b|b|3|.|7|b|−|7|.|9|
```

```
|ᵬ|1|2|.|8|ᵬ|3|6|.|2|
```

Notice that both components of an element of the array are read before input of the next element begins. The values are read in the order in which they are stored.

Output

Output of complex values can be done using either the F, E, or G specifications. The following example shows the use of the F specification. Given the program segment and data

```
      COMPLEX A,B,C                        let A = 8.62 + 9.86i
              .                                B = 18.65 + 10.81i
              .                                C = 13.16 − 9.75i
              .
      WRITE (*,1000) A,B,C
1000  FORMAT(1X,2F6.2,2F8.2,2F6.2)
```

the output is printed as:

```
|ᵬᵬ8.62|ᵬᵬ9.86|ᵬᵬᵬ18.65|ᵬᵬᵬ10.81|ᵬ13.16|ᵬ-9.75|
  re  |  imag  |   re   |   imag   |  re  |  imag
    A              B              C
```

The real component of each value is printed ahead of the imaginary component; the letter i is not printed. There is nothing in the output to show that the numbers are paired. The output would be more readable with the following format:

```
      COMPLEX A,B,C                        let A = 8.62 + 9.86i
              .                                B = 18.65 + 10.81i
              .                                C = 13.16 − 9.75i
              .
      WRITE (*,1000) A,B,C
1000  FORMAT(1X,2F6.2,'I',2F8.2,'I',2F6.2,'I')
```

The output is printed as:

```
|ᵬᵬ8.62|ᵬᵬ9.86I|ᵬᵬᵬ18.65|ᵬᵬᵬ10.81I|ᵬ13.16|ᵬ-9.75I|
  re  |  imag   |   re   |   imag    |  re  |  imag
    A               B               C
```

10.2.3 Arithmetic and Library Functions

In FORTRAN 77, complex numbers can be used in arithmetic expressions in the same way other numbers are used. For example,

```
COMPLEX A,B,C,D
   .                          let  A = 8.6 + 9.7i
   .                               B = 13.4 + 10.1i
   .                               C = 2.0 + 0.0i
D = (A + B) / C               then D = 11.0 + 9.9i
```

Arithmetic operations on complex numbers are defined as follows:

Mathematics	*FORTRAN*
$(w+xi) + (y+zi) = (w+y) +$ $(x+z)i$	$(W,X) + (Y,Z) = (W+Y,X+Z)$
ex. $2.5+3.2i + 6.5+4.6i =$ $9.0+7.8i$	$(2.5,3.2) + (6.5,4.6) = (9.0,7.8)$
$(w+xi) - (y+zi) = (w-y) +$ $(x-z)i$	$(W,X) - (Y,Z) = (W-Y,X-Z)$
ex. $9.2+6.7i - (5.2+3.7i) =$ $4.0+3.0i$	$(9.2,6.7) - (5.2,3.7) = (4.0,3.0)$
$(w+xi)(y+zi) = (wy-xz) +$ $(wz+xy)i$	$(W,X) * (Y,Z) =$ $(W*Y-X*Z,W*Z+X*Y)$
ex. $(2.0+3.0i)(5.0+2.0i) =$ $4.0+19.0i$	$(2.0,3.0) * (5.0,2.0) = (4.0,19.0)$
$(w+xi) / (y+zi) = (wy+xz)/$ $(y^2+z^2) + (-wz+xy)/$ $(y^2+z^2)i$	$(W,X) / (Y,Z) = ((W*Y+X*Z)/$ $(Y*Y+Z*Z),$ $(-W*Z+X*Y)/(Y*Y+Z*Z))$
ex. $(3.0+4.0i)/(2.0+1.0i) =$ $2.0+1.0i$	$(3.0,4.0) / (2.0,1.0) = (2.0,1.0)$

Ordinary real numbers are equivalent to complex numbers with the imaginary part zero. Assignment of a real value to a complex variable has the following result:

```
COMPLEX A
A = -27.3                     A has the value (-27.3,0.0)
```

Assignment of a complex value to a real variable has the following result:

```
REAL A
A = (14.6,1.89)               A has the value 14.6
```

The imaginary part of the value is discarded. Therefore, when complex numbers are used in mixed mode arithmetic, any real numbers are converted to complex before the arithmetic operation is performed:

$(6.0,3.0) + 5.2$ becomes $(6.0,3.0) + (5.2,0.0) = (11.2,3.0)$
$(8.5,6.2) - 5.2$ becomes $(8.5,6.2) - (5.2,0.0) = (3.3,6.2)$

Then the result is converted to the storage type of the receiving variable:

```
REAL A,B
COMPLEX Y,Z
A = 5.2
Y = (6.0,3.0)
```

```
B = A + Y                B has the value 11.2
Z = A + Y                Z has the value (11.2,3.0)
```

Complex numbers may also be used in logical expressions. For example,

```
COMPLEX A,B
. . .
IF (A .EQ. B) . . .
```

Complex numbers may only be compared for equality and inequality. For complex A and B,

```
(A .EQ. B)
```

is equivalent to

```
(REAL(A) .EQ. REAL(B) .AND. AIMAG(A) .EQ.
AIMAG(B))
```

while

```
(A .NE. B)
```

is equivalent to

```
(REAL(A) .NE. REAL(B) .OR. AIMAG(A) .NE. AIMAG(B))
```

Library Functions

The FORTRAN library includes versions of most of the scientific functions needed for complex number computations. The generic function cannot be used; but there is a specific version designed to provide complex results. The name of this version is the same as the name of the single-precision real function, except that it is preceded by a C. For example,

```
SQRT(X)          single precision real argument and result
CSQRT(X)         complex argument and result
```

These functions must have arguments of the correct type. For example,

```
COMPLEX X,Y
X = 3.0D0
Y = CSQRT(X)
```

Since 3.0 is a whole number, it would not seem to make any difference whether it is used as an integer, single-precision real, or complex. However, the CSQRT function requires a complex argument. The value stored in X is the complex number (3.0,0.0). The result stored in Y is in the form of a complex number even though the imaginary part is zero.

Table 10.2 shows the complex forms of the more common library functions. The complete list of functions is found in Appendix B.

User-Defined Subprograms

The programmer may write function subprograms that return complex values by declaring the function to be complex in the function header. The arguments of the function may be of any type, provided that the argument list matches the parameter

Table 10.2

FUNCTION	ARGUMENT TYPE	RESULT TYPE
CABS(C)	complex	real
CONJG(C)	"	complex
CSQRT(C)	"	"
CEXP(C)	"	"
CLOG(C)	"	"
CSIN(C)	"	"
CCOS(C)	"	"

list as to type, number, and order of the arguments. The function name is used to return the value of the computation. This is shown in the following example of the computation of a complex tangent:

```
****************************************************
*                                                  *
*   DRIVER                                         *
*                                                  *
****************************************************

        COMPLEX X,Y
        COMPLEX CCTAN

        . . .
        Y = CCTAN(X)
        . . .
        END


****************************************************
*                                                  *
*   COMPLEX TANGENT                                *
*                                                  *
*   PARAMETER                                      *
*      INPUT:  Z                                   *
*                                                  *
****************************************************

        COMPLEX FUNCTION CCTAN(Z)

        IF (CCOS(Z) .NE. 0.0) THEN
           CCTAN = CSIN(Z) / CCOS(Z)
           RETURN
        ELSE
           WRITE (*,*) 'ERROR IN CCTAN'
           STOP
        ENDIF
        END
```

Note that the calling program must know the type of argument being returned by the function.

Following is an example of a subroutine with complex arguments. It computes complex cube roots.

```
*******************************************************
*                                                     *
*    COMPLEX CUBE ROOTS                               *
*                                                     *
*    PARAMETER                                        *
*       INPUT:   Z                                    *
*       OUTPUT:  W                                    *
*                                                     *
*******************************************************

        SUBROUTINE CCBRT(Z,W)
        COMPLEX Z,W(3)
        REAL ABSZ,A,RAD,FRACPI
        PARAMETER (PI=3.14159)

        ABSZ = CABS(Z) ** (1.0/3.0)
        RAD = ATAN2(AIMAG(Z)/REAL(Z))
        FRACPI = 2.0 * PI / 3.0
        A = RAD / 3.0
        W(1) = ABSZ*(CMPLX(COS(A),SIN(A)))
        A = A + FRACPI
        W(2) = ABSZ*(CMPLX(COS(A),SIN(A)))
        A = A + FRACPI
        W(3) = ABSZ*(CMPLX(COS(A),SIN(A)))
        RETURN
        END
```

10.2.4 Review Questions

1. Write declarations for the following complex variables:

   a. a, b, c, p, r
   b. x_i i = 1 through 10, y_j j = 1 through 20
   c. $a_{i,j}$ i = 1 through 5, j = 1 through 10

2. Show the storage allocated by the following declarations:

   a. `COMPLEX W,X,Y(3)`
   b. `COMPLEX A(3),B(2),C`

3. Write program segments to calculate each of the following:

   a. the value of a complex polynomial $ax^2 + bx + c$
   b. the tangent of a complex number
   c. the hyperbolic sine of a complex number where

   $$\sinh(x + yi) = \sinh(x)\cos(y) + i\cosh(x)\sin(y)$$

   d. the complex root of a real polynomial $ax^2 + bx + c$

10.3 Miscellaneous Special Statements

In this section we discuss the DATA and EQUIVALENCE statements. This completes the presentation of all the data definition features available in FORTRAN 77.

10.3.1 Data Initialization (DATA statement)

The DATA statement was introduced in Sections 6.1.5 and 7.1.2. It may be used for initializing variables in common areas and for initializing other variables. In particular, it was used in the examples of the SAVE statement in Section 5.5.3. In other situations, either the PARAMETER or the DATA statement can be used for initialization.

The general form of the DATA statement is:

DATA var-list1/val-list1/var-list2/val-list2/...

The values in the val-list1 are stored in the variables in var-list1, the values in val-list2 in those of var-list2, and so forth. The values must match the variables as to type, number, and order. For example,

```
COMPLEX Y
REAL A,B,X(5)
INTEGER I,N
DATA A,B,I,N/3.5,8.6,9,10/X,Y/5*0.0,(0.0,1.0)/
```

initializes the variables as

$$A = 3.5$$
$$B = 8.6$$
$$I = 9$$
$$N = 10$$
$$X(1), \ldots, X(5) = 0.0$$
$$Y = (0.0, 1.0)$$

Unless the variables initialized by a DATA statement are in a common area or are saved, every time the routine containing them is loaded, the original values of the variables are loaded, and changes during previous activations of the routine are lost.

10.3.2 Storage Management (EQUIVALENCE statement)

The EQUIVALENCE statement is used to associate two or more data names with the same location in memory. The value stored at that location can then be accessed by either name. If the names are of different types, the bit pattern making up the value stored can be interpreted in several ways.

The EQUIVALENCE statement provides a way to access the parts of an array or of a complex number through scalar variable names. The general form of the EQUIVALENCE statement is:

EQUIVALENCE (var1,var2),(var3,var4),...

For example, EQUIVALENCE (A,B),(X,Y) assigns both the names A and B to the same data object and both the names X and Y to another data object. In the following example,

```
REAL W,X
EQUIVALENCE (W,X)
W = 10.5
WRITE (*,*) X
X = 8.5
WRITE (*,*) W
```

W,X | 10.5 |

W,X | 8.5 |

the output is:

```
10.5
 8.5
```

Only storage space for one variable is allocated. Both names are attached to it. Therefore when a value is assigned to W, it can also be accessed using the name X, and when a value is assigned to X, it can also be accessed using the name W.

The following examples show variations that are more useful:

```
COMPLEX X
REAL XPART(2)
EQUIVALENCE (X,XPART)
```

X   [   ]   XPART(1)
    [   ]   XPART(2)

XPART(1) is the real part of X; XPART(2) is the imaginary part of X.

```
REAL X(5)
REAL A,B,C,D,E
EQUIVALENCE (X(1),A),(X(2),B),(X(3),C),(X(4),D),(X(5),E)
```

X(1)   [   ]   A
X(2)   [   ]   B
X(3)   [   ]   C
X(4)   [   ]   D
X(5)   [   ]   E

Each element of X also has a scalar name.

```
REAL Q(4,2),COL1(4),COL2(4)
EQUIVALENCE (Q(1,1),COL1(4)),(Q(1,2),COL2(4))
```

Q(1,1)		COL1(1)
Q(2,1)		COL1(2)
Q(3,1)		COL1(3)
Q(4,1)		COL1(4)
Q(1,2)		COL2(1)
Q(2,2)		COL2(2)
Q(3,2)		COL2(3)
Q(4,2)		COL2(4)

COL1 is a one-dimensional array corresponding to the first column of Q. COL2 corresponds to the second column of Q.

The fact that in FORTRAN two-dimensional arrays are stored in column-major order permits single-dimensional arrays to be equivalenced to columns. It is not possible to equivalence one-dimensional arrays to the rows of larger arrays:

```
INTEGER N
PARAMETER (N=4)
REAL X(6),Y(N)
EQUIVALENCE (X,Y)
```

X(1)		Y(1)
X(2)		Y(2)
X(3)		Y(3)
X(4)		Y(4)
X(5)		
X(6)		

Arrays of different sizes start in the same memory location:

```
INTEGER N
PARAMETER (N=4)
REAL X(6),Y(N)
EQUIVALENCE (X(3),Y)
```

X(1)		
X(2)		
X(3)		Y(1)
X(4)		Y(2)
X(5)		Y(3)
X(6)		Y(4)

Arrays of different sizes start in different memory locations:

```
REAL X(4),Y(4)
EQUIVALENCE (X(3),Y(1))
```

X(1)		
X(2)		
X(3)		Y(1)
X(4)		Y(2)
		Y(3)
		Y(4)

Arrays of different sizes occupy overlapping memory locations:

```
CHARACTER*5 STR
CHARACTER*1 L(5)
EQUIVALENCE (STR,L)
STR = 'ABCDE'
```

STR $\boxed{A}\boxed{B}\boxed{C}\boxed{D}\boxed{E}$
L   1 2 3 4 5

L(1) = 'A', L(2) = 'B', L(3) = 'C', L(4) = 'D', L(5) = 'E'.

*Programming
Hint*

> Maintainability: Avoid using EQUIVALENCE statements unless it is necessary to save memory space or to access part of a variable or array. Then use them carefully.

The main use of EQUIVALENCE statements is to save space when several large arrays are used in the same routine but not at the same time. This is shown in the following example:

```
REAL X(100,100)              110,000 storage spaces allocated
REAL Y(1500),N(500)          2000 storage spaces needed
EQUIVALENCE (X,Y),(X(1,16),N)
```

The first 1500 places of X are reused by Y; the next 500 places of X are reused by N. Notice that neither Y nor N can be used while X is being used and X cannot be used after either Y or N has been initialized.

10.3.3 Review Questions

1. Write a DATA statement to initialize the following variables to the values given.

   a. A = 8.5, B = 9.8, C = 6.25
   b. X, W, Y, and Z to 13.8
   c. all elements of array X(10) to 12.6
   d. all elements of array A(10,10) to 10.5

2. Write EQUIVALENCE statements to make each of the following true:

   a. W, X, and Y share storage
   b. arrays A(10) and B(10) share storage
   c. arrays X(10) and W(20) share storage
   d. A is a name for the second element of array P(10), and B is a name for the ninth element

3. Show the storage allocation according to each of the following statements:

   a. EQUIVALENCE (P,Q), (Q,R), (S,T)
   b. EQUIVALENCE (X,Y) where X and Y are arrays of five elements each
   c. EQUIVALENCE (X(3),A), (A,B) where X is an array of four elements
   d. EQUIVALENCE (X(6),Y(2)) where X is an array of size 6 and Y is an array of size 3

10.4 Special Control Statements

This section contains descriptions of special control statements that are rarely used. The programmer is most likely to encounter them when modifying an existing program. The first five of these statements are the unconditional transfer (GO TO), the logical IF, the arithmetic IF, computed GO TO, and assigned GO TO implementation versions of the case statement. The next two, the PAUSE and STOP statements, provide for a small measure of user interaction with an executing program. In most batch systems, the PAUSE and STOP statements are disabled. The last two special statements to be considered are not executable statements, but a way of overcoming the "one entry—one exit" restriction of structured modular programming. To be fully useful, a programming language needs to restrict the programmer in order to minimize programming errors, but then it needs to provide ways around the restrictions for special situations.

Programming
Warning

> Maintainability: Avoid using these control statements unless no other way can be found to structure the program.

10.4.1 Unconditional Transfer (GO TO statement)

The unconditional control statement is a GO TO statement. Experts in structured programming methodology believe that GO TO statements are harmful. They should be used sparingly and in standard ways, as they make program control confusing to the reader. FORTRAN programmers cannot avoid the GO TO statement, but careful documentation can improve its readability.

The general form of the GO TO statement is:

GO TO n

where n is the number of the statement to be executed next. At statement n the computer resumes sequential execution. This is an unconditional transfer because the computer has no choice, but must transfer control to statement n. In the following example,

	Form		*Example*
	statement 1		$D = A + B * C$
	GO TO 10		GO TO 10
	statement 2		$X = Y * Z$
	statement 3		$Z = 8 - X$
	statement 4		$W = x + 5$
10	statement 5	10	WRITE (*,*) A, B, C, D
	statement 6		STOP

the order of execution is statements 1, 5, and 6. After statement 1 executes, the GO TO 10 statement executes, transferring control to statement 5 where sequential execution resumes. The value of D has been calculated but not the values of X, Z,

Figure 10.1

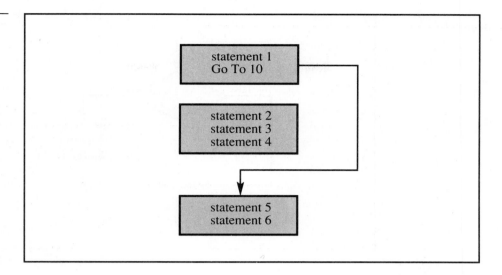

and W. This is shown in the structured flowchart of Fig. 10.1. This small example actually consists of three sequence structures, one of which is not executed at all. Notice that the statement label 10 is neither a line number nor a statement number. It is simply a number the programmer has chosen to mark a place in the program.

Good programming style supports the use of a CONTINUE statement to identify unconditional transfer of control. Using this, the example is rewritten as:

```
         statement 1
         GO TO 10

         statement 2
         statement 3
         statement 4

10       CONTINUE
         statement 5
         statement 6
```

The CONTINUE statement is simply used to place line numbers at particular places in the program. Control can be then transferred to this place. The CONTINUE statement itself is not an instruction for the computer to do anything. Note that in this example there is no way to get to statements 2–4. The blank comment lines before and after this block of code stress the lack of continuity.

10.4.2 Logical IF Statement

The logical IF statement is used with the GO TO statement to simulate a two-way selection structure. The logical IF statement has the form of a question that can be answered only "true" or "false." This question may be written as a relational

Figure 10.2

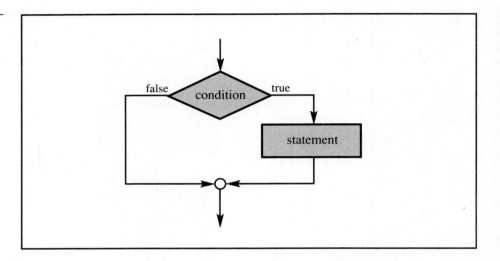

expression comparing two values, or it may be written as a logical expression using logical values. Relational and logical expressions were presented in detail in Section 4.3.

The general form of the logical IF statement is:

IF(condition) statement

This can be diagrammed as shown in Fig. 10.2.

Examples of the logical IF are:

```
IF (N .EQ. 0) GO TO 80
IF (Y .GT. 14.2) A = B + 5.0
IF (X .LT. Y) READ (*,*) A,B,C
IF (X .GE. 2*Y-7) WRITE (*,1500) W,X,Y,Z
IF (X .LE. 0.0) STOP
```

Any simple statement can be used in a logical IF, but structure control statements, such as another logical IF, cannot be used. The statement in the logical IF executes only if the evaluation of the condition results in a value of 'true.' If the result is 'false', the statement is skipped.

Since real numbers are rarely exactly equal inside a computer, real numbers should be checked for approximate equality, as in the following examples:

```
IF (ABS(X) .LT. .001) GO TO 10      X is approximately equal to 0
IF (ABS(X-Y) .LT. .001) GO TO 10    X is approximately equal to Y
```

The logical IF should only be used when there is a single statement to be executed, such as a GO TO, a flag to be set, a value to be computed, or a message to be printed.

10.4.3 Arithmetic IF Statement

A three-way case statement can be implemented by the arithmetic IF. It has two related forms:

IF (expr) n1,n2,n3

meaning

    go to n1 if expr $<$ 0   (value is negative)
    go to n2 if expr $=$ 0   (value is zero)
    go to n3 if expr $>$ 0   (value is positive)

and

IF (expr1 $-$ expr2) n1,n2,n3

meaning

    go to n1 if expr1 $<$ expr2
    go to n2 if expr1 $=$ expr2
    go to n3 if expr1 $>$ expr2

The expression in the parentheses is evaluated and control transfers, depending on the sign of the result.

    Since the line numbers referenced do not have to be different, special cases of this statement are equivalent to forms of logical IF statements:

	Arithmetic IF	*Logical IF*
	IF (expr)n1,n1,n2	IF (expr .GT. 0) GOTO n2
n1	. . .	
n2	statement	
	IF (expr)n2,n2,n1	IF(expr .LE. 0) GOTO n2
n1	. . .	
n2	statement	
	IF (expr)n1,n2,n2	IF(expr .GE. 0) GOTO n2
n1	. . .	
n2	statement	
	IF (expr)n2,n1,n1	IF(expr .LT. 0) GOTO n2
n1	. . .	
n2	statement	
	IF (expr)n2,n1,n2	IF(expr .NE. 0) GOTO n2
n1	. . .	
n2	statement	
	IF (expr)n1,n2,n1	IF(expr .EQ. 0) GOTO n2
n1	. . .	
n2	statement	

The following example shows the use of the arithmetic IF statement to implement a case statement:

```
        IF (X) 10,20,30
*                                X IS NEGATIVE
10      Y = X**2
        WRITE (*,*) X,Y
        GO TO 50
*                                X IS ZERO
20      WRITE (*,*) X
        GO TO 50
*                                X IS POSITIVE
30      Y = X**3
        WRITE (*,*) X,Y

50      CONTINUE
```

The computer will execute one of the three WRITE statements depending on the sign of X.

The following are valid arithmetic IF statements:

```
IF (K) 10,20,40
IF (K*N-M) 10,50,80
```

This can be interpreted as looking at the sign of K*N-M or as comparing K*N with M.

```
IF (A+C*D-E) 20,60,60
```

This can be interpreted as looking at the sign of A + C*D − E or as comparing A + C*D with E. Since it is unlikely they will be exactly equal, the comparison is looking for inequality.

10.4.4 Multibranch Transfer of Control

FORTRAN 77 has inherited from earlier versions of FORTRAN two multibranch transfer statements that are controlled by single variables. These are primarily useful when data contains numeric codes.

Computed GO TO

A computed GO TO statement implements a simple form of the case structure. An integer variable that has one of the values 1, 2, 3, . . . is used to indicate whether the 1st, 2nd, 3rd, . . . branch is to be taken. The value of the integer variable may be obtained from calculations or from input.

The general form of the computed GO TO statement is:

GO TO $(m_1, m_2, m_3, \ldots, m_n)$,intvar

where m_1, m_2, m_3, . . . m_n are the statement labels to which control is transferred based on the value of intvar. The index variable must be between 1 and n inclusive.

Figure 10.3

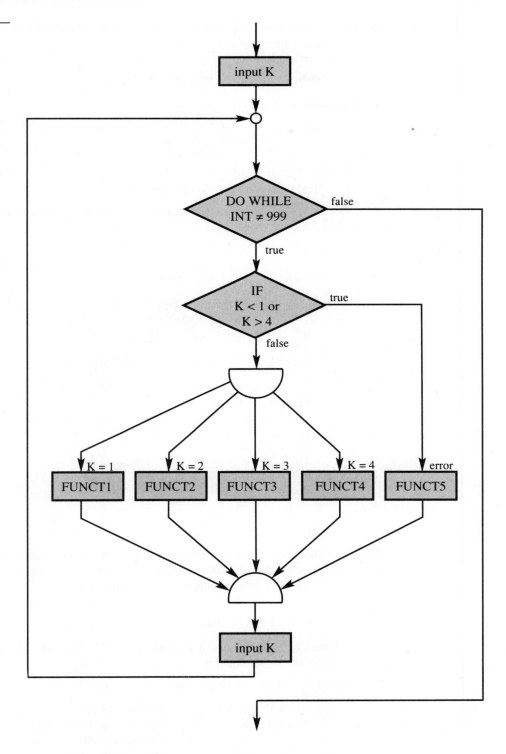

If there are n statement labels and intvar < 1 or intvar > n, the result of executing the statement is unpredictable.

In this example,

```
GO TO (10,20,30,50,90),INTVAR
```

control is transferred to:

statement label 10 when INTVAR = 1
statement label 20 when INTVAR = 2
statement label 30 when INTVAR = 3
statement label 50 when INTVAR = 4
statement label 90 when INTVAR = 5

The following examples show an input value being used to select one of the options of the case statement:

```
        READ (*,*) K

*       DO WHILE (K .NE. 999)

5       IF (K .NE. 999) THEN
          IF (K .LE. 0 .OR. K .GT. 4)GO TO 50
          GO TO (10,20,30,40),K
10        funct 1
          GO TO 100
20        funct 2
          GO TO 100
30        funct 3
          GO TO 100
40        funct 4
          GO TO 100
50        funct 5                     error messages
100       READ (*,*) K
          GOTO 5
        ENDIF

*       ENDDO
```

Fig. 10.3 shows the diagrams for this program segment. In this example funct n represents blocks of code that accomplish certain tasks. The value of the input variable K controls which function is to be performed.

Assigned GO TO Statement

The assigned GO TO statement is used as another form of case statement. The general form of the statement is:

GO TO labvar,($m_1,m_2,m_3,\ldots,m_n$)

where labvar is an INTEGER variable that has values assigned through the use of a special assignment statement. The values must be literals that are line labels. The list m_1, m_2, . . . , m_n gives the set of acceptable labels that are targets for the GO TO. The general form of the assignment statement is:

```
      ASSIGN label to labvar
```

The assigned label must exist in the program. If an illegal value is assigned, the result will be unpredictable. The assigned GO TO is hard to debug, so it should be avoided when possible.

In the following example,

```
      ASSIGN 300 TO IVAR
      GO TO IVAR,(40,100,90,300,170)
         . . .
300   CONTINUE
```

the GO TO statement transfers control to statement 300. This statement is used primarily to access an error routine from several different places in the program, then return to the place where the error was discovered. The following example shows this:

```
      READ (*,*) N
      IF (N .EQ. 0) THEN
         ASSIGN 10 TO LAB
         GO TO 100
      ENDIF
10    X = 1/N
      IF (X .LT. 0) THEN
         ASSIGN 20 TO LAB
         GO TO 100
      ENDIF
20    WRITE (*,*) SQRT(X)          prints N^{-1/2}  if N > 0
         . . .                            1      if N = 0
                                          0      if N < 0

*  PROCESS ERRORS

100   WRITE (*,*) 'ERROR'
      N = 1
      X = 0
      GO TO LAB,(10,20)
```

Unlike the computed GO TO, input values cannot be used with the assigned GO TO.

Programming Hint

> Maintainability: Use the computed GO TO rather than the assigned GO TO.

10.4.5 Execution Control (STOP and PAUSE Statements)

In the early days of computing, the STOP and PAUSE statements were used to halt the computer, returning control to the user. With large multiprocessing systems, control returns to the operating system. The user may not even be present when the program is running.

STOP Statement

The STOP statement has been used throughout this text to terminate normal processing of a program and in a few cases to terminate processing when data is invalid. The STOP statement can be used to assist the debugging process or to signal runtime errors by printing an error message before halting. The general form of the STOP statement is:

STOP [literal]

where the optional literal may be a positive integer of at most five digits, or a character literal of any length. For example,

```
STOP 67324
STOP 1532
STOP 'LINE12'
STOP 'NEGATIVE-ARGUMENT'
STOP 'NORMAL TERMINATION'
```

On some computers, when the STOP statement is executed, the associated literal is printed.

PAUSE Statement

The PAUSE statement is used to suspend program execution until the operator indicates that execution should continue. For example, it might be used when operator intervention is needed, such as mounting a tape or changing paper. The general form of the PAUSE statement is:

PAUSE [literal]

The optional literal may be a positive integer of at most five digits, or it may be a character literal. When the program pauses, the literal is printed. For example,

```
PAUSE 67324
PAUSE 1532
PAUSE 'LINE12'
PAUSE 'NEGATIVE-ARGUMENT'
```

The user can then abort the program or adjust the input according to the place in the program where the pause occurred. In interactive processing there is always a pause when the computer waits for input; therefore the PAUSE statement is of little value except when operator intervention is necessary.

10.4.6 Review Questions

1. Answer the following questions about the arithmetic IF statements:

   a. Given A = 5.0, B = 10.5, C = 8.2, D = 12.7 and

   ```
   IF (A + B - C * D) 10,20,30
   ```

   which statement will be executed next?

   b. Given X = 5.0, Y = 10.0, Z = 2.0 and

```
IF (Y - X * Z) 80,120,280
```

which statement will be executed next?
c. Given

```
IF (X - Y / X) 10,10,20
```

what is known about X and Y if control passes to statement 10?
d. Given

```
IF (A + B * A) 20,40,20
```

what is known about A and B if control passes to statement 20?

2. Indicate the valid range of values for I in each of the following:

   a. GO TO (80,250,670,980,400),I
   b. GO TO (20,30,40),I

3. Given

   GO TO (80,90,120,760,900),ICON

   what is the value of ICON if control passes to

   a. statement 90?
   b. statement 760?

4. Answer the following questions about the assigned GO TO statements:

   a. Given

      GO TO K,(10,80,95,70)

      what are the valid values for K?
   b. Given

      GO TO L,(180,360,780)

      what is the value of L if control passes to statement 780?

5. Indicate the syntax errors in the following statements:

   a. IF (10 - A * B) 89,90 120
   b. GO TO (10,20,30)I
   c. GO TO I(80,90,80)
   d. ASSIGN K TO L
   e. GO TO 10,20,30,40,K
   f. GO TO K+1(30,40,50)

10.5 Additional Subprogram Features

A FORTRAN subprogram may have more than one point of entry and more than one exit. The main use of multiple entries in structured programming is to package a data structure and the routines that access it. The main use of multiple exits is to provide an error exit for a function when an error flag is useless.

10.5.1 Multiple ENTRY Points

The ENTRY statement is not an executable statement. It simply marks a place in
the subprogram code where entry takes place when the ENTRY name is invoked.
Properly structured subprograms that have more than one entry point should have
an exit for each entry point, and should have separate executable code for each
entry-exit pair. The general form of an ENTRY statement is:

ENTRY name(par1,par2, . . . , parn)

The following example shows three entry points to a subroutine used to hide
the storage of the array X:

```
      SUBROUTINE XPACK
      REAL XMAX, XMIN
      REAL ARRAY X(1000)
      SAVE X

*   ROUTINE TO READ THE ARRAY X

      ENTRY GETX
      . . .
      RETURN

*   ROUTINE TO FIND THE MAXIMUM VALUE IN X

      ENTRY MAX(XMAX)
      . . .
      RETURN

*   ROUTINE TO FIND THE MINIMUM VALUE IN X

      ENTRY MIN(XMIN)
      . . .
      RETURN

      END
```

Notice that the first entry point does not have a parameter list; no parameters are
needed. The array X is saved so that it is available every time the subroutine is
called. The entry point GETX should be called first to input the values of X. Then
MAX(arg) and MIN(arg) can be called whenever the maximum or minimum is
needed. They return the maximum and minimum value, respectively, through their
arguments. All the declarations precede all the entry points. The subroutine name
XPACK will never be invoked. The full subroutine and a debugging driver follow:

```
**********************************************************
*                                                        *
*   DRIVER                                               *
*                                                        *
**********************************************************

      REAL XMAX, XMIN
```

```
          CALL GETX
          CALL MAX(XMAX)
          WRITE (*,*) XMAX
          CALL MIN(XMIN)
          WRITE (*,*) XMIN
          STOP
          END


*****************************************************
*                                                   *
*   PACKAGE HOLDING ARRAY X AND ITS ROUTINES        *
*                                                   *
*****************************************************

          SUBROUTINE XPACK
          REAL XMAX, XMIN
          INTEGER I,N
          REAL ARRAY X(1000)
          SAVE X

*   ROUTINE TO READ THE ARRAY X

          ENTRY GETX
          READ (*,1000) N
1000      FORMAT(I5)
          IF (N .LT. 1 .OR. N .GT. 1000) THEN
             STOP 'INVALID ''N'''
          READ (*,1100,END=100) (X(I),I=1,N)
1100      FORMAT(16F5.0)
          RETURN
100       STOP 'MISSING DATA'

*   ROUTINE TO FIND THE MAXIMUM VALUE IN X

          ENTRY MAX(XMAX)
          XMAX = X(1)
          DO 200 I= 1,N
            IF (X(I) .GT. XMAX) THEN
               XMAX = X(I)
            ENDIF
200       CONTINUE
          RETURN

*   ROUTINE TO FIND THE MINIMUM VALUE IN X

          ENTRY MIN(XMIN)
          XMIN = X(1)
          DO 300 I= 1,N
            IF (X(I) .LT. XMIN) THEN
               XMIN = X(I)
            ENDIF
300       CONTINUE
          RETURN

          END
```

The first time the subroutine package XPACK is called, no arguments are used, because the entry point does not define a parameter list. Each of the other calls passes one argument. The input routine uses two error stop statements, one for invalid values of N, the other for an inconsistency between the value of N and the amount of data present.

If a subprogram with multiple entry points is a function, the entry points may have different types. The following example returns either the larger or the smaller of two values:

```
      FUNCTION COMPAR(X,Y)
      INTEGER X,Y
      INTEGER GREAT, SMALL

*   ROUTINE TO RETURN THE LARGER VALUE

      ENTRY GREAT(X,Y)
      IF (X .GT. Y) THEN
        GREAT = X
      ELSE
        GREAT = Y
      ENDIF
      RETURN

*   ROUTINE TO RETURN THE SMALLER VALUE

      ENTRY SMALL(X,Y)
      IF (X .LT. Y) THEN
        SMALL = X
      ELSE
        SMALL = Y
      ENDIF
      RETURN
      END
```

The types of the entry points must also be declared in the calling program:

```
INTEGER GREAT,SMALL
. . .
K = GREAT(I,J)
L = SMALL(I,J)
```

10.5.2 Multiple Exits

The RETURN statement, as used so far, has always returned to the point where the subprogram was invoked. A subprogram that has multiple exits can return to the point of invocation or to other points specified in the call. An example of such a call is:

```
      CALL SUB1 (A,B,C,*S1,D,E,*S2,*S3)
```

where A, B, C, D, and E are ordinary variables and S1, S2, and S3 are the labels of the statements to which control may be returned. The matching subroutine header is:

```
SUBROUTINE SUB1 (X,Y,Z,*,W,V,*,*)
```

where X, Y, Z, W, and V are dummy variables and the asterisks correspond to the label arguments.

The corresponding RETURN statements are:

```
RETURN 1                returns control to statement S1
RETURN 2                returns control to statement S2
RETURN 3                returns control to statement S3
```

That is, the RETURN statements are numbered to correspond to the position of the desired return point in a list of return points.

10.5.3 BLOCK DATA Subprograms

The BLOCK DATA subprogram provides a way of preinitializing a shared data area. It plays the role for shared data that a PARAMETER statement plays for local data. Both may be used to initialize variables, but are more appropriately used for constants. Do not preinitialize both constants and variables because it makes it impossible for a person reading the program to distinguish between them.

Programming Hint

> Readability: Preinitialize constants, but do not preinitialize variables.

The general form of the BLOCK DATA subprogram is:

BLOCK DATA [subprogram name]

.

.   named COMMON statements

. .

.   type statements

.

.   DATA or PARAMETER statements

.

END

Any statements used in the declarative part of a program may be used in a BLOCK DATA subprogram, except an unnamed COMMON statement, but no executable statements may be used. A BLOCK DATA subprogram is not executed. Instead, it is used by the compiler to allocate and initialize an area of shared storage.

Folllowing is an example of a BLOCK DATA subprogram:

```
**********************************************************
*                                                        *
*   CONSTANTS USED IN MATHEMATICS AND PHYSICS,           *
*   AND SHARED TABLES                                    *
*                                                        *
**********************************************************

      BLOCK DATA
      COMMON /GEOM/PI,E,SEMIPI,LOG2
```

```
      REAL PI,E,SEMIPI,LOG2
      DATA PI,E,SEMIPI,LOG2/
     1      3.14159,2.71828,1.57080,.301030/

      COMMON /PHYS/G,ATPRES
      REAL G,ATPRES
      DATA G,APRES/32.0,14.7/

      COMMON /TABLES/N,X(100),Y(100)
      REAL X,Y
      INTEGER N
      END
```

BLOCK DATA subprograms may also contain uninitialized common areas to be used for storing variables. Separating the various common areas in the block data statement improves readability. Also, the descriptions of the various common areas can be easily copied to other places where they are needed. The following code shows the use of these common areas:

```
*     MAIN PROGRAM
      . . .
      STOP
      END

      SUBROUTINE A
      COMMON /GEOM/PI,E,SEMIPI,LOG2
      REAL PI,E,SEMIPI,LOG2
      COMMON /TABLES/N,X(100),Y(100)
      REAL X,Y
      INTEGER N
      . . .
      RETURN
      END

      SUBROUTINE B
      COMMON /TABLES/N,X(100),Y(100)
      REAL X,Y
      INTEGER N
      . . .
      RETURN
      END

      SUBROUTINE C
      COMMON /GEOM/PI,E,SEMIPI,LOG2
      REAL PI,E,SEMIPI,LOG2
      COMMON /PHYS/G,C
      REAL G,C
      . . .
      RETURN
      END

      SUBROUTINE D
      COMMON /PHYS/G,C
```

```
REAL G,C
 . . .
RETURN
END
```

As shown in this example, preinitialized shared data values are made available to subprograms the same way other common areas are made available. The BLOCK DATA subprogram provides an appropriate place to document the use of the common areas.

10.5.4 Review Questions

1. Indicate whether the following statements are true or false:

   a. A FORTRAN subprogram cannot have more than one entry point.
   b. The ENTRY statement is an executable statement.
   c. A FORTRAN subprogram can have more than one exit.
   d. Separate code with separate entry points and exits may not share the same data.
   e. It is possible for a subprogram to have several entry points and a single exit or several exits and a single entry point.
   f. BLOCK DATA subprograms may contain uninitialized common areas to be used for storing variables.
   g. Values in a BLOCK DATA subprogram are reinitialized every time they are used.

10.6 Sample Programs Using Advanced Features

These programs illustrate the use of the advanced data types and subroutine and function packages using multiple entries and exits. The programs were executed interactively on the Digital Equipment Corporation (DEC) computer model VAX 11/780.

10.6.1 Waterflow through Pipes

Problem

Write a program to compute the velocity and mass flow rate of water at 80°F through a pipe of diameter D flowing at a rate of G gal/min.

Pseudocode

Convert the flow rate from G gal/min into cu ft/min
$$1 \text{ cu ft} = 7.4909964 \text{ gal}$$
Compute the cross-sectional area of the pipe in sq ft
Compute the velocity in ft/sec
Compute the mass flow rate
$$M = \rho \, AV \qquad \text{where AV is volume rate of flow}$$
$$\rho \text{ is the density of the liquid}$$
$$\text{and } \rho = 1/V \qquad \text{V is the specific volume}$$

```
      ************************************************************
      *                                                          *
      *    PROGRAM TO CALCULATE VELOCITY AND MASS FLOW RATE      *
      *                                                          *
      ************************************************************
      *                                                          *
      *    INPUT VARIABLES:                                      *
      *                                                          *
      *       GAL    -   FLOW RATE (GALLONS PER MINUTE)          *
      *       DIAM   -   DIAMETER OF PIPE (FEET)                 *
      *       SPVOL  -   SPECIFIC VOLUME                         *
      *                                                          *
      *    OUTPUT VARIABLES:                                     *
      *                                                          *
      *       GAL    -   FLOW RATE (GALLONS PER MINUTE)          *
      *       QUANTY -   FLOW RATE (CUBIC FEET PER MINUTE)       *
      *       VELCTY -   VELOCITY (FEET PER MINUTE)              *
      *       MFRATE -   MASS FLOW RATE                          *
      *                                                          *
      ************************************************************

            DOUBLE PRECISION MFRATE,VELCTY,AREA,SPVOL,DIAM,
           1      GAL,QUANTY
            DOUBLE PRECISION PI,CBFT
            PARAMETER (PI=3.141592653,CBFT=7.4909964)

            WRITE (*,*) 'INPUT GALLONS, DIAMETER, AND ',
           1      'SPECIFIC VOLUME'
            READ (*,1000) GAL, DIAM, SPVOL
      1000  FORMAT(3D10.0)
            QUANTY = GAL / CBFT
            AREA = (PI * DIAM * DIAM) / 4.0D0
            VELCTY = QUANTY / AREA
            MFRATE = AREA * VELCTY / SPVOL
            WRITE (*,1500)
      1500  FORMAT(/1X,'OUTPUT OF THE RESULTS'/)
            WRITE (*,2000) QUANTY, VELCTY, MFRATE
      2000  FORMAT(1X,D14.8,4X,D14.8,4X,D14.8)
            STOP
            END
```

Output

```
 INPUT GALLONS, DIAMETER, AND SPECIFIC VOLUME
 10000.0    5.0         1.0

 OUTPUT OF THE RESULTS

 0.13349359D+04       0.67987943D+02       0.13349359D+04
```

10.6.2 Distance between Two Points in a Complex Plane

Problem

Write a function to calculate the distance between the points Z1 and Z2 in a complex plane.

Method

The formula for the distance between two points in a complex plane is:

$$\text{dist} = \sqrt{(Z1_{re} - Z2_{re})^2 + (Z1_{imag} - Z2_{imag})^2}$$

This is the same as the formula for the absolute value of $(Z1 - Z2)$. A statement function can be used because, even though the arguments are complex, the value returned is real.

Program

```
*****************************************************************
*                                                               *
*   DISTANCE BETWEEN TWO POINTS IN THE COMPLEX PLANE   *
*                                                               *
*****************************************************************
*                                                               *
*   INPUT VARIABLES:                                            *
*                                                               *
*     Z1,Z2        - COORDINATES OF THE POINTS                  *
*                                                               *
*   OUTPUT VARIABLES:                                           *
*                                                               *
*     CDIST        - DISTANCE BETWEEN THE POINTS                *
*                                                               *
*****************************************************************

        COMPLEX Z1,Z2
        REAL CDIST

        WRITE (*,1000)
1000    FORMAT(1X,'INPUT TWO COORDINATE POINTS IN A ',
       1        'COMPLEX PLANE')
        READ (*,2000) Z1,Z2
2000    FORMAT(4F8.2)
        CDIST = CABS(Z1-Z2)
        WRITE (*,3000) CDIST
3000    FORMAT(/1X,'THE DISTANCE BETWEEN THE POINTS ='
       1        ,F10.6)
        END
```

Output from Two Runs

```
INPUT TWO COORDINATE POINTS IN A COMPLEX PLANE
2.5      3.5      6.5      7.5

THE DISTANCE BETWEEN THE POINTS =  5.656854

INPUT TWO COORDINATE POINTS IN A COMPLEX PLANE
1.0      5.0      3.0      2.0

THE DISTANCE BETWEEN THE POINTS = 3.605551
```

10.6.3 Secant, Cosecant, Cotangent One

Problem

Write a function to calculate either a secant, cosecant, or cotangent of an angle.

Method

Two different methods are shown. First, a switch is used to show which function is wanted. Second, a different entry point is used for each trigonometric function. The formulas for the functions are:

$$\sec(\theta) = 1/\cos(\theta) \qquad \theta /= \pi/2, 3\pi/2, 5\pi/2, \ldots$$
$$\csc(\theta) = 1/\sin(\theta) \qquad \theta /= 0, \pi, 2\pi, \ldots$$
$$\cot(\theta) = 1/\tan(\theta) \qquad \theta /= 0, \pi, 2\pi, \ldots$$

An error return is used for invalid angles.

Program

```
*******************************************************
*                                                     *
*    MAIN DRIVER                                       *
*                                                     *
*******************************************************

      REAL ANGLE,VALUE
      INTEGER ISW
      CHARACTER FNC*3

      WRITE (*,1000)
1000  FORMAT(1X,'INPUT FUNCTION AND ANGLE')
      READ (*,2000) FNC,ANGLE
2000  FORMAT(A3,1X,F5.0)
```

```
          IF(FNC .EQ. 'SEC') ISW = 1
          IF(FNC .EQ. 'CSC') ISW = 2
          IF(FNC .EQ. 'COT') ISW = 3
          CALL TRIG(ANGLE,ISW,VALUE,*10)

          WRITE (*,3000) FNC,VALUE
3000      FORMAT(/X,'OUTPUT OF VALUE OF ',A3,' =',F10.2)
          STOP

10        CONTINUE
          STOP 'INVALID ANGLE'
          END


***************************************************************
*                                                             *
*    SUBROUTINE TO CALCULATE SECANT, COSECANT, OR             *
*    COTANGENT                                                *
*                                                             *
***************************************************************
*                                                             *
*    INPUT PARAMETERS:                                        *
*                                                             *
*       ANGLE   - ANGLE IN DEGREES                            *
*       SW      - SWITCH   1) SEC   2) CSC   3) COT           *
*                                                             *
*    OUTPUT PARAMETERS:                                       *
*                                                             *
*       VALUE   - VALUE OF SECANT, COSECANT, OR               *
*                 COTANGENT                                   *
*                                                             *
***************************************************************

          SUBROUTINE TRIG(ANGLE,SW,VALUE,*)
          REAL ANGLE,SINA,COSA,TANA,VALUE,PI,RADANG
          INTEGER SW
          PARAMETER (PI=3.14159)

          RADANG = ANGLE * PI / 180.0
          IF (SW .LT. 1 .OR. SW .GT. 3) STOP 'INVALID',
     1      ' SWITCH'
          GO TO (10,20,30),SW

*    CALCULATE SECANT

10        COSA = COS(RADANG)

          IF (ABS(COSA) .LE. 0.00001) RETURN 1
          VALUE = 1.0 / COSA
          RETURN

*    CALCULATE COSECANT
```

```
20      SINA = SIN(RADANG)
        IF (ABS(SINA) .LE. 0.00001) RETURN 1
        VALUE = 1.0 / SINA
        RETURN

*   CALCULATE COTANGENT

30      TANA = TAN(RADANG)
        IF (ABS(TANA) .LE. 0.00001) RETURN 1
        VALUE = 1.0 / TANA
        RETURN

        END
```

Output of Three Runs

```
INPUT FUNCTION AND ANGLE
CSC 60.0

OUTPUT OF VALUE OF CSC =         1.15


INPUT FUNCTION AND ANGLE
SEC 30.0

OUTPUT OF VALUE OF SEC =         1.15


INPUT FUNCTION AND ANGLE
SEC 90.0
INVALID ANGLE
```

10.6.4 Secant, Cosecant, Cotangent Two

Rather than using a switch to determine which function is being called, multiple entry points can be used, as in the following adaptation of the program of Section 10.6.3.

Program

```
**********************************************************
*                                                        *
*    MAIN DRIVER                                          *
*                                                        *
**********************************************************

        REAL ANGLE,VALUE
        CHARACTER FNC*3
```

```
          WRITE (*,1000)
1000      FORMAT(1X,'INPUT FUNCTION AND ANGLE')

          READ (*,2000) FNC,ANGLE
2000      FORMAT(A3,F5.0)

          IF(FNC .EQ. 'SEC') THEN
             CALL SEC(ANGLE,VALUE,*10)
          ELSEIF(FNC .EQ. 'CSC') THEN
             CALL CSC(ANGLE,VALUE,*10)
          ELSEIF(FNC .EQ. 'COT') THEN
             CALL COT(ANGLE,VALUE,*10)
          ELSE
             STOP 'INVALID FUNCTION'
          ENDIF
          WRITE (*,3000) FNC,VALUE
3000      FORMAT(/X,'OUTPUT OF VALUE OF ',A3,' =',F10.2)
          STOP

10        CONTINUE
          STOP 'INVALID ANGLE'
          END

*********************************************************
*                                                       *
*   SUBROUTINE TO CALCULATE SECANT, COSECANT, OR        *
*   COTANGENT                                           *
*                                                       *
*********************************************************
*                                                       *
*   INPUT PARAMETERS:                                   *
*                                                       *
*      ANGLE   - ANGLE IN DEGREES                       *
*      *       - ERROR RETURN                           *
*                                                       *
*   OUTPUT PARAMETERS:                                  *
*                                                       *
*      VALUE   - VALUE OF SECANT, COSECANT, OR          *
*                COTANGENT                              *
*                                                       *
*********************************************************

          SUBROUTINE TRIG(ANGLE,VALUE,*)
          REAL ANGLE,SINA,COSA,TANA,VALUE,PI,RADANG
          PARAMETER (PI=3.14159)

          ENTRY SEC(ANGLE,VALUE,*)
          RADANG = ANGLE * PI / 180.0
          COSA = COS(RADANG)
          IF (ABS(COSA) .LE. 0.00001) RETURN 1
          VALUE = 1.0 / COSA
          RETURN
```

```
     ENTRY CSC(ANGLE,VALUE,*)
     RADANG = ANGLE * PI / 180.0
     SINA = SIN(RADANG)
     IF (ABS(SINA) .LE. 0.00001) RETURN 1
     VALUE = 1.0 / SINA
     RETURN

     ENTRY COT(ANGLE,VALUE,*)
     RADANG = ANGLE * PI / 180.0
     TANA = TAN(RADANG)
     IF (ABS(TANA) .EQ. 0.00001) RETURN 1
     VALUE = 1.0 / TANA
     RETURN

     END
```

In this example it is very tempting to combine the code for the three functions, because they differ only in the call on the library function. However, if this were done, it would not be possible, for instance, to change the code for cot(θ) from $1/\tan(\theta)$ to $\cos(\theta)/\sin(\theta)$ without rewriting the entire program. The example with the separate entry points is preferred; not having a switch, it is less error prone. Abnormal exits are used because the functions are not defined for all values of the angle.

10.6.5 Sum of Positive and Sum of Negative Numbers One

Problem

Write a program to input an array of *n* elements. Write a subroutine to compute both the sum of the positive numbers and the sum of the negative numbers in the array and return the sum with the larger magnitude.

Method

Input the data
Invoke the subroutine passing the array
Print whichever sum is returned, labeled appropriately
The subroutine should use an arithmetic IF statement to compare the sums and select the correct exit

Program

```
******************************************************
*                                                    *
*   MAIN PROGRAM DRIVER                              *
*                                                    *
******************************************************

     REAL X(100),SUMX
     INTEGER N
```

```
          WRITE (*,1000)
1000   FORMAT(1X,'INPUT THE NUMBER OF VALUES OF ',
     1        'THE ARRAY X')
          READ (*,*) N
          WRITE (*,2000)
2000   FORMAT(/1X,'INPUT THE VALUES OF ARRAY X')
          READ (*,*) (X(I), I=1,N)
          WRITE (*,*)
          CALL MAXSUM(X,N,SUMX,*10,*20,*30)

10     WRITE (*,*) 'SUM OF POSITIVE NUMBERS =',SUMX
          STOP

20     WRITE (*,*) 'THE SUMS ARE EQUAL'
          STOP

30     WRITE (*,*) 'SUM OF NEGATIVE NUMBERS =',SUMX
          STOP
          END

*************************************************************
*                                                           *
*   SUBROUTINE TO FIND GREATER IN ABSOLUTE VALUE OF         *
*   SUM OF POSITIVE VALUES, SUM OF NEGATIVE VALUES          *
*   OF X                                                    *
*                                                           *
*************************************************************
*                                                           *
*   INPUT PARAMETERS:                                       *
*                                                           *
*     X(N)          - LIST OF NUMBERS                       *
*     N             - NUMBER OF VALUES IN LIST              *
*                                                           *
*   OUTPUT PARAMETERS:                                      *
*                                                           *
*     BIGSUM        - SUM WITH LARGER MAGNITUDE             *
*                                                           *
*   RETURNS:                                                *
*                                                           *
*     RETURN 1                      POSITIVE SUM            *
*     RETURN 2                      SUMS ARE EQUAL          *
*     RETURN 3                      NEGATIVE SUM            *
*                                                           *
*************************************************************

          SUBROUTINE MAXSUM(X,N,BIGSUM,*,*,*)
          REAL X(N),PSUM,NSUM,BIGSUM
          INTEGER I,N

          PSUM = 0.0
          NSUM = 0.0
          BIGSUM = 0.0
          DO 30 I = 1,N
```

```
           IF (X(I))10,30,20
10            NSUM = NSUM + X(I)
           GO TO 30

20            PSUM = PSUM + X(I)

30         CONTINUE
           IF (PSUM + NSUM)40,50,60
40            BIGSUM = NSUM
           RETURN 3

50            RETURN 2

60            BIGSUM = PSUM
           RETURN 1
           END
```

Output from Three Runs

```
INPUT THE NUMBER OF VALUES OF THE ARRAY X
5

INPUT THE VALUES OF ARRAY X
-9,3,-6,5,-10

SUM OF NEGATIVE NUMBERS =   -25.00000


INPUT THE NUMBER OF VALUES OF THE ARRAY X
5

INPUT THE VALUES OF ARRAY X
3,9,-6,5,-8

SUM OF POSITIVE NUMBERS =    17.00000
INPUT THE NUMBER OF VALUES OF THE ARRAY X
5

INPUT THE VALUES OF ARRAY X
-5,-5,-5,7,8

THE SUMS ARE EQUAL
```

Nonstructured features such as these returns must always be carefully documented, as they are error prone. RETURN 1 returns control to statement 10 of the calling program, RETURN 2 returns control to statement 20, and RETURN 3 returns control to statement 30. Rather than using multiple returns, the value of XSUM could be tested in the calling program and the appropriate output printed. This subroutine demonstrates a natural use of the arithmetic IF statement.

10.6.6 Sum of Positive and Sum of Negative Numbers Two

Problem

Write a program to input an array of *n* elements and store it in a COMMON area. Write a subroutine to compute either the sum of the positive numbers or the sum of the negative numbers in the array, depending on the entry point used.

Method

Write the subroutine so that it computes either the sum of the positive numbers or the sum of the negative numbers but not both. Note that in this program there are no values to save since the array is in COMMON and only one sum is being computed.

Program

```
*******************************************************
*                                                     *
*   MAIN PROGRAM DRIVER                               *
*                                                     *
*******************************************************
      COMMON X(100)
      REAL POSSUM,NEGSUM
      INTEGER I,N

      WRITE (*,1000)
1000  FORMAT(1X,'INPUT THE NUMBER OF VALUES OF THE ',
     1        'ARRAY X')
      READ (*,*) N
      WRITE (*,2000)
2000  FORMAT(/1X,'INPUT THE VALUES OF ARRAY X')
      READ (*,*) (X(I), I=1,N)
      WRITE (*,3000)
3000  FORMAT(/1X,'OUTPUT OF RESULTS'/)
      WRITE (*,*) 'SUM OF POSITIVE NUMBERS ='
     1        ,POSSUM(N)
      WRITE (*,*) 'SUM OF NEGATIVE NUMBERS ='
     1        ,NEGSUM(N)
      STOP
      END
```

```
*************************************************************
*                                                           *
*    SUBROUTINE TO CALCULATE SUM OF POSITIVE VALUES         *
*    OF X AND SUM OF NEGATIVE VALUES OF X                   *
*                                                           *
*************************************************************
*                                                           *
*    COMMON:                                                *
*                                                           *
*      X(N)            - LIST OF NUMBERS                     *
*                                                           *
*    INPUT PARAMETERS:                                      *
*                                                           *
*      N               - NUMBER OF VALUES IN LIST           *
*                                                           *
*    OUTPUT PARAMETERS:                                     *
*                                                           *
*      POSSUM OR NEGSUM - SUM OF POSITIVE OR NEGATIVE        *
*                              NUMBERS                       *
*                                                           *
*************************************************************

       REAL FUNCTION SUM(N)
       COMMON X(100)
       REAL PSUM,NSUM,POSSUM,NEGSUM
       INTEGER I,N

       ENTRY POSSUM(N)
       PSUM = 0.0
       DO 10 I = 1,N
         IF (X(I) .GT. 0) THEN
           PSUM = PSUM + X(I)
         ENDIF
10       CONTINUE
       SUM = PSUM
       RETURN

       ENTRY NEGSUM(N)
       NSUM = 0.0
       DO 20 I = 1,N
         IF (X(I) .LT. 0) THEN
           NSUM = NSUM + X(I)
         ENDIF
20       CONTINUE
       SUM = NSUM
       RETURN
       END
```

Output

```
INPUT THE NUMBER OF VALUES OF THE ARRAY X
5

INPUT THE VALUES OF ARRAY X
1.0,2.0,30.0,-5.0,-3.0

OUTPUT OF THE RESULTS

SUM OF POSITIVE NUMBERS =   33.00000
SUM OF NEGATIVE NUMBERS =   -8.000000
```

Notice that the result of the function is always assigned to the function name SUM in order to be returned.

Summary

Chapter 10 introduced two FORTRAN 77 advanced data types:

DOUBLE PRECISION var1,var2,...,varn

which makes it possible to carry out calculations to more significant digits than REAL variables, and

COMPLEX var1,var2,...,varn

which implements complex numbers. Addition, subtraction, multiplication, and division are supported for these variable types. In addition, they may be used as the base number in exponentiation.

Two other declarative statements were discussed:

DATA var-list1/val-list1/var-list2/val-list2/...

is used to initialize variables. The computer does not distinguish between its use and that of the PARAMETER statement except in BLOCK DATA subprograms, where the DATA statement must be used. Limit your use of the DATA statement to initializing variables and the PARAMETER statement to initializing constants.

EQUIVALENCE (var1,var2),(var3,var4),...

is used to associate more than one name and data description with the same location in memory. If the associated variables are not of the same type, the bit pattern in that location will represent two different values.

The unconditional transfer of control,

GO TO label

should only be used to implement standard structured programming constructs.

The logical IF statement and three versions of the case statement were discussed:

IF (logical value) statement

executes a single statement if the logical value is true;

IF (arith value)label1,label2,label3

effects a three-way branch depending on the sign of the value;

GO TO (label1,label2,...,labeln),expr

effects an n-way branch depending on the value of the expression, whether it is 1, 2, . . . , or $n;$

ASSIGN label TO var

. . .

GO TO var,(label1,label2, . . . , labeln)

effects a multiway branch depending on which label matches the value of the variable.

The PAUSE and PAUSE n statements were discussed, and the STOP and STOP n statements, which are used for output of error messages.

Packages of subroutines and functions can be constructed by using multiple entries and exits. In general, good programming style requires each entry point to have its own set of code and its own exits. Mingling code and multiple use of a single exit can lead to programming errors.

The BLOCK DATA subprogram is used to initialize values in a shared data area. It does not contain any executable statements, only data declarations. The general form of the BLOCK DATA subprogram is:

BLOCK DATA subname
    named COMMON statements
    type declarations
    DATA or PARAMETER statements
    END

Exercises

1. Write a subroutine package that implements matrix addition, subtraction, and multiplication. It should accept matrices of any size as input. Be sure to validate the matrix sizes for each operation.

2. Write a subroutine ROOT(N,Z,R) that returns the N nth roots of a complex number Z.

3. Write a program that finds all the real roots of a general cubic polynomial $f(x) = ax^3 + bx^2 + cx + d = 0$. Note that there must be either one real root or three real roots. If there are three distinct real roots, one of them is between the values of x for which $3ax^2 + 2bx + c = 0$ (the relative maximum and minimum); one is less than those values of x; and one is greater. Use double-precision values.

4. Write a subroutine package using multiple entries and exits to add, subtract, and multiply $n \times n$ matrices.

5. Write a program that computes the paychecks of employees of an industrial firm. Use a code to indicate the frequency of payment for each employee: 1 for weekly, 2 for biweekly, and 3 for monthly. Deduct .5% for taxes from each weekly paycheck, 1% from each biweekly paycheck, and 2% from each monthly paycheck. The input on a formatted sequential file EMPLYE has the layout:

cols.   1– 9   social security number
          10   code for paycheck frequency
        11–15   amount earned per pay period (dollars)

Use a computed GO TO to separate the categories of employees.

6. Write a function subprogram AVG(X) that returns the MEAN, MEDIAN, or MODE of the list X of measurements, depending on which entry name is used. The three averages are defined as follows:

$$\text{mean} = \sum_{i=1}^{n} x_i$$

median = middle value when the list is sorted
mode = most frequent value (assuming there is one)

Appendix A

Common Character Representations

CHAR-ACTER	BCD (6-BIT)	OCTAL	ASCII (7-BIT)	HEX	EBCDIC (8-BIT)	HEX
A	010 001	21	100 0001	41	1100 0001	C1
B	010 010	22	100 0010	42	1100 0010	C2
C	010 011	23	100 0011	43	1100 0011	C3
D	010 100	24	100 0100	44	1100 0100	C4
E	010 101	25	100 0101	45	1100 0101	C5
F	010 110	26	100 0110	46	1100 0110	C6
G	010 111	27	100 0111	47	1100 0111	C7
H	011 000	30	100 1000	48	1100 1000	C8
I	011 001	31	100 1001	49	1100 1001	C9
J	100 001	41	100 1010	4A	1101 0001	D1
K	100 010	42	100 1011	4B	1101 0010	D2
L	100 011	43	100 1100	4C	1101 0011	D3
M	100 100	44	100 1101	4D	1101 0100	D4
N	100 101	45	100 1110	4E	1101 0101	D5
O	100 110	46	100 1111	4F	1101 0110	D6
P	100 111	47	101 0000	50	1101 0111	D7
Q	101 000	50	101 0001	51	1101 1000	D8
R	101 001	51	101 0010	52	1101 1001	D9
S	110 010	62	101 0011	53	1110 0010	E2
T	110 011	63	101 0100	54	1110 0011	E3
U	110 100	64	101 0101	55	1110 0100	E4
V	110 101	65	101 0110	56	1110 0101	E5
W	110 110	66	101 0111	57	1110 0110	E6
X	110 111	67	101 1000	58	1110 0111	E7
Y	111 000	70	101 1001	59	1110 1000	E8
Z	111 001	71	101 1010	5A	1110 1001	E9
0	000 000	00	011 0000	30	1111 0000	F0
1	000 001	01	011 0001	31	1111 0001	F1
2	000 010	02	011 0010	32	1111 0010	F2
3	000 011	02	011 0011	33	1111 0011	F3
4	000 100	04	011 0100	34	1111 0100	F4
5	000 101	05	011 0101	35	1111 0101	F5
6	000 110	06	011 0110	36	1111 0110	F6
7	000 111	07	011 0111	37	1111 0111	F7
8	001 000	10	011 1000	38	1111 1000	F8
9	001 001	11	011 1001	39	1111 1001	F9
b	110 000	60	010 0000	20	0100 0000	40
$	101 011	53	010 0100	24	0101 1011	5B
+	010 000	20	010 1011	2B	0100 1110	4E
−	100 000	40	010 1101	2D	0110 0000	60

CHAR-ACTER	BCD (6-BIT)	OCTAL	ASCII (7-BIT)	HEX	EBCDIC (8-BIT)	HEX
*	101 100	54	010 1010	2A	0101 1100	5C
/	110 001	61	010 1111	2F	0110 0001	61
=	001 011	13	011 1101	3D	0111 1110	7E
.	011 011	33	010 1110	2E	0100 1011	4B
,	111 011	73	010 1100	2C	0110 1011	6B
:	001 001	11	011 1010	3A	0111 1010	7A
(	111 100	74	010 1000	28	0100 1101	4D
)	011 100	34	010 1001	29	0101 1101	5D
,			010 0111	27	0111 1101	7D

Common Numeric Representations

DECIMAL	BINARY	OCTAL	BINARY	HEXADECIMAL	BINARY
0	0000	00	000 000	0	0000
1	0001	01	000 001	1	0001
2	0010	02	000 010	2	0010
3	0011	02	000 011	3	0011
4	0100	04	000 100	4	0100
5	0101	05	000 101	5	0101
6	0110	06	000 110	6	0110
7	0111	07	000 111	7	0111
8	1000	10	001 000	8	1000
9	1001	11	001 001	9	1001
10	1010	12	001 010	A	1010
11	1011	13	001 011	B	1011
12	1100	14	001 100	C	1100
13	1101	15	001 101	D	1101
14	1110	16	001 110	E	1110
15	1111	17	001 111	F	1111

Appendix B

Standard FORTRAN 77 Library Functions

Key: Argument types are:
- N integer
- X real
- D double precision
- Z complex
- S character string

Type Conversion Functions

RESULT TYPE	ARGUMENT TYPE				
	INTEGER	REAL	DOUBLE	COMPLEX	CHAR-ACTER
INTEGER		INT (X) IFIX (X) NINT (X)	INT (D) IDINT (D) IDNINT (D)	INT (Z)	ICHAR (S)
REAL	REAL (N) FLOAT (N)	AINT (X) ANINT (X)	REAL (D) SNGL (D)	REAL (Z) AIMAG (Z)	
DOUBLE	DBLE (N)	DBLE (X)	DINT (D) DNINT (D)	DBLE (Z)	
COMPLEX	CMPLX (N1,N2)	CMPLX (X1,X2)	CMPLX (D1,D2)		
CHAR	CHAR (N)				

FUNCTION TYPE	GENERIC	REAL	DOUBLE	COMPLEX
Trigonometric functions				
sine	SIN	SIN (X)	DSIN (D)	CSIN (Z)
cosine	COS	COS (X)	DCOS (D)	CCOS (Z)
tangent	TAN	TAN (X)	DTAN (D)	
arc sine	ASIN	ASIN (X)	DASIN (D)	
arc cosine	ACOS	ACOS (X)	DACOS (D)	
arc tangent	ATAN	ATAN (X)	DATAN (D)	
hyperbolic sine	SINH	SINH (X)	DSINH (D)	
hyperbolic cosine	COSH	COSH (X)	DCOSH (D)	
hyperbolic tangent	TANH	TANH (X)	DTANH (D)	

Other mathematical functions

FUNCTION TYPE	GENERIC	REAL	DOUBLE	COMPLEX
exponent of e	EXP	EXP (X)	DEXP (D)	CEXP (Z)
natural logarithm	LOG	ALOG (X)	DLOG (D)	CLOG (Z)
common logarithm	LOG10	ALOG10 (X)	DLOG10 (D)	
complex conjugate				CONJG (Z)
square root	SQRT	SQRT (X)	DSQRT (D)	CSQRT (Z)
positive difference	DIM	DIM (X1,X2)	DDIM (D1,D2)	
IDIM (N1,N1) integer				
product			DPROD (D1,D2)	
maximum value	MAX	AMAX1 (X1, . . . ,Xn)	DMAX1 (D1, . . . ,Dn)	
MAX0 (N1, . . . ,Nn) integer				
minimum value	MIN	AMIN1 (X1, . . . ,Xn)	DMIN1 (D1, . . . ,Dn)	
MIN0 (N1, . . . ,Nn) integer				
sign	SIGN	ASIGN (X)	DSIGN (D)	
ISIGN (N) integer				
remainder	MOD	AMOD (X1,X2)	DMOD (D1,D2)	
absolute value	ABS	ABS (X)	DABS (D)	CABS (Z)
IABS (N) integer				
truncated		AINT (X)	DINT (D)	
rounded		ANINT (X)	DNINT (D)	

Character string functions

LEN (S)	returns length of character string
INDEX (S1,S2)	returns position of substring S2 in S1
LGE (S1,S2)	returns logical value of comparison S1 $\geq$ S2
LGT (S1,S2)	returns logical value of comparison S1 $>$ S2
LLE (S1,S2)	returns logical value of comparison S1 $\leq$ S2
LLT (S1,S2)	returns logical value of comparison S1 $<$ S2

Rules for Mixed Mode Arithmetic

Type used for arithmetic and type of result

FIRST OPERAND	SECOND OPERAND			
	INTEGER	REAL	DOUBLE	COMPLEX
INTEGER	integer	real	double	complex
REAL	real	real	double	complex
DOUBLE	double	double	double	ERROR
COMPLEX	complex	complex	ERROR	complex

Appendix C

FORTRAN 77 Structures and Statements

Program structures

```
PROGRAM progname
    declarations
    initializations
    statement functions
    executable code
STOP
END

fncname(arg1,arg2,...) = expr

type FUNCTION fncname(arg1,arg2,...)
    declarations
    initializations
    statement functions
    executable code
    fncname = expr
RETURN
END

SUBROUTINE subname(arg1,arg2,...)
    declarations
    initializations
    statement functions
    executablecode
RETURN
END

BLOCK DATA
COMMON ...
    declarations
    initializations
END
```

Declarative statements

```
scalar variables
REAL var1,var2,...
INTEGER var1,var2,...
COMPLEX var1,var2,...
DOUBLE PRECISION var1,var2,...
LOGICAL var1,var2,...
CHARACTER var1*k1,var2*k2,...
CHARACTER*k var1,var2,...
```

arrays
DIMENSION arr1(d1,...),arr2(d2,...),...
REAL arr1(d1,...),arr2(d2,...),...
INTEGER arr1(d1,...),arr2(d2,...),...
COMPLEX arr1(d1,...),arr2(d2,...),...
DOUBLE PRECISION arr1(d1,...),arr2(d2,...),...
LOGICAL arr1(d1,...),arr2(d2,...),...
CHARACTER*k arr1*k1(d1,...),arr2*k2(d2,...),...

initialization
DATA varlist1/valuelist1/varlist2/valuelist2/...
PARAMETER (var1 = val1,var2 = val2,...)

miscellaneous
IMPLICIT type (ch1-ch2,ch3-ch4,...)
EQUIVALENCE (var1,var2),(var3,var4),...
COMMON var1,var2,...,varn
COMMON /name1/varlist1/name2/varlist2...
SAVE var1,var2,...
ENTRY entryname(arg1,arg2,...)
FORMAT(spec1,spec2,...)

Executable statements

assignment statement
var = expr
ASSIGN label TO labelvar

control statements
GO TO label
GO TO (label1,label2,...), expr
GO TO labelvar, (label1,label2,...)
IF (arith expr)label1,label2,label3
IF (condition) executable instruction
STOP
STOP n
PAUSE
PAUSE n
CALL entryname(arglist)
RETURN
RETURN n
END

file statements
READ(*,*) inputlist
READ fmt, inputlist
READ (lun,FORMAT = fmt,END = label1,ERR = label2,
        IOSTAT = var) inputlist
READ (lun,FORMAT = fmt,END = label1,ERR = label2,
        IOSTAT = var,REC = bytes) inputlist
PRINT fmt, outputlist
WRITE(*,*) outputlist
WRITE (lun,FORMAT = fmt,ERR = label1,IOSTAT = var)
        outputlist

```
WRITE (lun,FORMAT = fmt,ERR = label1,IOSTAT = var,
        REC = bytes) outputlist
OPEN (UNIT = lun,ERR = label,IOSTAT = var,FILE = file,
        STATUS = stat,BLANK = ch)
OPEN (UNIT = lun,ERR = label,IOSTAT = var,FILE = file,
        STATUS = stat,ACCESS = 'DIRECT',FORM = form,
        RECL = bytes,BLANK = ch)
CLOSE (UNIT = lun,ERR = label,IOSTAT = var,STATUS = stat)
INQUIRY (FILE = file, querylist)
INQUIRY (UNIT = lun, querylist)
REWIND lun
REWIND (UNIT = lun,ERR = label,IOSTAT = var)
BACKSPACE lun
BACKSPACE (UNIT = lun,ERR = label,IOSTAT = var)
ENDFILE lun
ENDFILE (UNIT = lun,ERR = label,IOSTAT = var)
```

Format Specifications	Control characters	
Iw	ƀ	single space
Aw	0	double space
Fw.d	1	advance page
Ew.d	+	overprint
Dw.d		
Gw.d		
nX		
Tn		
'...'		
/		
n(...)		

Relational operators	Logical operators
.LT.	.NOT.
.LE.	.AND.
.EQ.	.OR.
.NE.	.EQV.
.GT.	.NEQV.
.GE.	

Control structures

```
DO label var = init,final,step

    . . .


label CONTINUE


    IF (condition) THEN

        . . .

    ENDIF
```

```
      IF (condition) THEN
        . . .

      ELSE
        . . .

      ENDIF


*     DO WHILE (condition)

label IF (condition) THEN
        . . .

      GO TO label
      ENDIF

*     ENDDO


*     REPEAT UNTIL (condition)

label   . . .

      IF (.NOT. (condition)) GO TO label

*     END REPEAT
```

Appendix D

Answers to Odd-numbered Questions

Chapter 1

1.1.4 Review questions
1. hardware, software
3. machine language
5. control
7. character
9. application
11. memory, processor, files, devices
13. firmware
15. sequence

1.2.5 Review questions
1. An algorithm is a procedure consisting of a finite number of precisely defined steps for solving a problem.
3. Top-down design methodology starts with a single statement of the solution to be designed. This is then broken down into steps, which are then further broken down, until each step is simple enough to be implemented in a computer language.
5. A move instruction copies information from one memory location in a computer to another.
7. The four fundamental types of instructions are assignment, arithmetic, control, and input/output.
9. input data
11. internal data
13. Pseudocode is used to describe a problem solution in semi-formal terms.
15. A flow chart is used to describe a problem solution in graphic form, emphasizing the order of execution.
17. Test data is used to test a computer algorithm or program to be sure it produces the correct output.
19. Control instructions are used to switch execution from one set of computer instructions to another, or cause a set of instructions to be executed repeatedly.

1.3.5 Review questions
1. A linker builds an executable module from user routines and library routines.
3. object
5. specification and design errors
   compilation errors
   linkage errors
   execution errors
7. debugging
9. One should test a program with error-containing data to discover if the program can detect incorrect input

1.4.3 Review questions
1. Time-sharing is done when several users run different programs at the same time.
3. Multi-programming is done when several users have different programs in the computer at the same time, but the programs take turns executing.

5. Real-time processing is important because it allows a computer to respond almost instantly to changing conditions.
7. Interactive permits several users to access data immediately and interact with it while batch processing does not involve any user interaction.

Chapter 2

2.1.4 Review questions
1. a) true   b) true   c) true   d) true   e) false   f) false   g) true
3. Each structure is represented by a box.
5. A glossary is a list of data names and corresponding data descriptions.
7. sign, size, and value

2.2.4 Review questions
1. forty-nine
3. six
5. integer
7. CONSTANT is illegal $MONEY is illegal
   (too many characters)   (first character is not alphabetic)

   MAXIM is legal   COUNT is legal
   5VALUE is illegal   VAL8X is legal
   (first character is not alphabetic)

   N57*XY is illegal   BLN + 5 is illegal
   (special characters not allowed)   (special characters not allowed)
   BALbNC is legal   MANY6 is legal
   (embedded blank is ignored)
9. INTEGER AMAX,ACON,BSTR,CVAL,CONST1,AMIN5
11. PARAMETER (N = 10,K = 25)

2.3.6 Review questions
1. **
3. a) 61.0   b) −25.0   c) 262.5   d) 75.0   e) 89.0
5. a) (W + X)/(Y + Z) + X * T
   b) (A + B + C)/(D + E − (F + G)/(H + I))
   c) A * X ** 3 + B * X ** 2 − C * X + D
   d) FORCE = MASS * ACC
   e) VOLUME = LENGTH * WIDTH * HEIGHT
7. a) P = M * R * T / V
   b) P1 = P2 * V2 / V1
   c) M = P * V / (R * T)
   d) R = SQRT(A / (4 * PI)) or SQRT(A/12.5664)
      or SQRT(A/3.1416) /2.0
   e) M = A / (0.5 * R**2) or 2.0 * A / (R * R)
   f) P = RHO * R * T
   g) H = F*L*V*V / (2.0*D*G)
   h) Q = K * SQRT(2.0*G*L) * H **(3.0/2.0)
   i) R = 1 /(1/R1 + 1/R2 + 1/R3 + 1/R4 + 1/R5)

2.4.4 Review questions
1. a) 5.0   b) 91.7   c) 64.6   d) −18.0   e) 64   f) 65   g) 45.0
   h) 25.0   i) −2.0

2.5.3 Answers to Review Questions
1. C   THIS IS AN EXAMPLE
           A = 5.0
           STOP
           END

Chapter 3

3.1.5 Review questions
1. `READ(*,*) P,K,L R`

```
   10.5      18      11      28.75
```

3. a) `WRITE(*,*) UBOUND,LBOUND,KVA`

```
   18.35        19        7854
```

b) `WRITE(*,*) A,B,SQRT(A+B)`
```
   17.0        -1.0      4.0
```

c) `WRITE(*,*) X,Y,MAX(X,Y)`
```
   -45.9          -13.11        -13.11
```

5. `WRITE (*,*,ERR=50) A,B,A*B`

3.2.4 Review questions
1. a)   `READ(*,1000) I,J,K,L,M`
  `1000` `FORMAT(I3,I3,I5,I2,I2)`

```
   389793-391585-9
```

b)   `READ(*,1000) I,J,K,L,M`
  `1000` `FORMAT(I3,I8,I10,I7,I7)`

```
   389      793      -3915      85      -9
```

c)   `READ(*,1000) I,J,K,L,M`
  `1000` `FORMAT(5I5)`

```
   389   793-3915    85    -9
```

d)   `READ(*,1000) I,J,K,L,M`
  `1000` `FORMAT(I3,5X,I3,5X,I5,5X,I2,5X,I2)`

```
   389      793      -3915      85      -9
```

e)   `READ(*,1000) I,J,K,L,M`
`1000    FORMAT(I3,I3/I5,I2,I2)`

```
 389793
-391585-9
```

3. a)   `READ(*,1000) ACON,BMAX,CVAL,BMIN`
`1000    FORMAT(F7.3,F6.3,F6.3,F6.5)`

```
 3856854-31085785984000375
```

b)   `READ(*,1000) ACON,BMAX,CVAL,BMIN`
`1000    FORMAT(F12.7,F12.7,F12.7,F12.7)`
or
`1000    FORMAT (4F12.7)`

```
 38568540000  -310850000  7859840000     00037500
```

c)   `READ(*,1000) ACON,BMAX,CVAL,BMIN`
`1000    FORMAT(F7.3,5X,F6.3,5X,F6.3,5X,F6.5)`

```
 3856854      -31085      785984      000375
```

d)   `READ(*,1000) ACON,BMAX,CVAL,BMIN`
`1000    FORMAT(F8.0,F7.0,F7.0,F7.0)`

```
 3856.854-31.085785.9840.00375
```

e)   `READ(*,1000) ACON,BMAX,CVAL,BMIN`
`1000    FORMAT(4F12.0)`

```
 3856.854     -31.085      785.984      0.00375
```

5. a) K = 12345, L = 678901, M = 2345678, N = 901
   b) A = 62.514, B = 769.35217, C = 3189.321, D = 160.75
   c) X = 312.672E03 or 312672.0, Y = 189.54E02 or 18954.0
   d) p = 12.3E-4 or .00123, Q = 567.89E-13

3.3.5 Review questions

1. a)

```
78546385    7615-895932
```

   b)

```
78546      385      7615        -895932
```

   c)

```
78546      385      7615        -895932
```

   d)

```
     78546          385       7615    -895932
```

   e)

```
78546385
7615-895932
```

   f)

```
        78546          385
        7615    -895932
```

3. a) `FORMAT(4X,I5,4X,I3,3X,F7.2,4X,F6.4)`
      or `FORMAT(1X I8,I7,F10.2,F10.4)`
   b) `FORMAT(8X,E12.6,6X,E11.6)`
   c) `FORMAT(6X,'TOTAL = ',I8)`
   d) `FORMAT(1X,T5,'NAME:',T22,'DATE:'/'+',T5,`
      `'____',T22,'____')`
      or `FORMAT(4X,'NAME:',12X,'DATE:'/'+',3X,`
      `'____',12X,'____')`

Chapter 4

4.1.5 Review questions

  1. a)

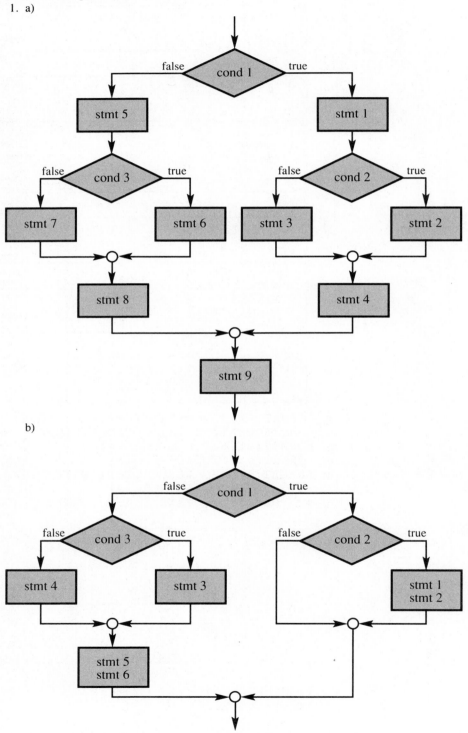

  b)

c)

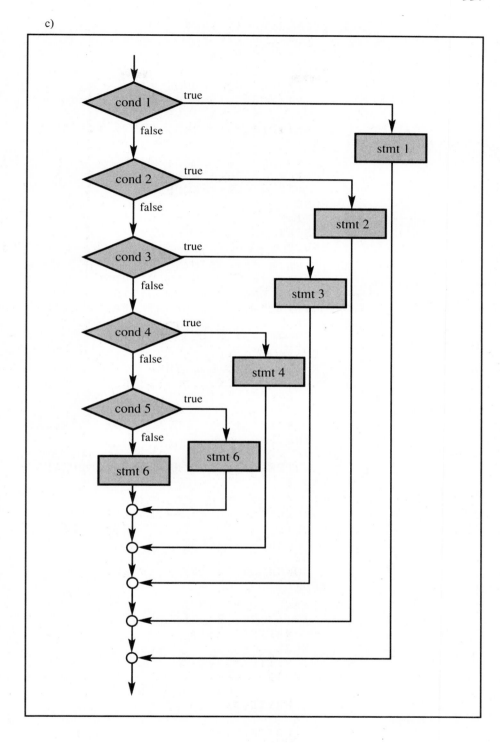

```
3. a) IF(A .GT. B) THEN
         Z = W * X + Y
         R = Z + 10.5
      ENDIF

   b) IF(WKSAL .GT. 2000) THEN
         NETINC = .15 * COST
         SALES = COST + NETINC
         WRITE(*,*) SALES, COST, NETINC
      ENDIF

   c) IF(MONSAL .GT.5000) THEN
         FTAX = .25 * MONSAL
         STAX = .08 * MONSAL
      ELSE
         FTAX = .20 * MONSAL
         STAX = .06 * MONSAL
      ENDIF

   d) IF(RAIN .LT. 1.0) THEN
         WRITE(*,*) 'LIGHT RAINFALL'
      ELSEIF (RAIN .LE. 2.0) THEN
         WRITE(*,*) 'MODERATE RAINFALL'
      ELSE
         WRITE(*,*) 'HEAVY RAINFALL'
      ENDIF

   e) IF(TEMP .GT. 60) THEN
         IF(TEMP .LT. 100) THEN
            WRITE(*,*) TEMP
         ELSE
            WRITE(*,*) 'DO NOT USE COMPUTER'
         ENDIF
      ELSE
         WRITE(*,*) 'DO NOT USE COMPUTER'
      ENDIF

5. a) IF (SALARY .LE. 50) THEN
         MONSAL = 40 * 4 * SALARY
      ELSEIF (SALARY .LE. 50000) THEN
         MONSAL = SALARY
      ELSE
         MONSAL = SALARY / 12
      ENDIF

   b) IF(A .GT. B) THEN
         IF(A .GT. C) THEN
            WRITE(*,*) A
         ELSE
            WRITE(*,*)C
         ENDIF
      ELSEIF (B .GT. C) THEN
            WRITE(*,*) B
      ELSE
            WRITE(*,*) C
      ENDIF

   c) IF(TEMP .LT. 40) THEN
         WRITE(*,*) 'LOW'
```

```
      ELSEIF (TEMP .LT. 80) THEN
        WRITE(*,*) 'AVERAGE'
      ELSEIF (TEMP .GT. 80) THEN
        WRITE(*,*) 'HIGH'
        WRITE(*,*) 'WARNING'
      ELSE
        WRITE(*,*) 'HIGH'
      ENDIF
```

4.2.4 Review questions

1. a) output is

        1 2, 2 4, 3 6, 4 8, 5 10, 6 12, 7 14, 8 16, 9 18

```
        I = 1
10      IF(I .LT. 10) THEN
          WRITE(*,*) I, 2*I
          I = I + 1
          GO TO 10
        ENDIF
```

   b) output is

   1 2, 2 4, 3 6, 4 8, 5 10, 6 12, 7 14, 8 16, 9 18, 10 20

```
        I = 1
10      IF(I .LE. 10) THEN
          WRITE(*,*) I, 2*I
          I = I + 1
          GO TO 10
        ENDIF
```

   c) output is

        5 10, 7 14, 9 18

```
        I = 5
10      IF(I .LE. 10) THEN
          WRITE(*,*) I, 2*I
          I = I + 2
          GO TO 10
        ENDIF
```

3. a) 1 3, 2 4, 3 5, 4 6, 5 7, 6 8, 7 9, 8 10, 9 11, 10 12
   b) 0 0, 1 2, 2 4, 3 6, 4 8, 5 10, 6 12, 7 14, 8 16, 9 18
   c) 5   10, 6 12, 7 14, 8 16, 9 18

5. a) line number missing
   b) must have positive step to count up from 5 to 15
   c) must have negative step to count down from 15 to 5
   d) must have negative step to count down from -5 to -20
   e) $1-$ is not a line number
   f) must have negative step to count down from 50.0 to 10.0
   g) correct

4.3.4 Review questions

1. a) true   b) true   c) true
3. a) false   b) true   c) true   d) true   e) true

Chapter 5

5.1.2 Review questions

1. It represents a procedure (program) or subprocedure (subprogram).
3. Modular design is a way of developing a program as a collection of functional routines.
5. Function subprograms are used to calculate a single value.

5.2.3 Review questions

1. a) F(X,Y) = X * (X * (X + 1) + Y) + Y * (Y + 1) + X) + 18
   b) F(S,T) = X * (A * X + B) + C
   c) F(P,Q,R) = P * P + ABS(Q − R) + SQRT(2*R)

5.3.3 Review questions

1. a) A = 1.7, B = − 13.5, K = 9
   b) A = − 13.5, B = − 27.0, K = 2
   c) A = 3.0, B = − 11.8, K = 5
3. REAL FUNCTION SLOPE(X1,Y1,X2,Y2)
   REAL X1,Y1,X2,Y2
   SLOPE = (Y2 − Y1) / (X2 − X1)
   RETURN
   END
5. REAL FUNCTION HIGH(H0,V0)
   REAL H0,V0,T
   T = − V0 / 32.0
   HIGH = H0 + V0 * T + A * T * T / 2.0
   RETURN
   END

5.4.4 Review questions

1. a) true   b) false   c) false   d) true   e) true   f) false   g) false
3. SUBROUTINE ANGLE(SIDEA,SIDEB,SIDEC,ANGLEA,ANGLEB,ANGLEC)
   REAL SIDEA,SIDEB,SIDEC,ANGLEA,ANGLEB,ANGLEC)
   ANGLEA = VALUE(SIDEA,SIDEB,SIDEC)
   ANGLEB = VALUE(SIDEB,SIDEC,SIDEA)
   ANGLEC = VALUE(SIDEC,SIDEA,SIDEB)
   RETURN
   END

   REAL FUNCTION VALUE(X,Y,Z)
   REAL X,Y,Z
   VALUE = ACOS((Y*Y + Z*Z − X*X)/(2.0*Y*Z))
   RETURN
   END

5.5.4 Review questions

1. a) true,   b) false,   c) true,   d) true
3. SUBROUTINE CNTR
   INTEGER K
   DATA K/1/
   SAVE K
   WRITE(*,*) K
   K = K + 1
   RETURN
   END

Chapter 6

6.1.6 Review questions

1. a) REAL X(15),Y(25)   X has 15 elements, Y has 25 elements
   b) INTEGER A(8),B(8:35)   A has 8 elements, B has 28 elements
   c) LOGICAL P(−20:−5),Q(15:25)   P has 16 elements, Q has 11 elements
   d) REAL W(−30:−15),Z(20:30)   W has 16 elements, Z has 11 elements
      INTEGER Y(−3:45)   Y has 49 elements

3. a) (X(K), K=1,20)
   b) (Y(K), K=10,30)
   c) (Z(K), K=−15,−4)
   d) (W(K), K=−5,25)

6.2.3 Review questions

1. a) `READ(*,*) CONS`

```
     10.5   8.6   5.2   9.7   20.7   2.5   −6.9
```

   b)   `DO 10 K=1,7`
                  `READ(*,*) CONS(K)`
         `10      CONTINUE`

```
     10.5
     8.6
     5.2
     9.7
     20.7
     2.5
     −6.9
```

   c) `READ(*,*) (CONS(K), K=1,7)`

```
     10.5   8.6   5.2   9.7   20.7   2.5   −6.9
```

3. a) i. 20, ii. four, iii. two, iv. three
   b) 20
   c) 20
   d) i. 20 ii. four iii. two iv. three

5. a) K = 10 when array full, K = N+1 when array not full and N values read, N < 10
   b) K = 11 when array full, K = N+1 when array not full and N values read, N < 10
   c) K undefined when array full, K = N+1 when array not full and N values read, N < 10

6.3.3 Review questions

1. a)
```
     1    3    5    7    9   11   13   15   17   19
```

   b)
```
     1    2    3    4    5
```

c)
```
   10   9   8   7   6   5   4   3   2   1
```

d)
```
   10   14   18
```

e)
```
    5   6   7   8   9
```

3. a)
```
    1    2    3    4    5    6    7    8    9   10
   11   12   13   14   15
```

b)
```
   1 1   1 2   1 3   1 4   1 5
   2 1   2 2   2 3   2 4   2 5
```

c)
```
   1   1   1   3   1   5   1   7   1   9
   2   1   2   3   2   5   2   7   2   9
   3   1   3   3   3   5   3   7   3   9
```

d)
```
   1   2   3   4   5   1   2   3   4   5
```

e)
```
   1   1   2   3   4   5
   2   1   2   3   4   5
   3   1   2   3   4   5
```

5. a) The 20 values of Y are printed in order using default spacing.
   b) The first 10 values of Y are printed on the first line, the next 10 on the next line.
   c) The 20 values of Y are printed in order, each on a separate line.
   d) The values of $Y(1), Y(5), Y(9), Y(13), Y(17)$ are printed on each of four consecutive lines.

7. a)
```
       DO 10 K=1,100
          WRITE(*,1000) XVAL(K),YVAL(K),ZVAL(K)
1000      FORMAT(1X,3F6.3)
10     CONTINUE
```

b)
```
     WRITE(*,1000)          (XVAL(K),YVAL(K),ZVAL(K),
  K=1,100)
1000 FORMAT(1X,3F6.3)
```

9.
```
          KGO = 1
          KSTOP = 100
          DO 50 PAGE = 1,4
             WRITE(*,1000) (SALE(K), K=KGO,KSTOP)
1000         FORMAT('1',(10F7.2/))
             KGO = KGO + 100
             KSTOP = KSTOP + 100
50        CONTINUE
```

6.4.3 Review questions

1. a)

X	Y
7.2	−5.7
9.2	−4.7
11.2	−3.7

b)

X	Y
3.0	1.5
3.9	2.4
−4.5	−6.0

c)

X	Y
12.8	8.9
21.7	8.9
12.8	8.9

6.5.4 Review questions

1. a)
```
          SUBROUTINE SUB1(K,L,Y,YSUM)
          INTEGER K,L
          REAL Y(10),YSUM
```

b)
```
          SUBROUTINE SUBSUM(X,Y)
          REAL X(10),Y(10)
```

c)
```
          SUBROUTINE CALC(R,RLIM)
          REAL R(RLIM)
```

3.
```
          LOGICAL VALID(ARR,N,LB,UB)
          REAL ARR(N),LB,UB
          INTEGER K

          VALID = .TRUE.
          DO 10 K=1,N
             IF (ARR(K) .LT. LB .OR. ARR(K) .GT. UB) THEN
                VALID = .FALSE.
                RETURN
             ENDIF
10        CONTINUE
          RETURN
          END
```

5.
```
          SUBROUTINE OUTPUT(A,N)
          REAL A(N)
          INTEGER K

          DO 10 K=1,N
             WRITE(*,*) A(K)
10        CONTINUE
          RETURN
          END
```

Chapter 7

7.1.3 Review questions

1. a) REAL X(5,8)   b) INTEGER Y(-2:7,12)
   c) LOGICAL P(3:8,0:6), Q(3:8,0:6)

3. a) X(I,J) $1 \leq I \leq 8$, $1 \leq J \leq 6$
   b) Y(I,J) $3 \leq I \leq 7$, $8 \leq J \leq 16$
   c) Z(I,J) $-5 \leq I \leq 3$, $-7 \leq J \leq -2$

5. a)
```
        DO 20 I = 1,6
          DO 10 J = 1,7
            . . . X(I,J) . . .
   10       CONTINUE
   20     CONTINUE
```
   b)
```
        DO 20 I = 5,8
          DO 10 J = 6,12
            . . . Y(I,J) . . .
   10       CONTINUE
   20     CONTINUE
```
   c)
```
        DO 20 I = -5,2
          DO 10 J = -6,-2
            . . . Z(I,J) . . .
   10       CONTINUE
   20     CONTINUE
```
   d)
```
        DO 20 I = -8,-2
          DO 10 J = 9,11
            . . . W(I,J) . . .
   10       CONTINUE
   20     CONTINUE
```

7.2.3 Review questions

1. a)
```
        READ (*,1000) N
   1000 FORMAT(4I5)
```

input

```
   1     2     3     4
```
```
   5     6     7     8
```
```
   9    10    11    12
```
```
  13    14    15    16
```

storage
1
2
3
4
5
6
7
8
9
10
11
12
13
14
15
16

b)
```
        READ (*,1000) N
   1000 FORMAT(AI5)
```

input

```
   1     5     9    13
```
```
   2     6    10    14
```
```
   3     7    11    15
```
```
   4     8    12    16
```

storage
1
5
9
13
2
6
10
14
3
7
11
15
4
8
12
16

```
3.           READ (*,1000) ((X(I,J) J=1,5),I=1,10)
   1000      FORMAT(5F8.0)
```

5. a) 50   b) 50   c) 10   d) five   e) 10

7.3.2 Review questions

1. a)
```
             DO 10 I = 1,4
                WRITE(*,*) ((N(I,J), J = 1,3)
   10        CONTINUE
```

b)
```
             DO 10 J=1,3
                WRITE(*,*) (N(I,J), I = 1,4)
   10        CONTINUE
```

c)
```
             DO 10 I = 1,4
                WRITE(*,*) I,(N(I,J), J = 1,3)
   10        CONTINUE
```

d)
```
             WRITE(*,*)(J,J=1,3)
             DO 10 I=1,3
                WRITE(*,*) J, (N(I,J), J = 1,4)
   10        CONTINUE
```

3. a)
```
    25     7   -27
    -8    62   780
   286     0     5
    23   116   176
```

b)
```
   1    25     7   -27
   2    -8    62   780
   3   286     0     5
   4    23   116   176
```

c)
```
   1    25   2     7   3   -27
   1    -8   2    62   3   780
   1   286   2     0   3     5
   1    23   2   116   3   176
```

7.4.3 Review questions

1. a)
```
      3.5  18.4   9.2    b)        2.0  3.0  4.0
  A = 8.5  25.4  12.7        B =   8.0  7.0  9.0
      5.2  14.4   7.2              7.0  5.0  3.0
```

c)
```
      3.5   6.0   8.0    d)        5.5   9.8  13.2
  A = 8.5   4.0  12.0        B =   9.5   9.6  18.7
      5.2  10.0   6.0             12.2   9.6  10.2
```

3. a)   `SUM = 0.0`

```
                  DO 10 K = 1,10
                     SUM = SUM + X(K,K) + X(K,11-K)
          10      CONTINUE


     b)           SUM = 0.0
                  DO 20 I = 1,9
                    DO 10 J = I+1,10
                       SUM = SUM + X(I,J)
          10        CONTINUE
          20      CONTINUE


     c)           SUM = 0.0
                  DO 20 I = 2,10
                    DO 10 J = 1,I-1
                       SUM = SUM + X(I,J)
          10        CONTINUE
          20      CONTINUE
```

7.5.4 Review questions

1. a) REAL X(5,-1:0,4)   X contains 40 values
   b) REAL Y(-5:5,-3:2,4:8)   Y contains 330 values
   c) INTEGER A(0:5,0:2,0:10)   A contains 198 values

3. a)
```
                  DO 20 K = 1,10
                     WRITE(*,1000)
          1000       FORMAT('1')
                     DO 10 I = 1,40
                        WRITE(*,1100) (N(I,J,K), J = 1,20)
          1100         FORMAT(1X,20I6)
          10        CONTINUE
          20      CONTINUE
```

7.6.3 Review questions

1. a) true   b) false   c) true   d) true   e) true   f) false
   g) true   h) true   i) true

3.
```
                  SUBROUTINE XTRANS(X,N,M,Y)
                  REAL X(N,M),Y(M,N)
                  INTEGER N,M,I,J
                  DO 20 I = 1,N
                    DO 10 J = 1,M
                       Y(J,I) = X(I,J)
          10        CONTINUE
          20      CONTINUE
                  RETURN
                  END
```

5.
```
                  SUBROUTINE OUTPUT(MAT)
                  INTEGER MAT(9,9),I,J
                  DO 10 I = 1,9
                     WRITE(*,1000) (I, J, MAT(I,J), J=1,9)
          1000       FORMAT(1X,9(3X,'(',I1,',',I1,')',I4))
          10      CONTINUE
                  RETURN
                  END
```

Chapter 8

8.1.5 Review questions

1. a) CHARACTER STR1*10
   b) CHARACTER STR2*18
   c) CHARACTER STR1*3
   d) CHARACTER STR4*4
   e) CHARACTER STR5*0

3. a) CHARACTER TITLE*13
      PARAMETER (TITLE = 'ANNUAL REPORT')
   b) CHARACTER DEPT*11
      PARAMETER (DEPT = 'ENGINEERING')
   c) CHARACTER SECT*14
      PARAMETER (SECT = 'PRODUCT REVIEW')
   d) CHARACTER YEAR*4
      PARAMETER (YEAR = '1989')

5. a) READ(*,*) METAL1,METAL2,METAL3,METAL4
   b) READ(*,*) PART1,PART2,PART3,PART4
   c) READ(*,*) DIM1,DIM2,DIM3

7.
```
        L = -1
        DO 10 N = 5,1,-1
          L = L + 2
          WRITE(*,*) (' ', K = 1,N),('*', K = 1,L)
10      CONTINUE
        DO 20 N = 2,5
          L = L - 2
          WRITE(*,*) (' ', K = 1,N),('*', K = 1,L)
20      CONTINUE
```

8.2.4 Review questions

1. a) WATERbISbAbLIQUID
   b) LIQUIDWATER
   c) WATERbISbWATER.
3. a) 25 b) five c) 16 d) 31
5. a) ROSERED b) three c) four d) five e) OSE

8.3.4 Review questions

1. a) CHARACTER*20 XSTR(15)   or   CHARACTER XSTR(15)*20
   b) CHARACTER STRX(10)*8,STRY(15)*12,STRZ(20)*15
   c) CHARACTER*10 ST1(40),ST2(40),ST3(40)*15,ST4(40)*20

3.   assume data is in TEXT
```
        CHARACTER SENTEN(6)*36
        INTEGER I,K
        DO 10 K = 1,6
          I = INDEX(TEXT,'.')
          SENTEN(K) = TEXT(:I)
          TEXT = TEXT(I+2:)
10      CONTINUE
```

8.4.3 Review questions

1. a) true b) false c) false d) true e) true
3.
```
            SUBROUTINE REVERS(INSTR,OUTSTR,N)
            CHARACTER INSTR*(*),OUTSTR*(*)
            INTEGER N,K,L
            L = N
```

```
                 DO 10 k = 1,N
                    OUTSTR(L:L) = INSTR(K:K)
                    L = L - 1
          10     CONTINUE
```

```
5.        SUBROUTINE INPUT(DATA,SORTED)
          CHARACTER DATA(20)*10
          INTEGER K
          LOGICAL SORTED
          READ(*,*) DATA
          SORTED = .TRUE.
          DO 10 K = 2,20
             SORTED = DATA(K) .GE. DATA(K-1)
   10     CONTINUE
          RETURN
          END
```

Chapter 9

9.1.5 Review questions
1. a) true b) false c) false d) false e) true f) false
   g) true h) true i) false j) false k) true l) true

3. a) CLOSE(UNIT = 15,STATUS = 'DELETE')
   b) CLOSE(UNIT = 12,STATUS = 'KEEP')

```
5. a)       WRITE(13,1000,ERR=500,IOSTAT=ERRKEY)
          1        STUDID,STNAME,T1,T2,T3,T4,AVGT,GRADE
       1000   FORMAT(A8,1X,A16,T31,4I3,2X,F6.2,4X,A1)
```

```
   b)       WRITE(18,1000,ERR=500,IOSTAT=ERRKEY,REC=3127)
          1        LOCAT, DIST,BRIGHT
       1000   FORMAT(A25,A6,A9)
```

```
7.        READ(15,1000,ERR=500,REC=32) INFO
          WRITE(23,1000,REC=32) DATA
              . . .
   500    WRITE(*,*) 'RECORD NOT FOUND'
   1000   FORMAT(A80)
```

9.2.4 Review questions
1. a) false b) false c) true d) false e) false f) true
   g) true h) false i) false

```
3.        OPEN(UNIT=8,FILE='INFIL',STATUS='OLD')
          OPEN(UNIT=9,FILE='OUTFIL',STATUS='NEW')

   *      DO WHILE (MORE DATA)

   10     READ(8,END=20)  (X(K), K=1,10)
             WRITE(9)  (X(K), K=1,10)
             GO TO 10

   *      ENDDO
```

```
      20      CONTINUE
```

9.3.5 Review questions

1. a) INQUIRE(FILE = 'MYOUTF',IOSTAT = N)
   b) INQUIRE(FILE = 'MYOUTF',ACCESS = STR)
   c) INQUIRE(FILE = 'MYOUTF',NUMBER = N)
   d) INQUIRE(FILE = 'MYOUTF',FORM = STR)
   e) INQUIRE(FILE = 'MYOUTF',RECL = N)

3.
```
         CHARACTER*80 CHDATA
         INTEGER K

         OPEN (UNIT=15,FILE='SEQTMP',STATUS='NEW')
         DO 10 K = 1,100
            READ(5) CHDATA
            WRITE(15) CHDATA
   10    CONTINUE
         REWIND 15
         DO 20 K=1,100
            READ(15) CHDATA
            PRINT 1000, CHDATA
 1000       FORMAT(1X,A80)
   20    CONTINUE
         CLOSE(UNIT=15,STATUS='KEEP')
         STOP
         END
```

5.
```
         CHARACTER*40 BLANKS
         INTEGER K
         PARAMETER (BLANKS=' ')
         OPEN (UNIT=15,FILE='ENGDAT',STATUS='NEW',
     1         FORM='UNFORMATTED',ACCESS='DIRECT',RECL=10)
         DO 10 K = 1,100
            WRITE(15,REC=K) BLANKS
   10    CONTINUE
         CLOSE(UNIT=15,STATUS='KEEP')
         STOP
         END
```

Chapter 10

10.1.4 Review questions

1. a) DOUBLE PRECISION AMAX,AVAL,CONST,CALC,VAL
   b) DOUBLE PRECISION X(10),Y(25)
   c) DOUBLE PRECISION A(20,30),B(30,40)

3. a)
```
   WRITE(*,1000) W,X,Y
 1000  FORMAT(T21,D16.9,T41,D16.9,T61,D16.9)
```
   b)
```
   WRITE(*,1000) P,Q,R
 1000  FORMAT(T21,D16.9,T41,D16.9,T61,D16.9)
```
   c)
```
   WRITE(*,1000) E,F,G
 1000  FORMAT(T21,D16.9,T41,D16.9,T61,D16.9)
```

5. a) exact value   b) 16 digits   c) five digits
   d) exact value   e) exact value   f) two digits

10.2.4 Review questions
1. a) COMPLEX A,B,C,P,R
   b) COMPLEX X(10),Y(20)
   c) COMPLEX A(5,10)

3. a) CVALUE = X * (A*X + B) + C
   b) CVALUE = CSIN(Z) / CCOS(Z)
   c) X = REAL(Z)
      Y = AIMAG(Z)
      CSINH = CMPLX(SINH(X) * COS(Y) , COSH(X) * SIN(Y))
   d) CROOT = CMPLX($-$B/(2*A),SQRT(B*B $-$ 4.0*A*C)/(2*A))

10.3.3 Review questions
1. a) DATA A,B,C/8.5,9.8,6.25/
   b) DATA X,W,Y,Z/4*13.8/
   c) DATA X/10*12.6/
   d) DATA A/100*10.5/

3. a)

P,Q,R	
S,T	

b)

X(1),Y(1)	
X(2),Y(2)	
X(3),Y(3)	
X(4),Y(4)	
X(5),Y(5)	

c)

X(1)	
X(2)	
A,B,X(3)	
X(4)	

d)

X(1)	
X(2)	
X(3)	
X(4)	
Y(1),X(5)	
Y(2),X(6)	
Y(3)	

10.4.6 Review questions
1. a) 10   b) 120   c) $Y \geqslant X^2$ d) A $\neq$ 0.0 and B $\neq -1.0$
3. a) two,   b) four
5. a) comma missing between 90 and 120
   b) comma missing between) and I
   c) duplicate line numbers
   d) cannot assign a variable to L
   e) parentheses missing
   f) label variables cannot be used in expressions

10.5.4 Review questions
1. a) false   b) false   c) true   d) false   e) true   f) true
   g) false

Appendix E

List of Sample Programs

The sample programs are listed by name and by the primary FORTRAN features that they illustrate.

551

Appendix F

Proposed FORTRAN 8x Standard

The new proposed FORTRAN 8x is an extension of FORTRAN 77, including some of the features found in current extensions, with additional features borrowed from other languages. The major new features are given below.

Basic concepts of FORTRAN

The eleven characters ! " & % ; < > ? [ ] _ are added to the FORTRAN character set. Their uses are as follows:

!	separates executable code from an inline comment
"	an alternative form of quotation mark
&	used at the end of a line to indicate continuation
%	indicates a field of a user-defined data type
;	separates statements on a line
< >	used as relational operators
?	
[ ]	used in array initialization
_	embedded in names for readability

Names may consist of at most 31 characters, including embedded underscores, for example:

$$AMT\_OF\_BAL$$
$$TEMP\_CENT$$

REAL and COMPLEX numbers can be defined to any desired precision. This eliminates the need for DOUBLE PRECISION.

It is possible for the user to define new data types. This makes it possible to do the following:
1. define a type MATRIX and therefore be able to have arrays of matrices

```
TYPE MATRIX (M,N)
   REAL R(M,N)
END TYPE
```

2. define a record as consisting of various elements, for example

```
TYPE RECORD
   CHARACTER NAME*20
   CHARACTER ADDR*20
   REAL SALARY
END TYPE RECORD
```

which can be used in declarations, for example

```
TYPE (RECORD) EMPLOYEE
```

and can be accessed as a whole as EMPLOYEE or in parts as

EMPLOYEE%NAME, EMPLOYEE%ADDR, and EMPLOYEE%SALARY

Labels may be either numbers or character strings, for example

> LOOP_START: . . .
>
> GO TO LOOP_START

FORTRAN programs may be written in free format. But free format code and code which uses the special meanings of columns 1−5 and 6 may not be mixed.

Comments may be placed inline, separated by exclamation points, for example

> READ(*,*) X   ! GET VELOCITY MEASUREMENTS

Input/Output Specifications

The only major new input/output feature is the ability to give a name to a list, for example

> NAMELIST /INDATA/X,Y,Z
>
> . . .
>
> READ (*,*, NML = INDATA)

reads values into the variables X, Y, and Z.

Besides the NML namelist option, there is a PROMPT option for interactive input, for example:

> READ (*,*, PROMPT = ' INPUT AN INTEGER:') N

Control Structures

The pseudo-mathematical symbols $<$, $>$, $<=$, $>=$, $==$, and $<>$ may be used as relational operators.

The case statement is implemented in the form

> SELECT CASE (var)
>   CASE (value1)
>
>   . . .
>
>   CASE (value2)
>
>   . . .
>
> DEFAULT
>
>   . . .
>
> END SELECT

Repetition structures are implemented that can be used to repeat a body of code a certain number of times without explicitly counting

> LOOP: DO (N) TIMES
>
>   . . .
>
>   END DO LOOP

or to repeat a body of code, stopping the repetition when a particular condition arises

> LOOP: DO
>
>   . . .
>
>   IF (condition_1) EXIT LOOP
>
>   . . .
>
>   IF (condition_2) CYCLE LOOP
>
>   . . .
>
>   END DO

The statement EXIT LOOP causes an immediate exit of the loop when the corresponding condition is true. The statement CYCLE LOOP causes an immediate restart of the loop when the corresponding condition is true. These two statements can be used to implement a DO . . . WHILE loop and a REPEAT . . . UNTIL loop as follows:

```
        LOOP: DO                                      !  DO WHILE (condition)
                IF (.NOT. condition) EXIT LOOP
                  . . .
                CYCLE LOOP
        END DO

        LOOP: DO                                      !  REPEAT UNTIL (condition)
                  . . .
                IF (.NOT. condition) CYCLE LOOP
        END DO
```

Modular Design and Subprograms

Subroutines and functions may be recursive, that is, they may call themselves.

A new subprogram type MODULE may be defined, similar to the packages described in Chapter 5. Modules are used to hide data structures and the routines that process them. These modules can be added to a program library as a way of providing controlled access to data or new data types. Eventually the MODULE subprograms will replace COMMON, as they provide a way of sharing data without having to include declarations in all of the routines.

Subprograms may be defined inside other routines rather than separately. This limits their availability to those routines where they are defined. For example:

```
        SUBROUTINE A
          . . .
        CONTAINS
          SUBROUTINE B
            . . .
          END SUBROUTINE B
        END SUBROUTINE A
```

implies that only subroutine A and routines defined inside it may invoke subroutine B.

One-dimensional and multi-dimensional arrays

Arithmetic operations are defined for arrays. Two arrays of the same size and shape may be added, subtracted, multiplied, divided, or compared on an element by element basis. The result is another array of the same size. For example:

```
        REAL A(N,M),B(N,M),C(N,M)
        LOGICAL L(N,M)

        C = A + B
        C = A − B
        C = A * B
        C = A / B
        L = A .LT. B
```

Library functions for arrays are included such as functions to compute the matrix product MATMUL of two arrays or the transpose TRANSPOSE of an array. These functions return arrays as values. User-defined functions may also be written to return arrays.

Subarrays may be defined and named, for example:

```
        REAL ARR (10,10)
        IDENTIFY (TOP(I,J) = ARR(I,J), I = 1:5,J = 1:10)
```

defines the first five rows of array ARR to be the array TOP.

```
        IDENTIFY (DIAG(K) = ARR(K,K), K = 1:N)
```

which defines the one-dimensional array DIAG(N) to be the major diagonal of the N × N array ARR. This makes is possible to reference the major diagonal of array ARR as though it were a one-dimensional array.

Selective operations may be performed on arrays using a form of filtering through a mask. The following two examples replace every element of array ARR by its absolute value.

WHERE (ARR < 0.0) ARR = − ARR

WHERE (ARR < 0.0)
 ARR = − ARR
ELSEWHERE
END WHERE

References

A Review and Analysis of Fortran 8X, edited by Brian T. Smith, 1987

Fortran 8X, The New Fortran Standard, J. K. Reid, September 1987

Fortran F8 (X3.9-198X) Revision of X3.9-1978, American National Standard for Information Systems Programming Language

Index